Donald E. Knuth, on Bottom-UP.

(excerpted from the preface to "The Art of Computer Programming, Fascicle 1: MMIX"
http://www.cs-faculty.Stanford.EDU/~knuth/fasc1.ps.gz with his permission)

Why have a machine language?

Many readers are no doubt thinking, "Why does Knuth replace MIX by another machine instead of just sticking to a high-level programming language? Hardly anybody uses assemblers these days."

Such people are entitled to their opinions, and they need not bother reading the machine-language parts of my books. But the reasons for machine language that I gave in the preface to Volume 1, written in the early 1960s, remain valid today:

> One of the principal goals of my books is to show how high-level constructions are actually implemented in machines, not simply to show how they are applied. I explain coroutine linkage, tree structures, random number generation, high-precision arithmetic, radix conversion, packing of data, combinatorial searching, recursion, etc., from the ground up.
>
> The programs needed in my books are generally so short that their main points can be grasped easily.
>
> People who are more than casually interested in computers should have at least some idea of what the underlying hardware is like. Otherwise the programs they write will be pretty weird.

Machine language is necessary in any case, as output of some software that I describe.

> Expressing basic methods like algorithms for sorting and searching in machine language makes it possible to carry out meaningful studies of the effects of cache and RAM size and other hardware characteristics (memory speed, pipelining, multiple issue, lookaside buffers, the size of cache blocks, etc.) when comparing different schemes.

INTRODUCTION TO COMPUTING SYSTEMS:

From Bits and Gates to C and Beyond

INTRODUCTION TO COMPUTING SYSTEMS:

From Bits and Gates to C and Beyond

Yale N. Patt
The University of Texas at Austin

Sanjay J. Patel
University of Illinois at Urbana-Champaign

Boston   Burr Ridge, IL   Dubuque, IA   Madison, WI
New York   San Francisco   St. Louis
Bangkok   Bogotá   Caracas   Lisbon   London   Madrid   Mexico City
Milan   New Delhi   Seoul   Singapore   Sydney   Taipei   Toronto

McGraw-Hill Higher Education

A Division of The McGraw-Hill Companies

INTRODUCTION TO COMPUTING SYSTEMS:
FROM BITS AND GATES TO C AND BEYOND
Published by McGraw-Hill, an imprint of The McGraw-Hill Companies, Inc. 1221 Avenue of the
Americas, New York, NY, 10020. Copyright ©2001, by The McGraw-Hill Companies, Inc. All rights
reserved. No part of this publication may be reproduced or distributed in any form or by any means, or
stored in a data base or retrieval system, without the prior written consent of The McGraw-Hill
Companies, Inc., including, but not limited to, in any network or other electronic storage or transmission,
or broadcast for distance learning.

Some ancillaries, including electronic and print components, may not be available to customers outside
the United States.

This book is printed on acid-free paper.

1 2 3 4 5 6 7 8 9 0 FGR/FGR 0 9 8 7 6 5 4 3 2 1 0

ISBN 0-07-237690-2

Vice president/Editor-in-chief: *Thomas Casson*
Executive editor: *Betsy Jones*
Development editor: *Michelle Flomenhoft*
Marketing manager: *John T. Wannemacher*
Project managers: *Laura M. Healy* and *Laura Ward Majersky*
Production supervisor: *Rose Hepburn*
Coordinator freelance design: *Matt Baldwin*
Cover design: *Andrew Curtis*
Compositor: *Techsetters, Inc.*
Typeface: *10/12 Times Roman*
Printer: *Quebecor Printing Book Company/Fairfield*

Library of Congress Cataloging-in-Publication Data

Patt, Yale N.
    Introduction to computing systems : from bits and gates to C and beyond / Yale N. Patt
and Sanjay J. Patel.
    p. cm. – (McGraw-Hill series in computer science)
    ISBN 0-07-237690-2 (alk. paper)
    1. Computer science. 2. C (Computer program language) I. Patel, Sanjay J. II. Title.
III. Series
QA76.P367 2001
004–dc21
                                                                            00-56615

http://www.mhhe.com

To the memory of my parents,
Abraham Walter Patt A"H and Sarah Clara Patt A"H,
who taught me to value "learning"
even before they taught me to ride a bicycle.

To Mira and her grandparents,
Sharda Patel and Jeram Patel.

CONTENTS

Chapter 13

Control Structures   275

Chapter 14

Functions   311

Chapter 15

Debugging   335

Chapter 16

Recursion   347

PREFACE

This textbook has evolved from EECS 100, the first computing course for computer science, computer engineering, and electrical engineering majors at the University of Michigan, that Kevin Compton and the first author introduced for the first time in the fall term, 1995.

EECS 100 happened because Computer Science and Engineering faculty had been dissatisfied for many years with the lack of student comprehension of some very basic concepts. For example, students had a lot of trouble with pointer variables. Recursion seemed to be "magic," beyond understanding.

We decided in 1993 that the conventional wisdom of starting with a high-level programming language, which was the way we (and most universities) were doing it, had its shortcomings. We decided that the reason students were not getting it was that they were forced to memorize technical details when they did not understand the basic underpinnings.

The result is the bottom-up approach taken in this book. We treat (in order) MOS transistors (very briefly, long enough for students to grasp their global switch-level behavior), logic gates, latches, logic structures (MUX, Decoder, Adder, gated latches), finally culminating in an implementation of memory. From there, we move on to the Von Neumann model of execution, then a simple computer (the LC-2), machine language programming of the LC-2, assembly language programming of the LC-2, the high level language C, recursion, pointers, arrays, and finally some elementary data structures.

We do not endorse today's popular information hiding approach when it comes to learning. Information hiding is a useful productivity enhancement technique after one understands what is going on. But until one gets to that point, we insist that information hiding gets in the way of understanding. Thus, we continually build on what has gone before, so that nothing is magic, and everything can be tied to the foundation that has already been laid.

We should point out that we do not disagree with the notion of top-down *design*. On the contrary, we believe strongly that top-down design is correct design. But there is a clear difference between how one approaches a design problem (after one understands the underlying building blocks), and what it takes to get to the point where one does understand the building blocks. In short, we believe in top-down design, but bottom-up learning for understanding.

WHAT IS IN THE BOOK

The book breaks down into two major segments, a) the underlying structure of a computer, as manifested in the LC-2; and b) programming in a high level language, in our case C.

The LC-2

We start with the underpinnings that are needed to understand the workings of a real computer. Chapter 2 introduces the bit and arithmetic and logical operations on bits. Then we begin to build the structure needed to understand the LC-2. Chapter 3 takes the student from MOS transistor, step by step, to a real memory. Our real memory consists of 4 words of 3 bits each, rather than 64 megabytes. The picture fits on a single page (Figure 3.20), making it easy for a student to grasp. By the time the students get there, they have been exposed to all the elements that make memory work. Chapter 4 introduces the Von Neumann execution model, as a lead-in to Chapter 5, the LC-2.

The LC-2 is a 16-bit architecture that includes physical I/O via keyboard and monitor; TRAPs to the operating system for handling service calls; conditional branches on N, Z, and P condition codes; a subroutine call/return mechanism; a minimal set of operate instructions (ADD, AND, and NOT); and various addressing modes for loads and stores (direct, indirect, base+offset, and an immediate mode for loading effective addresses).

Chapter 6 is devoted to programming methodology (stepwise refinement) and debugging, and Chapter 7 is an introduction to assembly language programming. We have developed a simulator and an assembler for the LC-2. Actually, we have developed two simulators, one that runs on Windows platforms and one that runs on UNIX. The Windows simulator is available on the website and on the CD-ROM. Students who would rather use the UNIX version can download and install the software from the web at no charge.

Students use the simulator to test and debug programs written in LC-2 machine language and in LC-2 assembly language. The simulator allows on-line debugging (deposit, examine, single-step, set breakpoint, and so on). The simulator can be used for simple LC-2 machine language and assembly language programming assignments, which are essential for students to master the concepts presented throughout the first 10 chapters.

Assembly language is taught, but not to train expert assembly language programmers. Indeed, if the purpose was to train assembly language programmers, the material would be presented in an upper-level course, not in an introductory course for freshmen. Rather, the material is presented in Chapter 7 because it is consistent with the paradigm of the book. In our bottom-up approach, by the time the student reaches Chapter 7, he/she can handle the process of transforming assembly language programs to sequences of 0s and 1s. We go through the process of assembly step-by-step for a very simple LC-2 Assembler. By hand assembling, the student (at a very small additional cost in time) reinforces the important fundamental concept of translation.

It is also the case that assembly language provides a user-friendly notation to describe machine instructions, something that is particularly useful for the second half of the book. Starting in Chapter 11, when we teach the semantics of C statements, it is far easier for the reader to deal with ADD R1, R2, R3 than with 0001001010000011.

Chapter 8 deals with physical input (from a keyboard) and output (to a monitor). Chapter 9 deals with TRAPs to the operating system, and subroutine calls and returns. Students study the operating system routines (written in LC-2 code) for carrying out physical I/O invoked by the TRAP instruction.

The first half of the book concludes with Chapter 10, a treatment of stacks and data conversion at the LC-2 level, and a comprehensive example that makes use of both. The example is the simulation of a calculator, which is implemented by a main program and 11 subroutines.

The Language C

From there, we move on to C. The C programming language occupies the second half of the book. By the time the student gets to C, he/she has an understanding of the layers below.

The C programming language fits very nicely with our bottom-up approach. Its low-level nature allows students to see clearly the connection between software and the underlying hardware. In this book we focus on basic concepts such as control structures, functions, and arrays. Once basic programming concepts are mastered, it is a short step for students to learn more advanced concepts such as objects and abstraction.

Each time a new construct in C is introduced, the student is shown the LC-2 code that a compiler would produce. We cover the basic constructs of C (variables, operators, control, functions), pointers, recursion, arrays, structures, I/O, complex data structures, and dynamic allocation.

Chapter 11 is a gentle introduction to high-level programming languages. At this point, students have dealt heavily with assembly language and can understand the motivation behind what high-level programming languages provide. Chapter 11 also contains a simple C program, which we use to kick-start the process of learning C.

Chapter 12 deals with values, variables, constants, and operators. Chapter 13 introduces C control structures. We provide many complete program examples to give students a sample of how each of these concepts are used in practice. LC-2 code is used to demonstrate how each C construct affects the machine at the lower levels.

In Chapter 14, students are exposed to techniques for debugging high-level source code. Chapter 15 introduces functions in C. Students are not merely exposed to the syntax of functions. Rather they learn how functions are actually executed using a run-time stack. A number of examples are provided.

Chapter 16 teaches recursion, using the student's newly gained knowledge of functions, activation records, and the run-time stack. Chapter 17 teaches pointers and arrays, relying heavily on the students' understanding of how memory is organized. Chapter 18 introduces the details of I/O functions in C, in particular, streams, variable length argument lists, and how C I/O is affected by the various format specifications. This chapter relies on the student's earlier exposure to physical I/O in Chapter 8. Chapter 19 concludes the coverage of C with structures, dynamic memory allocation, and linked lists.

Along the way, we have tried to emphasize good programming style and coding methodology by means of examples. Novice programmers probably learn at least as much from the programming examples they read as from the rules they are forced to study. Insights that accompany these examples are highlighted by means of lightbulb icons that are included in the margins.

We have found that the concept of pointer variables (Chapter 17) is not at all a problem. By the time students encounter it, they have a good understanding of what memory is all about, since they have analyzed the logic design of a small memory (Chapter 3). They know the difference, for example, between a memory location's address and the data stored there.

Recursion ceases to be magic since, by the time a student gets to that point (Chapter 16), he/she has already encountered all the underpinnings. Students understand how stacks work at the machine level (Chapter 10), and they understand the call/return mechanism from their LC-2 machine language programming experience, and the need for linkages between a called program and the return to the caller (Chapter 9). From this foundation, it is not a large step to explain functions by introducing run-time activation records (Chapter 15), with a lot of the mystery about argument passing, dynamic declarations, and so on, going away. Since a function can call a function, it is one additional small step (certainly no magic involved) for a function to call itself.

How to Use this Book

We have discovered over the past two years that there are many ways the material in this book can be presented in class effectively. We suggest six presentations below.

1. The Michigan model. First course, no formal prerequisites. Very intensive, this course covers the entire book. We have found that with talented, very highly motivated students, this works best.

2. Normal usage. First course, no prerequisites. This course is also intensive, although less so. It covers most of the book, leaving out Sections 10.3 and 10.4 of Chapter 10, Chapters 16 (recursion), 18 (the details of C I/O), and 19 (data structures).

3. Second course. Several schools have successfully used the book in their second course, after the students have been exposed to programming with an object-oriented programming language in a milder first course. In this second course, the entire book is covered, spending the first two-thirds of the semester on the first 10 chapters, and the last one-third of the semester on the second half of the book. The second half of the book can move more quickly, given that it follows both Chapter 1–10 and the introductory programming course, which the student has already taken. Since students have experience with programming, lengthier programming projects can be assigned. This model allows students who were introduced to programming via an object-oriented language to pick up C, which they will certainly need if they plan to go on to advanced software courses such as operating systems.

4. Two quarters. An excellent use of the book. No prerequisites, the entire book can be covered easily in two quarters, the first quarter for Chapters 1–10, the second quarter for Chapters 11–19.

5. Two semesters. Perhaps the optimal use of the book. A two-semester sequence for freshmen. No formal prerequisites. First semester, Chapters 1–10, with supplemental material from Appendix C, the Microarchitecture of the LC-2. Second semester, Chapters 11–19 with additional substantial programming projects so that the students can solidify the concepts they learn in lectures.

6. A sophomore course in computer hardware. Some universities have found the book useful for a sophomore level breadth-first survey of computer hardware. They wish to introduce students in one semester to number systems, digital logic, computer organization, machine language and assembly language programming, finishing up with the material on stacks, activation records, recursion, and linked lists. The idea is to tie the hardware knowledge the students have acquired in the first part of the course to some of the harder to understand concepts that they struggled with in their freshman programming course. We strongly believe the better paradigm is to study the material in this book before tackling an object-oriented language. Nonetheless, we have seen this approach used successfully, where the sophomore student gets to understand the concepts in this course, after struggling with them during the freshman year.

Some Observations

Understanding, not Memorizing   Since the course builds from the bottom up, we have found that less memorization of seemingly arbitrary rules is required than in traditional programming courses. Students understand that the rules make sense since by the time a topic is taught, they have an awareness of how that topic is implemented at the levels below it. This approach is good preparation for later courses in design, where understanding of and insights gained from fundamental underpinnings is essential to making the required design tradeoffs.

The Student Debugs the Student's Program   We hear complaints from industry all the time about CS graduates not being able to program. Part of the problem is the helpful teaching assistant, who contributes far too much of the intellectual component of the student's program, so the student never has to really master the art. Our approach is to push the student to do the job without the teaching assistant (TA). Part of this comes from the bottom-up approach where memorizing is minimized and the student builds on what he/she already knows. Part of this is the simulator, which the student uses from day one. The student is taught debugging from the beginning and is required to use the debugging tools of the simulator to get his/her programs to work from the very beginning. The combination of the simulator and the order in which the subject material is taught results in students actually debugging their own programs instead of taking their programs to the TA for help . . . and the common result that the TAs end up writing the programs for the students.

Preparation for the Future: Cutting Through Protective Layers   In today's real world, professionals who use computers in systems but remain ignorant of what is going on underneath are likely to discover the hard way that the effectiveness of their solutions is impacted adversely by things other than the actual programs they write. This is true for the sophisticated computer programmer as well as the sophisticated engineer.

Serious programmers will write more efficient code if they understand what is going on beyond the statements in their high-level language. Engineers, and not just computer engineers, are having to interact with their computer systems today more and more at the device or pin level. In systems where the computer is being used to sample data from some metering device such as a weather meter or feedback control system, the engineer needs to know more than just how to program in FORTRAN. This is true of mechanical, chemical, and aeronautical engineers today, not just electrical engineers. Consequently, the high-level programming language course, where the compiler protects the student from everything "ugly" underneath, does not serve most engineering students well, and certainly does not prepare them for the future.

Rippling Effects Through the Curriculum   The material of this text clearly has a rippling effect on what can be taught in subsequent courses. Subsequent programming courses can not only assume the students know the syntax of C but also understand how it relates to the underlying architecture. Consequently, the focus can be on problem solving and more sophisticated data structures. On the hardware side, a similar effect is seen in courses in digital logic design and in computer organization. Students start the logic design course with an appreciation of what the logic circuits they master are good for. In the computer organization course, the starting point is much further along than when students are seeing the term Program Counter for the first time. Feedback from Michigan faculty members in the follow-on courses have noticed substantial improvement in student's comprehension, compared to what they saw before students took EECS 100.

ACKNOWLEDGMENTS

This book has benefited greatly from important contributions of many, many people. At the risk of leaving out some, we would at least like to acknowledge the following.

First, Professor Kevin Compton. Kevin believed in the concept of the book since it was first introduced at a curriculum committee meeting that he chaired at Michigan in 1993. The book grew out of a course (EECS 100) that he and the first author developed together, and co-taught the first three semesters it was offered at Michigan in fall 1995, winter 1996, and fall 1996. Kevin's insights into programming methodology (independent of the syntax of the particular language) provided a sound foundation for the beginning student. The course at Michigan and this book would be a lot less were it not for Kevin's influence.

Several other students and faculty at Michigan were involved in the early years of EECS 100 and the early stages of the book. We are particularly grateful for the help of Professor David Kieras, Brian Hartman, David Armstrong, Matt Postiff, Dan Friendly, Rob Chappell, David Cybulski, Sangwook Kim, Don Winsor, and Ann Ford.

We also benefited enormously from TAs who were committed to helping students learn. The focus was always on how to explain the concept so the student gets it. We acknowledge, in particular, Fadi Aloul, David Armstrong, David Baker, Rob Chappell, David Cybulski, Amolika Gurujee, Brian Hartman, Sangwook Kim, Steve Maciejewski, Paul Racunas, David Telehowski, Francis Tseng, Aaron Wagner, and Paul Watkins.

We were delighted with the response from the publishing world to our manuscript. We ultimately decided on McGraw-Hill in large part because of the editor, Betsy Jones. Once she checked us out, she became a strong believer in what we are trying to accomplish. Throughout the process, her commitment and energy level have been greatly appreciated. We also appreciate what Michelle Flomenhoft has brought to the project. It has been a pleasure to work with her.

Our book has benefited from extensive reviews provided by faculty members at many universities. We gratefully acknowledge reviews provided by Carl D. Crane III, Florida, Nat Davis, Virginia Tech, Renee Elio, University of Alberta, Kelly Flangan, BYU, George Friedman, UIUC, Franco Fummi, Universita di Verona, Dale Grit, Colorado State, Thor Gulsrud, Stavanger College, Brad Hutchings, BYU, Dave Kaeli, Northeastern, Rasool Kenarangui, UT at Arlington, Joel Kraft, Case Western Reserve, Wei-Ming Lin, UT at San Antonio, Roderick Loss, Montgomery College, Ron Meleshko, Grant MacEwan Community College, Andreas Moshovos, Northwestern, Tom Murphy, The Citadel, Murali Narayanan, Kansas State, Carla Purdy, Cincinnati, T. N. Rajashekhara, Camden County College, Nello Scarabottolo, Universita degli Studi di Milano, Robert Schaefer, Daniel Webster College, Tage Stabell-Kuloe, University of Tromsoe, Jean-Pierre Steger, Burgdorf School of Engineering, Bill Sverdlik, Eastern Michigan, John Tronto, St. Michael's College, Murali Varansi, University of South Florida, Montanez Wade, Tennessee State, and Carl Wick, US Naval Academy.

In addition to all these people, there were others who contributed in many different and sometimes unique ways. Space dictates that we simply list them and say thank you. Susan Kornfield, Ed DeFranco, Evan Gsell, Rich Belgard, Tom Conte, Dave Nagle, Bruce Shriver, Bill Sayle, Steve Lumetta, Dharma Agarwal, and David Lilia.

Finally, if you will indulge the first author a bit: This book is about developing a strong foundation in the fundamentals with the fervent belief that once that is accomplished, students can go as far as their talent and energy can take them. This objective was instilled in me by the professor who taught me how to be a professor, Professor William K. Linvill. It has been more than 35 years since I was in his classroom, but I still treasure the example he set.

A FINAL WORD

We hope you will enjoy the approach taken in this book. Nonetheless, we are mindful that the current version will always be a work in progress, and both of us welcome your comments on any aspect of it. You can reach us by email at patt@ece.utexas.edu and sjp@crhc.uiuc.edu. We hope you will.

Yale N. Patt
Sanjay J. Patel

1

Welcome Aboard

1.1 WHAT WE WILL TRY TO DO

Welcome to "From Bits and Gates to C and Beyond." Our intent is to introduce you over the next 515 pages to the world of computing. As we do so, we have one objective above all others: to show you very clearly that there is no magic to computing. The computer is a deterministic system—every time we hit it over the head in the same way and in the same place (provided, of course, it was in the same starting condition), we get the same response. The computer is not an electronic genius; on the contrary, if anything, it is an electronic idiot, doing exactly what we tell it to do. It has no mind of its own.

What appears to be a very complex organism is really just a huge, systematically interconnected collection of very simple parts. Our job throughout this book is to introduce you to those very simple parts, and, step-by-step, build the interconnected structure that you know by the name *computer*. Like a house, we will start at the bottom, construct the foundation first, and then go on to add layers and layers, as we get closer and closer to what most people know as a full-blown computer. Each time we add a layer, we will explain what we are doing, tying the new ideas to the underlying fabric. Our goal is that when we are done, you will be able to write programs in a computer language such as C, using the sophisticated features of that language, and understand what is going on underneath, inside the computer.

1.2   HOW WE WILL GET THERE

We will start (in Chapter 2) by noting that the computer is a piece of electronic equipment and, as such, consists of electronic parts interconnected by wires. Every wire in the computer, at every moment in time, is either at a high voltage or a low voltage. We do not differentiate exactly how high. For example, we do not distinguish voltages of 115 volts from voltages of 118 volts. We only care whether there is or whether there is not a large voltage relative to 0 volts. That absence or presence of a large voltage relative to 0 volts is represented as 0 or 1.

We will encode all information as sequences of 0s and 1s. For example, one encoding of the letter *a* that is commonly used is the sequence 01100001. One encoding of the decimal number *35* is the sequence 00100011. We will see how to perform operations on such encoded information.

Once we are comfortable with information represented as codes made up of 0s and 1s and operations (addition, for example) being performed on these representations, we will begin the process of showing how a computer works. In Chapter 3, we will see how the transistors that make up today's microprocessors work. We will further see how those transistors are combined into larger structures that perform operations, such as addition, and into structures that allow us to save information for later use. In Chapter 4, we will combine these larger structures into the Von Neumann machine, a basic model that describes how a computer works. In Chapter 5, we will begin to study a simple computer, the LC-2. *LC-2* stands for Little Computer 2; we started with LC-1 but needed a second chance before we got it right! The LC-2 has all the important characteristics of the microprocessors that you may have already heard of, for example, the Intel 8088, which was used in the first IBM PCs back in 1981. Or the Motorola 68000, which was used in the Macintosh, vintage 1984. Or the Pentium III, one of the high-performance microprocessors of choice in the PC of the year 2000. That is, the LC-2 has all the important characteristics of these "real" microprocessors, without being so complicated that it gets in the way of your understanding.

Once we understand how the LC-2 works, the next step is to program it, first in its own language (Chapter 6), then in a language called *assembly language* that is a little bit easier for humans to work with (Chapter 7). Chapter 8 deals with the problem of getting information into (input) and out of (output) the LC-2. Chapter 9 covers two sophisticated LC-2 mechanisms, TRAPs and subroutines.

We conclude our introduction to programming the LC-2 in Chapter 10 by first introducing two important concepts (stacks and data conversion), and then by showing a sophisticated example: an LC-2 program that carries out the work of a handheld calculator.

In the second half of the book (Chapters 11–19), we turn our attention to a high-level programming language, C. We include many aspects of C that are usually not dealt with in an introductory textbook. In almost all cases, we try to tie high-level C constructs to the underlying LC-2, so that you will understand what you demand of the computer when you use a particular construct in a C program.

Our treatment of C starts with basic topics such as variables and operators (Chapter 12), control structures (Chapter 13), and functions (Chapter 14). We then move on to the more advanced topics of debugging C programs (Chapter 15), recursion (Chapter 16), and pointers and arrays (Chapter 17).

We conclude our introduction to C by examining two very common high-level constructs, input/output in C (Chapter 18) and the linked list (Chapter 19).

1.3   A COMPUTER SYSTEM

We have used the word *computer* many times in the preceding paragraphs, and although we did not say so explicitly, we used it to mean a mechanism that does two things: It directs the processing of information and it performs the actual processing of information. It does both these things in response to a computer program. When we say "directing the processing of information," we mean figuring out which task should get carried out next. When we say "performing the actual processing," we mean doing the actual additions, multiplications, and so forth that are necessary to get the job done. A more precise term for this mechanism is a central processing unit (cpu), or simply a processor. This textbook is primarily about the processor and the programs that are executed by the processor.

Twenty years ago, the processor was constructed out of ten or more 18-inch electronic boards, each containing 50 or more electronic parts known as integrated circuit packages (see Figure 1.1). Today, a processor usually consists of a single microprocessor chip, built on a piece of silicon material, measuring less than an inch square, and containing many millions of transistors (see Figure 1.2).

However, when most people use the word *computer*, they usually mean more than the processor. They usually mean the collection of parts that in combination form their "computer system" (see Figure 1.3). A computer system usually includes, in addition to the processor, a keyboard for typing commands, a mouse for clicking on menu entries, a monitor for displaying information that the computer system has produced, a printer for obtaining paper copies of that information, memory for temporarily storing information, disks and CD-ROMs of one sort or another for storing information for a very long time, even after the computer has been turned off, and the collection of programs (the software) that the user wishes to execute.

These additional items are useful to help the computer user do his/her job. Without a printer, for example, the user would have to copy by hand what is displayed on the monitor. Without a mouse, the user would have to type each command, rather than simply click on the mouse button.

So, as we begin our journey which focuses on how we get less than 1 square inch of silicon to do our bidding, we note that the computer systems we use contain a lot of other components to make our life more comfortable.

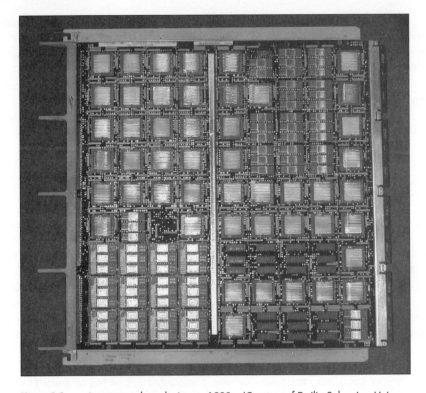

Figure 1.1   A processor board, vintage 1980s. (Courtesy of Emilio Salgueiro, Unisys Corporation.)

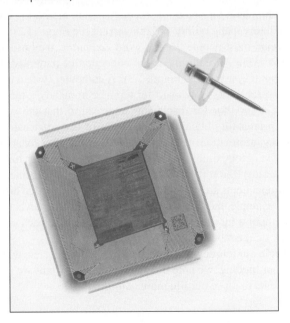

Figure 1.2   A microprocessor, vintage 1998. (Courtesy of Intel Corporation.)

Figure 1.3   A personal computer. (Courtesy of Dell Computer.)

1.4   TWO VERY IMPORTANT IDEAS

Before we leave this first chapter, there are two very important ideas that we would like you to understand, ideas that are at the core of what computing is all about.

IDEA 1: All computers (the biggest and the smallest, the fastest and the slowest, the most expensive and the cheapest) are capable of computing exactly the same things if they are given enough time and enough memory. That is, anything a fast computer can do, a slow computer can do also. The slow computer just does it more slowly. A more expensive computer cannot figure out something that a cheaper computer is unable to figure out as long as the cheap computer can access enough memory. (You may have to go to the store to buy disks whenever it runs out of memory in order to keep increasing memory.) *All* computers are able to do *exactly* the same things. Some computers can do things faster, but none can do *more* than any other.

IDEA 2: We describe our problems in English or some other language spoken by people. Yet the problems are solved by electrons running around inside the computer. It is necessary to transform our problem from the language of humans to the voltages that influence the flow of electrons. This transformation is really a sequence of systematic transformations, developed and improved over the last 50 years, which combine to give the computer the ability to carry out what appears to be some very complicated tasks. In reality, these tasks are simple and straightforward.

The rest of this chapter is devoted to discussing these two ideas.

1.5   COMPUTERS AS UNIVERSAL COMPUTATIONAL DEVICES

It may seem strange that an introductory textbook begins by describing how computers work. After all, mechanical engineering students begin by studying physics, not how car engines work. Chemical engineering students begin by studying chemistry, not oil refineries. Why should computing students begin by studying computers?

The answer is that computers are different. To learn the fundamental principles of computing, you must study computers or machines that can do what computers can do. The reason for this has to do with the notion that computers are *universal computational devices*. Let's see what that means.

Before modern computers, there were many kinds of calculating machines. Some were *analog machines*—machines that produced an answer by measuring some physical quantity such as distance or voltage. For example, a slide rule is an analog machine that multiplies numbers by sliding one logarithmically graded ruler next to another. The user can read a logarithmic "distance" on the second ruler. Some early analog adding machines worked by dropping weights on a scale. The difficulty with analog machines is that it is very hard to increase their accuracy.

This is why *digital machines*—machines that perform computations by manipulating a fixed finite set of digits or letters—came to dominate computing. You are familiar with the distinction between analog and digital watches. An analog watch has hour and minute hands, and perhaps a second hand. It gives the time by the positions of its hands, which are really angular measures. Digital watches give the time in digits. You can increase accuracy just by adding more digits. For example, if it is important for you to measure time in hundredths of a second, you can buy a watch that gives a reading like 10:35.16 rather than just 10:35. How would you get an analog watch that would give you an accurate reading to one one-hundredth of a second? You could do it, but it would take a mighty long second hand. When we talk about computers in this book, we will always mean digital machines.

Before modern digital computers, the most common digital machines in the West were adding machines. In other parts of the world another digital machine, the abacus, was common. Digital adding machines were mechanical or electromechanical devices that could perform a specific kind of computation: adding integers. There were also digital machines that could multiply integers. There were digital machines that could put a stack of cards with punched names in alphabetical order. The main limitation of all of these machines is that they could do only one specific kind of computation. If you owned only an adding machine and wanted to multiply two integers, you had some pencil and paper work to do.

This is why computers are different. You can tell a computer how to add numbers. You can tell it how to multiply. You can tell it how to alphabetize a list or perform any computation you like. When you think of a new kind of computation, you do not have to buy or design a new computer. You just give the old computer a new set of instructions (or program) to carry out the computation. This is why we say the computer is a *universal computational device*. Computer scientists believe that *anything that can be computed, can be computed by a computer* provided it has enough time and enough memory. When we study computers, we study the fundamentals of all computing. We learn what computation is and what can be computed.

The idea of a universal computational device is due to Alan Turing. Turing proposed in 1937 that all computations could be carried out by a particular kind of machine, which is now called a Turing machine. He gave a mathematical description of this kind of machine, but did not actually build one. Digital computers were not operating until 1946. Turing was more interested in solving a philosophical problem: defining computation. He began by looking at the kinds of actions that people perform when they compute; these include making marks on paper, writing symbols according to certain rules when other symbols are present, and so on. He abstracted these actions and specified a mechanism that could carry them out. He gave some examples of the kinds of things that these machines could do. One Turing machine could add two integers; another could multiply two integers.

Figure 1.4 provides what we call "black box" models of Turing machines that add and multiply. In each case, the operation to be performed is described in the box. The data on which to operate is shown as input to the box. The result of the operation is shown as output from the box. A black box model provides no information as to exactly how the operation is performed, and indeed, there are many ways to add or multiply two numbers.

Turing proposed that every computation can be performed by some Turing machine. We call this *Turing's thesis*. Although Turing's thesis has never been proved, there does exist a lot of evidence to suggest it is true. We know, for example, that various enhancements one can make to Turing machines do not result in machines that can compute more.

Perhaps the best argument to support Turing's thesis was provided by Turing himself in his original paper. He said that one way to try to construct a machine more powerful than any particular Turing machine was to make a machine U that could simulate *all* Turing machines. You would simply describe to U the particular Turing machine you wanted it to simulate, say a machine to add two integers, give U the input data, and U would compute the appropriate output, in this case the sum of the inputs. Turing then showed that there was, in fact, a Turing machine that could do

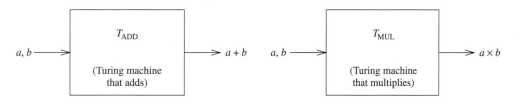

Figure 1.4   Black box models of Turing machines

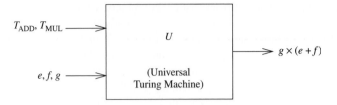

Figure 1.5   Black box model of a universal turing machine

this; so even this attempt to find something that could not be computed by Turing machines failed.

Figure 1.5 further illustrates the point. Suppose you wanted to compute $g \cdot (e + f)$. You would simply provide to U descriptions of the Turing machines to add and to multiply, and the three inputs, e, f, and g. U would do the rest.

In specifying U, Turing had provided us with a deep insight: He had given us the first description of what computers do. In fact, both a computer (with as much memory as it wants) and a universal Turing machine can compute exactly the same things. In both cases you give the machine a description of a computation and the data it needs, and the machine computes the appropriate answer. Computers and universal Turing machines can compute anything that can be computed because they are *programmable*.

This is the reason that a big or expensive computer cannot do more than a small, cheap computer. More money may buy you a faster computer, a monitor with higher resolution, or a nice sound system. But if you have a small, cheap computer, you already have a universal computational device.

1.6   HOW DO WE GET THE ELECTRONS TO DO THE WORK?

Figure 1.6 shows the process we must go through to get the electrons (which actually do the work) to do our bidding. We call the steps of this process the "Levels of Transformation." As we will see, at each level we have choices. If we ignore any of the levels, our ability to make best use of our computing system can be very adversely affected.

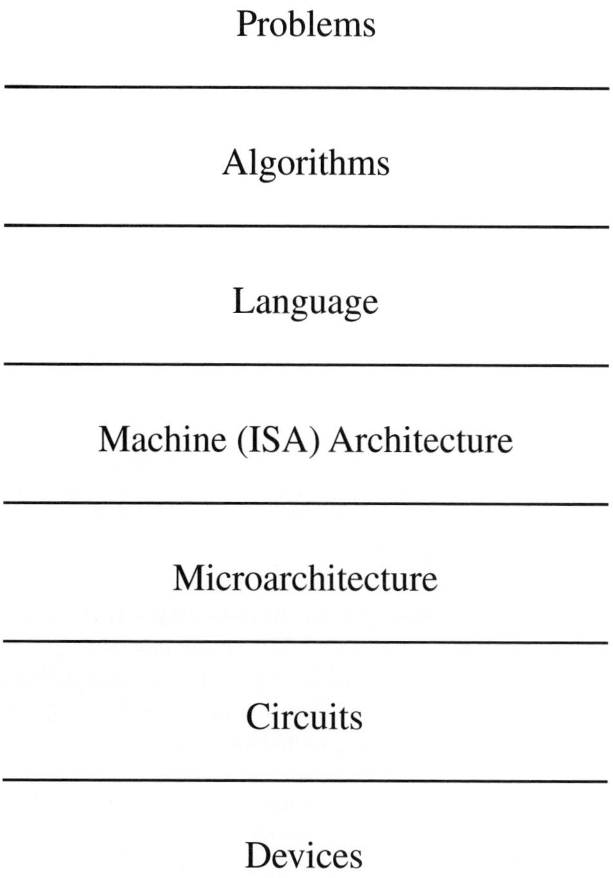

Problems

Algorithms

Language

Machine (ISA) Architecture

Microarchitecture

Circuits

Devices

Figure 1.6   Levels of transformation

1.6.1   The Statement of the Problem

We describe the problems we wish to solve with a computer in a "natural language." Natural languages are languages that people speak, like English, French, Japanese, Italian, and so on. They have evolved over centuries in accordance with their usage. They are fraught with a lot of things unacceptable for providing instructions to a computer. Most important of these unacceptable attributes is ambiguity. Natural language is filled with ambiguity. To infer the meaning of a sentence, a listener is often helped by the tone of voice of the speaker, or at the very least, the context of the sentence.

An example of ambiguity in English is the sentence, "Time flies like an arrow." At least three interpretations are possible, depending on whether (1) one is noticing how fast time passes, (2) one is at a track meet for insects, or (3) one is writing a letter to the Dear Abby of Insectville. In the first case, a simile, one is comparing the speed of time passing to the speed of an arrow that has been released. In the second case, one is giving instructions to the timekeeper that he/she do his/her job much like an arrow would. In the third case, one is relating that a particular group of flies (time flies, as opposed to fruit flies) are all in love with the same arrow.

Such ambiguity would be unacceptable in instructions provided to a computer. The computer, electronic idiot that it is, can only do as it is told. To tell it to do something where there are multiple interpretations would cause the computer to not know which interpretation to follow.

1.6.2   The Algorithm

The first step in the sequence of transformations is to transform the natural language description of the problem to an algorithm, and in so doing, get rid of the objectional characteristics. An algorithm is a step-by-step procedure that is guaranteed to terminate, such that each step is precisely stated and can be carried out by the computer. There are terms to describe each of these properties.

We use the term *definiteness* to describe the notion that each step is precisely stated. A recipe for excellent pancakes that instructs the preparer to "stir until lumpy" lacks definiteness, since the notion of lumpiness is not precise.

We use the term *effective computability* to describe the notion that each step can be carried out by a computer. A procedure that instructs the computer to "take the largest prime number" lacks effective computability, since there is no largest prime number.

We use the term *finiteness* to describe the notion that the procedure terminates.

For every problem there are usually many different algorithms for solving that problem. One algorithm may require the fewest number of steps. Another algorithm may allow some steps to be performed concurrently. A computer that allows more than one thing to be done at a time can often solve the problem in less time, even though it is likely that the total number of steps to be performed has increased.

1.6.3   The Program

The next step is to transform the algorithm into a computer program, in one of the programming languages that are available. Programming languages are "mechanical languages." That is, unlike natural languages, mechanical languages did not evolve through human discourse. Rather, they were invented for use in specifying a sequence of instructions to a computer. Therefore, mechanical languages do not suffer from failings such as ambiguity that would make them unacceptable for specifying a computer program.

There are more than 1,000 programming languages. Some have been designed for use with particular applications, such as Fortran for solving scientific calculations and COBOL for solving business data-processing problems. In the second half of this book, we will use C, a language that was designed for manipulating low-level hardware structures.

Other languages are useful for still other purposes. Prolog is the language of choice for many applications that require the design of an expert system. LISP was for years the language of choice of a substantial number of people working on problems dealing with Artificial Intelligence. Pascal is a language invented as a vehicle for teaching beginning students how to program.

There are two kinds of programming languages, high-level languages and low-level languages. High-level languages are at a distance (a high level) from the underlying computer. At their best, they are independent of the computer on which the programs will execute. We say the language is "machine independent." All the languages mentioned thus far are high-level languages. Low-level languages are tied to the computer on which the programs will execute. There is generally one such low-level language for each computer. That language is called the *assembly language* for that computer.

1.6.4   The ISA

The next step is to translate the program into the instruction set of the particular computer that will be used to carry out the work of the program. The instruction set architecture (ISA) is the complete specification of the interface between programs that have been written and the underlying computer hardware that must carry out the work of those programs.

The ISA specifies the set of instructions the computer can carry out, that is, what operations the computer can perform and what data is needed by each operation. The term *operand* is used to describe individual data values. The ISA specifies the acceptable representations for operands. They are called *data types*. A *data type* is a legitimate representation for an operand such that the computer can perform operations on that representation. The ISA specifies the mechanisms that the computer can use to figure out where the operands are located. These mechanisms are called *addressing modes*.

The number of operations, data types, and addressing modes specified by an ISA varies among the different ISAs. Some ISAs have as few as a half dozen operations, whereas others have as many as several hundred. Some ISAs have only one data type, while others have more than a dozen. Some ISAs have one or two addressing modes, whereas others have more than 20. The IA-32 has more than 100 operations, more than a dozen data types, and more than two dozen addressing modes.

The ISA also specifies the number of unique locations that comprise the computer's memory, and the number of individual 0s and 1s that are contained in each location.

Many ISAs are in use today. The most common example, the one used in the PC, is the IA-32 ISA, introduced by Intel Corporation in 1979, and currently also manufactured by AMD and other companies. Other ISAs are the PowerPC (IBM and Motorola), Alpha (Compaq Computer Corporation), PA-RISC (Hewlett-Packard), and SPARC (SUN Microsystems and HAL Computer Systems).

The translation from a high-level language (such as C) to the ISA of the computer on which the program will execute (such as IA-32) is usually done by a translating program called a *compiler*. To translate from a program written in C to the IA-32 ISA, one would need an IA-32 C compiler. For each high-level language and each desired target computer, one must provide a corresponding compiler.

The translation from the unique assembly language of a computer to its ISA is done by an assembler.

1.6.5 The Microarchitecture

The next step is to transform the ISA into an implementation. The detailed organization of an implementation is called its *microarchitecture*. So, for example, the IA-32 has been implemented by several different microprocessors over the years, each having its own unique microarchitecture. The original implementation was the 8086 in 1979. More recently, in 1999, Intel introduced the Pentium III microprocessor. Compaq Computer Corporation has implemented its Alpha ISA with four different microprocessors, each having its own microarchitecture, the 21064, the 21164, the 21264, and the 21364.

Each implementation is an opportunity for computer designers to make different trade-offs between the cost of the microprocessor and the performance that microprocessor will provide. Computer design is always an exercise in trade-offs, as the designer opts for higher (or lower) performance at greater (or lesser) cost.

The automobile provides a good analogy of the relationship between an ISA and a microarchitecture that implements that ISA. The ISA describes what the driver sees as he/she sits inside the automobile. All automobiles provide the same interface (an ISA different from the ISA for boats and the ISA for airplanes). Of the three pedals on the floor, the middle one is always the brake. The one on the right is the accelerator, and when it is depressed, the car will move faster. The ISA is about basic functionality. All cars can get from point A to point B, can move forward and backward, and can turn to the right and to the left.

The implementation of the ISA is about what goes on under the hood. Here all automobile makes and models are different, depending on what cost/performance trade-offs the automobile designer made before the car was manufactured. So, some automobiles come with disk brakes, others (in the past, at least) with drums. Some automobiles have eight cylinders, others run on six cylinders, and still others have four. Some are turbocharged, some are not. In each case, the "microarchitecture" of the specific automobile is a result of the automobile designers' decisions regarding cost and performance.

1.6.6 The Logic Circuit

The next step is to implement each element of the microarchitecture out of simple logic circuits. Here, also, there are choices, as the logic designer decides how to best make the trade-offs between cost and performance. So, for example, even for the simple operation of addition, there are several choices of logic circuits to perform this operation at differing speeds and corresponding costs.

1.6.7   The Devices

Finally, each basic logic circuit is implemented in accordance with the requirements of the particular device technology used. So, CMOS circuits are different from NMOS circuits, which are different, in turn, from gallium arsenide circuits.

1.6.8   Putting It Together

In summary, from the natural language description of a problem to the electrons running around that actually solve the problem, many transformations need to be performed. If we could speak electron, or the electrons could understand English, perhaps we could just walk up to the computer and get the electrons to do our bidding. Since we can't speak electron and they can't speak English, the best we can do is this systematic sequence of transformations. At each level of transformation, there are choices as to how to proceed. Our handling of those choices determine the resulting cost and performance of our resulting computer.

In this book, we describe each of these transformations. We show how transistors combine to form logic circuits, how logic circuits combine to form the microarchitecture, and how the microarchitecture implements a particular ISA, in our case, the LC-2. We complete the process by going from the English language description of a problem to a C program that solves the problem, and show how that C program is translated (i.e., compiled) to the ISA of the LC-2.

We hope you enjoy the ride.

PROBLEMS

1.1.   Explain the first of the two important ideas stated in Section 1.4.

1.2.   Can a higher level programming language instruct a computer to compute more than a lower level programming language?

1.3.   What difficulty with analog computers encourages computer designers to use digital designs?

1.4.   Say we had a "black box," which takes two numbers as input and outputs their sum. See Figure 1.7a. Say we had another box capable of multiplying two numbers together. See Figure 1.7b. We can connect these boxes together to calculate $p \times (m + n)$. See Figure 1.7c. Assume we have an unlimited number of these boxes. Show how to connect them together to calculate:

1. $ax + b$
2. The average of the four input numbers w, x, y, and z.
3. $a^2 + 2ab + b^2$. (Can you do it with one add box and one multiply box?)

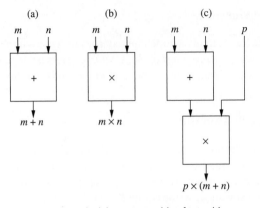

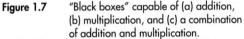

Figure 1.7   "Black boxes" capable of (a) addition, (b) multiplication, and (c) a combination of addition and multiplication.

1.5.   Name one characteristic of natural languages that prevents them from being used as programming languages.

1.6.   Write a statement in a natural language and offer two different interpretations of that statement.

1.7.   Are natural languages capable of expressing algorithms?

1.8.   Name three characteristics of algorithms. Briefly explain each of these three characteristics.

1.9.   For each characteristic of an algorithm, give an example of a procedure that does not have the characteristic, and is therefore not an algorithm.

1.10.   Are items 1 to 4 in the list below algorithms? If not, what qualities required of algorithms do they lack?

1.   Add the first row of the following matrix to another row whose first column contains a nonzero entry. (*Reminder*: Columns run vertically; rows run horizontally.)

$$\begin{bmatrix} 1 & 2 & 0 & 4 \\ 0 & 3 & 2 & 4 \\ 2 & 3 & 10 & 22 \\ 12 & 4 & 3 & 4 \end{bmatrix}$$

2.   In order to show that there are as many prime numbers as there are natural numbers, match each prime number with a natural number in the following manner. Create pairs of prime and natural numbers by matching the first prime number with 1 (which is the first natural number) and the second prime number with 2, the third with 3, and so forth. If, in the end, it turns out that each prime number can be paired with each natural number, then it is shown that there are as many prime numbers as natural numbers.

3. Suppose you're given two vectors each with 20 elements and asked to perform the following operation. Take the first element of the first vector and multiply it by the first element of the second vector. Do the same to the second elements, and so forth. Add all the individual products together to derive the dot product.

4. Lynne and Calvin are trying to decided who will take the dog for a walk. Lynne suggests that they flip a coin and pulls a quarter out of her pocket. Calvin does not trust Lynne and suspects that the quarter may be weighted (meaning that it might favor a particular outcome when tossed) and suggests the following procedure to fairly determine who will walk the dog.

   • Flip the quarter twice.

   • If the outcome is heads on the first flip and tails on the second, then I will walk the dog.

   • If the outcome is tails on the first flip, and heads on the second, then you will walk the dog.

   • If both outcomes are tails or both outcomes are heads, then we flip twice again.

   Is Calvin's technique an algorithm?

1.11. Generate an algorithm to search for a particular book title in a library. Explain how this algorithm satisfies the three conditions required of algorithms.

1.12. Suppose we wish to put a set of names in alphabetical order. We call the act of doing so *sorting*. One algorithm that can accomplish that is called the bubble sort. We could then program our bubble sort algorithm in C, and compile the C program to execute on an IA-32 ISA. The IA-32 ISA can be implemented with an Intel Pentium III microarchitecture. Let us call the sequence "Bubble Sort, C program, IA-32 ISA, Pentium III microarchitecture" one *transformation process*.

Assume we have available four sorting algorithms and can program in C, C++, Pascal, Fortran, and COBOL, and have available compilers that can translate from each of these to either IA-32 or SPARC, and have available three different microarchitectures for IA-32 and three different microarchitectures for SPARC.

1. How many transformation processes are possible?

2. Write three examples of transformation processes.

3. How many transformation processes are possible if instead of three different microarchitectures for IA-32 and three different microarchitectures for SPARC, there were two for IA-32 and four for SPARC?

1.13. Name at least three things specified by an ISA.

1.14. Identify one advantage of programming in a higher level language over a lower level language. Identify one disadvantage.

1.15. Briefly describe the difference between an ISA and a microarchitecture.

1.16. How many ISAs are normally implemented by a single microarchitecture? Conversely, how many microarchitectures could exist for a single ISA?

1.17. List the levels of transformation and name an example for each level.

1.18. Say you go to the store and buy the some word processing software. What form is the software actually in? Is it in a high-level programming language? Is it in assembly language? Is it in the ISA of the computer on which you'll run it? Justify your answer.

1.19. Why is an ISA unlikely to change between successive generations of microarchitectures that implement it? For example, why would Intel want to make certain that the ISA implemented by the Pentium III is the same as the one implemented by Pentium II? *Hint:* When you upgrade your computer (or buy one with a newer CPU), do you need to throw out all your old software?

chapter
2
Bits, Data Types, and Operations

2.1 BITS AND DATA TYPES

2.1.1 The Bit as the Unit of Information

We noted in Chapter 1 that the computer was organized as a system with several levels of transformation. A problem stated in a natural language such as English is actually solved by the electrons moving around inside the electronics of the computer.

Inside the computer, millions of very tiny, very fast devices control the movement of those electrons. These devices react to the presence or absence of voltages in electronic circuits. They could react to the actual voltages, rather than simply to the presence or absence of voltages. However, this would make the control and detection circuits more complex than they need to be. It is much easier simply to detect whether or not a voltage exists between a pair of points in a circuit than it is to measure exactly what that voltage is.

To understand this, consider any wall outlet in your home. You could measure the exact voltage it is carrying, whether 120 volts or 115 volts, or 118.6 volts, for example. However, the detection circuitry to determine *only* whether there is a voltage (any of the above three will do) or whether there is no voltage is much simpler. Your finger casually inserted into the wall socket, for example, will suffice.

We symbolically represent the presence of a voltage as "1" and the absence of a voltage as "0." We refer to each 0 and each 1 as a "bit," which is a shortened form of binary digit. Recall the digits you have been using since you were a child—0,1,2,3, ..., 9. There are 10 of them, and they are referred to as decimal digits. In the case of binary digits, there are two of them, 0 and 1.

To be perfectly precise, it is not really the case that the computer differentiates the *absolute* absence of a voltage (that is, 0) from the *absolute* presence of a voltage (that is, 1). Actually, the electronic circuits in the computer differentiate voltages *close to* 0 from voltages *far from* 0. So, for example, if the computer expects a voltage of 2.9 volts or a voltage of 0 volts (2.9 volts signifying 1 and 0 volts signifying 0), then a voltage of 2.6 volts will be taken as a 1 and 0.2 volts will be taken as a 0.

To get useful work done by the computer, it is necessary to be able to identify uniquely a large number of distinct values. The voltage on one wire can represent uniquely one of only two things. One thing can be represented by 0, the other thing can be represented by 1. Thus, to identify uniquely many things, it is necessary to combine multiple bits. For example, if we use 8 bits (corresponding to the voltage present on 8 wires), we can represent one particular value as 01001110, and another value as 11100111. In fact, if we are limited to eight bits, we can differentiate at most only 256 (that is, 2^8) different values. In general, with k bits, we can distinguish at most 2^k distinct items. Each pattern of these k bits is a code; that is, it corresponds to a particular value.

2.1.2 Data Types

There are many ways to represent the same value. For example, the number five can be written as a 5. This is the standard decimal notation that you are used to. The value five can also be represented by someone holding up one hand, with all fingers and thumb extended. The person is saying, "The number I wish to communicate can be determined by counting the number of fingers I am showing." A written version of that scheme would be the value 11111. This notation has a name also—*unary*. The Romans had yet another notation for five—the character V. We will see momentarily that a fourth notation for five is the binary representation 00000101.

It is not enough simply to represent values, we must be able to operate on those values. We say a particular representation is a *data type* if there are operations in the computer that can operate on information that is encoded in that representation. Each ISA has its own set of data types and its own set of instructions that can operate on those data types. In this book, we will mainly use two data types: *2's complement integers* for representing positive and negative integers that we wish to perform arithmetic on, and *ASCII codes* for representing characters on the keyboard that we wish to input to a computer or display on the computer's monitor. Both data types will be explained shortly.

There are other representations of information that could be used, and indeed that are present in most computers. Recall the "scientific notation" from high school chemistry where you were admonished to represent the decimal number 621 as $6.21 \cdot 10^2$. There are computers that represent numbers in that form, and provide operations that can operate on numbers so represented. That data type is usually called *floating point*. We will show you its representation in Section 2.6.

2.2 INTEGER DATA TYPES

2.2.1 Unsigned Integers

The first representation of information, or data type, that we shall look at is the unsigned integer. Unsigned integers have many uses in a computer. If we wish to perform a task some specific number of times, unsigned integers enable us to keep track of this number easily by simply counting how many times we have performed the task "so far." Unsigned integers also provide a means for identifying different memory locations in the computer, in the same way that house numbers differentiate 129 Main Street from 131 Main Street.

We can represent unsigned integers as strings of binary digits. To do this, we use a positional notation much like the decimal system that you have been using since you were three years old.

You are familiar with the decimal number 329, which also uses positional notation. The 3 is worth much more than the 9, even though the absolute value of 3 standing alone is only worth 1/3 the value of 9 standing alone. This is because, as you know, the 3 stands for 300 ($3 \cdot 10^2$) due to its position in the decimal string 329, while the 9 stands for $9 \cdot 10^0$.

The 2's complement representation works the same way, only the digits used are the binary digits 0 and 1, and the base is 2, rather than 10. So, for example, if we have five bits available to represent our values, the number 6 is represented as 00110, corresponding to

$$0 \cdot 2^4 + 0 \cdot 2^3 + 1 \cdot 2^2 + 1 \cdot 2^1 + 0 \cdot 2^0.$$

With k bits, we can represent in this positional notation exactly 2^k integers, ranging from 0 to $2^k - 1$. In our five-bit example, we can represent the integers from 0 to 31.

2.2.2 Signed Integers

However, to do useful arithmetic, it is often (although not always) necessary to be able to deal with negative quantities as well as positive. We could take our 2^k distinct patterns of k bits and separate them in half, half for positive numbers, and half for negative numbers. In this way, with five-bit codes, instead of representing integers from 0 to +31, we could choose to represent positive integers from +1 to +15 and negative integers from −1 to −15. There are 30 such integers. Since 2^5 is 32, we still have two 5-bit codes unassigned. One of them, 00000 we would presumably assign to the value 0, giving us the full range of integer values from −15 to +15. That leaves one more five-bit code to assign, and there are different ways to do this, as we will see momentarily.

We are still left with the problem of determining what codes to assign to what values. That is, we have 32 codes, but which value should go with which code?

Positive integers are represented in the straightforward positional scheme. Since there are k bits, and we wish to use exactly half of the 2^k codes to represent the integers from 0 to $2^{k-1} - 1$, all positive integers will have a leading 0 in their representation. In our example (with $k = 5$), the largest positive integer $+15$ is represented as 01111.

Note that in all three data types shown in Figure 2.1, the representation for 0 and all the positive integers start with a leading 0. What about the representations for the negative numbers (in our five-bit example, -1 to -15)? The first thought that usually comes to mind is: If a leading 0 signifies a *positive* integer, how about letting a leading 1 signify a *negative* integer? The result is the *Signed-Magnitude* data type shown in Figure 2.1. A second idea (that was actually used on some early computers such as the Control Data Corporation 6600) was the following: Let a negative number be represented by taking the representation of the positive number having the same

Representation	Value Represented		
	Signed Mag.	1's Compl.	2's Compl.
00000	0	0	0
00001	1	1	1
00010	2	2	2
00011	3	3	3
00100	4	4	4
00101	5	5	5
00110	6	6	6
00111	7	7	7
01000	8	8	8
01001	9	9	9
01010	10	10	10
01011	11	11	11
01100	12	12	12
01101	13	13	13
01110	14	14	14
01111	15	15	15
10000	-0	-15	-16
10001	-1	-14	-15
10010	-2	-13	-14
10011	-3	-12	-13
10100	-4	-11	-12
10101	-5	-10	-11
10110	-6	-9	-10
10111	-7	-8	-9
11000	-8	-7	-8
11001	-9	-6	-7
11010	-10	-5	-6
11011	-11	-4	-5
11100	-12	-3	-4
11101	-13	-2	-3
11110	-14	-1	-2
11111	-15	-0	-1

Figure 2.1   Three representation of signed integers

magnitude, and "flipping all the bits." So, for example, since +5 is represented as 00101, we designate −5 as 11010. This data type is referred to in the computer engineering community as *1's complement*, and is also shown in Figure 2.1.

At this point, you might think that a computer designer could assign any bit pattern to represent any integer he/she wants. And, you would be right! Unfortunately, that could complicate matters when we try to build a logic circuit to add two integers. In fact, the signed-magnitude and 1's complement data types both require unnecessarily cumbersome hardware to do addition. Because computer designers knew what it would take to design a logic circuit to add two integers, they chose representations that simplified that logic circuit. The result is the *2's complement* data type, also shown in Figure 2.1. It is used on just about every computer manufactured today.

2.3   2'S COMPLEMENT INTEGERS

We see in Figure 2.1 the representations of the integers from −16 to +15 for the 2's complement data type. Why were the representations chosen that way?

The positive integers, we saw, are represented in the straightforward positional scheme. With 5 bits, we use exactly half of the 2^5 codes to represent the integers from 0 to $2^4 - 1$.

The choice of representations for the negative integers was based, as we said above, on the wish to keep the logic circuits as simple as possible. Almost all computers use the same basic mechanism to do addition. It is called an *Arithmetic and Logic Unit*, usually known by its acronym ALU. We will get into the actual structure of the ALU in Chapters 3 and 4. What is relevant right now is that an ALU has two inputs and one output. It performs addition by adding the binary bit patterns at its inputs, producing a bit pattern at its output that is the sum of the two input bit patterns.

For example, if the ALU processed five-bit input patterns, and the two inputs were 00110 and 00101, the result (output of the ALU) would be 01011. The addition is shown below.

```
00110
00101
─────
01011
```

Addition of two binary strings is performed in the same way addition of two decimal strings is performed, from right to left, column by column. If the addition in a column generates a carry, the carry is added to the column immediately to its left.

What is particularly relevant is that the binary ALU does not know (and does not care) what the two patterns it is adding represent. It simply adds the two binary patterns. Since the binary ALU only ADDs and does not CARE, it would be a "nice" benefit of our assignment of codes to the integers if it resulted in the ALU doing the right thing.

For starters, it would be nice if, when the ALU adds the representation for an arbitrary integer to the integer of the same magnitude and opposite sign, the sum is

0. That is, if the inputs to the ALU are the representations of A and $-A$, the output of the ALU should be 00000.

To accomplish that, the 2's complement data type specifies the representation for each negative integer so that when the ALU adds it to the representation of the positive integer of the same magnitude, the result will be the representation for 0. For example, since 00101 is the representation of $+5$, 11011 is chosen as the representation for -5.

Moreover, and more importantly, as we sequence from representations of -15 to $+15$, the ALU is adding 00001 to each successive representation.

We can express this mathematically as:

$$\text{REPRESENTATION(value} + 1) =$$
$$\text{REPRESENTATION(value)} + \text{REPRESENTATION(1)}.$$

This is sufficient to guarantee (as long as we do not get a result larger than $+15$ or smaller than -16) that the binary ALU will perform addition correctly.

Note in particular, the representations for -1 and 0, that is, 11111 and 00000. When we add 00001 to the representation for -1, we do get 00000, but we also generate a carry. That carry does not influence the result. That is, the correct result of adding 00001 to the representation for -1 is 0, not 100000. Therefore, the carry is ignored. In fact, because the carry obtained by adding 00001 to 11111 is ignored, the carry can *always* be ignored when dealing with 2's complement arithmetic.

Note: A shortcut for figuring out the representation for $-A$, if we know the representation for A is as follows: Flip all the bits of A (the term for "flipping" is *complement*), and add A to the complement of A. The result is 11111. If we then add 00001 to 11111, the final result is 00000. Thus, the representation for $-A$ can be easily obtained by adding 1 to the complement of A.

For example, if A is $+13$, its representation is

```
01101.
```

The complement of A is

```
10010.
```

Adding 1 to 10010 gives us

```
10011.
```

The ALU, if presented with bit strings 01101 and 10011, would produce the binary sum 00000,

```
  01101
  10011
  ─────
  00000
```

from which we know that the representation for -13 is 10011.

You may have noticed that the addition of 01101 and 10011, in addition to producing 00000, also produces a carry out of the five-bit ALU. That is, the binary addition of 01101 and 10011 is really 100000. However, as we saw above, in the case of the 2's complement data type, this carry out can be ignored.

At this point, we have identified in our five-bit scheme, 15 positive integers. We have constructed 15 negative integers. We also have a representation for 0. With $k = 5$, we can uniquely identify 32 distinct quantities, and we have accounted for only 31 $(15 + 15 + 1)$. The remaining representation is 10000. What value shall we assign to it?

We note that -1 is 11111, -2 is 11110, -3 is 11101, and so on. If we continue this, we note that -15 is 10001. Note that as in the case of the positive representations, as we sequence backwards from representations of -1 to -15, the ALU is subtracting 00001 from each successive representation. Thus, it seems to make sense to assign to 10000 the value -16; that is the value one gets by subtracting 00001 from 10001 (the representation for -15).

In Chapter 5 we will specify a computer that we affectionately have named the LC-2 (for little computer 2). The LC-2 operates on 16-bit values. Therefore, the 2's complement integers that can be represented in the LC-2 are the integers from $-32,768$ to $+32,767$.

2.4   BINARY-DECIMAL CONVERSION

It is often useful to convert integers between the 2's complement data type and the decimal representation that you have used all your life.

2.4.1   Binary to Decimal Conversion

We convert from 2's complement to a decimal representation as follows: For purposes of illustration, we will assume 2's complement representations of 8 bits, corresponding to decimal integer values, from -128 to $+127$.

Recall that an 8-bit 2's complement number takes the form

$$a_7 \; a_6 \; a_5 \; a_4 \; a_3 \; a_2 \; a_1 \; a_0,$$

where each of the bits a_i is either 0 or 1.

1. Examine the leading bit a_7. If it is a 0, the integer is positive, and we can begin evaluating its magnitude. If it is 1, the integer is negative. In that case, we need to first obtain the 2's complement representation of the positive number having the same magnitude.

2. The magnitude is simply

$$a_6 \cdot 2^6 + a_5 \cdot 2^5 + a_4 \cdot 2^4 + a_3 \cdot 2^3 + a_2 \cdot 2^2 + a_1 \cdot 2^1 + a_0 \cdot 2^0.$$

    which we obtain by simply adding the powers of 2 that have coefficients of 1.

3. Finally, if the original number is negative, we affix a minus sign in front. Done!

Example 2.1 | Convert the 2's complement integer 11000111 to a decimal integer value.

1. Since the leading binary digit is a 1, the number is negative. We first find the 2's complement representation of the positive number of the same magnitude. This is 00111001.

2. The magnitude can be represented as

$$0 \cdot 2^6 + 1 \cdot 2^5 + 1 \cdot 2^4 + 1 \cdot 2^3 + 0 \cdot 2^2 + 0 \cdot 2^1 + 1 \cdot 2^0.$$

or, $32 + 16 + 8 + 1$.

3. The decimal integer value corresponding to 11000111 is -57.

2.4.2   Decimal to Binary Conversion

Converting from decimal to 2's complement is a little more complicated. The crux of the method is to note that a positive binary number is *odd* if the right-most digit is 1, and *even* if the right-most digit is 0.

Consider again, our generic eight-bit representation:

$$a_7 \cdot 2^7 + a_6 \cdot 2^6 + a_5 \cdot 2^5 + a_4 \cdot 2^4 + a_3 \cdot 2^3 + a_2 \cdot 2^2 + a_1 \cdot 2^1 + a_0 \cdot 2^0.$$

We can illustrate the conversion best by first working through an example.

Suppose we wish to convert the value $+105$ to a 2's complement binary code. We note that $+105$ is positive. We first find values for a_i, representing the magnitude 105. Since the value is positive, we will then obtain the 2's complement result by simply appending a_7, which we know is 0.

Our first step is to find values for a_i that satisfies the following:

$$105 = a_6 \cdot 2^6 + a_5 \cdot 2^5 + a_4 \cdot 2^4 + a_3 \cdot 2^3 + a_2 \cdot 2^2 + a_1 \cdot 2^1 + a_0 \cdot 2^0.$$

Since 105 is odd, we know that a_0 is 1. We subtract 1 from both sides of the equation, yielding

$$104 = a_6 \cdot 2^6 + a_5 \cdot 2^5 + a_4 \cdot 2^4 + a_3 \cdot 2^3 + a_2 \cdot 2^2 + a_1 \cdot 2^1.$$

We next divide both sides of the equation by 2, yielding

$$52 = a_6 \cdot 2^5 + a_5 \cdot 2^4 + a_4 \cdot 2^3 + a_3 \cdot 2^2 + a_2 \cdot 2^1 + a_1 \cdot 2^0.$$

We note that 52 is even, so a_1, the only coefficient not multiplied by a power of 2, must be equal to 0.

We now iterate the process, each time subtracting the right-most digit from both sides of the equation, dividing both sides by 2, and then noting whether the new decimal number on the left side is odd or even. Starting where we left off, with

$$52 = a_6 \cdot 2^5 + a_5 \cdot 2^4 + a_4 \cdot 2^3 + a_3 \cdot 2^2 + a_2 \cdot 2^1.$$

the process produces, in turn:

$$26 = a_6 \cdot 2^4 + a_5 \cdot 2^3 + a_4 \cdot 2^2 + a_3 \cdot 2^1 + a_2 \cdot 2^0.$$

Therefore, $a_2 = 0$.

$$13 = a_6 \cdot 2^3 + a_5 \cdot 2^2 + a_4 \cdot 2^1 + a_3 \cdot 2^0.$$

Therefore, $a_3 = 1$.

$$6 = a_6 \cdot 2^2 + a_5 \cdot 2^1 + a_4 \cdot 2^0.$$

Therefore, $a_4 = 0$.

$$3 = a_6 \cdot 2^1 + a_5 \cdot 2^0.$$

Therefore $a_5 = 1$.

$$1 = a_6 \cdot 2^0$$

Therefore, $a_6 = 1$, and we are done. The binary representation is 01101001.

We can summarize the process as follows: If we are given a decimal integer value N, we construct the 2's complement representation as follows:

1. We first obtain the binary representation of the magnitude of N by forming the equation

    $$N = a_6 \cdot 2^6 + a_5 \cdot 2^5 + a_4 \cdot 2^4 + a_3 \cdot 2^3 + a_2 \cdot 2^2 + a_1 \cdot 2^1 + a_0 \cdot 2^0.$$

    and repeating the following, until the left side of the equation is 0:
    a. If N is odd, the right-most bit is 1. If N is even, the right most bit is 0.
    b. Subtract 1 or 0 (according to whether N is odd or even) from N, and divide both sides of the equation by 2.
    Each iteration produces the value of one coefficient a_i.

2. If the original decimal number is positive, append a leading 0 sign bit, and you are done.

3. If the original decimal number is negative, append a leading 0 and then form the negative of this 2's complement representation, and then you are done.

2.5   OPERATIONS ON BITS—PART I: ARITHMETIC

2.5.1   Addition and Subtraction

Arithmetic on 2's complement numbers is very much like the arithmetic on decimal numbers that you have been doing for a long time.

Addition still proceeds from right to left, one digit at a time. At each point, we generate a sum digit and a carry. Instead of generating a carry after 9, since 9 is the largest decimal digit, we generate a carry after 1 since 1 is the largest digit.

Using our five-bit notation, what is $11 + 3$?   **Example 2.2**

```
The decimal value 11 is represented as  01011
The decimal value 3 is represented      00011

The sum is                              01110
which is the value 14.
```

Subtraction is simply addition, preceded by determining the negative of the subtrahend first. That is, $A - B$ is simply $A + (-B)$.

Example 2.3 | **W**hat is $14 - 9$?

```
The decimal value 14 is represented as    01110
The decimal value 9 is represented        01001

First we form the negative, that is -9:    10111

Adding 14 to -9, we get                    01110
                                           10111


which results in                           00101
which is the value 5.
```

Note again that the carry out is ignored.

Example 2.4 | **W**hat happens when we add a number to itself (e.g., $x + x$).

Let's again assume for this example eight-bit codes, which would allow us to represent integers from -128 to 127. Consider a value for x, the integer 59, represented as 00111011. If we add 59 to itself, we get the code 01110110. Note that the bits have all shifted to the left by one position. Is that a curiosity, or will that happen all the time as long as the sum $x + x$ is not too large to represent with the available number of bits?

Using our positional notation, the number 59 is formed, as

$$0 \cdot 2^6 + 1 \cdot 2^5 + 1 \cdot 2^4 + 1 \cdot 2^3 + 0 \cdot 2^2 + 1 \cdot 2^1 + 1 \cdot 2^0.$$

The sum $59 + 59$ is $2 \cdot 59$, which, in our representation, is

$$2 \cdot (0 \cdot 2^6 + 1 \cdot 2^5 + 1 \cdot 2^4 + 1 \cdot 2^3 + 0 \cdot 2^2 + 1 \cdot 2^1 + 1 \cdot 2^0).$$

But that is nothing more than

$$0 \cdot 2^7 + 1 \cdot 2^6 + 1 \cdot 2^5 + 1 \cdot 2^4 + 0 \cdot 2^3 + 1 \cdot 2^2 + 1 \cdot 2^1,$$

which shifts each digit one position to the left. Thus, adding a number to itself (provided there are enough bits to represent the result) is equivalent to shifting the representation one bit position to the left.

2.5.2 Sign-extension

It is often useful to represent a small number with fewer bits. For example, rather than represent the value 5 as 0000000000000101, there are times when it is useful to allocate only six bits to represent the value 5: 000101. There is little confusion, since we are all used to adding leading zeroes without affecting the value of a number. A check for $456.78 and a check for $0000456.78 are checks having the same value.

What about negative representations?   We obtained the negative representa-tion from its positive counterpart by complementing the positive representation and adding 1. Thus, the representation for −5, given that 5 is represented as 000101, is 111011. If 5 is represented as 0000000000000101, then the representation for −5 is 1111111111111011. In the same way that leading 0s do not affect the value of a positive number, leading 1s do not affect the value of a negative number.

In order to add representations of different lengths, it is first necessary to represent them with the same number of bits. For example, suppose we wish to add the number 13 to −5, where 13 is represented as 0000000000001101 and −5 is represented as 111011. If we do not represent the two values with the same number of bits, we have:

$$
\begin{array}{r}
0000000000001101 \\
+ \qquad\qquad 111011 \\
\hline
\end{array}
$$

When we attempt to perform the addition, what shall we do with the missing bits in the representation for −5? If we take the absence of a bit to be a 0, then we are no longer adding −5 to 13. On the contrary, if we take the absence of bits to be 0s, we have changed the −5 to the number represented as 0000000000111011, that is +59. Not surprising, then, our result turns out to be the representation for 72.

However, if we understand that a six-bit −5 and a 16-bit −5 differ only in the number of meaningless leading 1s, then we first extend the value of −5 to 16-bit before we perform the addition. Thus, we have:

$$
\begin{array}{r}
0000000000001101 \\
+ \quad 1111111111111011 \\
\hline
\end{array}
$$

and the result is   0000000000001000
which is +8, as we should expect.

The value of a positive number does not change if we extend the sign bit 0 as many bit positions to the left as desired. Similarly, the value of a negative number does not change its value by extending the sign bit 1 as many bit positions to the left as desired. Since in both cases, it is the sign bit that is extended, we refer to the operation as *Sign-EXTension*, often abbreviated SEXT. Sign-extension is performed in order to be able to operate on bit patterns of different lengths. It does not affect the values of the numbers being represented.

2.5.3   Overflow

Up to now, we have always insisted that the sum of two integers be small enough to be represented by the available bits. What happens if such is not the case?

You are undoubtedly familiar with the odometer on the front dashboard of your automobile. It keeps track of how many miles your car has been driven—but only up to a point. In the old days, when the odometer registered 99992 and you drove it 100 miles, its new reading became 00092. A brand new car! The problem, as you know, is that the largest value the odometer could store was 99999, so the value 100092 showed up as 00092. The carry out of the ten-thousands digit was lost. (Of course, if you grew up in Boston, the carry out was not lost at all—it was in full display in the rusted chrome all over the car.)

We say the odometer OVERFLOWed. Representing 100092 as 00092 is unacceptable. As more and more cars lasted more than 100,000 miles, car makers felt the pressure to add a digit to the odometer. Today, practically all cars overflow at one million miles, rather than one hundred thousand miles.

The odometer provides an example of unsigned arithmetic. The miles you add are always positive miles. The odometer reads 000129 and you drive 50 miles. The odometer now reads 000179. Overflow is a carry out of the leading digit.

In the case of signed arithmetic, or more particularly, 2's complement arithmetic, overflow is a little more subtle.

Let's return to our five-bit 2's complement data type, which allowed us to represent integers from −16 to +15. Suppose we wish to add +9 and +11. Our arithmetic takes the following form:

$$
\begin{array}{r}
01001 \\
01011 \\
\hline
10100
\end{array}
$$

Note that the sum is larger than +15, and therefore too large to represent with our 2's complement scheme. The fact that the number is too large means that the number is larger than 01111, the largest positive number we can represent with a five-bit 2's complement data type. Note that because our positive result was larger than +15, it generated a carry into the leading bit position. But this bit position is used to indicate the sign of a value. Thus detecting that the result is too large is an easy matter. Since we are adding two positive numbers, the result must be positive. Since the ALU has produced a negative result, something must be wrong. The thing that is wrong is that the sum of the two positive numbers is too large to be represented with the available bits. We say that the result has OVERFLOWed the capacity of the representation.

Suppose instead, we had started with negative numbers, for example, −12 and −6. In this case our arithmetic takes the following form:

$$
\begin{array}{r}
10100 \\
11010 \\
\hline
01110
\end{array}
$$

Here, too, the result has overflowed the capacity of the machine, since −12 + −6 equals −18, which is "more negative" than −16, the negative number with the largest allowable magnitude. The ALU obliges by producing a positive result. Again, this is easy to detect since the sum of two negative numbers cannot be positive.

Note that the sum of a negative number and a positive number never presents a problem. Why is that?

2.6   OPERATIONS ON BITS—PART II: LOGICAL OPERATIONS

We have seen that it is possible to perform arithmetic (e.g., add, subtract) on values represented as binary patterns. Another class of operations that it is useful to perform on binary patterns is the set of *logical* operations.

Logical operations operate on logical variables. A logical variable can have one of two values, 0 or 1. The name *logical* is a historical one; it comes from the fact that the two values 0 and 1 can represent the two logical values *false* and *true*, but the use of logical operations have traveled far from this original meaning.

There are several basic logic functions, and most ALUs perform all of them.

2.6.1   The AND Function

AND is a binary function. This means it requires two pieces of input data. Said another way, AND requires two source operands. Each source is a logical variable, taking the value 0 or 1. The output of AND is 1 only if both sources have the value 1. Otherwise, the output is 0. We can think of the AND operation as the ALL operation; that is, the output is 1 only if ALL two inputs are 1. Otherwise, the output is 0.

A convenient mechanism for representing the behavior of a logical operation is the *truth table*. A truth table consists of $n + 1$ columns and 2^n rows. The first n columns correspond to the n source operands. Since each source operand is a logical variable and can have one of two values, there are 2^n unique values that these source operands can have. Each such set of values (sometimes called an input combination) is represented as one row of the truth table. The final column in the truth table shows the output for each input combination.

In the case of a two-input AND function, the truth table has two columns for source operands, and four (2^2) rows for unique input combinations.

A	B	AND
0	0	0
0	1	0
1	0	0
1	1	1

We can apply the logical operation AND to two-bit patterns of m bits each. This involves applying the operation individually to each corresponding pair of bits in the two source operands. For example, if a and b, shown below, are 16-bit patterns, then c is the AND of a and b. This operation is often called a *bit-wise AND*.

```
a:    0011101001101001
b:    0101100100100001
      ────────────────
c:    0001100000100001
```

2.6.2   The OR Function

OR is also a binary function. It requires two source operands, both of which are logical variables. The output of OR is 1 if any source has the value 1. Only if both sources are 0 is the output 0. We can think of the OR operation as the ANY operation; that is, the output is 1 if ANY of the two inputs are 1.

The truth table for a two-input OR function is shown below.

A	B	OR
0	0	0
0	1	1
1	0	1
1	1	1

In the same way that we applied the logical operation AND to two m-bit patterns, we can apply the OR operation bit-wise to two m-bit patterns. For example, if a and b are as before, then c (shown below) is the OR of a and b.

```
a:    0011101001101001
b:    0101100100100001
      _____

c:    0111101101101001
```

Sometimes this OR operation is referred to as the *inclusive-OR* in order to distinguish it from the exclusive-OR function, which we will discuss momentarily.

2.6.3   The NOT Function

NOT is a unary function. This means it operates on only one source operand. It is also known as the *complement* operation. The output is formed by complementing the input. We sometimes say the output is formed by inverting the input. A 1 input results in a 0 output. A 0 input results in a 1 output.

The truth table for the NOT function is shown below.

A	NOT
0	1
1	0

In the same way that we applied the logical operation AND and OR to two m-bit patterns, we can apply the NOT operation bit-wise to one m-bit pattern. If a is as before, then c is the NOT of a.

```
a:    0011101001101001
      _____

c:    1100010110010110
```

2.6.4 The Exclusive-OR Function

Exclusive-OR, often abbreviated XOR, is a binary function. It, too, requires two source operands, both of which are logical variables. The output of XOR is 1 if the two sources are different. The output is 0 if the two sources are the same.

The truth table for the XOR function is shown below.

A	B	XOR
0	0	0
0	1	1
1	0	1
1	1	0

In the same way that we applied the logical operation AND to two m-bit patterns, we can apply the XOR operation bit-wise to two m-bit patterns. For example, if a and b are 16-bit patterns as before, then c (shown below) is the XOR of a and b.

```
a:   0011101001101001
b:   0101100100100001
     ─────────────────
c:   0110001101001000
```

Note the distinction between the truth table for XOR shown here and the truth table for OR shown earlier. In the case of exclusive-OR, if both source operands are 1, the output is 0. That is, the output is 1 if the first operand is 1 but the second operand is not 1 or if the second operand is 1 but the first operand is not 1. The term *exclusive* is used because the output is 1 *only* if one of the two sources is 1. The OR function, on the other hand, produces an output 1 if both sources are 1. Ergo, the name *inclusive-OR*.

2.6.5 Examples

The following examples illustrate the use of logical operations to perform useful functions in the computer.

Example 2.5

Consider a complex system made up of eight units that are independently busy or available. This system can be a manufacturing plant where each unit is a particular machine. Or the system could be a taxicab network where each unit is a particular taxicab. In both cases, it is important to identify which units are busy and which are available, so that work can be assigned as needed.

One can keep track of these eight units with an eight-bit binary BUSYNESS pattern, where a bit is 1 if the unit is free and 0 if the unit is busy. The bits are labeled, from right to left, from 0 to 7. The BUSYNESS pattern 11000010 corresponds to the situation where only units 7, 6, and 1 are free, and therefore available for work assignment.

Suppose work is assigned to unit 7. We can update our BUSYNESS pattern by performing the logical AND with sources 11000010 and 01111111. The result is the BUSYNESS pattern 01000010.

The second source 01111111 is an example of a *mask*. The purpose of a mask is to differentiate how some bits in a pattern will be handled from how other bits will be handled. In this instance, the mask leaves all bits except the leading bit unchanged. The leading bit is *cleared* (set to 0).

Suppose unit 5 finishes its task and becomes idle. We can reflect that by performing the logical OR with the BUSYNESS pattern and 00100000. The result is 01100010.

Example 2.6 | Suppose we have an eight-bit pattern in which the right-most two bits have particular significance. The computer could be asked to do one of four tasks depending on the value stored in the two right-most bits. We could isolate those two bits by ANDing the eight-bit pattern with the mask 00000011. For example, if the pattern is 01010110, the AND of 01010110 and 00000011 is 00000010, which highlights the two bits that are relevant, that is, 10.

Example 2.7 | Suppose we wish to know if two patterns are identical. Since the XOR function produces a 0 only if the corresponding pair of bits is identical, two patterns are identical if the output of the XOR is all zeroes.

2.7   OTHER REPRESENTATIONS

Three other representations of information that we will find useful in our work are the floating point data type, the ASCII codes, and the hexadecimal notation.

2.7.1   Floating Point Data Type

Most of the arithmetic we will do in this book uses integer values. For example, the LC-2 uses the 16-bit, 2's complement data type, which provides, in addition to one bit to identify positive or negative, 15 bits to represent the magnitude of the value. With 16 bits used in this way, we can express values between $-32,768$ and $+32,767$, that is, between -2^{15} and $+2^{15} - 1$. We say the *precision* of our value is 15 bits, and the *range* is 2^{15}. As you learned in high school chemistry or physics, sometimes we need to express much larger numbers, but we do not require so many digits of precision. In fact, recall the value $6.023 \cdot 10^{23}$ which you may have been required to memorize back then. The range required to express this value is far greater than the 2^{15} available with 16-bit 2's complement integers. On the other hand, the 15 bits of precision available with 16-bit 2's complement integers is overkill. We need only enough bits to express four significant decimal digits (6023).

So we have a problem. We have more bits than we need for precision. But we don't have enough bits to represent the range.

The *floating point* data type is the solution to the problem. Instead of using all the bits (except the sign bit) to represent the precision of a value, the floating point data type allocates some of the bits to the range of values (i.e., how big or small) that can be expressed. The rest of the bits (except for the sign bit) are used for precision.

Most ISAs today specify more than one floating point data type. One of them, usually called *float*, consists of 32 bits, allocated as follows:

```
 1 bit for the sign (positive or negative)
 8 bits for the range (the exponent field)
23 bits for precision (the fraction field)
```

In most computers manufactured today, these bits represent numbers according to the formula in Figure 2.2. This formula is part of the IEEE Standard for Floating Point Arithmetic.

Recall we said that the floating point data type was very much like the scientific notation you learned in high school, and we gave the example $6.023 \cdot 10^{23}$. This representation has three parts: the sign, which is positive, the significant digits 6.023, and the exponent 23. We call the significant digits the *fraction*. Note that the fraction is normalized, that is, exactly one nonzero decimal digit appears to the left of the decimal digit.

The data type and formula of Figure 2.2 also consist of these three parts. Instead of a fraction (i.e., significant digits) of four decimal digits, we have 23 binary digits. Note that the fraction is normalized, that is, exactly one nonzero binary digit appears to the left of the binary point. Since the nonzero binary digit has to be a 1 (1 is the only nonzero binary digit) there is no need to represent that bit explicitly. Thus, the formula of Figure 2.2 shows 24 bits of precision, the 23 bits from the data type and the leading one bit to the left of the binary point that is unnecessary to represent explicitly.

Instead of an exponent of two decimal digits as in $6.023 \cdot 10^{23}$, we have in Figure 2.2 eight binary digits. Instead of a radix of 10, we have a radix of 2. With eight bits to represent the exponent, we can represent 256 exponents. Note that the formula only gives meaning to 254 of them. If the exponent field contains 00000000 (that is, 0) or 11111111 (that is, 255), the formula does not tell you how to interpret the bits. We will look at those two special cases momentarily.

For the remaining 254 values in the exponent field of the floating point data type, the explanation is as follows: The actual exponent being represented is the unsigned number in the data type minus 127. For example, if the actual exponent is $+8$, the exponent field contains 10000111, which is the unsigned number 135. Note that $135 - 127 = 8$. If the actual exponent is -125, the exponent field contains 00000010, which is the unsigned number 2. Note that $2 - 127 = -125$.

$N = -1^S \times 1.\text{fraction} \times 2^{\text{exponent} - 127},\ 1 \leq \text{exponent} \leq 254$

Figure 2.2   The floating point data type

The third part is the sign bit: 0 for positive numbers, 1 for negative numbers. The formula contains the factor -1^s, which evaluates to $+1$ if $s = 0$, and -1 if $s = 1$.

Example 2.8

How is the number $-6\frac{5}{8}$ represented in the floating point data type?

First, we express $6\frac{5}{8}$ as a binary number: -110.101.

$$-\left(1 \cdot 2^2 + 1 \cdot 2^1 + 0 \cdot 2^0 + 1 \cdot 2^{-1} + 0 \cdot 2^{-2} + 1 \cdot 2^{-3}\right)$$

Then we normalize the value, yielding $-1.10101 \cdot 2^2$

The sign bit is 1, reflecting the fact that $-6\frac{5}{8}$ is a negative number. The exponent field contains 10000011, the unsigned number 129, reflecting the fact that the real exponent is $+2$ ($129 - 127 = +2$). The fraction is the 23 bits of precision, after removing the leading 1. That is, the fraction is 10101000000000000000000. The result is the number $-6\frac{5}{8}$, expressed as a floating point number:

1 10000011 10101000000000000000000

Example 2.9

What does the floating point data type

00111101100000000000000000000000

represent?

The leading bit is a 0. This signifies a positive number. The next eight bits represent the unsigned number 123. If we subtract 127, we get the actual exponent -4. The last 23 bits are all 0. Therefore the number being represented is $+1.00000000000000000000000 \cdot 2^{-4}$, which is $\frac{1}{16}$.

Recall we noted that the interpretation of the 32 bits required that the exponent field contained neither 00000000 nor 11111111. The IEEE Standard for Floating Point Arithmetic also specifies how to interpret the 32 bits if the exponent field contains 00000000 or 11111111.

If the exponent field contains 00000000, the exponent is -126, and the significant digits are obtained by starting with a leading 0, followed by a binary point, followed by the 23 bits of the fraction field, as shown below:

$$-1^s \cdot 0.\, fraction \,\cdot 2^{-126}$$

For example, the floating point data representation

0 00000000 00001000000000000000000

can be evaluated as follows: The leading 0 means the number is positive. The next eight bits, a zero exponent, means the exponent is -126. The last 23 bits form the number 0.00001000000000000000000, which equals 2^{-5}. Thus, the number represented is $2^{-5} \cdot 2^{-126}$, which is 2^{-131}.

This allows very tiny numbers to be represented.

Example 2.10

The following four examples provide further illustrations of the interpretation of the 32-bit floating point data type according to the rules of the IEEE standard.

   0 10000011 00101000000000000000000 is $1.00101 \cdot 2^4 = 18.5$

The exponent field contains the unsigned number 131. Since $131 - 127$ is 4, the exponent is $+4$. Combining a 1 to the left of the binary point with the fraction field to the right of the binary point yields 1.00101. If we move the binary point four positions to the right, we get 10010.1, which is 18.5.

   1 10000010 00101000000000000000000 is $-1 \cdot 1.00101 \cdot 2^3 = -9.25$

The sign bit is 1, signifying a negative number. The exponent is 130, signifying an exponent of $130 - 127$, or $+3$. Combining a 1 to the left of the binary point with the fraction field to the right of the binary point yields 1.00101. Moving the binary point three positions to the right, we get 1001.01, which is -9.25.

   0 11111110 11111111111111111111111 is $\sim 2^{128}$

The sign is $+$. The exponent is $254 - 127$, or $+127$. Combining a 1 to the left of the binary point with the fraction field to the right of the binary point yields 1.11111111111111111111111, which is approximately 2. Therefore, the result is approximately 2^{128}.

   1 00000000 00000000000000000000001 is -2^{-149}

The sign is $-$. The exponent field contains all 0s, signifying an exponent of -126. Combining a 0 to the left of the binary point with the fraction field to the right of the binary point yields 2^{-23} for the fraction. Therefore, the number represented is $-2^{-23} \cdot 2^{-126}$, which equals -2^{-149}.

A detailed understanding of IEEE Floating Point Arithmetic is well beyond what should be expected in this first course. Indeed, we have not even considered how to interpret the 32 bits if the exponent field contains 11111111. Our purpose in including this section in the textbook is to at least let you know that there is, in addition to 2's complement integers, another very important data type available in almost all ISAs. This data type is called *floating point*; it allows very large and very tiny numbers to be expressed at the expense of reducing the number of binary digits of precision.

2.7.2 ASCII Codes

Another representation of information is the standard code that almost all computer equipment manufacturers have agreed to use for transferring character codes between the main computer processing unit and the input and output devices. That code is a seven-bit code referred to as *ASCII*. ASCII stands for American Standard Code for Information Interchange. It (ASCII) greatly simplifies the interface between a keyboard manufactured by one company, a computer made by another company, and a monitor made by a third company.

In almost all uses of ASCII today, each seven-bit code is appended with a leading 0 and stored as an eight-bit code. Each key on the keyboard is identified by its unique ASCII code. So, for example the digit 3 expanded to 8 bits with a leading 0 is 00110011, the digit 2 is 00110010, the lower case *e* is 01100101, and the carriage return is 00001101. The entire set of seven-bit ASCII codes is listed in Figure E.3 of Appendix E. When you type a key on the keyboard, the corresponding eight-bit code is stored and made available to the computer. Where it is stored and how it gets into the computer is part of the subject matter of Chapter 8.

In order to display a particular character on the monitor, the computer must transfer the ASCII code for that character to the electronics associated with the monitor. That, too, is part of the subject matter of Chapter 8.

2.7.3 Hexadecimal Notation

We have seen that information can be represented as 2's complement integers, or in floating point format, or as an ASCII code. There are other representations also, but we will leave them for another book. However, before we leave this topic, we would like to introduce you to a representation that is used more as a convenience for humans than as a data type to support operations being performed by the computer. This is the *hexadecimal* notation. As we will see, it evolves nicely from the positional binary notation and is useful for dealing with long strings of binary digits without making errors.

It will be particularly useful in dealing with the LC-2 where 16-bit binary strings will be encountered frequently.

An example of such a binary string is

$$0011110101101110.$$

Let's try an experiment. Cover the 16-bit binary string of 0s and 1s with one hand, and try to write it down from memory. How did you do? Hexadecimal notation is about being able to do this without making mistakes. We shall see how.

In general, a 16-bit binary string takes the form

$$a_{15}\, a_{14}\, a_{13}\, a_{12}\, a_{11}\, a_{10}\, a_9\, a_8\, a_7\, a_6\, a_5\, a_4\, a_3\, a_2\, a_1\, a_0,$$

where each of the bits a_i is either 0 or 1.

If we think of this binary string as an unsigned integer, its value can be computed as

$$a_{15} \cdot 2^{15} + a_{14} \cdot 2^{14} + a_{13} \cdot 2^{13} + a_{12} \cdot 2^{12} + a_{11} \cdot 2^{11} + a_{10} \cdot 2^{10}$$
$$+ a_9 \cdot 2^9 + a_8 \cdot 2^8 + a_7 \cdot 2^7 + a_6 \cdot 2^6 + a_5 \cdot 2^5 + a_4 \cdot 2^4 + a_3 \cdot 2^3$$
$$+ a_2 \cdot 2^2 + a_1 \cdot 2^1 + a_0 \cdot 2^0.$$

We can factor 2^{12} from the first four terms, 2^8 from the second four terms, 2^4 from the third set of four terms, and 2^0 from the last four terms, yielding

$$2^{12}[a_{15} \cdot 2^3 + a_{14} \cdot 2^2 + a_{13} \cdot 2^1 + a_{12} \cdot 2^0]$$
$$+ 2^8[a_{11} \cdot 2^3 + a_{10} \cdot 2^2 + a_9 \cdot 2^1 + a_8 \cdot 2^0]$$
$$+ 2^4[a_7 \cdot 2^3 + a_6 \cdot 2^2 + a_5 \cdot 2^1 + a_4 \cdot 2^0]$$
$$+ 2^0[a_3 \cdot 2^3 + a_2 \cdot 2^2 + a_1 \cdot 2^1 + a_0 \cdot 2^0].$$

Note that the largest value inside a set of square brackets is 15, which would be the case if each of the four bits is 1. If we replace what is inside each square bracket by a symbol representing its value (from 0 to 15), and we replace 2^{12} by its equivalent 16^3, 2^8 by 16^2, 2^4 by 16^1 and 2^0 by 16^0, we have

$$h_3 \cdot 16^3 + h_2 \cdot 16^2 + h_1 \cdot 16^1 + h_0 \cdot 16^0,$$

where h_3 is a symbol representing

$$a_{15} \cdot 2^3 + a_{14} \cdot 2^2 + a_{13} \cdot 2^1 + a_{12} \cdot 2^0.$$

Since the symbols must represent values from 0 to 15, we assign symbols to these values as follows: 0, 1, 2, 3, 4, 5, 6, 7, 8, 9, A, B, C, D, E, F. That is, we represent 0000 with the symbol 0, 0001 with the symbol 1, ... 1001 with 9, 1010 with A, 1011 with B, ... 1111 with F. The resulting notation is hexadecimal, or base 16.

So, for example, if the hex digits E92F represent a 16-bit 2's complement integer, is the value of that integer positive or negative? How do you know?

Now, then, what is this hexadecimal representation good for, anyway? It seems like just another way to represent a number without adding any benefit. Let's return to the exercise where you tried to write from memory the string

0011110101101110.

If we had first broken the string at four-bit boundaries

0011   1101   0110   1110

and then converted each four-bit string to its equivalent hex digit

3   D   6   E,

it would have been no problem to jot down (with the string covered) 3D6E.

In summary, hexadecimal notation is mainly used as a convenience for humans. It can be used to represent binary strings that are integers or floating point numbers or sequences of ASCII codes, or bit vectors. It simply reduces the number of digits by a factor of four, where each digit is in hex (0, 1, 2, ... F) instead of binary (0, 1). The usual result is far fewer copying errors due to too many 0s and 1s.

PROBLEMS

2.1. Given n bits, how many distinct combinations of the n bits exist?

2.2. There are 26 characters in the English alphabet. What is the least number of bits needed to have a unique bit pattern for each of the 26 characters? What if we need to distinguish between upper- and lowercase characters? How many bits are needed to distinguish between these 52 characters?

2.3.
1. Assume that there are about 400 students in your class. If every student is to be assigned a unique bit pattern, what is the minimum number of bits required to do this?
2. How many more students can be admitted to the class without requiring additional bits for each student's unique bit pattern?

2.4. Given n bits, how many unsigned integers can be represented with the n bits? What is the range of these integers?

2.5. Write the representations of 7 and -7 in 1's complement, signed magnitude, and 2's complement integers.

2.6. Write the six-bit 2's complement representation of -32.

2.7. Create a table showing the decimal values of all four-bit 2's complement numbers.

2.8.
1. What is the largest positive number one can represent in an eight-bit 2's complement code? Write your result in binary and decimal.
2. What is the greatest magnitude negative number one can represent in eight-bit 2's complement code? Write your result in binary and decimal.
3. What is the largest positive number one can represent in n-bit 2's complement code?
4. What is the greatest magnitude negative number one can represent in n-bit 2's complement code?

2.9. Convert the following 2's complement binary numbers to decimal.
1. `1010`
2. `01011010`
3. `11111110`
4. `0011100111010011`

2.10. Convert these decimal numbers to eight-bit 2's complement binary numbers.

1. 102
2. 64
3. 33
4. −128
5. 127

2.11. If the last digit of a 2's complement binary number is 0, then the number is even. If the last two digits of a 2's complement binary number are 00 (e.g., the binary number 01100), what does that tell you about the number?

2.12. Without changing their values, convert the following 2's complement binary numbers into eight-bit 2's complement numbers.

1. `1010`
2. `011001`
3. `1111111000`
4. `01`

2.13. Add the following binary numbers. Leave your results in binary form.

1. `1011 + 0001`
2. `0000 + 1010`
3. `1100 + 0011`
4. `0101 + 0110`
5. `1111 + 0001`

2.14. Write the results of the following computations both as binary and decimal numbers.

1. Using standard binary addition, add the 1's complement representation of 7 to the 1's complement representation of −7.
2. Using standard binary addition, add the signed magnitude representation of 7 to the signed magnitude representation of −7.
3. Using standard binary addition, add the 2's complement representation of 7 to the 2's complement representation of −7.

2.15. It was demonstrated in Example 2.4 that shifting a binary number one bit to the left is equivalent to multiplying the number by two. What operation is performed when a binary number is shifted one bit to the right?

2.16. Add the following 2's complement binary numbers. Also express the answer in decimal.

1. `01 + 1011`
2. `11 + 01010101`
3. `0101 + 110`
4. `01 + 10`

2.17. Add the following unsigned binary numbers. Also, express the answer in decimal.

1. `01 + 1011`
2. `11 + 01010101`
3. `0101 + 110`
4. `01 + 10`

2.18. Sign extension does not affect the value of a 2's complement number. Does it affect the value of an unsigned number, a 1's complement number, or a signed magnitude number? If it does change the value of a number in one of these datatypes, give an example to demonstrate.

2.19. The following binary numbers are 2's complement binary numbers. Which of the following operations generate overflow? Justify your answer by translating the operands and results into decimal.

1. `1100 + 0011`
2. `1100 + 0100`
3. `0111 + 0001`
4. `1000 - 0001`
5. `0111 + 1001`

2.20. Describe in English what conditions indicate overflow has occurred when two 2's complement numbers are added.

2.21. Create two 16-bit 2's complement integers such that their sum causes an overflow.

2.22. Describe in English what conditions indicate overflow has occurred when two unsigned numbers are added.

2.23. Create two 16-bit unsigned integers such that their sum causes an overflow.

2.24. Why does the sum of a negative 2's complement number and a positive 2's complement number never generate an overflow?

2.25. When is the output of an AND operation equal to 1?

2.26. Fill in the following truth table for a one-bit AND operation.

X	Y	X AND Y
0	0	
0	1	
1	0	
1	1	

2.27. Compute the following. Write your results in binary.

1. `01010111 AND 11010111`

    2. `101 AND 110`

    3. `11100000 AND 10110100`

    4. `00011111 AND 10110100`

    5. `(0011 AND 0110) AND 1101`

    6. `0011 AND (0110 AND 1101)`

2.28. When is the output of an OR operation equal to 1?

2.29. Fill in the following truth table for a one-bit OR operation.

X	Y	X OR Y
0	0	
0	1	
1	0	
1	1	

2.30. Compute the following:

    1. `01010111 OR 11010111`

    2. `101 OR 110`

    3. `11100000 OR 10110100`

    4. `00011111 OR 10110100`

    5. `(0101 OR 1100) OR 1101`

    6. `0101 OR (1100 OR 1101)`

2.31. Compute the following:

    1. `NOT(1011) OR NOT(1100)`

    2. `NOT(1000 AND (1100 OR 0101))`

    3. `NOT(NOT(1101))`

    4. `(0110 OR 0000) AND 1111`

2.32. In Example 2.5, what is the mask used for?

2.33. Refer to Example 2.5 for the following questions.

    1. What mask value and what operation would one use to indicate that machine 2 is busy?

    2. What mask value and what operation would one use to indicate that machines 2 and 6 are no longer busy? (Note: This can be done with only one operation.)

    3. What mask value and what operation would one use to indicate that all machines are busy?

    4. What mask value and what operation would one use to indicate that no machines are busy?

5. Develop a procedure to isolate the status bit of machine 2 as the sign bit. For example, if the BUSYNESS pattern is 01011100, then the output of this procedure is 10000000. If the BUSYNESS pattern is 01110011, then the output is 00000000. In general, if the BUSYNESS pattern is:

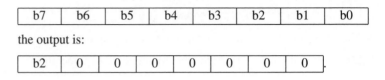

b7	b6	b5	b4	b3	b2	b1	b0

the output is:

b2	0	0	0	0	0	0	0

Hint: What happens when you ADD a bit pattern to itself?

2.34. If n and m are both four-bit 2's complement numbers, and s is the four-bit result of adding them together, how can we determine, using only the logical operations described in Section 2.6, if an overflow occurred during the addition? Develop a "procedure" for doing so. The inputs to the procedure are n, m, and s, and the output will be a bit pattern of all zeros (0000) if no overflow occurred and 1000 if an overflow did occur.

2.35. If n and m are both four-bit unsigned numbers, and s is the four-bit result of adding them together, how can we determine, using only the logical operations described in Section 2.6, if an overflow occurred during the addition? Develop a "procedure" for doing so. The inputs to the procedure are n, m, and s, and the output will be a bit pattern of all zeros (0000) if no overflow occurred and 1000 if an overflow did occur.

2.36. Write IEEE floating point representation of the following decimal numbers:

1. 3.75
2. $-55\frac{23}{64}$
3. 3.1415927
4. 64, 000

2.37. Write the decimal equivalents for these IEEE floating point numbers:

1. 0 10000000 00000000000000000000000
2. 1 10000011 00010000000000000000000
3. 0 11111111 00000000000000000000000
4. 1 10000000 10010000000000000000000

2.38. 1. What is the largest exponent the IEEE standard allows for a 32-bit floating point number?

2. What is the smallest exponent the IEEE standard allows for a 32-bit floating point number?

2.39. A computer programmer wrote a program that adds two numbers. He/she ran the program and observed that when 5 is added to 8, the result is the character *m*. Explain why this program is behaving erroneously.

2.40. Translate the following ASCII codes into strings of characters by interpreting each group of eight bits as an ASCII character.

1. x48656c6c6f21
2. x68454c4c4f21
3. x436f6d70757465727321
4. x4c432d32

2.41. What operation(s) can be used to convert the binary representation for 3 (i.e., 0000 0011) into the ASCII representation for 3 (i.e., 0110 0011)? What about the binary 4 into the ASCII 4? What about any digit?

2.42. Convert the following unsigned binary numbers to hexadecimal:

1. **1101 0001 1010 1111**
2. **001 1111**
3. **1**
4. **1110 1101 1011 0010**

2.43. Convert the following hexadecimal numbers to binary.

1. x10
2. x801
3. xF731
4. x0F1E2D
5. xBCAD

2.44. Convert the following hexadecimal representations of 2's complement binary numbers to decimal numbers:

1. xF0
2. x7FF
3. x16
4. x8000

2.45. Convert the following decimal numbers to hexadecimal representations of 2's complement numbers:

1. 256
2. 111
3. 123,456,789
4. −44

2.46. Perform the following additions. The corresponding 16-bit binary numbers are in 2's complement notation. Provide your answers in hexadecimal.

1. x025B + x26DE
2. x7D96 + xF0A0

3.   xA397 + xA35D

4.   x7D96 + x7412

5.   What else can you say about the answers to parts (3) and (4)?

2.47.   Perform the following logical operations. Express your answers in hexadecimal notation.

1.   x5478 AND xFDEA

2.   xABCD OR x1234

3.   NOT((NOT(xDEFA)) AND (NOT(xFFFF)))

4.   x00FF XOR x325C

2.48.   What is the hexadecimal representation of the following numbers:

1.   25,675

2.   675.625 (that is, $675\frac{5}{8}$), in the IEEE 754 floating point standard

3.   The ASCII string: Hello

2.49.   Consider two hexadecimal numbers: x434F4D50 and x55544552. What values do they represent for each of the five data types shown?

	x434F4D50	x55544552
Unsigned binary		
1's complement		
2's complement		
IEEE 754 floating point		
ASCII string		

2.50.   Fill in the truth table for the equations given below. The first line is done as an example.

$$Q_1 = \text{NOT(A AND B)}$$
$$Q_2 = \text{NOT(NOT(A) AND NOT(B))}$$

A	B	Q_1	Q_2
0	0	1	0

Express Q_2 another way.

2.51. Fill in the truth table for the equations given below. The first line is done as an example.

$$Q_1 = \text{NOT}(\text{NOT}(X) \text{ OR } (X \text{ AND } Y \text{ AND } Z))$$
$$Q_2 = \text{NOT}((Y \text{ OR } Z) \text{ AND } (X \text{ AND } Y \text{ AND } Z))$$

X	Y	Z	Q_1	Q_2
0	0	0	0	1

3

Digital Logic Structures

In Chapter 1, we stated that computers were constructed out of very large numbers of very simple structures. For example, Intel's Pentium II microprocessor, first offered for sale in 1998, is made up of more than 7 million MOS transistors. The Compaq Alpha 21264 consists of more than 15 million MOS transistors. In this chapter, we will explain how the MOS transistor works (as a logic element), show how these transistors are connected to form logic gates, and then show how logic gates are interconnected to form larger units that are needed to construct a computer. In Chapter 4, we will connect those larger units into a computer.

But first, the transistor.

3.1 THE TRANSISTOR

Most computers today, or rather most microprocessors (which form the core of the corresponding computer) are constructed out of MOS transistors. MOS stands for *metal-oxide semiconductor.* The electrical properties of metal-oxide semiconductors are well beyond the scope of what we want to understand in this course. However, it is useful to know that there are two types of MOS transistors: P-type and N-type. They both operate "logically," very similar to the way wall switches works.

Figure 3.1 shows the most basic of electrical circuits: a power supply (in this case, the 120 volts that come into your house), a wall switch, and a lamp (plugged into an outlet in the wall). In order for the lamp to glow, electrons must flow; in order for electrons to flow, there must be a closed circuit from the power supply to the lamp

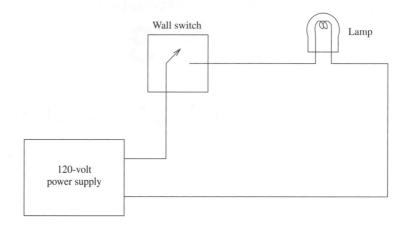

Figure 3.1   A simple electric circuit showing the use of a wall switch

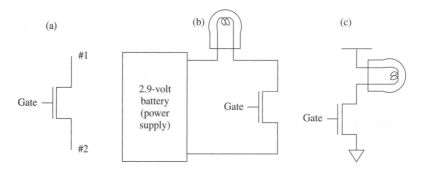

Figure 3.2   The N-type MOS transistor

and back to the power supply. The lamp can be turned on and off by simply making or breaking the closed circuit by manipulating the wall switch.

Instead of the wall switch, we could use an N-type or a P-type MOS transistor to make or break the closed circuit. Figure 3.2 shows a schematic rendering of an N-type transistor, (a) by itself, and (b) in a circuit. Note (Figure 3.2a) that the transistor has three terminals. If the gate of the transistor is supplied with 2.9 volts, terminals 1 and 2 act like a piece of wire. We say (in the language of electricity) that we have a *closed circuit* between terminals 1 and 2. If the gate of the transistor is supplied with 0 volts, terminals 1 and 2 act like a broken connection. We say that between terminals 1 and 2 we have an *open circuit*.

Figure 3.2b shows the N-type transistor in a circuit with a battery and a bulb. When the gate is supplied with 2.9 volts, the transistor acts like a piece of wire, completing the circuit and causing the bulb to glow. When the gate is supplied with

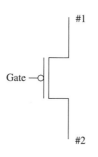

Figure 3.3   A P-type MOS transistor

0 volts, the transistor acts like an open circuit, breaking the circuit, and causing the bulb to not glow.

Figure 3.2c is a shorthand notation for describing the circuit of Figure 3.2b. Rather than always showing the power supply and the complete circuit, electrical engineers usually show only the terminals of the power supply. The fact that the power supply itself provides the completion of the completed circuit is well understood, and so is not usually shown.

The P-type transistor works exactly the opposite of the N-type transistor. Figure 3.3 shows the schematic representation of a P-type transistor. When the gate is supplied with 0 volts, the P-type transistor acts (more or less) like a piece of wire, closing the circuit. When the gate is supplied with 2.9 volts, the P-type transistor acts like an open circuit. Because the P-type and N-type transistors act in this complementary way, we refer to circuits that contain both P-type and N-type transistors as CMOS circuits, for *complementary metal oxide semiconductor*.

3.2 LOGIC GATES

One step up from the transistor is the logic gate. That is, we construct basic logic structures out of individual MOS transistors. In Chapter 2, we studied the behavior of the AND, the OR, and the NOT functions. In this chapter we construct transistor circuits that implement each of these functions. The corresponding circuits are called AND, OR, and NOT gates.

3.2.1   The NOT Gate (or, Inverter)

Figure 3.4 shows the simplest logic structure that exists in a computer. It is constructed from two MOS transistors, one P-type and one N-type. Figure 3.4a is the schematic representation of that circuit. Figure 3.4b shows the behavior of the circuit if the input is supplied with 0 volts. Note that the P-type transistor conducts and the N-type transistor does not conduct. The output is, therefore, connected to 2.9 volts. On the other hand, if the input is supplied with 2.9 volts, the P-type transistor does not

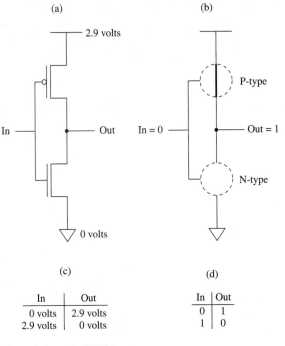

(a)   (b)

2.9 volts   P-type

In ——— Out   In = 0 ———— Out = 1

N-type

0 volts

(c)   (d)

In	Out
0 volts	2.9 volts
2.9 volts	0 volts

In	Out
0	1
1	0

Figure 3.4   A CMOS inverter

conduct, but the N-type transistor does conduct. The output in this case is connected to ground (i.e., 0 volts). The complete behavior of the circuit can be described by means of a table, as shown in Figure 3.4c. If we replace 0 volts by the symbol 0 and 2.9 volts by the symbol 1, we have the truth table (Figure 3.4d) for the complement or NOT function, which we discussed in Chapter 2.

In other words, we have just shown how to construct an electronic circuit that implements the NOT logic function discussed in Chapter 2. We call this circuit a *NOT gate*, or an *inverter*.

3.2.2   OR and NOR Gates

First examine Figure 3.5. Figure 3.5a is a schematic containing two P-type and two N-type transistors.

Figure 3.5b shows the behavior of the circuit if *A* is supplied with 0 volts and *B* is supplied with 2.9 volts. In this case, the lower of the two P-type transistors produces an open circuit, and the output *C* is disconnected from the 2.9-volt power supply. However, the left-most N-type transistor acts like a piece of wire, connecting the output *C* to 0 volts.

Note that if both *A* and *B* are supplied with 0 volts, the two P-type transistors conduct, and the output *C* is connected to 2.9 volts. Note, further, that there is no ambiguity here, since both N-type transistors act as open circuits, and so *C* is disconnected from ground.

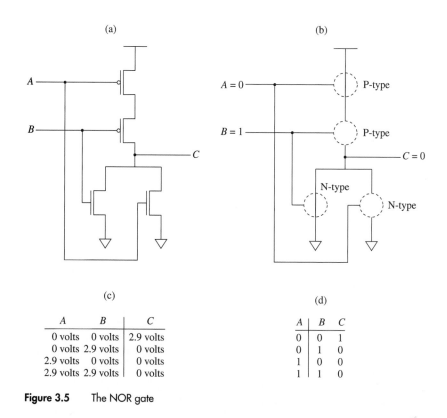

Figure 3.5 The NOR gate

If either A or B is supplied with 2.9 volts, the corresponding P-type transistor results in an open circuit. That is sufficient to break the connection from C to the 2.9-volt source. However, 2.9 volts supplied to the gate of one of the N-type transistors is sufficient to cause that transistor to conduct, resulting in C being connected to ground (i.e., 0 volts).

Figure 3.5c summarizes the complete behavior of the circuit of Figure 3.5a. It shows the behavior of the circuit for each of the four pairs of voltages with which A and B can be supplied. That is,

$$A = 0 \text{ volts}, \qquad B = 0 \text{ volts}$$
$$A = 0 \text{ volts}, \qquad B = 2.9 \text{ volts}$$
$$A = 2.9 \text{ volts}, \qquad B = 0 \text{ volts}$$
$$A = 2.9 \text{ volts}, \qquad B = 2.9 \text{ volts}$$

If we replace the voltages with their logical equivalents, we have the truth table of Figure 3.5d. Note that the output C is exactly the opposite of the logical OR function discussed in Chapter 2. In fact, it is the NOT-OR function, more typically abbreviated as NOR. We refer to the circuit that implements the NOR function as a NOR gate.

If we augment the circuit of Figure 3.5a by adding an inverter at the output, as shown in Figure 3.6a, we have at the output D the logical function OR. Figure 3.6a is the circuit for an OR gate. Figure 3.6b describes the behavior of this circuit if the

(a)

(c)

A	B	C	D
0	0	1	0
0	1	0	1
1	0	0	1
1	1	0	1

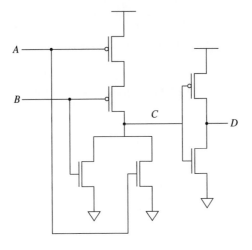

(b)

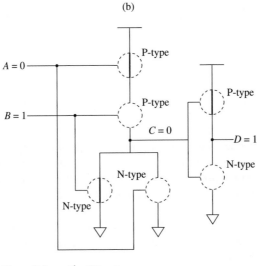

Figure 3.6   The OR gate

input variable A is set to 0 and the input variable B is set to 1. Figure 3.6c shows the circuit's truth table.

3.2.3 AND and NAND Gates

Next, we will examine Figure 3.7. Note that if either A or B is supplied with 0 volts, there is a direct connection from C to the 2.9-volt power supply. The fact that C is at 2.9 volts means the N-type transistor whose gate is connected to C provides a path

(a)   (b)

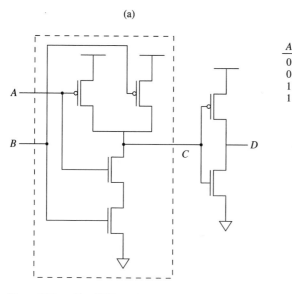

A	B	C	D
0	0	1	0
0	1	1	0
1	0	1	0
1	1	0	1

Figure 3.7   The AND gate

from D to ground. Therefore, if either A or B is supplied with 0 volts, the output D of the circuit of Figure 3.7 is 0 volts.

Again, we note that there is no ambiguity. The fact that at least one of the two inputs A or B is supplied with 0 volts means that at least one of the two N-type transistors whose gates are connected to A or B is open, and that consequently, C is disconnected from ground. Furthermore, the fact that C is at 2.9 volts means the P-type transistor whose gate is connected to C is open-circuited. Therefore, D is not connected to 2.9 volts.

On the other hand, if both A and B are supplied with 2.9 volts, then both of their corresponding P-type transistors are open. However, their corresponding N-type transistors act like pieces of wire, providing a direct connection from C to ground. Because C is at ground, the right-most P-type transistor acts like a closed circuit, forcing D to 2.9 volts.

Figure 3.7b summarizes in truth table form the behavior of the circuit of Figure 3.7a. Note that the circuit is an AND gate. The circuit shown within the dashed lines (i.e., having output C) is a NOT-AND gate, which we generally abbreviate as NAND.

The gates just discussed are very common in digital logic circuits and in digital computers. There are hundreds of thousands of inverters (NOT-gates) in the Pentium II microprocessor. As a convenience, we can represent each of the above gates by standard symbols, as shown in Figure 3.8. The bubble shown in the inverter, NAND, and NOR gates signifies the complement (i.e., NOT) function.

From now on, we will not draw circuits showing the individual transistors. Instead, we will use the symbols shown in Figure 3.8.

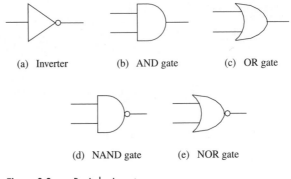

(a) Inverter   (b) AND gate   (c) OR gate

(d) NAND gate   (e) NOR gate

Figure 3.8   Basic logic gates

(a)   (b)

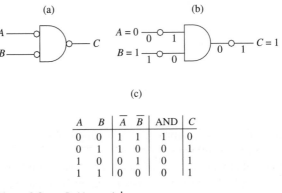

(c)

A	B	$\overline{A}$	$\overline{B}$	AND	C
0	0	1	1	1	0
0	1	1	0	0	1
1	0	0	1	0	1
1	1	0	0	0	1

Figure 3.9   DeMorgan's law

3.2.4   DeMorgan's Law

Note (see Figure 3.9a) that one can complement an input before applying it to a gate. Consider the effect on the two-input AND gate if we apply the complements of A and B as inputs to the gate, and also complement the output of the AND gate. The bubbles at the inputs to the AND gate designate that the inputs A and B are complemented before they are used as inputs to the AND gate.

Figure 3.9b shows the behavior of this structure for the input combination $A = 0$, $B = 1$. For ease of representation, we have moved the "bubbles" away from the inputs and the output of the AND gate. That way, we can more easily see what happens to each value as it passes through a bubble.

Figure 3.9c summarizes by means of a truth table the behavior of the logic circuit of Figure 3.9a for all four combinations of input values. Note that the NOT of A is represented as $\overline{A}$.

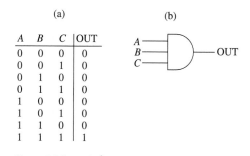

A	B	C	OUT
0	0	0	0
0	0	1	0
0	1	0	0
0	1	1	0
1	0	0	0
1	0	1	0
1	1	0	0
1	1	1	1

Figure 3.10   A three-input AND gate

We can describe the behavior of this circuit algebraically:

$$\overline{\overline{A} \text{ AND } \overline{B}} = A \text{ OR } B$$

This equivalence is known as DeMorgan's law. Is there a similar result if one inverts both inputs to an OR gate, and then inverts the output?

3.2.5 Larger Gates

Before we leave the topic of logic gates, we should note that the notion of AND, OR, NAND, and NOR gates extends to larger numbers of inputs. One could build a three-input AND gate or a four-input OR gate, for example. An n-input AND gate has an output value of 1 only if ALL the input variables have values of 1. If any of the n inputs has a value of 0, the output of the n-input AND gate is 0. An n-input OR gate has an output value of 1 if ANY of the input variables has a value of 1. That is, an n-input OR gate has an output value of 0 only if ALL n-input variables have values of 0.

Figure 3.10 illustrates a three-input AND gate. Figure 3.10a shows its truth table. Figure 3.10b shows the symbol for a three-input AND gate.

Can you draw a transistor-level circuit for a three-input AND gate? How about a four-input OR gate?

3.3   COMBINATIONAL LOGIC STRUCTURES

Now that we understand the workings of the basic logic gates, the next step is to build some of the logic structures that are important components of the microarchitecture of a computer.

There are fundamentally two kinds of logic structures, those that include the storage of information and those that do not. In Sections 3.4 and 3.5, we will deal with structures that store information. In this section, we will deal with those that do not. These structures are sometimes referred to as *decision elements*. Usually, they are referred to as *combinational logic structures*, because their outputs are strictly dependent on the combination of input values that are being applied to the structure *right now*. Their outputs are not at all dependent on any past history of information that is stored internally, since no information can be stored internally in a combinational logic circuit.

We will next examine a decoder, a mux, and a full adder.

3.3.1   Decoder

Figure 3.11 shows a logic gate description of a two-input decoder. A decoder has the property that it provides at its output exactly one 1 and all the rest 0s. The one output that is logically 1 is the output corresponding to the input pattern that it is expected to detect. In general, decoders have n inputs and 2^n outputs. We say the output line that detects the input pattern is *asserted*. That is, that output line has the value 1, rather than 0 as is the case for all the other output lines. In Figure 3.11, note that for each of the four possible combinations of inputs A and B, exactly one output has the value 1 at any one time. In Figure 3.11b, the input to the decoder is 10, resulting in the third output line being asserted.

The decoder is useful in determining how to interpret a bit pattern. We will see in Chapter 5 that the work to be carried out by each instruction in the LC-2 is determined by a four-bit pattern, called an *opcode*, that is part of the instruction. A 4-to-16 decoder is a simple combinational logic structure for identifying what work is to be performed by each instruction.

3.3.2   Mux

Figure 3.12a shows a gate-level description of a two-input multiplexer, more commonly referred to as a *mux*. The function of a mux is to select one of the inputs and

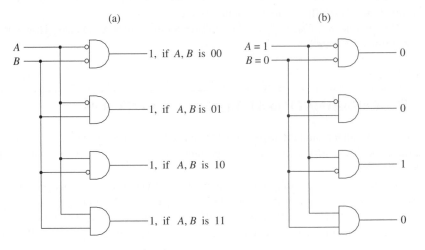

Figure 3.11   A two-input decoder

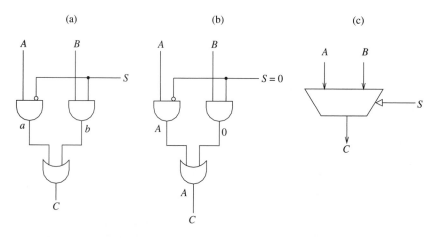

Figure 3.12   A 2-to-1 mux

connect it to the output. The select signal (S in Figure 3.12) determines which input is connected to the output.

The mux of Figure 3.12 works as follows: Suppose $S = 0$, as shown in Figure 3.12b. Since the output of an AND gate is 0 unless all inputs are 1, the output of the right-most AND gate is 0. Also, the output of the left-most AND gate is whatever the input A is. That is, if $A = 0$, then the output of the left-most AND gate is 0, and if $A = 1$, then the output is 1. Since the output of the right-most AND gate is 0, it has no effect on the OR gate. Consequently, the output at C is exactly the same as the output of the left-most AND gate. The net result of all this is that if $S = 0$, the output C is identical to the input A.

On the other hand, if $S = 1$, it is B that is ANDed with 1, resulting in the output of the OR gate having the value of B.

In summary, the output C is always connected to either the input A or the input B—which one depends on the value of the select line S. We say S selects the source of the mux (either A or B) to be routed through to the output C. Figure 3.12c shows the standard representation for a mux.

In general, a mux consists of 2^n inputs and n select lines. Figure 3.13a shows a gate-level description of a four-input mux. It requires two select lines. Figure 3.13b shows the standard representation for a four-input mux.

Can you construct the gate-level representation for an eight-input mux? How many select lines must you have?

3.3.3   Full Adder Circuit

In Chapter 2, we discussed binary addition. Recall that a simple algorithm for binary addition is simply to proceed as you have always done in the case of decimal addition, except one gets a carry after 1, rather than after 9.

Figure 3.14 is a truth table that describes the result of binary addition on *one column* of bits within two n-bit operands. At each column, there are three values that

(a)   (b)

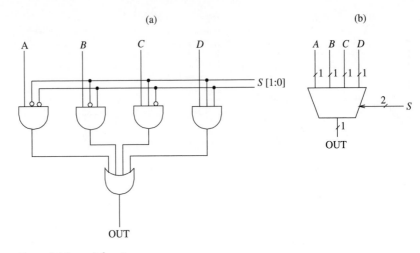

Figure 3.13   A four-input mux

a_i	b_i	$CARRY_i$	$CARRY_{i+1}$	S_i
0	0	0	0	0
0	0	1	0	1
0	1	0	0	1
0	1	1	1	0
1	0	0	0	1
1	0	1	1	0
1	1	0	1	0
1	1	1	1	1

Figure 3.14   A truth table for a
binary adder

must be added: one bit from each of the two operands and the carry from the previous column. We designate these three bits as a_i, b_i, and $carry_i$. There are two results, the sum bit (s_i) and the carry over to the next column, $carry_{i+1}$. Note that if only one of the three bits equals 1, we get a sum of 1, and no carry (i.e., $carry_{i+1} = 0$). If two of the three bits equal 1, we get a sum of 0, and a carry of 1. If all three bits equal 1, the sum is 3, which in binary addition corresponds to a sum of 1 and a carry of 1.

Figure 3.15 is the gate-level description of the truth table of Figure 3.14. We call a circuit that provides three inputs (a_i, b_i, and $carry_i$) and two outputs (the sum bit s_i and the carry over to the next column $carry_{i+1}$) a *full adder*.

Note that each input combination (a specific value associated with each of the three input variables) corresponds to a three-input AND gate with the inputs complemented if the corresponding variable is 0. The output of an AND gate is asserted (equals 1) if the corresponding input combination is present. Thus, to implement the logic circuit to perform the carry function, it is necessary only (as shown in Figure 3.15) (1) to construct AND gates that are asserted for each input combination that produces a carry out, and (2) to connect those AND gates as inputs to a single OR

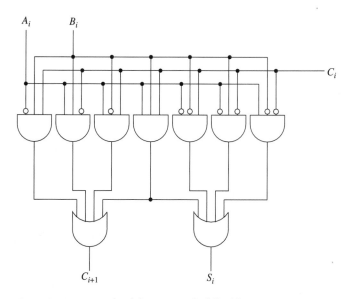

Figure 3.15 Gate-level description of a full adder

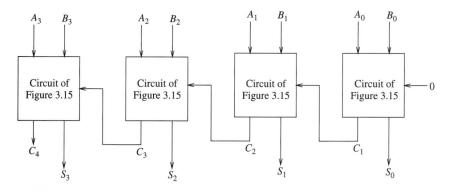

Figure 3.16 A circuit for adding 2 four-bit binary numbers

gate. The carry out is 1 if at least two of the three bits being added are 1s. That is, the carry out is 1 if the input combination is 011, 101, 110, or 111. Thus, we first construct AND gates that will produce an output 1 for each of these four input combinations. Since the output of an OR gate is 1 if any of its input combinations is 1, we connect these four AND gates as inputs to a single OR gate. The result is that if the input combination produces a carry out, the output of the OR gate will be 1. The logic circuit to perform the sum function is built in a similar way.

Figure 3.16 illustrates a circuit for adding two 4-bit binary numbers, using four of the full adder circuits of Figure 3.15. Note that the carry out of column i is an input to the addition performed in column $i + 1$.

3.3.4 Logical Completeness

Before we leave this section, it is worth noting that any arbitrary truth table can be implemented by a logic circuit, provided sufficiently many AND, OR, and NOT gates are available. We say that the set of gates {AND, OR, NOT} is *logically complete* because we can build a circuit to carry out the specification of any arbitrary truth table without using any other kind of gate. That is, the set of gates {AND, OR, and NOT} is logically complete because a barrel of AND gates, a barrel of OR gates, and a barrel of NOT gates are sufficient to build a logic circuit that carries out the specification of any desired truth table. The barrels may have to be big ones, but the point is, we do not need any other kind of gate to do the job.

We can prove this in the following way.

1. Choose any arbitrary specification of a truth table. There will be n input variables, 2^n input combinations, and 2^n entries in the output column, one for each input combination.

2. For each input combination that results in an output 1, construct an AND gate having n inputs. For each input that is a 1 in the input combination, apply the corresponding input directly to the input of the AND gate. For each input that is a 0 in the input combination, invert the input using a NOT gate before applying it to the corresponding input of the AND gate. The output of this AND gate equals 1 exactly when the inputs to the circuit are the corresponding input combination. The number of AND gates constructed in this step is equal to the number of 1s in the output column of the truth table. Note that this is exactly how we constructed the full adder circuit in the previous section.

3. Apply the outputs of each of the AND gates to an input of one (perhaps large) OR gate. The output of that OR gate will exactly carry out the truth table of step 1, as follows:
   a. Any input combination of the truth table that results in an output 1 corresponds (by construction in step 2) to an AND gate. The output of that AND gate equals 1. Since the output of that AND gate is an input to the OR gate, the output of the OR gate is likewise 1.
   b. Any input combination of the truth table that does not result in an output 1 does not correspond to any AND gate. Since the output of each AND is equal to 1 only if the input combination is the one specified for that AND gate, the outputs of all AND gates equal 0. Since all inputs to the OR gate are 0, the output of the OR gate is 0. Done!

3.4 BASIC STORAGE ELEMENTS

Recall our statement at the beginning of Section 3.3 that there are two kinds of logic structures, those that involve the storage of information and those that do not. We have discussed three examples of those that do not: the decoder, the mux, and the adder. Now we are ready to discuss logic structures that do include the storage of information.

3.4.1 The R-S Latch

A simple example of a storage element is the R-S latch. It can store one bit of information. The R-S latch can be implemented in many ways, the simplest being the one shown in Figure 3.17. Two two-input NAND gates are connected such that the output of each is connected to one of the inputs of the other. The remaining input S and R are normally held at a logic level 1.

The R-S latch works as follows: We start with what we call the *quiescent* (or quiet) state, where inputs S and R both have logic value 1. We consider first the case where the output a is 1. Since that means the input A equals 1 (and we know the input R equals 1 since we are in the quiescent state), the output b must be 0. That, in turn, means the input B must be 0, which results in the output a equal to 1. As long as the inputs S and R remain 1, the state of the circuit will not change. We say the R-S latch stores the value 1 (the value of the output a).

If, on the other hand, we assume the output a is 0, then the input A must be 0, and the output b must be 1. This, in turn, results in the input B equal to 1, and combined with the input S equal to 1 (again due to quiescence) results in the output a equal to 0. Again, as long as the inputs S and R remain 1, the state of the circuit will not change. In this case, we say the R-S latch stores the value 0.

The latch can be set to 1 by momentarily setting S to 0, provided we keep the value of R at 1. Similarly, the latch can be set to 0 by momentarily setting R to 0, provided we keep the value of S at 1. We use the term *set* to denote setting a variable to 0 or 1, as in "set to 0" or "set to 1." In addition, we often use the term *clear* to denote the act of setting a variable to 0.

If we clear S, then a equals 1, which in turn causes A to equal 1. Since R is also 1, the output at b must be 0. This causes B to be 0, which in turn makes a equal 1. If we now return S to 1, it does not affect a, since B is also 0, and only one input to a NAND gate must be 0 in order to guarantee that the output of the NAND gate is 1. Thus, the latch continues to store a 1 long after S returns to 1.

In the same way, we can clear the latch (set the latch to 0) by momentarily setting R to 0.

We should also note that in order for the R-S latch to work properly, one must take care that it is never the case that both S and R are allowed to be set to 0 at the same time. If that does happen, the outputs a and b are both 1, and the final state of the latch depends on the electrical properties of the transistors making up the gates

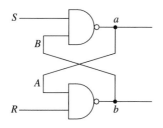

Figure 3.17   An R-S latch

and not on the logic being performed. How the electrical properties of the transistors will determine the final state in this case is a subject we will have to leave for a later semester.

3.4.2   The Gated D Latch

To be useful, it is necessary to control when a latch is set and when it is cleared. A simple way to accomplish this is with the gated latch.

Figure 3.18 shows a logic circuit that implements a gated D latch. It consists of the R-S latch of Figure 3.17, plus two additional gates that allow the latch to be set to the value of D, but *only* when WE is asserted. WE stands for *write enable*. When WE is not asserted (i.e., when WE equals 0), the outputs S and R are both equal to 1. Since S and R are also inputs to the R-S latch, if they are kept at 1, the value stored in the latch remains unchanged, as we explained above.

When WE is momentarily asserted (i.e., set to 1), exactly one of the outputs S or R is set to 0, depending on the value of D. If D equals 1, then S is set to 0. If D equals 0, then both inputs to the lower NAND gate are 1, resulting in R being set to 0. As we saw above, if S is set to 0, the R-S latch is set to 1. If R is set to 0, the R-S latch is set to 0. Thus, the R-S latch is set to 1 or 0 according to whether D is 1 or 0. When WE returns to 0, S and R return to 1, and the value stored in the R-S latch persists.

3.4.3   A Register

We have already seen in Chapter 2 that it is useful to deal with values consisting of more than 1 bit. In Chapter 5, we will introduce the LC-2 computer, where most values are represented by 16 bits. It is useful to be able to store these larger numbers of bits as a self-contained unit. The *register* is a structure that stores a number of bits, taken together as a unit. That number can be as large as is useful or as small as 1. In the LC-2, we will need many 16-bit registers, and also a few one-bit registers. We will see in Figure 3.22, which describes the internal structure of the LC-2, that PC, IR, and MAR are all 16-bit registers, and that N, Z, and P are all one-bit registers.

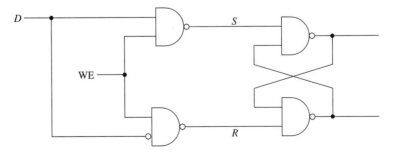

Figure 3.18   A gated D latch

Figure 3.19 shows a four-bit register made up of four gated D latches. The four-bit value stored in the register is Q_3, Q_2, Q_1, Q_0. The value D_3, D_2, D_1, D_0 can be written into the register when WE is asserted.

Note: A common shorthand notation to describe a sequence of bits that are numbered as above is $Q[3:0]$. That is, each bit is assigned its own bit number. The right-most bit is bit [0], and the numbering continues from right to left. If there are n bits, the left-most bit is bit $[n - 1]$. For example, in the following 16-bit pattern,

0011101100011110

bit [15] is 0, bit [14] is 0, bit [13] is 1, bit [12] is 1, and so on.

We can designate a subunit of this pattern with the notation $Q[l:r]$, where l is the left-most bit in the subunit and r is the right-most bit in the subunit. We call such a subunit a *field*.

In the above 16-bit pattern, if $A[15:0]$ is the entire 16-bit pattern, then, for example:

```
A[15:12] is 0011
A[13:7] is 1110110
A[2:0] is 110
A[1:1] is 1
```

We should also point out that the numbering scheme from right to left is purely arbitrary. We could just as easily have designated the left-most bit as bit [0] and numbered them from left to right. Indeed, many people do. So, it is not important whether the numbering scheme is left to right or right to left. But it is important that the bit numbering be consistent in a given setting, that is, that it is always done the same way. In our work, we will always number bits from right to left.

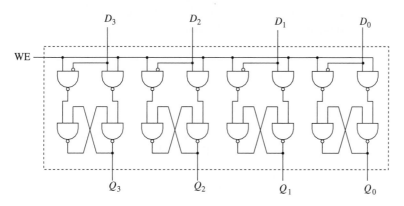

Figure 3.19   A four-bit register

3.5   THE CONCEPT OF MEMORY

We now have all the tools we need to describe what is perhaps the most important structure in the electronic digital computer, its *memory*. We will see in Chapter 4 how memory fits into the basic scheme of computer processing, and you will see throughout the rest of the book and indeed the rest of your work with computers how important the concept of memory is to computing.

Memory is made up of a (usually large) number of locations, each uniquely identifiable and each having the capability to store a value. We refer to the unique identifier associated with each memory location as its *address*. We refer to the number of bits of information stored in each location as its *addressability*.

For example, an advertisement for a personal computer might say, "This computer comes with 16 megabytes of memory." Actually, most ads generally use the abbreviation 16 MB. This statement means, as we will explain momentarily, that the computer system includes 16 million memory locations, each containing 1 byte of information.

3.5.1   Address Space

We refer to the total number of uniquely identifiable locations as the memory's *address space*. A 16-MB memory, for example, refers to a memory that consists of 16 million uniquely identifiable memory locations.

Actually, the number *16 million* is only an approximation, due to the way we identify memory locations. Since everything else in the computer is represented by sequences of 0s and 1s, it should not be surprising that memory locations are identified by binary addresses, as well. With n bits of address, we can uniquely identify 2^n locations. Ten bits provide 1,024 locations, which is approximately 1,000. If we have 20 bits to represent each address, we have 2^{20} uniquely identifiable locations, which is approximately 1 million. Thus 16 mega really corresponds to the number of uniquely identifiable locations that can be specified with 24 address bits. We say the address space is 2^{24}, which is *exactly* 16,777,216 locations, rather than 16,000,000 although we colloquially refer to it as 16 million.

3.5.2   Addressability

The number of bits stored in each memory location is the memory's addressability. A 16 megabyte memory is a memory consisting of 16,777,216 memory locations, each containing 1 byte (i.e., 8 bits) of storage. Most memories are byte-addressable. The reason is historical; most computers got their start processing data, and one character stroke on the keyboard corresponds to one 8-bit ASCII character, as we learned in Chapter 2. If the memory is byte-addressable, then each ASCII code occupies one location in memory. Uniquely identifying each byte of memory allowed individual bytes of stored information to be changed easily.

Many computers that have been designed specifically to perform large scientific calculations are 64-bit addressable. This is due to the fact that numbers used in scientific calculations are frequently represented as 64-bit floating point quantities. Recall we discussed the floating point data type in Chapter 2. Since scientific calculations are likely to use numbers that require 64 bits to represent them, it is reasonable to design a memory for such a computer that stores one such number in each uniquely identifiable memory location.

3.5.3   A 2^2-by-3-bit Memory

Figure 3.20 illustrates a memory of size 2^2 by 3 bits. That is, the memory has an address space of four locations, and an addressability of 3 bits. A memory of size 2^2 requires 2 bits to specify the address. A memory of addressability 3 stores 3 bits of information in each memory location.

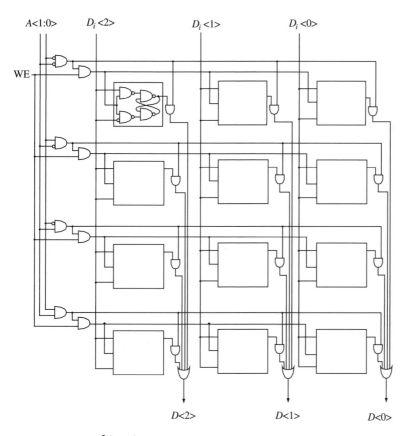

Figure 3.20   A 2^2-by-3-bit memory

Accesses of memory require decoding the address bits. Note that the address decoder takes as input $A[1:0]$ and asserts exactly one of its four outputs, corresponding to the *word line* being addressed. In Figure 3.20, each row of the memory corresponds to a unique 3-bit word; therefore, the term *word line*. Memory can be read by applying the address $A[1:0]$, which asserts the word line to be read. Note that each of the 12 bits in this memory is ANDed with its word line and then ORed with the corresponding bits of the other words. Since only one word line can be asserted at a time, the output of each *bit line* is the value stored in the corresponding bit of the word line that is asserted.

Figure 3.21 shows the process of reading location 3. The code for 3 is 11. The address $A[1:0] = 11$ is decoded, and the bottom word line is asserted. Note that the three other decoder outputs are not asserted. That is, they have the value 0. The value stored in location 3 is 101. These three bits are each ANDed with their word line producing the bits 101 which are supplied to the three output OR gates. Note that all other inputs to the OR gates are 0, since they have been produced by ANDing with unasserted word lines. The result is that $D[2:0] = 101$. That is, the value stored in location 3, is output by the OR gates.

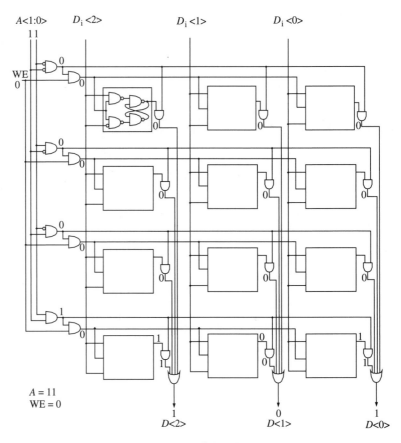

Figure 3.21   Reading location 3 in our 2^2-by-3-bit memory

Memory can be written in a similar fashion. The address specified by $A[1:0]$ is presented to the address decoder, resulting in the correct word line being asserted. With WE asserted as well, the three bits $D_i[2:0]$ can be written into the three gated latches corresponding to that word line.

3.6   THE DATA PATH OF THE LC-2

Preview of Coming Attractions: In Chapter 5, we will specify a computer, which we call the LC-2, and you will have the opportunity to write computer programs to execute on the LC-2. Figure 3.22 is a block diagram of what we call the *data path* of

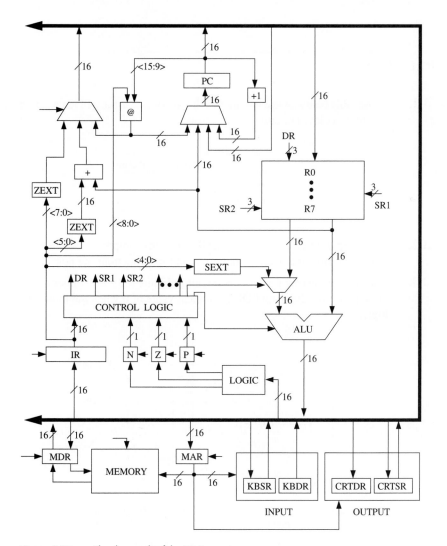

Figure 3.22   The data path of the LC-2 computer

the LC-2. The data path consists of all the logic structures that combine to process information in the core of the computer. Right now, Figure 3.22 is undoubtedly a little intimidating, and that is not surprising. You are not ready to analyze it yet. That will come in Chapter 5. We have included it here, however, to show you that you are already familiar with many of the basic structures that make up a computer. That is, you already know how many of the elements in the data path work, and furthermore, you know how those elements are constructed from gates. For example, PC, IR, MAR, and MDR are registers and store 16 bits of information each. Each wire that is labeled with a cross-hatch 16 represents 16 wires, each carrying one bit of information. N, Z, and P are one-bit registers. There are three muxes, one supplying a 16-bit value to the PC register. In Chapter 5, we will see why these elements must be connected as shown in order to execute the programs written for the LC-2 computer.

PROBLEMS

3.1. In the table below, write whether each type of transistor will act as an open circuit or a closed circuit.

	N-type	**P-type**
Gate = 1		
Gate = 0		

3.2. A two-input AND and a two-input OR are both examples of two-input logic functions. How many different two-input logic functions are possible?

3.3. Replace the missing parts in the circuit in Figure 3.23 with either a wire or no wire to give the output OUT a logical value of 0 when the input IN is a logical 1.

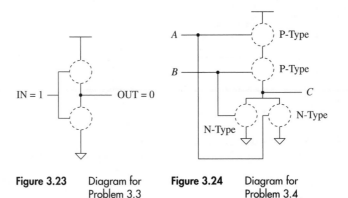

Figure 3.23   Diagram for Problem 3.3

Figure 3.24   Diagram for Problem 3.4

3.4. Replace the missing parts in the circuit in Figure 3.24 with either a wire or no wire to give the output *C* a logical value of 1.

Describe a set of inputs that give the output *C* a logical value of 0. Replace the missing parts with wires or no wires corresponding to that set of inputs.

3.5. Complete a truth table for the transistor-level circuit in Figure 3.25.

3.6. The circuit in Figure 3.26 has a major flaw. Can you identify it? *Hint*: Evaluate the circuit for all sets of inputs.

3.7. Fill in the truth table for the logical expression NOT(NOT(A) OR NOT(B)). What single logic gate has the same truth table?

A	B	NOT(NOT(A) OR NOT(B))
0	0	
0	1	
1	0	
1	1	

3.8. Fill in the truth table for a two-input NOR gate.

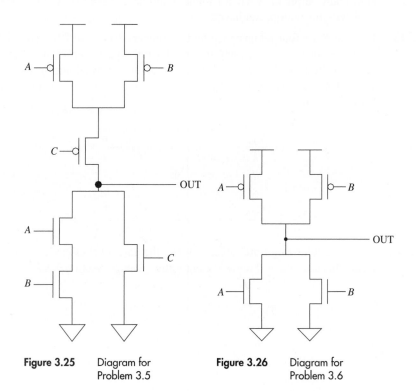

Figure 3.25 Diagram for Problem 3.5

Figure 3.26 Diagram for Problem 3.6

A	B	A NOR B
0	0	
0	1	
1	0	
1	1	

3.9.   1.   Draw a transistor-level diagram for a three-input AND gate and a three-input OR gate. Do this by extending the designs from Figures 3.6a and 3.7a.

2.   Replace the transistors in your diagrams from part 1 with either a wire or no wire to reflect the circuit's operation when the following inputs are applied.
   a. $A = 1, B = 0, C = 0$
   b. $A = 0, B = 0, C = 0$
   c. $A = 1, B = 1, C = 1$

3.10.   Following the example of Figure 3.11a, draw the gate-level schematic of a three-input decoder. For each output of this decoder, write the input conditions under which that output will be 1.

3.11.   How many output lines will a five-input decoder have?

3.12.   How many output lines will a 16-input multiplexer have? How many select lines will this multiplexer have?

3.13.   If A and B are four-bit unsigned binary numbers, 0111 and 1011, complete the table obtained when using the two-bit full adder from Figure 3.15 to calculate the sum, S, of A and B. Check your answer by adding the decimal value of A and B and comparing the sum with S. Are the answers the same? Why or why not?

C_{in}				0
A	0	1	1	1
B	1	0	1	1
S				
C_{out}				

3.14.   Given the following truth table, generate the gate-level circuit that implements this truth table. Follow the algorithm given in Section 3.3.4.

A	B	C	Z
0	0	0	1
0	0	1	0
0	1	0	0
0	1	1	1
1	0	0	0
1	0	1	1
1	1	0	1
1	1	1	0

3.15. 1. Given four inputs, A, B, C, and D and one output Z, create a truth table for a circuit with at least seven input combinations generating 1s at the output. (How many rows will this truth table have?)

2. Now that you have a truth table, generate the gate-level circuit that implements this truth table following the the algorithm given in steps (2) and (3) in Section 3.3.4.

3.16. Implement the following functions using AND, OR, and NOT logic gates. The inputs are A, B, and the output is F.

1. F has the value 1 only if A has the value 0 and B has the value 1.

2. F has the value 1 only if A has the value 1 and B has the value 0.

3. Use your answers from (1) and (2) to implement a one-bit adder. The truth table for the one-bit adder is given below.

A	B	Sum
0	0	0
0	1	1
1	0	1
1	1	0

4. Is it possible to create a four-bit adder (a circuit that will correctly add two 4-bit quantities) using only four copies of the logic diagram from (3)? If not, what information is missing? *Hint*: When $A = 1$ and $B = 1$, a sum of 0 is produced. What information is disregarded?

3.17. Logic circuit 1 in Figure 3.27 has inputs A, B, C. Logic circuit 2 in Figure 3.28 has inputs A and B. Both logic circuits have an output D. There is a fundamental difference between the behavioral characteristics of these two circuits. What is it? *Hint*: What happens when the voltage at input A goes from 0 to 1 in both circuits?

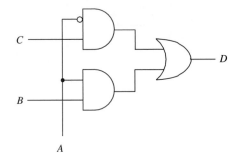

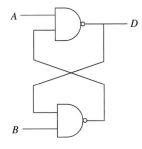

Figure 3.27   Circuit 1 for Problem 3.17   **Figure 3.28**   Circuit 2 for
                                                                               Problem 3.17

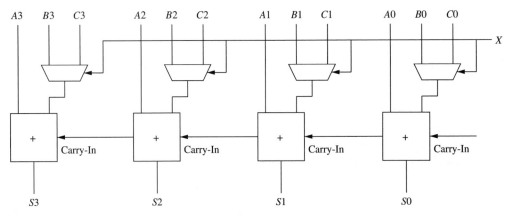

Figure 3.29   Diagram for Problem 3.19

3.18. You know a byte is 8 bits. We call a four-bit quantity a *nibble*. If a byte-addressable memory has a 14-bit address, how many nibbles of storage are in this memory?

3.19. 1. Figure 3.29 shows a logic circuit that appears in many of today's processors. Each of the boxes is a full adder circuit. What does the value on the wire X do? That is, what is the difference in the output of this circuit if $X = 0$ versus if $X = 1$?

2. Construct a logic diagram that implements an adder/subtracter. That is, the logic circuit will compute $A + B$ or $A - B$ depending on the value of X. *Hint*: Use the logic diagram of Figure 3.29 as a building block.

3.20. Given the logic circuit in Figure 3.30, fill in the truth table for the output value Z.

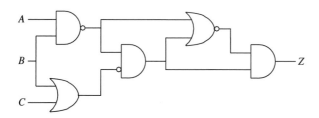

Figure 3.30   Diagram for Problem 3.20

A	B	C	Z
0	0	0	
0	0	1	
0	1	0	
0	1	1	
1	0	0	
1	0	1	
1	1	0	
1	1	1	

3.21. Say the speed of a logic structure depends on the largest number of logic gates through which any of the inputs must propagate to reach an output. Assume that a NOT, an AND, and an OR gate all count as one gate delay. For example, the propagation delay for a two-input decoder shown in Figure 3.11 is 2 because some inputs propagate through two gates.

1. What is the propagation delay for the two-input mux shown in Figure 3.12?

2. What is the propagation delay for the one-bit full adder in Figure 3.15?

3. What is the propagation delay for the four-bit adder shown in Figure 3.16?

4. What if the four-bit adder were extended to 32 bits?

3.22. For this question, refer to Figure 3.31.

1. Describe the output of this logic circuit when the select S is a logical 0. That is, what is the output Z for each value of A?

2. If the select line, S, is switched from a logical 0 to 1, what will the output be?

3. Is this logic circuit a storage element?

3.23. A 16-bit register contains a value. The value x75A2 is written into it. Can the original value be recovered?

3.24. Distinguish between a memory address and the memory's addressability.

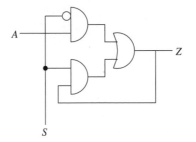

Figure 3.31   Diagram for Problem 3.22

3.25. If a computer has eight-byte addressability and needs three bits to access a location in memory, what is the total size of memory in bytes?

3.26. Using Figure 3.20, the diagram of the four-entry, three-bit memory,

1. To read from the fourth memory location, what must the values of $A[1:0]$, and WE be?

2. To change the number of entries in the memory from 4 to 60, how many total address lines would be needed? What would the addressability of the memory be after this change was made?

3. Suppose the minimum width (in bits) of the program counter (the program counter is a special register within a CPU and we will discuss it in detail in the next chapter) is the minimum number of bits needed to address all 60 locations in our memory from part (2). How many additional memory locations could be added to this memory without having to alter the width of the program counter.

3.27. Given a memory that is addressed by 22 bits and is three-bit addressable, how many bits of storage does the memory contain?

3.28. Generate the gate-level logic that implements the following truth table. From the gate-level structure, generate a transistor diagram that implements the logic structure. Verify that the transistor diagram implements the truth table.

in_0	in_1	$f(in_0, in_1)$
0	0	1
0	1	0
1	0	1
1	1	1

chapter

4

The Von Neumann Model

We are now ready to build on the logic structures that we studied in Chapter 3. We will need both decision elements and storage elements to construct the basic computer model first proposed by John Von Neumann in 1946.

4.1 BASIC COMPONENTS

Figure 4.1 shows the basic structure proposed by John Von Neumann for processing computer programs. We have taken a little poetic license and added a few of our own minor embellishments to Von Neumann's original diagram.

The Von Neumann model consists of five parts: *memory, a processing unit, input, output,* and *a control unit.* A computer program consists of a set of instructions, each specifying a well-defined piece of work for the computer to carry out. The *instruction* is the smallest piece of work specified in a computer program. That is, the computer either carries out the work specified by an instruction or it does not. The computer does not have the luxury of carrying out a piece of an instruction. The computer program is contained in the computer's memory. The control of the order in which the instructions are carried out is performed by the control unit.

We will describe each of the five parts of the Von Neumann model.

4.1.1 Memory

Recall that in Chapter 3 we examined a simple 2^2-by-3 bit memory that was constructed out of gates and latches. A more realistic memory for one of today's computer

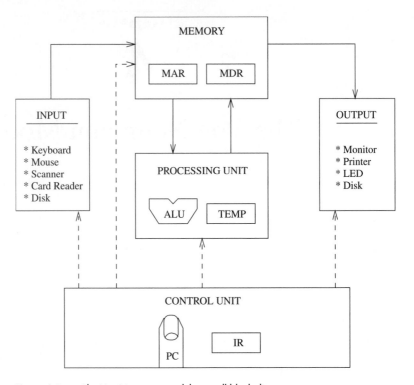

Figure 4.1   The Von Neumann model, overall block diagram

systems is 2^{28} by 8 bits. That is, a typical memory in today's world of computers consists of 2^{28} distinct memory locations, each of which is capable of storing 8 bits of information. We say that such a memory has an *address space* of 2^{28} uniquely identifiable locations, and an *addressability* of 8 bits. We refer to such a memory as a 256-megabyte memory (abbreviated, 256 MB). The "256 mega" refers to the 2^{28} locations, and the "byte" refers to the 8 bits stored in each location. The term *byte* is, by definition, the word used to describe 8 bits, much the way *gallon* describes four quarts.

We note (as we will note again and again) that with k bits, we can represent uniquely 2^k items. Thus, to uniquely identify 2^{28} memory locations, each location must have its own 28-bit address. In Chapter 5, we will begin the complete definition of the instruction set architecture (ISA) of the LC-2 computer. We will see that the memory address space of the LC-2 is 2^{16}, and the addressability is 16 bits.

Recall from Chapter 3 that we access memory by providing the address from which we wish to read, or to which we wish to write. To read the contents of a memory location, we first place the address of that location in the memory's address register (**MAR**), and then interrogate the computer's memory. The information stored in the location having that address will be provided in the memory's data register (**MDR**). To write (or store) a value in a memory location, we first write the address of the memory location in the MAR, and the value to be stored in the MDR. We

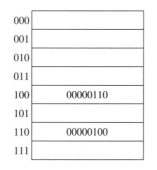

000	
001	
010	
011	
100	00000110
101	
110	00000100
111	

Figure 4.2   Location 6 contains the value 4; location 4 contains the value 6

then interrogate the computer's memory with the Write Enable signal asserted. The information contained in the MDR will be written into the memory location whose address is in the MAR.

Before we leave the notion of memory for the moment, let us again emphasize the two characteristics of a memory location: its address and what is stored there. Figure 4.2 shows a representation of a memory consisting of eight locations. Its addresses are shown at the left, numbered in binary from 0 to 7. Each location contains 8 bits of information. Note that we have stored the value 6 in the memory location whose address is 4, and we have stored the value 4 in the memory location whose address is 6. These represent two very different situations.

Finally, an analogy comes to mind: the post office boxes in your local post office. The box number is like the memory location's address. Each box number is unique. The information stored in the memory location is like the letters contained in the post office box. As time goes by, what is contained in the post office box at any particular moment can change. But the box number remains the same. So, too, with each memory location. The value stored in that location can be changed, but the location's memory address remains unchanged.

4.1.2   Processing Unit

The actual processing of information in the computer is carried out by the *processing unit*. The processing unit in a modern computer can consist of many sophisticated complex functional units, each performing one particular operation (divide, square root, etc.). The simplest processing unit, and the one normally thought of when discussing the basic Von Neumann model, is the **ALU**. *ALU* is the abbreviation for Arithmetic and Logic Unit, so called because it is usually capable of performing basic arithmetic functions (like ADD and SUBTRACT) and basic logic operations (like bit-wise AND, OR, and NOT that we have already studied in Chapter 2). As we will see in Chapter 5, the LC-2 has an ALU, which can perform ADD, AND, and NOT operations.

The size of the quantities normally processed by the ALU is often referred to as the *word length* of the computer, and each element is referred to as a *word*. In the LC-2, the ALU processes 16-bit quantities. We say the LC-2 has a word length of 16 bits. Each ISA has its own word length, depending on the intended use of the computer. Most microprocessors today that are used in PCs or workstations have a word length of either 32 bits (as is the case with Intel's Pentium III) or 64 bits (as is the case with Compaq's Alpha processors and Intel's Itanium processor). For some applications, like the microprocessors used in pagers, VCRs, and cellular telephones, 8 bits are usually enough. Such microprocessors, we say, have a word length of 8 bits.

It is almost always the case that a computer provides some small amount of storage very close to the ALU to allow results to be temporarily stored if they will be needed to produce other results in the near future. For example, if a computer is to calculate $(A + B) \cdot C$, it could store the result of $A + B$ in memory, and then subsequently read it in order to multiply that result by C. However, the time it takes to access memory is long compared to the time it takes to perform the ADD or MULTIPLY. Almost all computers, therefore, have temporary storage for storing the result of $A + B$ in order to avoid the unnecessarily longer access time that would be necessary when it came time to multiply. The most common form of temporary storage is a set of registers, like the register described in Section 3.4.3. Typically, the size of each register is identical to the size of values processed by the ALU, that is, they each contain one word. The LC-2 has eight registers (R0, R1, . . . R7), each consisting of 16 bits. The Alpha ISA has 32 registers (R0, R1, . . . R31), each containing 64 bits.

4.1.3   Input and Output

In order for a computer to process information, the information must get into the computer. In order to use the results of that processing, it must be displayed in some fashion outside the computer. Many devices exist for the purposes of input and output. They are generically referred to in computer jargon as *peripherals* because they are in some sense accessories to the processing function. Nonetheless, they are no less important.

In the LC-2 we will have the two most basic of input and output devices. For input, we will use the keyboard, and for output, we will use the monitor.

There are, of course, many other input and output devices present in computer systems today. For input we have among other things the mouse, digital scanners, and floppy disks. For output we have among other things printers, LED displays, and disks. In the old days, much input and output was carried out by punched cards. Fortunately, for those who would have to lug boxes of cards around, the use of punched cards has largely disappeared.

4.1.4   Control Unit

The control unit is like the conductor of an orchestra; it is in charge of making all the other parts play together. As we will see in the next section when we describe the step-by-step process of executing a computer program, it is the control unit that keeps track of both where we are within the process of executing the program and where we are in the process of executing each instruction.

To keep track of which instruction is being executed, the control unit has an *instruction register* to contain that instruction. To keep track of which instruction is to be processed next, the control unit has a register that contains the next instruction's address. For historical reasons, that register is called the *program counter* (abbreviated PC), although a simpler name for it would be the *instruction pointer*, since the contents of this register are, in some sense, "pointing" to the next instruction to be processed. Curiously, Intel does in fact call that register the instruction pointer, but the simple elegance of that name has not caught on.

4.1.5   Summary: The LC-2 as an Example of the Von Neumann Model

In Chapter 5, we will introduce the LC-2, a simple computer that we will study extensively. We have already introduced its data path in Chapter 3 (Figure 3.22). Figure 4.3 shows part of the data path of the LC-2. In fact, we constructed Figure 4.3 by starting with the full data path of the LC-2 (Figure 3.22) and removing all elements that are not essential to showing the presence of the basic components of the Von Neumann model.

Memory consists of the storage elements, along with the MAR for addressing individual locations and the MDR for holding the contents of a memory location on its way to/from the storage.

Input consists of a keyboard and output consists of a monitor. The simplest keyboard requires two registers, a data register (KBDR) for holding the ASCII codes of keys struck, and a status register (KBSR) for maintaining status information about the keys struck. The simplest monitor also requires two registers, one for holding the ASCII code of something to be displayed on the screen (CRTDR), and one for maintaining associated status information (CRTSR). The details of these input and output registers will be discussed in more detail in Chapter 8.

The processing unit consists of a functional unit that can perform arithmetic and logic operations (ALU) and eight registers (R0, ... R7) for storing temporary values that will be needed in the near future as operands for subsequent instructions.

The control unit contains the program counter (PC), instruction register (IR), and the control logic necessary for managing the control of all the activity going on.

4.2   INSTRUCTION PROCESSING

The central idea in the Von Neumann model of computer processing is that the program and data are both stored as sequences of bits in the computer's memory, and the program is executed one instruction at a time under the direction of the control unit.

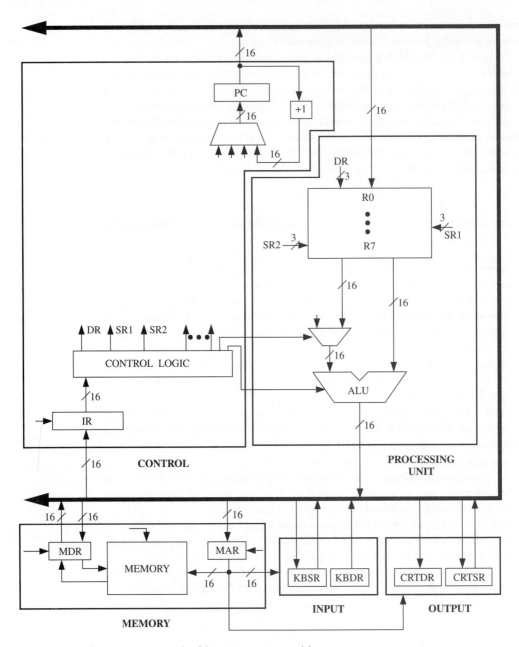

Figure 4.3   The LC-2 as an example of the Von Neumann model

4.2.1   The Instruction

The most basic unit of computer processing is the instruction. It is made up of two parts, the *opcode* (what the instruction does) and the *operands* (who it is to do it to).

In Chapter 5, we will see that each LC-2 instruction consists of 16 bits (one word), numbered from left to right, bit [15] to bit [0]. Bits [15:12] contain the opcode. This means there are at most 2^4 distinct opcodes. Bits [11:0] are used to figure out where the operands are.

The ADD Instruction   The ADD instruction requires three operands: two source operands (the data that is to be added) and one destination operand (the sum that is to be stored after the addition is performed). We said that the processing unit of the LC-2 contained eight registers for purposes of storing data that may be needed later. In fact, the ADD instruction **requires** that the two source operands be contained in these registers, and that the result of the ADD be put into one of these eight registers. Since there are eight registers, three bits are necessary to identify each one. Thus the 16-bit LC-2 ADD instruction has the following form (we say *format*):

Example 4.1

15	14	13	12	11	10	9	8	7	6	5	4	3	2	1	0
0	0	0	1	1	1	0	0	1	0	0	0	0	1	1	0
	ADD				R6			R2					R6		

The 4-bit opcode for ADD, contained in bits [15:12] is 0001. Bits [11:9] identify the location to be used for storing the result, in this case R6. Bits [8:6] and bits [2:0] identify the registers to be used to obtain the source operands, in this case R2 and R6. Bits [5:3] have a purpose that it is not necessary to understand in the context of this example. We will save the explanation of bits [5:3] for Section 5.2.

Thus, the instruction encoded above is interpreted, "Add the contents of R2 (register 2) to the contents of R6 and store the result back into R6."

The LDR Instruction   The LDR instruction requires two operands. *LD* stands for load, which is computerese for "go to a particular memory location, read the value that is contained there, and store it in one of the registers." The two operands that are required are the value to be read from memory and the destination register, which will contain that value after the instruction is processed. The *R* in LDR identifies the mechanism that will be used to calculate the address of the memory location to be read. That mechanism is called the *addressing mode*, and the particular addressing mode identified by the use of the letter *R* is called **BASE+offset**. Thus, the 16-bit LC-2 LDR instruction has the following format:

Example 4.2

15	14	13	12	11	10	9	8	7	6	5	4	3	2	1	0
0	1	1	0	0	1	0	0	1	1	0	0	0	1	1	0
	LDR				R2			R3				6			

The four-bit opcode for LDR is 0110. Bits [11:9] identify the register that will contain the value read from memory after the instruction is executed. Bits [8:0] are used to calculate the address of the location to be read. In particular, since the addressing mode is BASE+offset, the address is computed by adding the value 6 (the binary number contained in bits [5:0]) to the contents of R3 (Bits [8:6]). Thus, the instruction encoded above is interpreted: "Add the contents of R3 to the value 6 to form the address of a memory location. Load the contents stored in that memory location into R2."

4.2.2   The Instruction Cycle

Instructions are processed under the direction of the control unit in a very systematic step-by-step manner. The sequence of steps is called the *instruction cycle*, and each step is referred to as a *phase*. There are basically six phases to the instruction cycle, although many computers have been designed such that not all instructions require all six phases. We will discuss this momentarily.

But first, we will examine the six phases of the instruction cycle:

```
FETCH
DECODE
EVALUATE ADDRESS
FETCH OPERANDS
EXECUTE
STORE RESULT
```

The process is as follows (again refer to Figure 4.3, our simplified version of the LC-2 data path):

FETCH

The FETCH phase obtains the next instruction from memory and loads it into the instruction register (IR) of the control unit. Recall that a computer program consists of a collection of instructions, that each instruction is represented by a sequence of bits, and that the entire program (in the Von Neumann model) is stored in the computer's memory. In order to carry out the work of the next instruction, we must first identify where it is. The program counter (PC) contains the address of the next instruction. Thus, the FETCH phase takes multiple steps:

```
First the MAR is loaded with the contents of the PC.

Next, the memory is interrogated, which results
in the next instruction being placed by the memory
into the MDR.

Finally, the IR is loaded with the contents
of the MDR.
```

We are now ready for the next phase, decoding the instruction. However, when the instruction cycle is complete, and we wish to fetch the next instruction, we would like the PC to contain the address of the next instruction. Therefore, the final step in the FETCH phase is to increment the PC. In that way, at the completion of the execution of this instruction, the FETCH phase of the next instruction will load into IR the contents of the next memory location, provided the execution of the current instruction does not involve changing the value in the PC.

Note that the FETCH phase takes several steps.

Step 1: Load the MAR with the contents of the PC.

Step 2: Interrogate memory, resulting in the instruction being placed in the MDR.

Step 3: Load the IR with the contents of the MDR and simultaneously increment the PC.

Each of these steps is under the direction of the control unit, much like, as we said previously, the instruments in an orchestra are under the control of a conductor's baton. Each stroke of the conductor's baton corresponds to one *machine cycle*. Step 1 takes one machine cycle. Step 2 could take one machine cycle, or many machine cycles, depending on how long it takes to access the computer's memory. Step 3 takes one machine cycle. In a modern digital computer, a machine cycle takes a very small fraction of a second. Indeed, an 800-MHz Compaq Alpha completes 800 million cycles in one second. Said another way, one machine cycle takes 1.25 billionths of a second (1.25 nanoseconds). Recall that the light bulb that is helping you read this text is switching on and off at the rate of 120 times a second. Thus, in the time it takes a light bulb to switch on and off once, today's computers can complete 8 million machine cycles!

DECODE

The DECODE phase examines the instruction in order to figure out what the microarchitecture is being asked to do. Recall the decoder we studied in Chapter 3. In the LC-2, a 4-to-16 decoder identifies which of the 16 opcodes is to be processed. The corresponding output of the decoder is asserted. Depending on which output of the decoder is asserted (on the opcode), the remaining 12 bits identify what else is needed to process the instruction.

EVALUATE ADDRESS

This phase computes the address of the memory location that is needed to process the instruction. Recall the example of the LDR instruction: The LDR instruction causes a value stored in memory to be loaded into a register. In the previous example, the address was obtained by adding the value 6 to the contents of R3. This calculation was performed during the EVALUATE ADDRESS phase.

FETCH OPERANDS

This phase obtains the source operands needed to process the instruction. In the LDR example, this phase took two steps: loading MAR with the address calculated in the EVALUATE ADDRESS phase, and reading memory, which resulted in the source operand being placed in MDR.

In the ADD example, this phase consisted of obtaining the source operands from R2 and R6. [In most current microprocessors, this phase (for the ADD instruction) can be done at the same time the instruction is being decoded.

Exactly how we can speed up the processing of an instruction in this way is a fascinating subject, but one we are forced to leave for a later course.]

EXECUTE

This phase carries out the execution of the instruction. In the ADD example, this phase consisted of the single step of performing the addition in the ALU.

STORE RESULT

The final phase of an instruction's execution. The result is written to its designated destination.

Once the sixth phase (STORE RESULT) has been completed, the control unit begins anew the instruction cycle, starting from the top with the FETCH phase. Since the PC was updated during the previous instruction cycle, it contains at this point the address of the instruction stored in the next sequential memory location. Thus the next sequential instruction is fetched next. Processing continues in this way until something breaks this sequential flow.

4.2.3   Examples

Example 4.3   **ADD [eax], edx**   This is an example of an Intel IA-32 instruction that requires all six phases of the instruction cycle. All instructions require the first two phases, FETCH and DECODE. This instruction uses the eax register to calculate the address of a memory location (EVALUATE ADDRESS). The contents of that memory location are then read (FETCH OPERAND), added to the contents of the edx register (EXECUTE), and the result written into the memory location that originally contained the first source operand (STORE RESULT).

Example 4.4   The LC-2 ADD and LDR instructions do not require all six phases. In particular, the ADD instruction does not require an EVALUATE ADDRESS phase. The LDR instruction does not require an EXECUTE phase.

4.3   CHANGING THE SEQUENCE OF EXECUTION

Everything we have said thus far suggests that a computer program is executed in sequence. That is, the first instruction is executed, then the second instruction is executed, followed by the third instruction, and so on.

We have identified two types of instructions, the ADD, which is an example of an *operate instruction* in that it processes data, and the LDR, which is an example of a *data movement instruction* in that it moves data from one place to another. There are other examples of both operate instructions and data movement instructions, as we will discover in Chapter 5 when we study the LC-2.

There is a third type of instruction, the *control instruction*, whose purpose is to change the sequence of instruction execution. For example, there are times, as we shall see, when it is desirable to first execute the first instruction, then the second, then the third, then the first again, the second again, then the third again, then the first for the third time, and so on. As we know, each instruction cycle starts with loading the MAR with the PC. Thus, if we wish to change the sequence of instructions executed, we must change the PC between the time it is incremented (during the FETCH phase) of one instruction and the start of the FETCH phase of the next.

Control instructions perform that function by loading the PC during the EXE-CUTE phase, which wipes out the incremented PC that was loaded during the FETCH phase. The result is that, at the start of the next instruction cycle, when the computer accesses the PC to obtain the address of an instruction to fetch, it will get the address loaded during the previous EXECUTE phase, rather than the next sequential instruction in the computer's program.

Consider the LC-2 instruction JMPR, whose format is shown below. Assume this instruction is stored in memory location x36A2.   **Example 4.5**

15	14	13	12	11	10	9	8	7	6	5	4	3	2	1	0
1	1	0	0	0	0	0	0	1	1	0	0	0	1	1	0
JMPR								R3			6				

The four-bit opcode for JMPR is 1100. Bits [8:0] are used to calculate the address of the next instruction to be processed. In particular, since the addressing mode is BASE+offset (as was the case with the LDR), the address of the next instruction to be fetched is 6 (the binary number contained in bits [5:0] plus the contents of R3 (bits [8:6]). Thus, the instruction encoded above is interpreted, "Add the contents of R3 to the value 6 to form the address of a memory location. Load that address into the PC (during the EXECUTE phase) so that the next instruction processed will be at the address calculated."

Processing will go on as follows. Let's start at the beginning of the instruction cycle, with PC = x36A2. The FETCH phase results in the IR being loaded with the JMPR instruction and the PC updated to contain the address x36A3. Suppose the contents of R3 at the start of this instruction is x3440. During the EVALUATE ADDRESS phase, 6 is added to x3440, producing x3446. During the EXECUTE phase, the PC is loaded with x3446. Therefore, in the next instruction cycle, the instruction processed will be the one at address x3446, rather than the one at address x36A3.

4.4   STOPPING THE COMPUTER

From everything we have said, it appears that the computer will continue processing instructions, carrying out the instruction cycle again and again, ad nauseum. Since the computer does not have the capacity to be bored, must this continue until someone pulls the plug and disconnects power to the computer?

Usually, user programs execute under the control of an operating system. UNIX, DOS, and WindowsNT are all examples of operating systems. Operating systems are just computer programs themselves. So as far as the computer is concerned, the instruction cycle continues whether a user program is being processed or the operating system is being processed. This is fine as far as user programs are concerned since each user program terminates with a control instruction which changes the PC to again start processing the operating system—often to initiate the execution of another user program.

But what if we actually want to stop this infinite sequence of instruction cycles? Recall our analogy to the conductor's baton, beating at the rate of millions of machine cycles per second. Stopping the instruction sequencing requires stopping the conductor's baton. There is inside the computer, a component that corresponds very closely to the conductor's baton. It is called the CLOCK. The clock defines the machine cycle; it is the element of control that allows the control unit to continue on to the next machine cycle, whether that is the next step of the current phase, or the first step of the next phase of the instruction cycle. Stopping the instruction cycle requires stopping the clock. Figure 4.4 describes the behavior of the clock.

Figure 4.4a shows a block diagram of the clock circuit, consisting primarily of a clock generator and a RUN latch. The clock generator is a crystal oscillator, a piezoelectric device that you may have studied in your physics or chemistry class. For our purposes, the crystal oscillator is a black box (recall our definition of black box in Section 1.4) that produces the oscillating voltage shown in Figure 4.4b. Note the resemblance of that voltage to the conductor's baton. Every machine cycle, the voltage rises to 2.9 volts and then drops back to 0 volts.

If the RUN latch is in the 1 state (i.e., $Q = 1$), the output of the clock circuit is the same as the output of the clock generator. If the RUN latch is in the 0 state (i.e., $Q = 0$), the output of the clock circuit is 0.

Thus, stopping the instruction cycle requires only clearing the RUN latch. Every computer has some mechanism for doing that. In some older machines, it is done by executing a HALT instruction. In the LC-2, as in many other machines, it is done under control of the operating system, as we will see in Chapter 9.

Question: If a HALT instruction can clear the RUN latch, thereby stopping the instruction cycle, what instruction is needed to set the RUN latch, thereby reinitiating the instruction cycle?

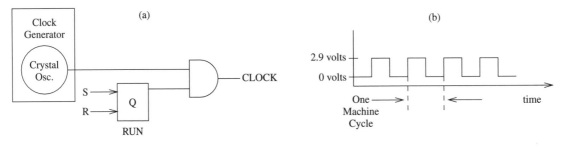

Figure 4.4   The clock circuit and its control

PROBLEMS

4.1. Name the five components of the Von Neumann model. For each component, state its purpose.

4.2. Briefly describe the interface between the memory and the processing unit. That is, describe the method by which the memory and the processing unit communicate.

4.3. What is misleading about the name *program counter*? Why is the name *instruction pointer* more insightful?

4.4. What is the word length of a computer? How does the word length of a computer affect what the computer is able to compute? That is, is it a valid argument, in light of what you learned in Chapter 1, to say that a computer with a larger word size can process more information and therefore is capable of computing more than a computer with a smaller word size?

4.5. The following table represents a small memory. Refer to this table for the following questions.

Address	Data
0000	0001 1110 0100 0011
0001	1111 0000 0010 0101
0010	0110 1111 0000 0001
0011	0000 0000 0000 0000
0100	0000 0000 0110 0101
0101	0000 0000 0000 0110
0110	1111 1110 1101 0011
0111	0000 0110 1101 1001

1. What binary value does location 3 contain? Location 6?

2. The binary value within each location can be interpreted in many ways. We have seen that binary values can represent unsigned numbers, 2's complement signed numbers, floating point numbers, and so forth.
   a. Interpret location 0 and location 1 as 2's complement integers.
   b. Interpret location 4 as an ASCII value.
   c. Interpret location 6 as a floating point number.
   d. Interpret location 5 as an unsigned value.

3. In the Von Neumann model, the contents of a memory location can also be an instruction. If the binary pattern in location 0 were interpreted as an instruction, what instruction would it represent?

    4.   A binary value can also be interpreted a memory address. Say the value stored in location 5 is a memory address. To which location does it refer? What binary value does that location contain?

4.6.   What are the two components of an instruction? What information do these two components contain?

4.7.   Suppose a 32-bit instruction takes the following format:

OPCODE	SR	DR	IMM

If there are 60 opcodes and 32 registers, what are the maximum and minimum values that the immediate (IMM) can take? Assume IMM is a 2's complement value.

4.8.   The FETCH phase of the instruction cycle does two important things. One is that it loads the instruction to be processed next into the IR. What is the other important thing?

4.9.   State the phases of the instruction cycle and briefly describe what operations occur in each phase.

4.10.   For these instructions, ADD, LD, NOP, write what operations occur in each phase of the instruction cycle.

4.11.   Say it takes 100 cycles to read from or write to memory and only one cycle to read from or write to a register. Calculate the number of cycles it takes for each phase of the instruction cycle for both the IA-32 instruction "ADD [eax], edx." Refer to Example 4.3 and the LC-2 instruction "ADD R6, R2, R6." Assume each phase (if required) takes one cycle, unless a memory access is required.

4.12.   Describe the execution of the JMPR instruction if R3 contains x369C. (Refer to Example 4.5.)

4.13.   If a HALT instruction can clear the RUN latch, thereby stopping the instruction cycle, what instruction is needed to set the RUN latch, thereby reinitiating the instruction cycle?

4.14.   1.   If a machine cycle is 2 nanoseconds (i.e., $2 \cdot 10^{-9}$ seconds), how many machine cycles occur each second?

        2.   If the computer requires on the average eight cycles to process each instruction, and the computer processes instructions one at a time from beginning to end, how many instructions can the computer process in 1 second?

        3.   Preview of future courses: In today's microprocessors, many features are added to increase the number of instructions processed each second. One such feature is the computer's equivalent of an assembly line. Each phase of the instruction cycle is implemented as one or more separate pieces of logic. Each step in the processing of an instruction picks up

where the previous step left off in the previous machine cycle. Using this feature, an instruction can be fetched from memory every machine cycle and handed off at the end of the machine cycle to the decoder, which performs the decoding function during the next machine cycle while the next instruction is being fetched. Ergo, the assembly line. Assuming instructions are located at sequential addresses in memory, and nothing breaks the sequential flow, how many instructions can the microprocessor execute each second if the assembly line is present? (The assembly line is called a pipeline, which you will encounter in your advanced courses. There are many reasons why the assembly line cannot operate at its maximum rate, a topic you will consider at length in some of these courses.)

chapter

5

The LC-2

In Chapter 4, we discussed the basic components of a computer—its memory, its processing unit including the associated temporary storage (usually a set of registers), input and output devices, and the control unit that directs the activity of all the units (including itself!). We also studied the six phases of the instruction cycle—FETCH, DECODE, ADDRESS EVALUATION, OPERAND FETCH, EXECUTE, and STORE RESULT. We are now ready to introduce a "real" computer, the LC-2. To be more nearly exact, we are ready to introduce the instruction set architecture (ISA) of the LC-2. We have already teased you with a few facts about the LC-2 and a few of its instructions. Now we are ready to examine the ISA of the LC-2 in a more comprehensive way.

Recall from Chapter 1 that the ISA is the interface between what the software commands and what the hardware actually carries out. In this chapter and in Chapters 8 and 9, we will point out the important features of the ISA of the LC-2. You will need these features to write programs in the LC-2's own language, that is, in the *machine language* of the LC-2.

A complete description of the ISA of the LC-2 is contained in Appendix A.

5.1   THE ISA: OVERVIEW

The ISA specifies all the information about the computer of which the software has to be aware. In other words, the ISA specifies everything in the computer that is available to a programmer that he/she can use when he/she writes programs in the computer's own machine language. Thus, the ISA also specifies everything in the computer that is available to someone who wishes to translate programs written in a high-level language like C or Pascal or Fortran or COBOL into the machine language of the computer.

The ISA specifies the memory organization, register set, and instruction set, including opcodes, data types, and addressing modes.

5.1.1   Memory Organization

The LC-2 memory has an address space of 2^{16} (i.e., 65,536) locations, and an addressibility of 16 bits. Not all 65,536 addresses are actually used for memory locations, but we will leave that discussion for Chapter 8.

We will see momentarily that it is often useful to think of memory as a sequence of pages, each containing a certain number of memory locations. In the LC-2, the 2^{16} addresses are sliced into 2^7 pages of size 2^9 locations each. Thus, bits [15:9] of an address specify the page number, and bits [8:0] specify the word on the page. The addresses of two locations that are on the same page have identical values in bits [15:9].

Since the normal unit of data that is processed in the LC-2 is 16 bits, we refer to 16 bits as one *word*, and we say the LC-2 is *word-addressable*.

5.1.2   Registers

Since it usually takes far more than one machine cycle to obtain data from memory, the LC-2 provides (like almost all computers) additional temporary storage locations that can be accessed in a single machine cycle.

The most common type of temporary storage locations and the one used in the LC-2 is the general purpose register set. Each register in the set is called a *general purpose register* (GPR). Registers have the same property as memory locations in that they are used to store information that can be later retrieved. The number of bits stored in each register is usually one word.

Registers must be uniquely identifiable. The LC-2 specifies eight GPRs, identified by a three-bit register number. They are referred to as R0, R1, . . . R7. Recall that the instruction to ADD the contents of R0 to R1 and store the result in R2 is specified as

15	14	13	12	11	10	9	8	7	6	5	4	3	2	1	0
0	0	0	1	0	1	0	0	0	0	0	0	0	0	0	1

ADD · · · · · R2 · · · R0 · · · · · R1

where the two *sources* of the ADD instruction are in bits [8:6] and bits [2:0]. The *destination* of the ADD result is specified in bits [11:9].

5.1.3   The Instruction Set

An instruction is made up of two things, its *opcode* (what the instruction is asking the computer to do) and its *operands* (who the computer is expected to do it to). The instruction set of an ISA is defined by its set of opcodes and the *data types* and *addressing modes* that determine the operands.

5.1.4   Opcodes

Some ISAs have a very large set of opcodes, one for each of a large number of tasks that a program may wish to carry out. Other ISAs have a very small set of opcodes. Some ISAs have specific opcodes to help with processing scientific calculations. For example, the Hewlett-Packard *Precision Architecture* has an instruction that performs a multiply, followed by an add $(A \cdot B) + C$ on three source operands. Other ISAs have instructions that process video images obtained from the World Wide Web. The Intel x86 ISA added a number of instructions Intel calls *MMX instructions* because they eXtend the ISA to assist with MultiMedia applications that use the Web. Still other ISAs have specific opcodes to help with handling the tasks of the operating system. For example, the VAX architecture, popular in the 1980s, had an opcode to save all the information pertaining to a program that was running prior to switching to another program. Almost all computers prefer to use a long sequence of instructions to ask the computer to carry out the task of saving all that information. Although that sounds counterintuitive, there is a rationale for it. Unfortunately, the topic will have to wait for a later semester. The decision as to which instructions to include or leave out of an ISA is usually a hotly debated topic in a company, when a new ISA is being specified.

The LC-2 ISA has 16 instructions, each identified by its unique opcode. The opcode is specified by bits [15:12] of the instruction. There are three different types of instructions, which means three different types of opcodes: *operates*, *data movement*, and *control*. Operate instructions process information. Data movement instructions move information between memory and the registers and between registers/memory and input/output devices. Control instructions change the sequence of instructions that will be executed. That is, they enable the execution of an instruction other than the one that is stored in the next sequential location in memory. Figure 5.1 lists the 16 instructions of the LC-2, the bit encoding [15:12] for each opcode, and the format of each instruction. The use of each of the formats will be further explained in Sections 5.2, 5.3, and 5.4 to come.

5.1.5   Data Types

A *data type* is a representation of information such that the ISA has opcodes that operate on that representation. There are many ways to represent the same information in a computer. That should not surprise us. We, in our daily lives, represent the same information in many different ways as well. For example, a child when asked how

	15 14 13 12	11 10 9	8 7 6	5	4 3	2 1 0
ADD+	0001	DR	SR1	0	00	SR2
ADD+	0001	DR	SR1	1	imm5	
AND+	0101	DR	SR1	0	00	SR2
AND+	0101	DR	SR1	1	imm5	
BR	0000	n z p	pgoffset9			
JSR	0100	L 00	pgoffset9			
JSRR	1100	L 00	BaseR	index6		
LD+	0010	DR	pgoffset9			
LDI+	1010	DR	pgoffset9			
LDR+	0110	DR	BaseR	index6		
LEA+	1110	DR	pgoffset9			
NOT+	1001	DR	SR	111111		
RET	1101	000000000000				
RTI*	1000	000000000000				
ST	0011	SR	pgoffset9			
STI	1011	SR	pgoffset9			
STR	0111	SR	BaseR	index6		
TRAP	1111	0000	trapvect8			

Figure 5.1   Formats of the 16 LC-2 instructions. NOTE: + indicates instructions that modify condition codes; * indicates that meaning and use of RTI is beyond the scope of this book.

old he is, might hold up three fingers, signifying he is three years old. If the child is particularly precocious, he might write the decimal digit *3* to indicate his age. Or, if he is a CS or CE major at the university, he might write 0000000000000011, the 16-bit binary representation for 3. If he is a chemistry major, he might write $3.0 \cdot 10^0$. All four represent the same entity: three.

If the ISA has an opcode that operates on information represented by a data type, then we say the ISA **supports** that data type. In Chapter 2, we introduced the only data type supported by the ISA of the LC-2: 2's complement integers.

5.1.6   Addressing Modes

An addressing mode is a mechanism for specifying where the operand is located. Operands can generally be found in one of three places: in memory, in a register, or as a part of the instruction. If the operand is a part of the instruction, we refer to it as a *literal* or as an *immediate* operand. The term *literal* comes from the fact that the bits of the instruction literally form the operand. The term *immediate* comes from the fact that we have the operand immediately, that is, we don't have to look elsewhere for it.

The LC-2 supports five addressing modes: immediate (or literal), register, and three memory addressing modes: *direct*, *indirect*, and *base+offset*. We will see in Section 5.2 that operate instructions use two addressing modes: register and immediate. We will see in Section 5.3 that data movement instructions use all five modes.

5.1.7   Condition Codes

One final item will complete our overview of the ISA of the LC-2: condition codes. Most ISAs (the x86 and SPARC, for example) allow the instruction sequencing to change on the basis of a previously generated result. The LC-2 has three single-bit registers that are set (set to 1) or cleared (set to 0) each time one of the eight general purpose registers is written. The three single-bit registers are called *N*, *Z*, and *P*, corresponding to their meaning: negative, zero, and positive. Each time a GPR is written, the N, Z, and P registers are individually set to 0 or 1, corresponding to whether the result written to the GPR is negative, zero, or positive. That is, if the result is negative, the N register is set, and Z and P are cleared. If the result is zero, Z is set and N and P are cleared. Finally, if the result is positive, P is set and N and Z are cleared.

Each of the three single-bit registers is referred to as a *condition code* because the condition of that bit can be used by one of the control instructions to change the sequence of instructions that get executed. We show how in Section 5.4.

5.2   OPERATE INSTRUCTIONS

Operate instructions process data. Arithmetic operations (like ADD, SUB, MUL, and DIV) and logical operations (like AND, OR, NOT, XOR) are common examples. The LC-2 has three operate instructions: ADD, AND, and NOT.

The **NOT** instruction is the only operate instruction that performs a *unary* operation, that is, the operation requires one source operand. The NOT instruction bitwise complements a 16-bit source operand and stores the result of this operation in a destination. NOT uses the register addressing mode for both its source and destination. Bits [8:6] specify the source register and bits [11:9] specify the destination register. Bits [5:0] must contain all 1s.

If R2 initially contains 0101000011110000, after executing the following instruction:

15	14	13	12	11	10	9	8	7	6	5	4	3	2	1	0
1	0	0	1	0	1	1	0	1	0	1	1	1	1	1	1

NOT   R3   R2

R3 will contain 1010111100001111.

The **ADD** and **AND** instructions both perform *binary* operations; they require two 16-bit source operands. The ADD instruction performs a 2's complement addition of its two source operands. The AND instruction performs a bitwise AND of each pair of bits in its two 16-bit operands. Like the NOT, the ADD and AND use the register addressing mode for one of the source operands and for the destination operand. Bits [8:6] specify the source register and bits [11:9] specify the destination register, that is, where the result will be written.

The second source operand for both ADD and AND can be specified by either register mode or as an immediate operand. Bit [5] determines which is used. If bit [5] is 0, then the second source operand uses a register, and bits [2:0] specify the register. In that case, bits [4:3] are set to 0 to complete the specification of the instruction.

For example, if R4 contains the value 6 and R5 contains the value −18, then after the following instruction is executed

15	14	13	12	11	10	9	8	7	6	5	4	3	2	1	0
0	0	0	1	0	0	1	1	0	0	0	0	0	1	0	1

ADD   R1   R4   R5

R1 will contain the value −12.

If Bit [5] is 1, the second source operand is contained within the instruction. In fact, the second source operand is obtained by sign-extending bits [4:0] to 16 bits before performing the ADD or AND. Note, then, that a 2's complement integer, represented as an immediate operand in an ADD instruction, can only be a value from −16 to +15. Why is that?

Example 5.1 | **W**hat does the instruction shown below do?

15	14	13	12	11	10	9	8	7	6	5	4	3	2	1	0
0	1	0	1	0	1	0	0	1	0	1	0	0	0	0	0

Answer

Register 2 is cleared (i.e., set to all 0s).

What does the following instruction do? | **Example 5.2**

15	14	13	12	11	10	9	8	7	6	5	4	3	2	1	0
0	0	0	1	1	1	0	1	1	0	1	0	0	0	0	1

Answer
Register 6 is incremented (i.e., R6 <— R6 + 1).
    Note that a register can be used as a source and also a destination in the same instruction. This is true for all the instructions in the LC-2.

Subtraction   Recall that the 2's complement of a number can be obtained by complementing | **Example 5.3**
the number and adding 1. Therefore, assuming the values A and B are in R0 and R1, what
sequence of three instructions performs "A minus B," and writes the result into R2?

Answer

15	14	13	12	11	10	9	8	7	6	5	4	3	2	1	0
1	0	0	1	0	0	1	0	0	1	1	1	1	1	1	1

    NOT   R1   R1   R1 ← NOT(B)

0	0	0	1	0	1	0	0	0	1	1	0	0	0	0	1

    ADD   R2   R1   1   R2 ← -B

0	0	0	1	0	1	0	0	0	0	0	0	0	0	1	0

    ADD   R2   R0   R2   R2 ← A +(-B)

Question: What distasteful result is also produced by this sequence? How can it easily be avoided?

5.3   DATA MOVEMENT INSTRUCTIONS

Data movement instructions move information between memory and the registers, and between memory/registers and the input/output devices. We will ignore for now the business of moving information from input devices to registers/memory and from registers/memory to output devices. This will be the major topic of Chapter 8 and an important part of Chapter 9 as well. In this chapter, we will confine ourselves to moving information between memory and the general purposes registers.
    The process of moving information from memory to a register is called a *load*, and the process of moving information data from a register to memory is called a *store*. In both cases, the contents of location of the source operand remains unchanged. In both cases, the contents of the location of the destination operand is overwritten with the source operand, destroying the old value in the process.
    The LC-2 contains seven instructions that move information: LD, LDR, LDI, LEA, ST, STR, and STI.

The format of the load and store instructions is as follows:

15	14	13	12	11	10	9	8	7	6	5	4	3	2	1	0
opcode				DR or SR			OPERAND SPECIFIER								

If the instruction is a load, *DR* refers to the destination register that will contain the value after it is read from memory (at the completion of the instruction cycle). If the instruction is a store, *SR* refers to the register that contains the value that will be written to memory.

Bits [8:0] contain the *operand specifier*. That is, bits [8:0] encode information that is used to obtain the memory operand. There are four ways to interpret the code in bits [8:0]. They are called *addressing modes*. The opcode specifies how to interpret bits [8:0]. That is, the opcode specifies which addressing mode should be used to obtain the operand from bits [8:0] of the instruction.

5.3.1   Immediate Mode

Immediate mode is used only with LEA. The LEA instruction loads the immediate value formed by concatenating bits [15:9] of the address of the instruction (i.e., PC [15:9]) with bits [8:0] of the instruction. Those 16 bits are loaded into the register specified by bits [11:9]. The instruction (Load Effective Address) is useful to initialize a register with an address on the same page as the instruction. Note that LEA is the *only* load instruction that does not access memory to obtain the information it will load into the DR. If instruction

15	14	13	12	11	10	9	8	7	6	5	4	3	2	1	0
1	1	1	0	1	0	1	1	1	1	1	1	1	1	0	1
LEA				R5			x1FD								

is contained in location x4018, after execution R5 will contain x41FD.

5.3.2   Direct Mode

LD and ST specify the *direct mode* addressing mode. Direct mode addressing is so named because the address of the operand is specified in the instruction. Actually, only bits [8:0] of the address are specified in the instruction. Bits [15:9] are implicit. They are identical to bits [15:9] of the address of the instruction. That is, LD and ST can refer only to memory locations on the same page as the instruction using the direct addressing mode.

If instruction

15	14	13	12	11	10	9	8	7	6	5	4	3	2	1	0
0	0	1	0	0	1	0	1	1	0	1	0	1	1	1	1
LD				R2			x1AF								

is located at x3018, it will cause the contents of x31AF to be loaded into R2.

5.3.3 Indirect Mode

LDI and STI specify the *indirect mode* addressing mode. An address is first formed exactly the same way as with LD and ST. However, instead of this *being* the address of the operand to be loaded or stored, it *contains* the address of the operand to be loaded or stored. Hence the name *indirect*. Note that the address of the operand can be anywhere in the computer's memory, not just on the same page as the instruction, as is the case for LD and ST.

If instruction

15	14	13	12	11	10	9	8	7	6	5	4	3	2	1	0
1	0	1	0	0	1	1	1	1	1	0	0	1	1	0	0

LDI   R3   x1CC

is in x4A1B, and the contents of x4BCC is x2110, execution of this instruction will result in the contents of x2110 being loaded into R3.

5.3.4 Base+Offset Mode

LDR and STR specify the *base+offset mode* addressing mode. Base+offset mode is so named because the address of the operand is obtained by adding the zero-extended six-bit offset to the base register. The six-bit offset is **literally** taken from the instruction, bits [5:0]. The base register is identified by bits [8:6] in the instruction.

Since bits [5:0] consist of six bits, and the register specified by bits [8:6] contains 16 bits, the six-bit quantity must first be expanded to 16 bits before the addition can take place. Base+offset addressing uses the six-bit value as a positive integer between 0 and 63. Thus, expanding it to 16 bits involves appending 10 leading 0s. Expanding by appending leading 0s is called *zero-extending*.

If R2 contains the 16-bit quantity x2345, the instruction

15	14	13	12	11	10	9	8	7	6	5	4	3	2	1	0
0	1	1	0	0	0	1	0	0	1	0	1	1	1	0	1

LDR   R1   R2   x1D

loads R1 with the contents of x2362.

Note that the base+offset addressing mode also allows the address of the operand to be anywhere in the computer's memory.

5.3.5 An Example

We conclude our study of addressing modes with a comprehensive example. Assume the contents of memory locations x30F6 through x30FC are as shown in Figure 5.2, and the PC contains x30F6. We will examine the effects of carrying out the instruction cycle seven times. Since the PC points initially to location x30F6, that is, since the contents of the PC is the address x30F6, the first instruction to be executed is the one stored in location x30F6. The opcode 1110 identifies the load effective address

Address	15	14	13	12	11	10	9	8	7	6	5	4	3	2	1	0
30F6	1	1	1	0	0	0	1	0	1	1	1	1	0	1	0	0
30F7	0	0	0	1	0	1	0	0	0	1	1	0	1	1	1	0
30F8	0	0	1	1	0	1	0	0	1	1	1	1	0	1	0	0
30F9	0	1	0	1	0	1	0	0	1	0	1	0	0	0	0	0
30FA	0	0	0	1	0	1	0	0	1	0	1	0	0	1	0	1
30FB	0	1	1	1	0	1	0	0	0	1	0	0	1	1	1	0
30FC	1	0	1	0	0	1	1	0	1	1	1	1	0	1	0	0

Figure 5.2   Addressing mode example

instruction (LEA), which loads the register identified by bits [11:9] with the address formed by the high seven bits (i.e., the page number) of the address of the instruction (in this case 0011000) concatenated with bits [8:0] of the instruction (in this case 011110100). Therefore, at the end of execution of this instruction, R1 contains 0011000011110100 (which is x30F4), and the PC contains x30F7.

The second instruction to be executed is the one stored in location x30F7. The opcode 0001 identifies the ADD instruction, which stores in the register identified by bits [11:9] the sum of the contents of the register identified in bits [8:6] added to the sign-extended immediate in bits [4:0] (since bit [5] is 1). At the end of execution, R2 contains the value x3102, and the PC contains x30F8. R1 still contains x30F4.

The third instruction to be executed is the one stored in location x30F8. The opcode 0011 identifies the ST instruction, which stores the contents of the register identified in bits [11:9] into the memory location whose address is formed using the direct addressing mode. Recall, direct addressing obtains the address by concatenating the high seven bits of the instruction's address (in this case 0011000) and bits [8:0] of the instruction (in this case 011110100). At the end of execution of this instruction, location x30F4 contains the value x3102, and the PC contains x30F9.

At x30F9, we find the opcode 0101, which represents the AND instruction. After execution, R2 contains the value 0, and the PC contains x30FA.

At x30FA, we find the opcode 0001, signifying the ADD instruction. After execution, R2 contains the value 5, and the PC contains x30FB.

At x30FB, we find the opcode 0111, signifying the STR instruction. The STR instruction (like the LDR instruction) uses the base+offset addressing mode. The memory address is obtained by adding the contents of the register specified by bits [8:6] (the BASE register) to the zero-extended offset contained in bits [5:0]. The STR instruction stores in that memory location the contents of the register specified by bits [11:9]. After execution of this instruction, memory location x3102 contains the value 5 (0000000000000101), and the PC contains x30FC.

At x30FC, we find the opcode 1010, signifying the LDI instruction. The LDI instruction (like the STI instruction) uses the indirect addressing mode. The memory address is obtained by first forming an address as is done in the direct addressing mode. That is, the page number (bits [15:9] of the address of the instruction) is concatenated with bits [8:0] of the instruction to form an address. The memory location at that address contains the address of the operand. The LDI instruction loads the value found at that address into the register identified by bits [11:9] of the instruction. After execution, R3 contains the value 5 and the PC contains x30FD.

5.4   CONTROL INSTRUCTIONS

Control instructions change the sequence of the instructions that are executed. Up to now the PC has been incremented in the FETCH phase of the instruction and not changed for the duration of the instruction cycle. Thus, when the next instruction cycle starts, the PC directs the FETCH of the instruction located in the next sequential memory location. We will see momentarily that it is often useful to be able to break that sequence.

The LC-2 has five instructions that enable the sequential flow to be broken: BRx, JMP/JSR, JMPR/JSRR, RET, and TRAP. In this section, we will deal almost exclusively with the most common control instruction, the *conditional branch*, BRx. We will also introduce the TRAP instruction because of its immediate usefulness to getting information into and out of the computer. However, most of the discussion on the TRAP instruction and all of the discussion on JMP/JSR, JMPR/JSRR, and RET we will save for Chapter 9.

5.4.1   Conditional Branches

The format of the conditional branch instruction (opcode = 0000) is shown below:

15	14	13	12	11	10	9	8	7	6	5	4	3	2	1	0
0	0	0	0	N	Z	P				page offset					

Bits [11], [10], and [9] correspond to the three condition codes discussed in Section 5.2. Recall that in the LC-2 **all** instructions that write values into registers set the three condition codes (i.e., the single-bit registers N, Z, P) in accordance with whether the value written is negative, zero, or positive. These instructions are ADD, AND, NOT, LD, LDI, LDR, and LEA.

The condition codes are used by the conditional branch instruction to determine whether to change the instruction flow; that is, whether to depart from the usual sequential execution of instructions that we get as a result of incrementing PC during the FETCH phase of each instruction.

The instruction cycle is as follows: FETCH and DECODE are the same as for all instructions. The PC is incremented during FETCH. The EVALUATE ADDRESS phase is the same as that for LD and ST: The page number (bits [15:9] of the instruction address) is concatenated with bits [8:0] of the instruction to form an address.

During the EXECUTE phase, the processor examines the condition codes whose corresponding bits in the instruction are 1. That is, if bit [11] is 1, condition code N is examined. If bit [10] is 1, condition code Z is examined. If bit [9] is 1, condition code P is examined. If any of bits [11:9] are 0, the corresponding condition codes are not examined. If any of the condition codes that are examined are in state 1, then the PC is loaded with the address obtained in the EVALUATE ADDRESS phase. If none of the condition codes which are examined are in state 1, the PC is left unchanged. In that case, in the next instruction cycle the next sequential instruction will be fetched.

For example, if the previous instruction loaded the value 0 into R5, then the current instruction (located at x4027) shown below

15	14	13	12	11	10	9	8	7	6	5	4	3	2	1	0
0	0	0	0	0	1	0	1	0	0	0	0	0	0	0	1

BR   n z p   x101

will load the PC with x4101, and the next instruction to be executed will be the one at x4101 rather than the one at x4028.

If all three bits [11:9] are 1, then all three condition codes are examined. In this case, since the last result stored into a register had to be either negative, zero, or positive (there are no other choices), one of the three condition codes must be in state 1. Since all three are examined, the PC is loaded with the address obtained in the EVALUATE ADDRESS phase. We call this an *un*conditional branch since the instruction flow is changed unconditionally, that is, independent of the data that is being processed.

For example, if the following instruction,

15	14	13	12	11	10	9	8	7	6	5	4	3	2	1	0
0	0	0	0	1	1	1	0	0	0	0	0	0	0	0	1

BR   n z p   x001

located at x507B is executed, the PC is loaded with x5001.

What happens if all three bits [11:9] in the BR instruction are 0?

5.4.2   An Example

Suppose we know that the 12 locations x3100 to x310B contain integers, and we wish to compute the sum of these 12 integers.

A flowchart for an algorithm to solve the problem is shown in Figure 5.3.

First, as in all algorithms, we must *initialize our variables*. That is, we must set up the initial values of the variables that the computer will use in executing the program that solves the problem. There are three such variables: the address of the next integer to be added (assigned to R1), the running sum (assigned to R4), and the number of integers left to be added (assigned to R2). The three variables are initialized as follows: The address of the first integer to be added is put in R1. R4, which will keep track of the running sum, is initialized to 0. R2, which will keep track of the number of integers left to be added, is intialized to 12. Then the process of adding begins.

The program repeats the process of loading into R4 one of the 12 integers, and adding it to R3. Each time we perform the ADD, we increment R1 so it will point to (i.e., contain the address of) the next number to be added and decrement R2 so

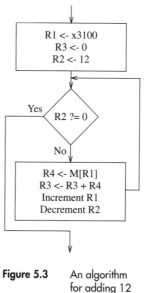

Figure 5.3   An algorithm for adding 12 integers

we will know how many additions are still needed. When R2 becomes zero, the Z condition code is set, and therefore we can detect that we are done.

The 10-instruction program shown in Figure 5.4 accomplishes the task.

The details of the program execution are as follows: The program starts with PC = x3000. The first instruction (at location x3000) loads R1 with the address x3100 (page number is 0011000 and bits [8:0] is 100000000).

The instruction at x3001 clears R3. R3 will keep track of the running sum, so it must start off with the value zero. As we said above, this is called *initializing* the SUM to zero.

The instructions at x3002 and x3003 set the value of R2 to 12, the number of integers to be added. R2 will keep track of how many numbers have already been added. This will be done (by the instruction contained in x3008 below) by decrementing R2 after each addition takes place.

The instruction at x3004 is a conditional branch instruction. Note that bit [10] is a 1. That means that the Z condition code will be examined. If it is set, we know R2 must have just been decremented to zero. That means there are no more numbers to be added and we are done. If it is clear, we know we still have work to do and we continue.

The instruction at x3005 loads the contents of x3100 (i.e., the first integer) into R4, and the instruction at x3006 adds it to R3.

The instructions at x3007 and x3008 perform the necessary bookkeeping. The instruction at x3007 increments R1, so R1 will point to the next location in memory containing an integer to be added (in this case, x3101). The instruction at x3008

Address	15	14	13	12	11	10	9	8	7	6	5	4	3	2	1	0	
3000	1	1	1	0	0	0	1	1	0	0	0	0	0	0	0	0	R1<- 3100
3001	0	1	0	1	0	1	1	0	1	1	1	0	0	0	0	0	R3 <- 0
3002	0	1	0	1	0	1	0	0	1	0	1	0	0	0	0	0	R2 <- 0
3003	0	0	0	1	0	1	0	0	1	0	1	0	1	1	0	0	R2 <- 12
3004	0	0	0	0	0	1	0	0	0	0	0	0	1	0	1	0	BRz x300A
3005	0	1	1	0	1	0	0	0	0	1	0	0	0	0	0	0	R4 <- M[R1]
3006	0	0	0	1	0	1	1	0	1	1	0	0	0	1	0	0	R3 <- R3+R4
3007	0	0	0	1	0	0	1	0	0	1	1	0	0	0	0	1	R1 <- R1+1
3008	0	0	0	1	0	1	0	0	1	0	1	1	1	1	1	1	R2 <- R2-1
3009	0	0	0	0	1	1	1	0	0	0	0	0	0	1	0	0	BRnzp x3004

Figure 5.4   A program that implements the algorithm of Figure 5.3

decrements R2, which is keeping track of the number of integers still to be added, as we have already explained, and sets the N, Z, and P condition codes.

The instruction at x3009 is an unconditional branch, since bits [11:9] are all 1. It loads the PC with x3004. It also does not affect the condition codes, so the next instruction to be executed (the conditional branch at x3004) will be based on the instruction executed at x3008.

This is worth saying again. The conditional branch instruction at x3004 follows the instruction at x3009, which does not affect condition codes, which in turn follows the instruction at x3008. Thus, the conditional branch instruction at x3004 will be based on the condition codes set by the instruction at x3008. The instruction at x3008 sets the condition codes depending on the value produced by decrementing R2. As long as there are still integers to be added, the ADD instruction at x3008 will produce a value greater than zero, and therefore clear the Z condition code. The conditional branch instruction at x3004 examines the Z condition code. As long as Z is clear, the PC will not be affected, and the next instruction cycle will start with an instruction fetch from x3005.

The conditional branch instruction causes the execution sequence to follow: x3000, x3001, x3002, x3003, x3004, x3005, x3006, x3007, x3008, x3009, x3004, x3005, x3006, x3007, x3008, x3009, x3004, x3005, and so on until the value in R2 becomes 0. At that point, the conditional branch instruction at x3004 leaves the PC at PC+1, and the program continues at x300A with its next activity.

5.4.3   Two Methods for Loop Control

We use the term *loop* to describe a sequence of instructions that get executed again and again under some controlling mechanism. The example of adding 12 integers contains a loop. Each time the *body* of the loop executes, one more integer is added to the running total, and the counter is decremented so we can detect whether there are any more integers left to add. Each time the loop body executes is called one *iteration* of the loop.

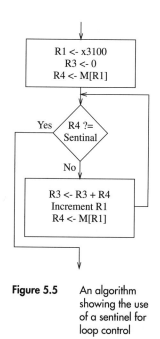

Figure 5.5   An algorithm
showing the use
of a sentinel for
loop control

There are two common methods for controlling the number of iterations of a loop. One method we just examined: the use of a counter. If we know we wish to execute a loop *n* times, we simply set a counter to *n*, then after each execution of the loop, we decrement the counter and check to see if it is zero. If it is not zero, we set the PC to the start of the loop and continue with another iteration.

A second method for controlling the number of executions of a loop is to use a *sentinel*. This method is particularly effective if we do not know ahead of time how many iterations we will want to perform. Each iteration is usually based on processing a value. We append to our sequence of values to be processed a value that we know ahead of time can never occur (i.e., the sentinel). For example, if we are adding a sequence of numbers, a sentinel could be a # or a *, that is, something that is not a number. Our loop test is simply a test for the occurrence of the sentinel. When we find it, we know we are done.

5.4.4   Example: Adding a Column of Numbers Using a Sentinel

Suppose in our example of Section 5.4.2, we know the values stored in x3100 to x310B are all positive. Then we could use any negative number as a sentinel. Let's say the sentinel stored at memory address x310C is −1. The resulting flowchart for the program is shown in Figure 5.5 and the resulting program is shown in Figure 5.6.

As before, the instruction at x3000 loads R1 with the address of the first value to be added, and x3101 initializes R3 (which keeps track of the sum) to zero.

Address	15	14	13	12	11	10	9	8	7	6	5	4	3	2	1	0	
x3000	1	1	1	0	0	0	1	1	0	0	0	0	0	0	0	0	R1<- x3100
x3001	0	1	0	1	0	1	1	0	1	1	1	0	0	0	0	0	R3 <- 0
x3002	0	1	1	0	1	0	0	0	0	1	0	0	0	0	0	0	R4 <- M[R1]
x3003	0	0	0	0	1	0	0	0	0	0	0	0	1	0	0	0	BRn x3008
x3004	0	0	0	1	0	1	1	0	1	1	0	0	0	1	0	0	R3 <- R3+R4
x3005	0	0	0	1	0	0	1	0	0	1	1	0	0	0	0	1	R1 <- R1+1
x3006	0	1	1	0	1	0	0	0	0	1	0	0	0	0	0	0	R4 <- M[R1]
x3007	0	0	0	0	1	1	1	0	0	0	0	0	0	0	1	1	BRnzp x3003

Figure 5.6   A program that implements the algorithm of Figure 5.5

At x3002, we load the contents of the next memory location into R4. If the sentinel is loaded, the N condition code is set.

The conditional branch at x3003 examines the N condition code, and if it is set, sets PC to x3008 and onto the next task to be done. If the N condition code is clear, R4 must contain a valid number to be added. In this case, the number is added to R3 (x3004), R1 is incremented to point to the next memory location (x3005), R4 is loaded with the contents of the next memory location (x3006), and the PC is loaded with x3003 to begin the next iteration (x3007).

5.4.5   The TRAP Instruction

Finally, because it will be useful long before Chapter 9 to get data in and out of the computer, we introduce the TRAP instruction now. The TRAP instruction changes the PC to a memory address which is part of the operating system in order for the operating system to perform some task in behalf of the program that is executing. In the language of operating system jargon, we say the TRAP instruction invokes an operating system SERVICE CALL. Bits [7:0] of the TRAP instruction, called the *trapvector*, identifies the service call that the program wishes the operating system to perform. Table A.3 contains the trapvectors for all the service calls that we will use with the LC-2 in this book.

15	14	13	12	11	10	9	8	7	6	5	4	3	2	1	0
1	1	1	1	0	0	0	0				trapvector				

Once the operating system is finished performing the service call, the program counter is set to the address of the instruction following the TRAP instruction and the program continues. In this way, a program can, during its execution, request services from the operating system and continue processing after each such service is performed. The services we will require for now are

```
* Input a character from keyboard (trapvector = x23).
* Output a character to monitor (trapvector = x21).
* Halt the program (trapvector = x25).
```

Exactly how the LC-2 carries out that interaction between operating system and executing programs is an important topic for Chapter 9.

5.5   ANOTHER EXAMPLE: COUNTING OCCURRENCES OF A CHARACTER

We will finish our introduction to the ISA of the LC-2 with another example program. We would like to be able to input a character from the keyboard and then count the number of occurrences of that character in a file. Finally, we would like to display that count on the monitor. We will simplify the problem by assuming that the number of occurrences of any character that we would be interested in is small. That is, there will be at most nine occurrences. This simplification allows us to not have to worry about complex conversion routines between the binary count and the ASCII display on the monitor—a subject we will get into in Chapter 10, but not today.

Figure 5.7 is a flow chart of the algorithm that solves this problem. Note that each step is expressed both in English and also (in parentheses) in terms of an LC-2 implementation.

The first step is (as always) to initialize all the variables. This means providing starting values (called *initial values*) for R0, R1, R2, and R3, the four registers the computer will use to execute program that will solve the problem. R2 will keep track of the number of occurrences; in Figure 5.7, it is referred to as *count*. It is initialized to zero. R3 will point to the next character in the file that is being examined. We refer to it as *pointer* since it contains the **address** of the location where the next character of the file that we wish to examine resides. The pointer is initialized with the address of the **first** character in the file. R0 will hold the character that is being counted; we will input that character from the keyboard and put it in R0. R1 will hold, in turn, each character that we get from the file being examined.

The next step is to count the number of occurrences of the input character. This is done by processing, in turn, each character in the file being examined, until the file is exhausted. Processing each character requires one iteration of a loop. Recall from Section 5.4 that there are two common methods for keeping track of iterations of a loop. We will use the sentinel method, using the ASCII code for EOT (End of Text) (00000100) as the sentinel.

In each iteration of the loop, the contents of R1 are first compared to the ASCII code for EOT. If yes, the loop is exited, and the program moves on to the final step, displaying on the screen the number of occurrences. If no, there is work to do. R1 (the current character under examination) is compared to R0 (the character input from the keyboard). If they match, R2 is incremented. In either case, we get the next character, that is, R3 is incremented, the next character is loaded into R1, and the program returns to the test that checks for the sentinel at the end of the file.

When the end of the file is reached, all the characters have been examined, and the count is contained as a binary number in R2. In order to display it on the monitor, it is necessary to first convert it to an ASCII code. Since we have assumed the count

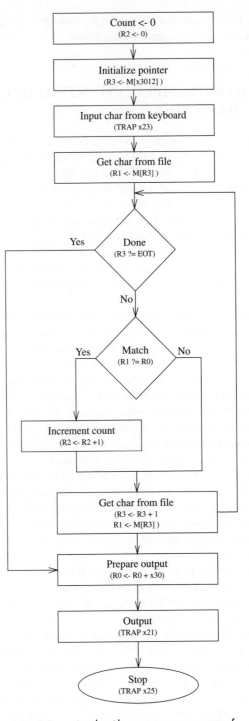

Figure 5.7   An algorithm to count occurrences of a character

is less than 10, that is, simply putting a leading 0011 in front of the four-bit binary representation of the count. Figure E.2 contains a table of ASCII codes. Note the relationship between the binary value of each decimal digit between 0 and 9 and its corresponding ASCII code. Finally, the count is output to the monitor, and the program terminates.

Figure 5.8 is a machine language program that implements the flow chart of Figure 5.7.

First the initialization steps. The instruction at x3000 clears R2 by ANDing it with x0000; the instruction at x3001 loads the value stored in x3012 into R3. Initially, x3012 contains the address of the first character in the file that is to be examined for occurrences of our character. x3002 contains the TRAP instruction, which requests the operating system to perform a service call on behalf of this program. The function requested, as identified by the eight-bit trapvector 00100011 (or, x23), is to input a character from the keyboard and load it into R0. Table A.3 lists trapvectors for all operating system service calls that can be performed on behalf of a user program. Note (from Table A.3) that x23 directs the operating system to perform the service call that reads the next character struck and loads it into R0. The instruction at x3003 loads the character pointed to by R3 into R1.

Address	15	14	13	12	11	10	9	8	7	6	5	4	3	2	1	0	
x3000	0	1	0	1	0	1	0	0	1	0	1	0	0	0	0	0	R2 <- 0
x3001	0	0	1	0	0	1	1	0	0	0	0	1	0	0	1	0	R3 <- M[x3012]
x3002	1	1	1	1	0	0	0	0	0	0	1	0	0	0	1	1	TRAP x23
x3003	0	1	1	0	0	0	1	0	1	1	0	0	0	0	0	0	R1 <- M[R3]
x3004	0	0	0	1	1	0	0	0	0	1	1	1	1	1	0	0	R4 <- R1-4
x3005	0	0	0	0	0	1	0	0	0	0	0	1	1	1	1	0	BRz x300E
x3006	1	0	0	1	0	0	1	0	0	1	1	1	1	1	1	1	R1 <- NOT R1
x3007	0	0	0	1	0	0	1	0	0	1	1	0	0	0	0	1	R1 <- R1 + 1
x3008	0	0	0	1	0	0	1	0	0	1	0	0	0	0	0	0	R1 <- R1 + R0
x3009	0	0	0	0	1	0	1	0	0	0	0	0	1	0	1	1	BRnp x300B
x300A	0	0	0	1	0	1	0	0	1	0	1	0	0	0	0	1	R2 <- R2 + 1
x300B	0	0	0	1	0	1	1	0	1	1	1	0	0	0	0	1	R3 <- R3 + 1
x300C	0	1	1	0	0	0	1	0	1	1	0	0	0	0	0	0	R1 <- M[R3]
x300D	0	0	0	0	1	1	1	0	0	0	0	0	0	1	0	0	BRnzp x3004
x300E	0	0	1	0	0	0	0	0	0	0	0	1	0	0	1	1	R0 <- M[x3013]
x300F	0	0	0	1	0	0	0	0	0	0	0	0	0	0	1	0	R0 <- R0 + R2
x3010	1	1	1	1	0	0	0	0	0	0	1	0	0	0	0	1	TRAP x21
x3011	1	1	1	1	0	0	0	0	0	0	1	0	0	1	0	1	TRAP x25
x3012	Starting Address of file																
x3013	0	0	0	0	0	0	0	0	0	0	1	1	0	0	0	0	ASCII TEMPLATE

Figure 5.8   A machine language program that implements the algorithm of Figure 5.7

Then the process of examining characters begins. We start (x3004) by subtracting 4 (the ASCII code for EOT) from R1, and storing it in R4. If the result is zero, the end of the file has been reached, and it is time to output the count. The instruction at x3005 conditionally branches to x300E, where the process of outputting the count begins.

If R4 is not equal to zero, the character in R1 is legitimate and must be examined. The sequence of instructions at locations x3006, x3007, and x3008 determine if the contents of R1 and R0 are identical. The sequence of instructions perform the following operation:

$$R0 + (NOT (R1) + 1)$$

This produces all zeroes only if the bit patterns of R1 and R0 are identical. If the bit patterns are not identical the conditional branch at x3009 branches to x300B, that is, it skips the instruction x300A, which increments the counter, R2.

The instruction at x300B increments R3, so it will point to the next character in the file being examined, the instruction at x300C loads that character into R1, and the instruction at x300D unconditionally takes us back to x3004 to start processing that character.

When the sentinel (EOT) is finally detected, the process of outputting the count begins (at x300E). The instruction at x300E loads 0011000 into R0, and the instruction at x300F adds the count to R0. This converts the binary representation of the count (in R2) to the ASCII representation of the count (in R0). The instruction at x3010 invokes a TRAP to the operating system to output the contents of R0 on the monitor. When that is done and the program resumes execution, the instruction at x3011 invokes a TRAP instruction to terminate the program.

5.6   THE DATA PATH REVISITED

Before we leave Chapter 5, let us revisit the data path diagram that we first encountered in Chapter 3 (Figure 3.22). Now we are ready to examine all the structures that are needed to implement the LC-2 ISA. We reproduce this diagram as Figure 5.9. Note at the outset that there are two kinds of arrows in the data path, those with arrowheads filled in, and those with arrowheads not filled in. Filled-in arrowheads designate information that is processed. Unfilled-in arrowheads designate control signals. Control signals emanate from the block labeled "Control Logic." The connections from Control Logic to most control signals have been left off Figure 5.9 to reduce unnecessary clutter in the diagram.

5.6.1   Basic Components of the Data Path

The Global Bus   You undoubtedly first notice the heavy black structure with arrowheads at both ends. This represents the data path's global bus. The LC-2 global bus consists of 16 wires and associated electronics. It allows one structure to transfer up to 16 bits of information to another structure by making the necessary electronic connections on the bus. Exactly one value can be transferred on the bus at one time. Note

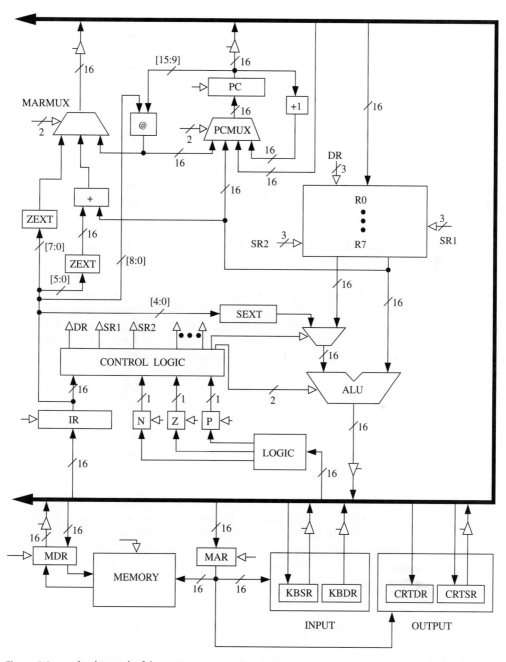

Figure 5.9   The data path of the LC-2

that each structure that supplies values to the bus has a triangle just behind its input arrow to the bus. This triangle (called a *tri-state device*) allows the computer's control logic to enable exactly one supplier to provide information to the bus at any one time.

The structure wishing to obtain the value being supplied can do so by asserting its WE (write enable) signal (recall our discussion of gated latches in Section 3.4.2). Not all computers have a single global bus. The pros and cons of a single global bus is yet another one of those topics that will have to wait for a later course.

Memory   One of the most important parts of any computer is the memory that contains both instructions and data. Memory is accessed by loading the memory address register (MAR) with the address of the location to be accessed. If a load is being performed, control signals then read the memory, and the result of that read is delivered by the memory to the memory data register (MDR). On the other hand, if a store is being performed, the data to be stored is first loaded into the MDR. Then the control signals specify that WE is asserted in order to store into that memory location (as you saw in Figure 3.20).

The ALU and the Register File   The ALU is the processing element. It has two inputs, source 1 from a register and source 2 from either a register or the sign-extended immediate value provided by the instruction. The registers (R0 through R7) can provide two values, source 1, which is controlled by the three-bit register number SR1, and source 2, which is controlled by the three-bit register number SR2. SR1 and SR2 are fields in the LC-2 operate instruction. The selection of a second register operand or a sign-extended immediate operand is determined by bit [5] of the LC-2 instruction. Note the MUX that provides source 2 to the ALU. The select line of that MUX, coming from the control logic, is bit [5] of the LC-2 operate instruction.

The result of an ALU operation is a result that is stored in one of the registers, and the three single-bit condition codes. Note that the ALU can supply 16 bits to the bus, and that value can then be written into the the register specified by the three-bit register number DR. Also, note that the 16 bits supplied to the bus are also input to logic that determines whether that 16-bit quantity is negative, zero, or positive, and sets the three registers N, Z, and P accordingly.

The PC and the PCMUX   The PC supplies via the global bus to the MAR the address of the instruction to be fetched at the start of the instruction cycle. The PC, in turn, is supplied via the four-to-one PCMUX, depending on the instruction being executed. During the FETCH phase of the instruction cycle, the PC is incremented and written into the PC. That is shown as the right-most input to the PCMUX.

If the current instruction is a control instruction, then the relevant source of the PCMUX depends on which control instruction is currently being processed. If the current instruction is a conditional branch and the branch is taken, then the PC is loaded with PC [15:9] (the page number) concatenated with INST [8:0] (the pg9offset). That is shown as the left-most input to PCMUX. The other two inputs to PCMUX are used to obtain the new PC when the TRAP instruction, a RET instruction, or a JSRR instruction is being executed. They will be covered in Chapter 9.

The MARMUX   As you know, memory is accessed by supplying the address to the MAR. The MARMUX controls which of three sources will supply the MAR with the appropriate address during the execution of a load, a store, or a TRAP instruction. The right-most input to the MARMUX is obtained by concatenating PC [15:9] with INST [8:0] in the same way the address of a conditional branch instruction is generated. This address is used in the case of LD and ST instructions to obtain source and destination addresses of the data to be loaded and stored, respectively. It is also used with LDI and STI instructions to obtain the address of the source or destination address. The left-most input to MARMUX provides the zero-extended trapvector, which is needed to invoke service calls, as will be discussed in further detail in Chapter 9. The middle input to MARMUX provides the zero-extended bits [5:0] of the instruction (index6) to the base register to obtain the address of source data for the LDR instruction and the address of destination data for the STR instruction.

5.6.2   The Instruction Cycle

We complete our tour of the LC-2 data path by following the flow through an instruction cycle. Suppose the contents of the PC is x3456 and the contents of location x3456 is 0110011010000100. And suppose the LC-2 has just completed processing the instruction at x3455, which happened to be an ADD instruction.

FETCH   As you know, the instruction cycle starts with the FETCH phase. That is, the instruction is obtained by accessing memory with the address contained in the PC. In the first cycle, the contents of the PC is loaded via the global bus into the MAR, and the PC is incremented and loaded into the PC. At the end of this cycle, the PC contains x3457. In the next cycle (if memory can provide information in one cycle), the memory is read, and the instruction 0110011010000100 is loaded into the MDR. In the next cycle, the contents of the MDR is loaded into the instruction register (IR), completing the FETCH phase.

DECODE   In the next cycle, the contents of the IR are decoded, resulting in the control logic providing the correct control signals (unfilled arrowheads) to control the processing of the rest of this instruction. The opcode is 0110, identifying the LDR instruction. This means that the base+offset addressing mode is to be used to determine the address of data to be loaded into the destination register R3.

EVALUATE ADDRESS   In the next cycle, the contents of R2 (the base register) and the zero-extended bits [5:0] of the IR are added and supplied via the MARMUX to the MAR. The SR1 field specifies 010, the register to be read to obtain the base address.

OPERAND FETCH   In the next cycle (or more than one, if memory access takes more than one cycle), the data at that address is loaded into the MDR.

EXECUTE   The LDR instruction does not require an EXECUTE phase, so this phase takes zero cycles.

STORE RESULT   In the last cycle, the contents of the MDR are loaded into R3. The DR control field specifies 011, the register to be loaded.

PROBLEMS

5.1.   Given instructions ADD, JMP, LEA, and NOP, identify whether the instructions are operate instructions, data movement instructions, or control instructions. For each instruction, list the addressing modes that can be used with the instruction.

5.2.   1.   State the page number for each of the following LC-2 memory addresses:
(*a*) x12FE
(*b*) xA931
(*c*) x3110
(*d*) x3210
(*e*) x3310
(*f*) x3610

2.   State the page offset for each of the above LC-2 memory addresses.

5.3.   Say we have a memory consisting of 256 locations, and each location contains 16 bits.

1.   How many bits are required for the address?

2.   If we divide this memory into eight pages, how many bits are required to represent the page number?

3.   How many bits specify the location of a word on the page?

4.   What is the address of the first word on page number 2 (remember page numbering starts with 0)?

5.   What is the address of the last word on the same page?

5.4.   1.   What is an addressing mode?

2.   Name three places an instruction's operands might be located.

3.   List the five addressing modes of the LC-2, and for each one state where the operand is located (from part 2).

4.   What addressing mode is used by the ADD instruction shown in Section 5.1.2?

5.5.   Recall the machine busy example from Section 2.6.5. We can use the LC-2 instruction 0101 011 010 1 00001 (AND R3, R2, #1) to determine whether machine 0 is busy or not. If the result of this instruction is 0, then machine 0 is busy.

1. Now write an instruction that determines whether machine 2 is busy.

2. Write an instruction that determines whether machines 2 or 3 are busy.

3. Write an LC-2 instruction that indicates all the machines are no longer busy.

4. Can you write an instruction that determines whether machine 13 is busy? Is there a problem here?

5.6. What is the largest positive number we can represent literally (i.e., as an IMMEDIATE value) within an LC-2 ADD instruction?

5.7. At location x3E00, we would like to put an instruction that does nothing. Many ISAs actually have an opcode devoted to doing nothing. It is usually called NOP, for NO OPERATION. The instruction is fetched, decoded, and executed. The execution phase is to do nothing! Which of the following three instructions could be used for NOP and have the program still work correctly?

1. 0001 001 001 1 00000

2. 0000 111 000000001

3. 0000 000 000000000

What does the ADD instruction do that the others do not do?

5.8. After executing the following LC-2 instruction: ADD R2, R0, R1, we notice that R0[15] equals R1[15], but is different from R2[15]. We are told that R0 and R1 contain UNSIGNED integers (that is, nonnegative integers between 0 and 65,535). Under what conditions can we trust the result in R2?

5.9. 1. How might one use a single LC-2 instruction to move the value in R2 into R3?

2. The LC-2 has no subtract instruction. How could one perform the following operation using only three LC-2 instructions:

$$R1 \leftarrow R2 - R3$$

3. Using only one instruction and without changing the contents of any register, how might one set the condition codes based on the value that resides in R1?

4. Is there a sequence of LC-2 instructions that will cause the condition codes at the end of the sequence to be N = 1, Z = 1, and P = 0? Explain.

5. Write an LC-2 instruction that clears the contents of R2.

5.10. State the contents of R1, R2, R3, and R4 after the program starting at location x3100 halts.

Address	Data
0011 0001 0000 0000	1110 001 100100011
0011 0001 0000 0001	0010 010 100100011
0011 0001 0000 0010	0110 011 010 000001
0011 0001 0000 0011	1010 100 100100011
0011 0001 0000 0100	1111 0000 0010 0101
:	:
:	:
0011 0001 0010 0011	0100 0101 0110 0111
:	:
:	:
0100 0101 0110 0111	1010 1011 1100 1101
0100 0101 0110 0111	1111 1110 1101 0011

5.11. Which addressing mode makes the most sense to use under the following conditions. (There may be more than one correct answer to each of these; therefore justify your answers with some explanation.)

1. If you want to load one value from the current page.

2. If you want to load one value from a page other than the current page.

3. If you want to load an array of sequential addresses on the current page.

5.12. How many times does the LC-2 make a read or write request to memory during the processing of the LD instruction? How many times during the processing of the LDI instruction? How many times during the processing of the LEA instruction?

5.13. The LC-2 program counter (PC) contains 16 bits, of which the least significant nine bits [8:0] represent the page offset. If we change the ISA so that bits [6:0] represent the page offset, how many pages will memory comprise?

5.14. If we made the LC-2 memory pages shorter by 384 locations, how many bits would be required for the page offset in the LD instruction?

5.15. What is the maximum number of TRAP service routines that the LC-2 ISA can support? Explain.

5.16. Suppose the following LC-2 program is loaded into memory starting at location x30FF:

```
30FF    1110001100000001
3100    0110010001000010
3101    1111000000100101
3102    0001010001000001
3103    0001010010000010
```

If the program is executed, what is the value in register 2 (R2) at the end of execution?

5.17. Write an LC-2 program that compares two numbers in R2 and R3 and puts the larger number in R1. If the numbers are equal, then R1 is set equal to zero.

5.18. Your task is to consider the successor to the LC-2. We will add 16 additional instructions to the ISA and expand the register set from 8 to 16. We would like our machine to have an addressability of 1 byte and a total memory size of 64K bytes. We will keep the size of an instruction at 16 bits. Also, we will encode all new instructions with the same five fields as the original 16 instructions, although it may be necessary to change the size of some of those fields.

1. How many bits do we need in the PC to be able to address all of memory?

2. Assuming we still support page-offset addressing, what is the size in bytes of a page? How many memory locations are on a page? How many pages are there?

3. What is the largest immediate value that can be represented in an arithmetic instruction?

4. If we want 128 different operating system routines to be able to be accessed with a trap instruction and we form the address of each of these routines by shifting the trap vector to the left by 5 bits, what is the minimum amount of memory required by the trap service routines?

5. If, in the new version of the LC-2, we reduced the number of registers from eight to four and did not change any of the opcodes, what is the largest immediate value we could represent in an ADD instruction on this new machine?

5.19. The LC-2 instruction **LDR DR, BaseR, Offset** can be broken down into the following constituent operations (called *micro-instructions*):

```
MAR ← BaseR + Offset ; set up the memory address
MDR ← Memory[MAR] ; read mem at BaseR + offset
DR  ← MDR ; load DR
```

Suppose that the architect of the LC-2 wanted to include an instruction **MOVE DR, SR** that would copy the memory location with address given by **SR** and store it into the memory location whose address is in **DR**.

1. Using regular LC-2 instructions, write code to carry out a **MOVE R0, R1** instruction. If necessary, use R2 for temporary storage.

2. List the constituent micro-instructions required to carry out the **MOVE** instruction.

5.20. 1. The LC-2 **JMP/JSR** instruction does not execute exactly the same if L = 0 and if L = 1. Why is the case L = 0 irrelevant to the LC-2 ISA?

2. Why is this not also true for **JMPR/JSRR** instruction pair?

5.21. Before the seven instructions are executed in the example of Section 3.5.5,
R2 contains the value xAAAA. How many different values are contained in
R2 during the execution of the seven instructions? What are they?

5.22. The following table shows a part of the LC-2's memory:

Address	Data
0011 0001 0000 0000	1001 001 001 111111
0011 0001 0000 0001	0001 010 000 000 001
0011 0001 0000 0010	1001 010 010 111111
0011 0001 0000 0011	0000 010 100000000

State what is known about R1 and R0 if the conditional branch redirects
control to location x3100.

chapter

6

Programming

We are now ready to start developing programs to solve problems with the computer. In this chapter we attempt to do two things: first, we develop a methodology for constructing programs; and second, we develop a methodology for fixing those programs under the likely condition that we did not get it right the first time. There is a long tradition that the errors present in programs are referred to as *bugs*, and the process of removing those errors *debugging*. The opportunities for introducing bugs into a complicated program are so great that it usually takes more time to get the program to work (debugging) than it does to create it in the first place.

6.1 PROBLEM SOLVING

6.1.1 Systematic Decomposition

Recall in Chapter 1 that in order for electrons to solve a problem, we need to go through several levels of transformation to get from a natural language description of the problem (in our case English, although some of you might prefer Italian, Mandarin, Hindi, or something else) to something electrons can deal with. Once we have a natural language description of the problem, the next step is to transform the problem statement into an algorithm. That is, the next step is to transform the problem statement into a step-by-step procedure that has the properties of finiteness (it terminates), definiteness (each step is precisely stated), and effective computability (each step can be carried out).

In the late 1960s, the concept of *structured programming* emerged as a way to improve the ability of average programmers to take a complex description of a problem and systematically decompose it into sufficiently smaller, manageable units that they could ultimately write a program that executed correctly. The mechanism has alternatively been called *systematic decomposition* because the larger tasks are systematically broken down into smaller ones.

We will find the systematic decomposition model a useful technique for designing computer programs to carry out complex tasks.

6.1.2   The Three Constructs: Sequential, Conditional, Iterative

Systematic decomposition is the process of taking a task, that is, a unit of work (see Figure 6.1a), and breaking it down into smaller units of work such that the collection of smaller units carry out the same task as the one larger unit. The idea is that if one starts with a large complex task and applies this process step by step, one will end up with very small units of work, and consequently, one will be able to easily write a program to carry out each of these small units of work. The process is also referred to as *stepwise refinement*, since each step refines one of the tasks that is still too complex into a collection of simpler subtasks.

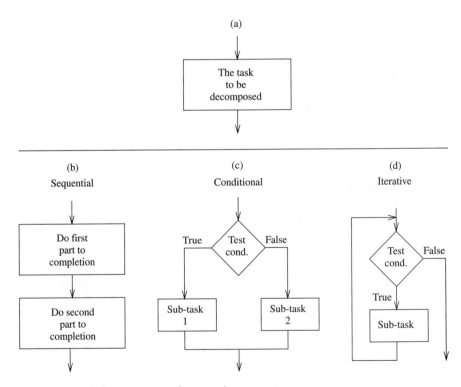

Figure 6.1   The basic constructs of structured programming

There are basically three constructs for doing this: *sequential*, *conditional*, and *iterative*. The idea is to replace the large unit of work with a construct that correctly decomposes it.

The **sequential** construct (Figure 6.1b) is the one to use if the designated task can be broken down into two subtasks, one following the other. That is, the computer is to carry out the first subtask completely, *then* go on and carry out the second subtask completely—never going back to the first subtask after starting the second subtask.

The **conditional** construct (Figure 6.1c) is the one to use if the task consists of doing one of two subtasks but not both, depending on some condition. If the condition is true, the computer is to carry out one subtask. If the condition is not true, the computer is to carry out a different subtask. Either subtask may be vacuous, that is, it may "do nothing." Regardless, after the correct subtask is completed, the program moves onward. The program never goes back and retests the condition.

The **iterative** construct (Figure 6.1d) is the one to use if the task consists of doing a subtask a number of times, but only as long as some condition is true. If the condition is true, do the subtask. After the subtask is finished, go back and test the condition again. As long as the result of the condition tested is true, the program continues to carry out the same subtask. The first time the test is not true, the program proceeds onward.

Note in Figure 6.1 that whatever the task of Figure 6.1a, work starts with the arrow into the top of the "box" representing the task and finishes with the arrow out of the bottom of the box. There is no mention of what goes on *inside* the box. In each of the three possible decompositions of Figure 6.1a (i.e., Figures 6.1b, 1c, and 1d), there is exactly *one entrance into the construct* and *one exit out of the construct*. Thus, it is easy to replace any task of the form of Figure 6.1a with whichever of its three decompositions apply. We will see how in the following example.

6.1.3   LC-2 Control Instructions to Implement the Three Constructs

Before we move on to an example, we illustrate in Figure 6.2 the use of LC-2 control instructions to direct the program counter to carry out each of the three decomposition constructs. That is, Figures 6.2b, 6.2c, and 6.2d correspond respectively to the three constructs shown in Figures 6.1b, 6.1c, and 6.1d.

We use the letters A, B, C, and D to represent addresses in memory containing LC-2 instructions. A, for example, is used in all three cases to represent the address of the first LC-2 instruction to be executed.

Figure 6.2b illustrates the control flow of the sequential decomposition. Note that no control instructions are needed since the PC is incremented from Address B1 to Address B1+1. The program continues to execute instructions through address D1. It does not return to the first subtask.

Figure 6.2c illustrates the control flow of the conditional decomposition. First, a condition is generated, resulting in the setting of one of the condition codes. This condition is tested by the conditional branch instruction at Address B2. If the condition is true, the PC is set to Address C2, and subtask 1 is executed. (*Note*: x corresponds

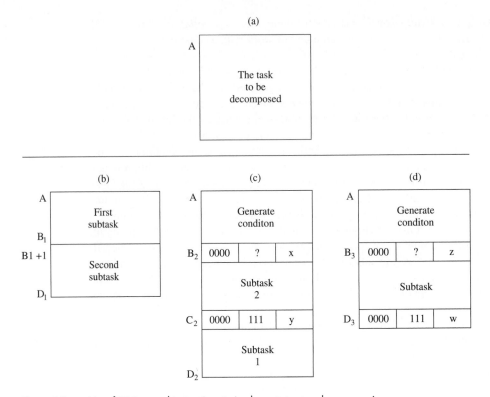

Figure 6.2   Use of LC-2 control instructions to implement structured programming

to bits [8:0] of the address represented by C2.) If the condition is false, the PC (which had been incremented during the FETCH phase of the branch instruction) fetches the instruction at Address B2+1, and subtask 2 is executed. Subtask 2 terminates in a branch instruction that unconditionally branches to D2+1. (*Note*: y corresponds to bits [8:0] of the address represented by D2+1.)

Figure 6.2d illustrates the control flow of the iterative decomposition. As in the case of the condition construct, first a condition is generated, a condition code is set, and a conditional branch is executed. In this case, the condition bits of the instruction at address B3 are set to cause a conditional branch if the condition generated is false. If the condition is false, the PC is set to address D3+1. (*Note*: z corresponds to bits [8:0] of the address represented by D3+1.) On the other hand, as long as the condition is true, the PC will be incremented to B3+1, and the subtask will be executed. The subtask terminates in an unconditional branch instruction at address D3, which sets the PC to A to again generate and test the condition. (*Note*: w corresponds to bits [8:0] of address A.)

Now, we are ready to move on to an example.

6.1.4 The Character Count Example from Chapter 5, Revisited

Recall the example of Section 5.5. The statement of the problem is as follows: "We wish to count the number of occurrences of a character in a file. The character in question is to be input from the keyboard; the result is to be displayed on the monitor."

The systematic decomposition of this English language statement of the problem to the final LC-2 implementation is shown in Figure 6.3. Figure 6.3a is a brief statement of the problem.

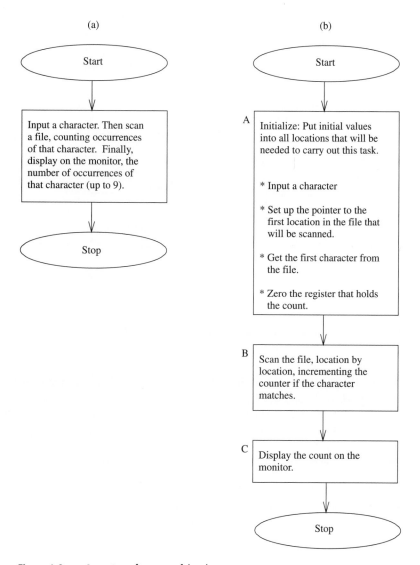

Figure 6.3   Stepwise refinement of the character count program

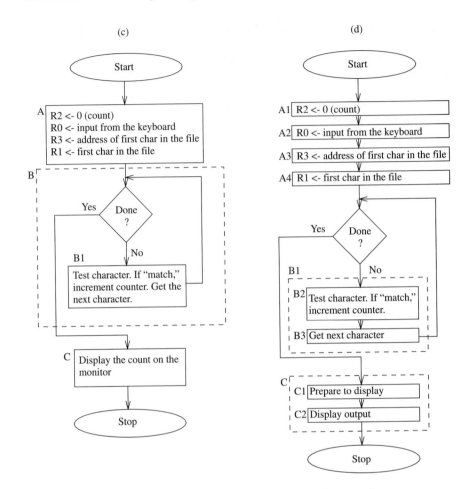

Figure 6.3   Stepwise refinement of the character count program *(Continued)*

In order to solve the problem, it is always a good idea first to examine exactly what is being asked for, and what is available to help solve the problem. In this case, the statement of the problem says that we will get the character of interest from the keyboard. We will scan all characters in a file, and when we find a match, we will increment a counter. Finally, we will output the result.

We will need places to hold the various pieces of information:

1. The character input from the keyboard.
2. Where we are (a pointer) in our scan of the file.
3. The character in the file that is currently being examined.
4. The count of the number of occurrences.

We will also need some mechanism for knowing when the file terminates.

The problem decomposes naturally (using the sequential construct) into three parts as shown in Figure 6.3b: (A) initialization, which includes keyboard input

(e)

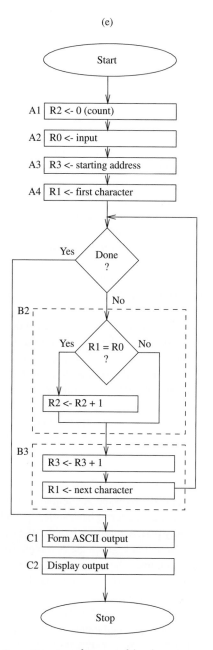

Figure 6.3   Stepwise refinement of the character count program *(Continued)*

of the character to be "counted," (B) the actual process of determining how many occurrences of the character are present in the file, and (C) displaying the count on the monitor.

We have seen the importance of proper initialization in several examples already. Before a computer program can get to the crux of the problem, it must have the correct initial values. These initial values do not just show up in the GPRs by magic. They get there as a result of the first set of steps in every algorithm: the initialization of its variables.

In this particular algorithm, initialization (as we said in Chapter 5) consists of starting the counter at 0, setting the pointer to the address of the first character in the file to be examined, getting an input character from the keyboard, and getting the first character from the file. Collectively, these four steps comprise the intialization of the algorithm shown in Figure 6.3b as A.

Figure 6.3c decomposes B into an iteration construct, such that as long as there are characters in the file to examine, the loop iterates. B1 shows what gets accomplished each iteration. The character is tested and the count incremented if there is a match. Then the next character is prepared for examination. Recall in Chapter 5 that there are two basic techniques for controlling the number of iterations of a loop: the sentinel method and the use of a counter. This program uses the sentinel method by terminating the file we are examining with an EOT (end of text) character. The test to see if there are more legitimate characters in the file is a test for the ASCII code for EOT.

Figure 6.3c also shows the initialization step in greater detail. Four LC-2 registers (R0, R1, R2, and R3) have been specified to handle the four requirements of the algorithm: the input character from the keyboard, the current character being tested, the counter, and the pointer to the next character to be tested.

Figure 6.3d decomposes both B1 and C using the sequential construct. In the case of B1, first the current character is tested (B2), and the counter incremented if we have a match, and then the next character is fetched (B3). In the case of C, first the count is prepared for display by converting it from a 2's complement integer to ASCII (C1), and then the actual character output is performed (C2).

Finally, Figure 6.3e completes the decomposition, replacing B2 with the elements of the condition construct and B3 with the sequential construct (first the pointer is incremented, and then the next character to be scanned is loaded).

The last step (and the easy part, actually) is to write the LC-2 code corresponding to each box in Figure 6.3e. Note that Figure 6.3e is essentially identical to Figure 5.7 of Chapter 5 (except now you know where it all came from!).

Before leaving this topic, it is worth pointing out that it is not always possible to understand everything at the outset. When you find that to be the case, it is not a signal simply to throw up your hands and quit. In such cases (which realistically are most cases), you should see if you can make sense of a piece of the problem, and expand from there. Problems are like puzzles; initially they can be opaque, but the more you work at it, the more they yield under your attack. Once you do understand what is given, what is being asked for, and how to proceed, you are ready to return to square one (Figure 6.3a) and restart the process of systematically decomposing the problem.

6.2   DEBUGGING

Debugging a program is pretty much applied common sense. A simple example comes to mind: You are driving to a place you have never visited, and somewhere along the way you made a wrong turn. What do you do now? One common "driving debugging" technique is to wander aimlessly, hoping to find your way back. When that does not work, and you are finally willing to listen to the person sitting next to you, you turn around and return to some "known" position on the route. Then, using a map (very difficult for some people) you follow the directions provided, periodically comparing where you are (from landmarks you see out the window) with where the map says you should be, until you reach your desired destination.

Debugging is somewhat like that. A logical error in a program can make you take a wrong turn. The simplest way to keep track of where you are as compared to where you want to be is to *trace* the program. This consists of keeping track of the **sequence** of instructions that have been executed and the **results** produced by each instruction executed. When you examine the sequence of instructions executed, you can detect errors in the control flow of the program. When you compare what each instruction has done to what it is supposed to do, you can detect logical errors in the program. In short, when the behavior of the program as it is executing is different from what it should be doing, you know there is a bug.

A useful technique is to partition the program into parts, often referred to as *modules*, and examine the results that have been computed at the end of execution of each module. In fact, the structured programming approach discussed in Section 6.1 can help you determine where in the program's execution you should examine results. This allows you to systematically get to the point where you are focusing your attention on the instruction or instructions that are causing the problem.

6.2.1   Debugging Operations

Many sophisticated debugging tools are offered in the marketplace, and undoubtedly you will use many of them in the years ahead. In Chapter 15, we will examine some debugging techniques available through **dbx**, the source-level debugger for the programming language C. For right now, however, we wish to stay at the level of the machine architecture, and so we will see what we can accomplish with a few very elementary interactive debugging operations. When debugging interactively, the user sits in front of the keyboard and monitor, and issues commands to the computer. In our case, this means operating an LC-2 simulator, using the menu available with the simulator.

It is important to be able to

1.   Deposit values in memory and in registers.

2.   Execute instruction sequences in a program.

3.   Stop execution when desired.

4. Examine what is in memory and registers, at any point in the program.

These few simple operations will go a long way toward debugging programs.

Set Values   It is useful to deposit values in memory and in registers in order to test the execution of a part of a program in isolation, without having to worry about parts of the program that come before it. For example, suppose one module in your program supplies input from a keyboard, and a subsequent module operates on that input. Suppose you want to test the second module before you have finished debugging the first module. If you know that the keyboard input module ends up with an ASCII code in R0, you can test the module that operates on that input by first placing an ASCII code in R0.

Execute Sequences   It is important to be able to execute a sequence of instructions and then stop execution in order to examine the values that the program has computed. Three simple mechanisms are usually available for doing this: run, step, and set breakpoints.

The **Run** command causes the program to execute until something makes it stop. This can be either a HALT instruction or a breakpoint (which is explained below).

The **Step** command causes the program to execute a fixed number of instructions and then stop. The interactive user enters the number of instructions he/she wishes the simulator to execute before it stops. When that number is one, the computer executes one instruction, then stops. Executing one instruction and then stopping is called *single-stepping*. It allows the person debugging the program to examine the individual results of every instruction executed.

The **Set Breakpoint** command causes the program to stop execution at a specific instruction in a program. Executing the debugging command Set Breakpoint consists of adding an address to a list maintained by the simulator. During the FETCH phase of each instruction, the Simulator compares the PC with the addresses in that list. If there is a match, execution stops. Thus, the effect of setting a breakpoint is to allow execution to proceed until the PC contains the address of the breakpoint. This is useful if one wishes to know what has been computed up to a particular point in the program. One sets a breakpoint at that address in the program, and executes the Run command. The program executes until that point, thereby allowing the user to examine what has been computed up to that point. (When one no longer wishes to have the program stop execution at that point, one can remove the breakpoint by executing the Clear Breakpoint command.)

Display Values   Finally, it is useful to examine the results of execution when the simulator has stopped execution. The Display command allows the user to examine the contents of any memory location or any register.

6.2.2   Examples: Use of the Interactive Debugger

We conclude this chapter with four examples, showing how the use of the interactive debugging operations can help us find errors in a program. We have chosen the following four errors: (1) incorrectly setting the loop control so that the loop executes

(a)

Address	15	14	13	12	11	10	9	8	7	6	5	4	3	2	1	0
x3200	0	1	0	1	0	1	0	0	1	0	1	0	0	0	0	0
x3201	0	0	0	1	0	1	0	0	1	0	0	0	0	1	0	0
x3202	0	0	0	1	1	0	1	1	0	1	1	1	1	1	1	1
x3203	0	0	0	0	0	1	1	0	0	0	0	0	0	0	0	1
x3204	1	1	1	1	0	0	0	0	0	0	1	0	0	1	0	1

(b)

PC	R2	R4	R5
x3201	0	10	3
x3202	10	10	3
x3203	10	10	2
x3201	10	10	2
x3202	20	10	2
x3203	20	10	1
x3201	20	10	1
x3202	30	10	1
x3203	30	10	0
x3201	30	10	0
x3202	40	10	0
x3203	40	10	−1
x3204	40	10	−1
	40	10	−1

(c)

PC	R2	R4	R5
x3203	10	10	2
x3203	20	10	1
x3203	30	10	0
x3203	40	10	−1

Figure 6.4   The use of interactive debugging to find the error in Example 1. (a) An LC-2 program to multiply (without a Multiply instruction). (b) A trace of the Multiply program. (c) Tracing with breakpoints.

an incorrect number of times, (2) confusing the load instruction 0100, which loads a register with the contents of a memory location with the load effective address instruction 1110, which loads a register with the address of a memory location, (3) forgetting which instructions set the condition codes, resulting in a branch instruction testing the wrong condition, and (4) not covering all possible cases of input values.

Example 1: Multiplying Without a Multiply Instruction   Consider the program of Figure 6.4. The goal of the program is to multiply the two positive numbers contained in R4 and R5. Given the fact that the LC-2 does not have a multiply instruction, the program clears R2 (that is, initializes R2 to zero), and then attempts to perform the multiplication by adding R4 to itself a number of times equal to the initial value in R5. Each time an add is performed, R5 is decremented. When R5 = 0, the program terminates.

It sounds like the program should work! Upon execution, however, we find that if R4 is initially 10 and R5 is initially 3, the program produces the value 40. What went wrong?

Figure 6.4b shows a trace of the program, which we can obtain by single-stepping. The column labeled *PC* shows the contents of the PC at the start of each instruction.

R2, R4, and R5 show the values in those three registers at the start of each instruction. If we examine the contents of the registers, we see that the branch condition codes were set wrong; that is, the conditional branch should be taken as long as R5 is positive, not as long as R5 is nonnegative, as is the case in x3203. That causes an extra iteration of the loop, resulting in 10 being added to itself four times, rather than three.

The program can be corrected by simply replacing the instruction at x3203 with

15	14	13	12	11	10	9	8	7	6	5	4	3	2	1	0
0	0	0	0	0	0	1	0	0	0	0	0	0	0	0	1

| | BR | | | n | z | p | | | | x001 | | | | | |

Figure 6.4c shows how setting a breakpoint at x3203 could have saved some of the tedium. Instead of examining the results of **each instruction**, a breakpoint at x3203 allows us to examine the results of **each iteration** of the loop. We see that the loop executed four times rather than three, as it should have.

Example 2: Adding a column of numbers   The program of Figure 6.5 is supposed to add the numbers stored in the 10 locations starting with x3100, and leave the result in R1. The contents of the 20 memory locations starting at location x3100 are shown in Figure 6.6.

The program should work as follows. The instructions in x3000 to x3003 initialize the variables. In x3000, the sum (R1) is initialized to 0. In x3001 and x3002,

(a)

Address	15	14	13	12	11	10	9	8	7	6	5	4	3	2	1	0
x3000	0	1	0	1	0	0	1	0	0	1	1	0	0	0	0	0
x3001	0	1	0	1	1	0	0	1	0	0	1	0	0	0	0	0
x3002	0	0	0	1	1	0	0	1	0	0	1	0	1	0	1	0
x3003	0	0	1	0	0	1	0	1	0	0	0	0	0	0	0	0
x3004	0	1	1	0	0	1	1	0	1	0	0	0	0	0	0	0
x3005	0	0	0	1	0	1	0	0	1	0	1	0	0	0	0	1
x3006	0	0	0	1	0	0	1	0	0	1	0	0	0	0	1	1
x3007	0	0	0	1	1	0	0	1	0	0	1	1	1	1	1	1
x3008	0	0	0	0	0	0	1	0	0	0	0	0	0	1	0	0
x3009	1	1	1	1	0	0	0	0	0	0	1	0	0	1	0	1

(b)

PC	R1	R2	R4
x3001	0	x	x
x3002	0	x	0
x3003	0	x	#10
x3004	0	x3107	#10

Figure 6.5   The use of interactive debugging to find the error in Example 2. (a) An LC-2 program to add 10 integers. (b) A trace of the first four instructions of the Add program.

Address	Contents
x3100	x3107
x3101	x2819
x3102	x0110
x3103	x0310
x3104	x0110
x3105	x1110
x3106	x11B1
x3107	x0019
x3108	x0007
x3109	x0004
x310A	x0000
x310B	x0000
x310C	x0000
x310D	x0000
x310E	x0000
x310F	x0000
x3110	x0000
x3111	x0000
x3112	x0000
x3113	x0000

Figure 6.6   Contents of memory locations x3100 to x3113 for Example 2

the loop control (R4), which counts the number of values added to R1, is initialized to #10. The program subtracts 1 each time through the loop, and repeats until R4 contains 0. In x3003, the base register (R2) is initialized to the starting location of the values to be added: x3100.

From there, each time through the loop, one value is loaded into R3 (in x3004), the base register is incremented to get ready for the next iteration (x3005), the value in R3 is added to R1, which contains the running sum (x3006), the counter is decremented (x3007), the P bit is tested, and if true, the PC is set to x3004 to begin the loop again (x3008). After ten times through the loop, R4 contains 0, the P bit is 0, the branch is not taken, and the program terminates (x3009).

It looks like the program should work. However, when we execute the program and then check the value in R1, we find the number x0024, which is not x8135, the sum of the numbers stored in locations x3100 to x3109. What went wrong?

We turn to the debugger and trace the program. Figure 6.5b shows a trace of the first four instructions executed. Note that after the instruction at x3003 has executed, the contents of R2 is x3107, not x3100, as we had expected. The problem is that the opcode 0100 loaded the **contents** of x3100 into R2, not the **address** x3100. Our mistake: We should have used the opcode 1110, which would have loaded the address of x3100 into R2. We correct the bug by replacing the opcode 0100 with 1110, and the program runs correctly.

Example 3: Determining Whether a Sequence of Memory Locations Contains a 5   The program of Figure 6.7 has been written to examine the contents of the ten memory locations starting at address x3100, and store a 1 in R0 if any of them contains a 5 and a 0 in R0 if none of them contains a 5.

The program is supposed to work as follows: The first six instructions (at x3000 to x3005) initialize R0 to 1, R1 to −5, and R3 to 10. In each case, the register is first cleared by ANDing it with 0, and then ADDing the corresponding immediate value. For example, in x3003, −5 is added to R1, and the result stored in R1.

The instruction at x3006 initializes R4 to the starting address (x3100) of the values to be tested, and x3007 loads the contents of x3100 into R2.

x3008 and x3009 determine if R2 contains the value 5 by adding −5 to it and branching to x300F if the result is 0. Since R0 is initialized to 1, the program terminates with R0 reporting the presence of a 5 among the locations tested.

x300A increments R4, preparing to load the next value. x300B decrements R3, indicating the number of values remaining to be tested. x300C loads the next value into R2. x300D branches back to x3008 to repeat the process if R3 still indicates more values to be tested. If R3 = 0, we have exhausted our tests, so R0 is set to 0 (x300E), and the program terminates (x300F).

(a)

Address	15	14	13	12	11	10	9	8	7	6	5	4	3	2	1	0
x3000	0	1	0	1	0	0	0	0	0	0	1	0	0	0	0	0
x3001	0	0	0	1	0	0	0	0	0	0	1	0	0	0	0	1
x3002	0	1	0	1	0	0	1	0	0	1	1	0	0	0	0	0
x3003	0	0	0	1	0	0	1	0	0	1	1	1	1	0	1	1
x3004	0	1	0	1	0	1	1	0	1	1	1	0	0	0	0	0
x3005	0	0	0	1	0	1	1	0	1	1	1	0	1	0	1	0
x3006	0	0	1	0	1	0	0	0	0	0	0	1	0	0	0	0
x3007	0	1	1	0	0	1	0	1	0	0	0	0	0	0	0	0
x3008	0	0	0	1	0	1	0	0	1	0	0	0	0	0	0	1
x3009	0	0	0	0	0	1	0	0	0	0	0	0	1	1	1	1
x300A	0	0	0	1	1	0	0	1	0	0	1	0	0	0	0	1
x300B	0	0	0	1	0	1	1	0	1	1	1	1	1	1	1	1
x300C	0	1	1	0	0	1	0	1	0	0	0	0	0	0	0	0
x300D	0	0	0	0	0	0	1	0	0	0	0	0	1	0	0	0
x300E	0	1	0	1	0	0	0	0	0	0	1	0	0	0	0	0
x300F	1	1	1	1	0	0	0	0	0	0	1	0	0	1	0	1
x3010	0	0	1	1	0	0	0	1	0	0	0	0	0	0	0	0

(b)

PC	R1	R2	R3	R4
x300D	−5	7	9	3101
x300D	−5	32	8	3102
x300D	−5	0	7	3013

Figure 6.7   The use of interactive debugging to find the error in Example 3. (a) An LC-2 program to detect the presence of a 5. (b) Tracing Example 3 with a breakpoint at x300D.

When we run the program for some sample data that contains a 5 in location x3108, the program terminates with R0 = 0, indicating there were no 5s in locations x3100 to x310A.

What went wrong? We examine a trace of the program, with a breakpoint set at x300D. The results are shown in Figure 6.7b.

The first time the PC is at x300D, we have already tested the value stored in x3100, we have loaded 7 (the contents of x3101) into R2, and R3 indicates there are still nine values to be tested. R4 contains the address from which we most recently loaded R2.

The second time the PC is at x300D, we have loaded 32 (the contents of x3102) into R2, and R3 indicates there are eight values still to be tested. The third time the PC is at x300D, we have loaded 0 (the contents of x3103) into R2, and R3 indicates seven values still to be tested.

However, the value 0 stored in x3103 causes the load instruction at x300C to clear the P condition code. This, in turn, causes the branch at x300D to be not taken, R0 is set to 0 (x300E) and the program terminates (x300F).

The error in the program was putting a load instruction at x300C between x300B, which kept track of how many values still needed to be tested, and x300D, the branch instruction that returned to x3008 to perform the next test. The load instruction sets condition codes. Therefore, the branch at x300D was based on the value loaded into R2, rather than on the count of how many values remained to be tested. If we remove the instruction at x300C and change the target of the branch in x300D to x3007, the program executes correctly.

Example 4: Finding the First 1 in a Word   Our last example contains an error that is usually one of the hardest to find, as we will see presently. The program of Figure 6.8 has been written to examine the contents of a memory location, find the first bit (reading left to right) that is set, and store the bit position of that bit into R1. If no bit is set, the program is to store −1 in R1. For example, if the location examined contained 0010000000000000, the program would terminate with R1 = 13. If the location contained 0000000000000100, the program would terminate with R1 = 2.

The program is supposed to work as follows (and it usually does): x3000 and x3001 intialize R1 in the same way as we have done in the previous examples. In this case, R1 is initialized to 15.

x3002 loads R2 with the contents of x3100, the value to be examined. It does this by the load indirect instruction, which finds the location of the value to be loaded in x3009.

x3003 tests the high bit of that value, and if it is a 1, it branches to x3008, where the program terminates with R1 = 15. If the high bit is a 0, the branch is not taken and R1 is decremented (x3004), indicating the next bit to be tested is bit [14].

In x3005, the value in R2 is added to itself, and the result stored back in R2. That is, the value in R2 is multiplied by 2. This is the same as shifting the contents of R2 one bit to the left. This causes the value in bit [14] to move into the bit [15] position, where it can be tested by a branch on negative instruction. x3006 performs the test of bit [14] (now in position bit [15]), and if the bit is 1, the branch is taken, and the program terminates with R1 = 14.

(a)

Address	15	14	13	12	11	10	9	8	7	6	5	4	3	2	1	0
x3000	0	1	0	1	0	0	1	0	0	1	1	0	0	0	0	0
x3001	0	0	0	1	0	0	1	0	0	1	1	0	1	1	1	1
x3002	1	0	1	0	0	1	0	0	0	0	0	0	1	0	0	1
x3003	0	0	0	0	1	0	0	0	0	0	0	0	1	0	0	0
x3004	0	0	0	1	0	0	1	0	0	1	1	1	1	1	1	1
x3005	0	0	0	1	0	1	0	0	1	0	0	0	0	0	1	0
x3006	0	0	0	0	1	0	0	0	0	0	0	0	1	0	0	0
x3007	0	0	0	0	1	1	1	0	0	0	0	0	0	1	0	0
x3008	1	1	1	1	0	0	0	0	0	0	1	0	0	1	0	1
x3009	0	0	1	1	0	0	0	1	0	0	0	0	0	0	0	0

(b)

PC	R1
x3007	14
x3007	13
x3007	12
x3007	11
x3007	10
x3007	9
x3007	8
x3007	7
x3007	6
x3007	5
x3007	4
x3007	3
x3007	2
x3007	1
x3007	0
x3007	−1
x3007	−2
x3007	−3
x3007	−4

Figure 6.8   The use of interactive debugging to find the error in Example 4. (a) An LC-2 program to find the first 1 in a word. (b) Tracing Example 4 with a breakpoint at x3007.

If the bit is 0, x3007 takes an unconditional branch to x3004, where the process repeats. That is, R1 is decremented (x3004), indicating the next lower bit number, R2, is shifted one bit to the left (x3005), and the new occupant of bit [15] is tested (x3006).

The process continues until the first 1 is found. The program works almost all the time. However, when we ran the program on our data, the program failed to terminate. What went wrong?

A trace of the program, with a breakpoint set at x3007, is illuminating. Each time the PC contained the address x3007, R1 contained a value smaller by one than the previous time. The reason is as follows: After R1 was decremented and the value in R2 shifted left, the bit tested was a 0, and so the program did not terminate. This continued for values in R1 equal to 14, 13, 12, 11, 10, 9, 8, 7, 6, 5, 4, 3, 2, 1, 0, -1, -2, -3, -4, and so forth.

The problem was that the initial value in x3100 was x0000, that is, there were no 1s present. The program worked fine as long as there was at least one 1 present. For the case where x3100 contained all zeroes, the conditional branch at x3006 was never taken, and so the program continued with execution of x3007, then x3004, x3005, x3006, x3007, and then back again to x3004. There was no way to break out of the sequence x3004, x3005, x3006, x3007, and back again to x3004. We call the sequence x3004 to x3007 a loop. Because there is no way for the program execution to break out of this loop, we call it an *infinite loop*. Thus, the program never terminates, and so we can never get the correct answer.

Again, we emphasize that this is often the hardest error to detect. It is also often the most important one. That is, it is not enough for a program to execute correctly most of the time; it must execute correctly all the time, independent of the data that the program is asked to process. We will see more examples of this kind of error later in the book.

PROBLEMS

6.1. Can a procedure that is *not* an algorithm be constructed from the three basic constructs of structured programming? If so, demonstrate through an example.

6.2. The LC-2 has no Subtract instruction. If a programmer needed to subtract two numbers he/she would have to write a routine to handle it. Show the systematic decomposition of the process of subtracting two integers.

6.3. Write a short LC-2 program that compares two numbers and puts the larger of the two in R1 and the smaller of the two in R2.

6.4. Which of the two algorithms for multiplying two numbers is preferable and why? $88 \cdot 3 = 88 + 88 + 88$ OR $3 + 3 + 3 + 3 + \ldots + 3$?

6.5. Use your answers from the last two problems to develop a program that efficiently multiplies two integers and places the result in R3. Show the complete systematic decomposition, from the problem statement to the final program.

6.6. Recall the machine busy example from previous chapters. Suppose memory location x4000 contains an integer between 0 and 15 identifying a particular machine that has just become busy. Suppose further that the value in memory location x4001 tells which machines are busy and which machines are idle.

Write an LC-2 machine language program that sets the appropriate bit in x4001 indicating that the machine in x4000 is busy.

For example, if x4000 contains a x0005 and x4001 contains x3101 at the start of execution, 0x4001 should contain x3121 after your program terminates.

6.7. What does the following LC-2 program do?

x3000	0011000000000000
x3001	1110000000001110
x3002	1110001000010011
x3003	0101010010100000
x3004	0010010000001101
x3005	0110011000000000
x3006	0110100001000000
x3007	0001011011000100
x3008	0111011000000000
x3009	0001000000100001
x300a	0001001001100001
x300b	0001010010111111
x300c	0000001000000100
x300d	1111000000100101
x300e	0000000000000101
x300f	0000000000000100
x3010	0000000000000011
x3011	0000000000000110
x3012	0000000000000010
x3013	0000000000000100
x3014	0000000000000111
x3015	0000000000000110
x3016	0000000000001000
x3017	0000000000000111
x3018	0000000000000101

6.8. Why is it necessary to initialize R2 in the character counting example in Section 6.1.4? In other words, in what manner might the program behave incorrectly if the R2 ← 0 step were removed from the routine?

6.9. Using the iteration construct, write an LC-2 machine language routine that displays exactly 100 Zs on the screen.

6.10. Using the conditional construct, write an LC-2 machine language routine that determines if a number stored in R2 is odd.

6.11. Write an LC-2 machine language routine to increment each of the numbers stored in memory location A through memory location B. Assume these locations have already been initialized with meaningful numbers. The addresses A and B can be found in memory locations x3100 and x3101.

6.12. 1. Write an LC-2 machine language routine that echoes the last character typed at the keyboard. If the user types an R, the program then immediately outputs an R on the screen.

2. Expand the routine from part (1) such that it echoes a line at a time. For example, if the user types:

    The quick brown fox jumps over the lazy dog.

    then the program waits for the user to press the Enter key (the ASCII code for which is x0A) and then outputs the same line.

6.13. Notice that we can shift a number to the left by one bit position by adding it to itself. For example, when the binary number 0011 is added to itself, the result is 0110. Shifting a number one bit pattern to the right is not as easy. Devise a routine in LC-2 machine code to shift the contents of memory location x3100 to the right by one bit.

6.14. Consider the following machine language program:

x3000	0101010010100000
x3001	0001001001111111
x3002	0001001001111111
x3003	0001001001111111
x3004	0000100000000111
x3005	0001010010100001
x3006	0000111000000001
x3007	1111000000100101

What are the possible initial values of R1 that cause the final value in R2 to be 3?

chapter
7

Assembly Language

By now, you are probably a little tired of 1s and 0s and keeping track of 0001 meaning ADD and 1001 meaning NOT. Also, wouldn't it be nice if we could refer to a memory location by some meaningful symbolic name instead of memorizing its 16-bit address. And, wouldn't it be nice if we could represent each instruction in some more easily comprehensible way, instead of having to keep track of which bit of the instruction conveys which individual piece of information about the instruction. It turns out that help is on the way.

In this chapter, we introduce Assembly Language, a mechanism that does all that, and more.

7.1 ASSEMBLY LANGUAGE PROGRAMMING—MOVING UP A LEVEL

Recall the levels of transformation identified in Figure 1.6 of Chapter 1. Algorithms are transformed into programs described in some mechanical language. This mechanical language can be, as it is in Chapter 5, the machine language of a particular computer. Recall that a program is in a computer's machine language if every instruction in the program is from the ISA of that computer.

On the other hand, the mechanical language can be more user-friendly. We generally partition mechanical languages into two classes, high-level and low-level. Of the two, high-level languages are much more user-friendly. Examples are C, C++, Fortran, COBOL, Pascal, plus more than a thousand others. Instructions in a high-level language almost (but not quite) resemble statements in a natural language such as English. High-level languages tend to be ISA independent. That is, once you learn how to program in C (or Fortran or Pascal) for one ISA, it is a small step to write programs in C (or Fortran or Pascal) for another ISA.

Before a program written in a high-level language can be executed, it must be translated into a program in the ISA of the particular computer on which it is expected to execute. It is usually the case that each statement in the high-level language specifies several instructions in the ISA of the computer. In Chapter 11, we will introduce the high-level language C, and in Chapters 12 through 19, we will show the relationship between various statements in C and their corresponding translations in LC-2 code. In this chapter, however, we will only move up a small step from the ISA we dealt with in Chapter 5.

A small step up from the ISA of a machine is that ISA's assembly language. Assembly language is a low-level language. There is no confusing an instruction in a low-level language with a statement in English. Each assembly language instruction usually specifies a single instruction in the ISA. Unlike high-level languages which are usually ISA independent, low-level languages are very ISA dependent. In fact, it is usually the case that each ISA has only one assembly language.

The purpose of assembly language is to make the programming process more user-friendly than programming in machine language (i.e., the ISA of the computer with which we are dealing), while still providing the programmer with detailed control over the individual instructions that the computer can execute. So, for example, while still retaining control over the detailed instructions the computer is to carry out, we are freed from having to remember what opcode is 0001 and what opcode is 1001, or what is being stored in memory location 0011111100001010 and what is being stored in location 0011111100000101. Assembly languages let us use mnemonic devices for opcodes, such as ADD and NOT, and let us give meaningful symbolic names to memory locations, such as SUM or PRODUCT, rather than use their 16-bit addresses. This makes it easier to differentiate which memory location is keeping track of a SUM and which memory location is keeping track of a PRODUCT.

We will see, starting in Chapter 11, that when we take the larger step of moving up to a higher level language (such as C), programming will be even more user-friendly, but we will relinquish control of exactly which detailed instructions are to be carried out in behalf of a high-level language statement.

7.2 AN ASSEMBLY LANGUAGE PROGRAM

We will describe LC-2 assembly language by means of an example. The following program multiplies a number by six by adding the number to itself six times. For example, if the number is 123, the program computes the product by adding 123 + 123 + 123 + 123 + 123 + 123.

The program consists of 20 lines of code. We have added a *line number* to each line of the program in order to be able to refer to individual lines easily. This is a common practice. These line numbers are not part of the program. Nine lines start with a semicolon, designating that they are strictly for the benefit of the human reader. More on this momentarily. Seven lines (05, 06, 07, 0B, 0C, 0D, and 0F) specify actual instructions to be translated into instructions in the ISA of the LC-2, which will actually be carried out when the program runs. The remaining four lines (04, 11, 12, and 14) contain pseudo-ops,which are messages from the programmer to the translation program to help in the translation process. The translation program is called an *assembler* (in this case the LC-2 assembler), and the translation process is called *assembly*.

```
01   ;
02   ; Program to multiply a number by the constant 6
03   ;
04           .ORIG   x3050
05           LD      R1,SIX
06           LD      R2,NUMBER
07           AND     R3,R3,#0      ; Clear R3. It will
08                                 ; contain the product.
09   ; The inner loop
0A   ;
0B   AGAIN   ADD     R3,R3,R2
0C           ADD     R1,R1,#-1     ; R1 keeps track of
0D           BRp     AGAIN         ; the iterations
0E   ;
0F           HALT
10   ;
11   NUMBER  .BLKW   1
12   SIX     .FILL   x0006
13   ;
14           .END
```

7.2.1   Instructions

Instead of an instruction being 16 0s and 1s, as is the case in the LC-2 ISA, an instruction in assembly language consists of four parts, as shown below:

LABEL   OPCODE   OPERANDS   ; COMMENTS

Two of the parts (LABEL and COMMENTS) are optional. More on this momentarily.

Opcodes and Operands   Two of the parts (OPCODE and OPERANDS) are **mandatory**. An instruction must have an OPCODE (the thing the instruction is to do), and the appropriate number of operands (the things it is supposed to do it to). Not surprisingly, this was exactly what we encountered in Chapter 5 when we studied the LC-2 ISA.

The OPCODE is a symbolic name for the opcode of the corresponding LC-2 instruction. The idea is that it is easier to remember an operation by the symbolic name ADD, AND, or LDR than by the four-bit quantity 0001,0101, or 0110. Figure 5.1 (also, Figure C.7) lists the OPCODES of the 16 LC-2 instructions. Pages 429 through 449 show the assembly language representations for the 16 LC-2 instructions.

The number of operands depends on the operation being performed. For example, the ADD instruction (line 0B) requires three operands (two sources to obtain the numbers being added, and one destination to designate where the result is to be placed). All three operands must be explicitly identified in the instruction.

```
AGAIN     ADD     R3,R3,R2
```

The operands to be added are obtained from register 2 and from register 3. The result is to be placed in register 3. We represent each of the registers 0 through 7 as R0, R2, ..., R7.

The LD instruction (line 06) requires two operands (the memory location from which the value is to be read) and the destination register which is to contain the value after the instruction completes execution. We will see momentarily that memory locations will be given symbolic addresses called *labels*. In this case, the location from which the value is to be read is given the label *NUMBER*. The destination into which the value is to be loaded is register 2.

```
LD   R2, NUMBER
```

As we discussed in Section 5.1.6, operands can be obtained from registers, from memory, or they may be literal (i.e., immediate) values in the instruction. In the case of register operands, the registers are explicitly represented (such as R2 and R3 in line 0B). In the case of memory operands, the symbolic name of the memory location is explicitly represented (such as NUMBER in line 6 and SIX in line 05). In the case of immediate operands, the actual value is explicitly represented (such as the value 0 in line 07).

```
AND  R3, R3, #0 ; Clear R3. It will contain the product.
```

A literal value must contain a symbol identifying the representation base of the number. We use # for decimal, x for hexadecimal, and b for binary. Sometimes there is no ambiguity, such as in the case 3F0A, which is a hex number. Nonetheless, we write it as x3F0A. Sometimes there is ambiguity, such as in the case 1000. x1000 represents the decimal number 4096, b1000 represents the decimal number 8, and #1000 represents the decimal number 1000.

Labels Labels are symbolic names which are used to identify memory locations that are referred to explicitly in the program. There are two reasons for explicitly referring to a memory location.

1. The location contains the target of a branch instruction (for example, AGAIN in line 0B).

2. The location contains a value that is loaded or stored (for example, NUMBER, line 11, and SIX, line 12).

The location AGAIN is specifically referenced by the branch instruction in line 0D.

```
BRp    AGAIN
```

If the result of ADD R1,R1,#−1 is positive (as evidenced by the P condition code being set), then the program branches to the location explicitly referenced as AGAIN to perform another iteration.

The location NUMBER is specifically referenced by the load instruction in line 06. The contents of the memory location explicitly referenced as NUMBER is loaded into R2.

If a location in the program is not explicitly referenced, then there is no need to give it a label.

Comments   Comments are messages intended only for human consumption. They have no effect on the translation process and indeed are not acted on by the LC-2 Assembler. They are identified in the program by semicolons. A semicolon signifies that the rest of the line is a comment and is to be ignored by the assembler. If the semicolon is the first nonblank character on the line, the entire line is ignored. If the semicolon follows the operands of an instruction, then only the comment is ignored by the assembler.

The purpose of comments is to make the program more comprehensible to the human reader. They help explain a nonintuitive aspect of an instruction or a set of instructions. In line 07, the comment "Clear R3; it will contain the product" lets the reader know that the instruction on line 07 is initializing R3 prior to accumulating the product of the two numbers. While the purpose of line 07 may be obvious to the programmer today, it may not be the case two years from now, after the programmer has written an additional 30,000 lines of code and cannot remember why he/she wrote AND R3,R3,#0. It may also be the case that two years from now, the programmer no longer works for the company and the company needs to modify the program in response to a product update. If the task is assigned to someone who has never seen the code before, comments go a long way to helping comprehension.

It is important to make comments that provide additional insight and not just restate the obvious. There are two reasons for this. First, comments that restate the obvious are a waste of everyone's time. Second, they tend to obscure the comments that say something important because they add clutter to the program. For example, in line 0C, the comment "Decrement R1" would be a bad idea. It would provide no additional insight to the instruction, and it would add clutter to the page.

Another purpose of comments, and also the judicious use of extra blank spaces to a line, is to make the visual presentation of a program easier to understand. So, for example, comments are used to separate pieces of the program from each other to make the program more readable. That is, lines of code that work together to compute a single result are placed on successive lines, while pieces of a program that produce separate results are separated from each other. For example, note that lines 0B through 0D are separated from the rest of the code by lines 0A and 0E. There is nothing on lines 0A and 0E other than the semicolons.

Extra spaces that are ignored by the assembler provide an opportunity to align elements of a program for easier readability. For example, all the opcodes start in the same column on the page.

7.2.2   Pseudo-ops (Assembler Directives)

The LC-2 assembler is a program that takes as input a string of characters representing a computer program written in LC-2 assembly language, and translates it into a program in the ISA of the LC-2. Pseudo-ops are helpful to the assembler in performing that task.

Actually, a more formal name for a pseudo-op is *assembler directive*. They are called pseudo-ops because they do not refer to operations that will be performed by the program during execution. Rather, the pseudo-op is strictly a message to the assembler to help the assembler in the assembly process. Once the assembler handles the message, the pseudo-op is discarded. The LC-2 assembler contains five pseudo-ops: .ORIG, .FILL, .BLKW, .STRINGZ, and .END. All are easily recognizable by the dot as their first character.

.ORIG

.ORIG tells the assembler where in memory to place the LC-2 program. In line 04, .ORIG x3050 says, start with location x3050. As a result, the LD R1,SIX instruction will be put in location x3050.

.FILL

.FILL tells the assembler to set aside the next location in the program and initialize it with the value of the operand. In line 12, the ninth location in the resultant LC-2 program is initialized to the value x0006.

.BLKW

.BLKW tells the assembler to set aside some number of sequential memory locations (i.e., a **BL**oc**K** of Words) in the program. The actual number is the operand of the .BLKW pseudo-op. In line 11, the pseudo-op instructs the assembler to set aside one location in memory (and also to label it NUMBER, incidentally).

The pseudo-op .BLKW is particularly useful when the actual value of the operand is not yet known. For example, one might want to set aside a location in memory for storing a character input from a keyboard. It will not be until the program is run that we will know the identity of that keystroke.

.STRINGZ

.STRINGZ tells the assembler to initialize a sequence of $n + 1$ memory locations. The argument is a sequence of n characters, inside double quotation marks. The first n words of memory are initialized with the zero-extended ASCII codes of the corresponding characters in the string. The final word of memory is initialized to zero. The last character, x0000, provides a convenient sentinel for processing the string of ASCII codes.

For example, the code fragment

```
                .ORIG     x3010
HELLO    .STRINGZ  "Hello, World!"
```

would result in the assembler initializing locations x3010 through x301D to the
following values:

```
x3010:  x0048
x3011:  x0065
x3012:  x006C
x3013:  x006C
x3014:  x006F
x3015:  x002C
x3016:  x0020
x3017:  x0057
x3018:  x006F
x3019:  x0072
x301A:  x006C
x301B:  x0064
x301C:  x0021
x301D:  x0000
```

.END

.END tells the assembler where the program ends. Any characters that come
after .END will not be utilized by the assembler. *Note:* .END does not stop the
program during execution. In fact, .END does not even exist at the time of
execution. It is simply a delimiter—it marks the end of the source program.

7.2.3   Example: The Character Count Example of Section 5.5, Revisited

Now we are ready for a complete example. Let's consider again the problem of
Section 5.5. We wish to write a program that will take a character that is input from
the keyboard and a file and count the number of occurrences of that character in that
file. As before, we first develop the algorithm by constructing the flowchart. Recall
that in Section 6.1, we showed how to decompose the problem systematically so as to
generate the flowchart of Figure 5.7. In fact, the final step of that process in Chapter 6
is the flowchart of Figure 6.3e, which is essentially identical to Figure 5.7. Next, we
use the flowchart to write the actual program. This time, however, we enjoy the luxury
of not worrying about 0s and 1s, and instead write the program in LC-2 assembly
language. The program is shown in Figure 7.1.

A few notes regarding this program:

Three times during this program, assistance in the form of a service call is required
of the operating system. In each case, a TRAP instruction is used. TRAP x23 causes
a character to be input from the keyboard and placed in R0 (line 0D). TRAP x21
causes the ASCII code in R0 to be displayed on the monitor (line 28). TRAP x25
causes the machine to be halted (line 29). As we said before, we will leave the details
of how the TRAP instruction is carried out until Chapter 9.

The ASCII codes for the decimal digits 0 to 9 (0000 to 1001) are 00110000 to
00111001. The conversion from binary to ASCII is done simply by adding 00110000

```
01      ;
02      ; Program to count occurrences of a character in a File.
03      ; Character to be input from the keyboard.
04      ; Result to be displayed on the monitor.
05      ; Program only works if no more than 9 occurrences are found.
06      ;
07      ;
08      ; Initialization
09      ;
0A              .ORIG    x3000
0B              AND      R2,R2,#0        ; R2 is counter, initialize to 0
0C              LD       R3,PTR          ; R3 is pointer to characters
0D              TRAP     x23             ; R0 gets character input
0E              LDR      R1,R3,#0        ; R1 gets the next character
0F      ;
10      ; Test character for end of file
11      ;
13      TEST    ADD      R4,R1,#-4       ; Test for EOT
14              BRZ      OUTPUT          ; If done, prepare the output
15      ;
16      ; Test character for match.  If a match, increment count.
17      ;
18              NOT      R1,R1
19              ADD      R1,R1,R0        ; If match, R1 = xFFFF
1A              NOT      R1,R1           ; If match, R1 = x0000
1B              BRnp     GETCHAR         ; If no match, do not increment
1C              ADD      R2,R2,#1
1D      ;
1E      ; Get next character from the file
1F      ;
20      GETCHAR ADD      R3,R3,#1        ; Increment the pointer
21              LDR      R1,R3,#0        ; R1 gets the next character to test
22              BR       TEST
23      ;
24      ; Output the count.
25      ;
26      OUTPUT  LD       R0,ASCII        ; Load the ASCII template
27              ADD      R0,R0,R2        ; Convert binary to ASCII
28              TRAP     x21             ; ASCII code in R0 is displayed
29              TRAP     x25             ; Halt machine
2A      ;
2B      ; Storage for pointer and ASCII template
2C      ;
2D      ASCII   .FILL    x0030
2E      PTR     .FILL    x4000
2F              .END
```

Figure 7.1   The assembly language program to count occurrences of a character

to the binary value of the decimal digit. Line 2D shows ASCII initialized to that value (i.e., x0030).

The file that is to be examined starts at address x4000 (see line 2E). Usually, this starting address would not be known to the programmer who is writing this program, since we would want the program to work on files that will become available in the future. That situation will be discussed in Section 7.4 to follow.

7.3   THE ASSEMBLY PROCESS

7.3.1   Introduction

Before an LC-2 assembly language program can be executed, it must first be translated into a machine language program, that is, one in which each instruction is in the LC-2 ISA. It is the job of the LC-2 assembler to perform that translation.

If you have available an LC-2 assembler, you can cause it to translate your assembly language program into a machine language program by executing an appropriate command. In the LC-2 assembler that is generally available via the Web, that command is *assemble* and requires as an argument the filename of your assembly language program. For example, if the filename is solution1.asm, then

```
assemble solution1.asm outfile
```

produces the file outfile, which is in the ISA of the LC-2. It is necessary to check with your local instructor for the correct command line for causing the LC-2 assembler to produce a file of 0s and 1s in the ISA of the LC-2.

7.3.2   A Two-Pass Process

In this section, we will see how the assembler goes through the process of translating an assembly language program into a machine language program. We start with the example of Figure 7.1.

Recall that there is in general a one-to-one correspondence between instructions in the assembly language program and instructions in the final machine language program. The process consists in making that one-to-one translation.

Starting at the top of Figure 7.1, the assembler sees (line 0A) that the machine language program starts at location x3000. The assembler can easily transform the first instruction (line 0B) to machine language, that is: 0101010010100000. At this point, we have

```
x3000:   0101010010100000
```

The LC-2 assembler moves on to the next instruction (line 0C). It would next want to translate this line but would be unable to, since it does not know the meaning of the symbolic address, PTR.

Consequently, the assembly process is done in **two steps**, or two passes, so named because the LC-2 assembler passes over the whole assembly language program twice, from beginning to end. The objective of the first pass is to identify the actual binary addresses corresponding to the symbolic names (or labels) so that the problem alluded to above (not knowing the 16-bit address corresponding to PTR) is removed. This set of correspondences is known as the *symbol table*. In pass one, we construct the symbol table. In pass two, we translate the individual assembly language instructions into their corresponding machine language instructions.

7.3.3   The First Pass: Creating the Symbol Table

For our purposes, the symbol table is simply a correspondence of symbolic names with their 16-bit memory addresses. We obtain these correspondences by passing through the assembly language program once, noting which instruction is assigned to which address, and identifying each label with the address of its assigned entry.

Recall that we provide labels in those cases where we have to refer to a location, either because it is the target of a branch instruction or because it contains data that must be loaded or stored. Consequently, if we have not made any programming mistakes, and if we identify all the labels, we will have identified all the symbolic addresses used in the program.

The above paragraph assumes that our entire program exists between our .ORIG and .END pseudo-ops: This is true at the moment. In Section 7.4, we will consider programs that consist of multiple parts, each with its own .ORIG and .END, and where each part is assembled separately.

The first pass starts by noting (line 0A) that the first instruction will be assigned to address x3000. We keep track of the location assigned to each instruction by means of a location counter (LC). The LC is initialized to the address specified in .ORIG, that is, x3000.

The assembler examines each instruction in sequence, and increments the LC once for each assembly language instruction. If the instruction examined contains a label, a symbol table entry is made for that label, specifying the current contents of LC as its address. The first pass terminates when the .END instruction is encountered.

The first instruction that has a label is at line 13. Since it is the fifth instruction in the program and the LC at that point contains x3004, a symbol table entry is constructed thus:

Symbol	Address
TEST	x3004

The second instruction that has a label is at line 20. At this point, the LC has been incremented to x300B. Thus a symbol table entry is constructed, as follows:

Symbol	Address
GETCHAR	x300B

At the conclusion of the first pass, the symbol table has the following entries:

Symbol	Address
TEST	x3004
GETCHAR	x300B
OUTPUT	x300E
ASCII	x3012
PTR	x3013

7.3.4   The Second Pass: Generating the Machine Language Program

The second pass consists of going through the assembly language program a second time, this time with the help of the symbol table. At each step, the assembly language instruction is translated into a machine language instruction (i.e., in the ISA of the LC-2).

Starting at line 0B, x3000 is set to 0101010010100000, and the LC is incremented to x3001.

This time, when we get to line 0C, we can completely assemble the instruction since we know that PTR corresponds to x3013. The instruction is LD, which has an opcode encoding of 0010. The Destination register (DR) is R3, that is, 011. Since PTR and the contents of LC (i.e., the address of this instruction) are on the same page (that is bits [15:9] are 0011000), LD is a legitimate opcode. The page offset of PTR is 000010011. Putting this all together, x3001 is set to 0010011000010011, and the LC is incremented to x3002.

Note: If the symbolic address of PTR had not been on the same page as the address assigned to the LD instruction, we could not have assembled the instruction. An assembly error would have occurred, preventing the assembly process from completing successfully. Fortunately, PTR is on the same page as x3001, so the instruction assembled correctly.

The second pass continues. At each step, the LC is incremented and the location specified by LC is assigned the translated LC-2 instruction or, in the case of .FILL, the value specified. When the second pass encounters the .END instruction, assembly terminates.

The resulting translated program is shown in Figure 7.2.

That process was, on a good day, merely tedious. Fortunately, you do not have to do it for a living—the LC-2 assembler does that. And, since you now know LC-2 assembly language, there is no need to program in machine language. Now we can write our programs symbolically in LC-2 assembly language and invoke the LC-2 assembler to create the machine language versions that can execute on an LC-2 computer.

7.4   BEYOND ASSEMBLY OF A SINGLE ASSEMBLY LANGUAGE PROGRAM

Our purpose in this chapter has been to take you one step up from the ISA of the computer and introduce assembly language. Although it is still quite a large step from C or C++, assembly language does, in fact, save us a good deal of pain. We have also shown how a rudimentary two-pass assembler actually works to translate an assembly language program into the machine language of the LC-2 ISA.

There are many more aspects to sophisticated assembly language programming that go well beyond an introductory course. However, our reason for teaching assembly language is not to deal with its sophistication, but rather to show its innate

Address	Binary
	0011000000000000
x3000	0101010010100000
x3001	0010011000010011
x3002	1111000000100011
x3003	0110001011000000
x3004	0001100001111100
x3005	0000010000001110
x3006	1001001001111111
x3007	0001001001000000
x3008	1001001001111111
x3009	0000110000001011
x300A	0001010010100001
x300B	0001011011100001
x300C	0110001011000000
x300D	0000111000000100
x300E	0010000000010010
x300F	0001000000000010
x3010	1111000000100001
x3011	1111000000100101
x3012	0000000000110000
x3013	0100000000000000

Figure 7.2   The machine language program
for the assembly language
program of Figure 7.1

simplicity. Before we leave this chapter, however, there are a few additional highlights
we should explore.

7.4.1 The Executable Image

When a computer begins execution of a program, the entity being executed is called
an *executable image*. The executable image is created from modules created by you
and others. Each module is translated separately into an object file. We have just
gone through the process of performing that translation ourselves by mimicking the
LC-2 assembler. Other modules, some written in C perhaps, are translated by the
C compiler. Some modules are written by users, and some modules are supplied as
library routines by the operating system. Each object file consists of instructions in
the ISA of the computer being utilized, along with its associated data. The final step
is to *link* all the object modules together into one executable image. During execution
of the program, the FETCH, DECODE, ... instruction cycle is applied to instructions
in the executable image.

7.4.2   More than One Object File

It is very common to form an executable image from more than one object file. In fact, in the real world, where most programs invoke libraries provided by the operating system as well as modules generated by other programmers, it is much more common to have multiple object files than a single one.

A case in point is our example character count program. The program counts the number of occurrences of a character in a file. A typical application can easily have the program as one module and the input data file as another. If this is the case, then the starting address of the file, shown as x4000 in line 2E of Figure 7.1, would not be known when the program was written. If we remove line 2E, then the program of Figure 7.1 will not assemble because there would be no symbol table entry for PTR. What can we do?

One solution is to identify PTR as the symbolic name of an address that is not known at the time the program of Figure 7.1 is assembled. We can do that by identifying PTR to the assembler. A pseudo-op such as

                         .EXTERNAL PTR

would send a message to the LC-2 assembler that the absence of label PTR is not an error in the program. Rather, PTR is a label in some other module that will be translated independently. In fact, in our case, it will be the label of the location of the first character in the file to be examined by our character count program.

With PTR designated .EXTERNAL, the LC-2 will create a symbol table entry for PTR, but instead of assigning it an address, it would mark it as belonging to another module. At *link time*, when all the modules are combined, the linker (the program that manages the "combining" process) would use the symbol table entry for PTR in another module to complete the translation of the instruction at line 0C in our character count module. In this way, references by one module to symbolic locations in another module do not present problems. They are resolved by the linker.

PROBLEMS

7.1.   An assembly language program contains the following two instructions. The assembler puts the translated version of the LDI instruction shown below into location x3025 of the object module. After assembly is complete, what is in location x3025?

```
PLACE     .FILL     x45A7
          LDI       R3, PLACE
```

7.2.   What is the problem with using the string AND as a label?

7.3.   Create the symbol table entries generated by the assembler when translating the following routine into machine code:

```
                         .ORIG    x301C
                         ST       R3, SAVE3
                         ST       R2, SAVE2
                         AND      R2, R2, #0
            TEST         IN
                         BRz      TEST
                         ADD      R1, R0, #-30
                         BRn      FINISH
                         ADD      R1, R0, #-40
                         NOT      R1
                         BRn      FINISH
                         HALT
            FINISH       ADD      R2, R2, #1
                         HALT
            SAVE3        .FILL    X0000
            SAVE2        .FILL    X0000
                         .END
```

7.4. 1. What does the following program do?

```
                         .ORIG    x3000
                         LD       R2, ZERO
                         LD       R0, M0
                         LD       R1, M1
            LOOP         BRz      DONE
                         ADD      R2, R2, R0
                         ADD      R1, R1, -1
                         BRnzp    LOOP
            DONE         ST       R2, RESULT
                         HALT
            RESULT       .FILL    x0000
            ZERO         .FILL    x0000
            M0           .FILL    x0004
            M1           .FILL    x0803
                         .END
```

2. What value will be contained in **RESULT** after the program runs to completion?

7.5. Write a program in LC-2 assembly language that counts the number of 1s in the value stored in R0 and stores the result into R1. For example, if R0 contains 0001001101110000, then after the program executes, the result stored in R1 would be 0000 0000 0000 0110.

7.6. What is the purpose of the .END pseudo-op? How does it differ from the HALT instruction?

7.7. The following program fragment has an error in it. Identify the error and explain how to fix it.

```
                         ADD      R3, R3, #30
                         ST       R3, A
                         HALT
            A            .FILL    #0
```

Will this error be detected when this code is assembled or when this code is run on the LC-2?

7.8. We want the following program fragment to shift R3 to the left by four bits, but it has an error in it. Identify the error and explain how to fix it.

```
              .ORIG    x3000
              AND      R2, R2, #0
              ADD      R2, R2, #4
      LOOP    BRz      DONE
              ADD      R2, R2, #-1
              ADD      R3, R3, R3
              BRnzp    LOOP
      DONE    HALT
              .END
```

7.9. What does the following program do?

```
              .ORIG    x3000
              AND      R5, R5, #0
              AND      R3, R3, #0
              ADD      R3, R3, #8
              LDI      R1, A
              ADD      R2, R1, #0
      AG      ADD      R2, R2, R2
              ADD      R3, R3, #-1
              BRnp     AG
              LD       R4, B
              AND      R1, R1, R4
              NOT      R1, R1
              ADD      R1, R1, #1
              ADD      R2, R2, R1
              BRnp     NO
              ADD      R5, R5, #1
      NO      HALT
      B       .FILL    xFF00
      A       .FILL    x4000
              .END
```

7.10. 1. Assemble the following program:

```
              .ORIG    x3000
              STI      R0, LABEL
              OUT
              HALT
      LABEL   .STRINGZ "%"
              .END
```

2. The programmer intended the program to output a % to the monitor, and then halt. Unfortunately, the programmer got confused about the semantics of each of the opcodes (that is, exactly what function is carried out by the LC-2 in response to each opcode). Replace exactly **one** opcode in the above program with the correct opcode, which will then make the program work as intended.

3. The original program from part 1 was executed. However, execution exhibited some very strange behavior. The strange behavior was in part due to the programming error, and in part due to the fact that the value in R0 when the program started executing was x3000. Explain what the strange behavior was and why the program behaved that way.

7.11. When the following LC-2 program is executed, how many times will the instruction at the memory address labeled **LOOP** execute?

```
            .ORIG     x3005
            LEA       R2, DATA
            LDR       R4, R2, #0
LOOP        ADD       R4, R4, #-3
            BRzp      LOOP
            TRAP      x25
DATA        .FILL     x000B
            .END
```

7.12. Assume a sequence of nonnegative integers is stored in consecutive memory locations, one integer per memory location, starting at location x4000. Each integer has a value between 0 and 30,000 (decimal). The sequence terminates with the value −1 (i.e., xFFFF).

What does the following program do?

```
            .ORIG     x3000
            AND       R4, R4, #0
            AND       R3, R3, #0
            LD        R0, NUMBERS
LOOP        LDR       R1, R0, #0
            NOT       R2, R1
            BRz       DONE
            AND       R2, R1, #1
            BRz       L1
            ADD       R4, R4, #1
            BRnzp     NEXT
L1          ADD       R3, R3, #1
NEXT        ADD       R0, R0, #1
            BRnzp     LOOP
DONE        TRAP      x25
NUMBERS     .FILL     x4000
            .END
```

7.13. The following is an LC-2 program that performs a function. Assume a sequence of integers is stored in consecutive memory locations, one integer per memory location, starting at the location x4000. The sequence terminates with the value x0000. What does the following program do?

```
.ORIG     x3000
          LD        R0, NUMBERS
          LD        R2, MASK
LOOP      LDR       R1, R0, #0
          BRz       DONE
          AND       R5, R1, R2
          BRz       L1
          BRnzp     NEXT
L1        ADD       R1, R1, R1
          STR       R1, R0, 0
NEXT      ADD       R0, R0, #1
          BRnzp     LOOP
DONE      HALT
NUMBERS   .FILL     x4000
MASK      .FILL     x8000
.END
```

7.14. The following LC-2 program compares two character strings of the same length. The source strings are in the `.STRINGZ` form. The first string starts at memory location `FIRST`, and the second string starts at memory location `SECOND`. If the strings are the same, the program terminates with the value 0 in R5. If the strings are different, the program terminates with the value 1 in R5. Fill in the blanks labeled (a), (b), and (c), that will complete the program.

```
            .ORIG   x3000
            LD      R1, FIRST
            LD      R2, SECOND
            AND     R0, R0, #0
    LOOP    ------------- (a)
            LDR     R4, R2, #0
            BRz     NEXT
            ADD     R1, R1, #1
            ADD     R2, R2, #1
            ------------- (b)
            ------------- (c)
            ADD     R3, R3, R4
            BRz     LOOP
            AND     R5, R5, #0
            BRnzp   DONE
    NEXT    AND     R5, R5, #0
            ADD     R5, R5, #1
    DONE    TRAP    x25
    FIRST   .FILL   x4000
    SECOND  .FILL   x4100
            .END
```

7.15. What does the pseudo-op `.FILL xFF004` do? Why?

7.16. Suppose you write two separate assembly language modules that you expect to be combined by the linker. Each module uses the label AGAIN, and neither module contains the pseudo-op `.EXTERNAL AGAIN`. Is there a problem using the label `AGAIN` in both modules? Why or why not?

7.17. 1. The LC-2 assembler must be able to map an instruction's mnemonic into its binary opcode. For instance, given an ADD, it must generate the binary pattern 0001. Write an LC-2 assembly language program that prompts the user to type in an LC-2 assembly language instruction and then displays its binary opcode. If the assembly language instruction is invalid, it displays an error message.

2. The LC-2 assembler must also convert constants represented in ASCII into their appropriate binary values. For instance, x2A translates into 101010 and #12 translates into 1100. Write an LC-2 assembly language program that reads a decimal or hexadecimal constant from the keyboard (i.e., it is preceded by a # character signifying it is a decimal, or x signifying it is HEX) and prints out the binary. Assume the constants can be expressed with no more than two digits.

chapter

8

I/O

Up to now, we have paid little attention to I/O. We did note (in Chapter 4) that input/output is an important component of the Von Neumann model. There must be a way to get information into the computer in order to process it, and there must be a way to get the result of that processing out of the computer so humans can use it. Figure 4.1 depicts a number of different input and output devices.

And we did suggest (in Chapter 5) that input and output can be accomplished by executing the TRAP instruction, which asks the operating system to do it for us. Figure 5.8 illustrates this for input (at address x3002) and for output (at address x3010).

In this chapter, we are ready to do I/O by ourselves. We have chosen to study the keyboard as our input device and the monitor display as our output device. Not only are they the simplest I/O devices and the most familiar to us, but they have characteristics that allow us to study important concepts about I/O without getting bogged down in unnecessary detail.

8.1   I/O BASICS

8.1.1   Device Registers

Although we often think of an I/O device as a single entity, interaction with a single I/O device usually means interacting with more than one *device register*. The simplest I/O devices usually have at least two device registers: one to hold the data being transferred between the device and the computer, and one to indicate status information about the device. An example of status information is whether the device is available or is still busy processing the most recent I/O task.

8.1.2   Memory-Mapped I/O Versus Special Input/Output Instructions

An instruction that interacts with an input or output device register must identify the particular input or output device register with which it is interacting. Two schemes are used. Some computers use special input and output instructions. Other computers prefer to use the same data movement instructions that are used to move data in and out of memory.

The Digital Equipment Corporation's PDP-8 is an example of a computer that used special input and output instructions. The 12-bit PDP-8 instruction contained a three-bit opcode. If the opcode was 110, an I/O instruction was indicated. The remaining nine bits of the PDP-8 instruction identified which I/O device register and what operation was to be performed.

Most computer designers prefer not to specify an additional set of instructions for dealing with input and output. They use the same data movement instructions that are used for loading and storing data between memory and the general purpose registers. For example, a load instruction, where the source address is that of an input device register, is an input instruction. Similarly, a store instruction where the destination address is that of an output device register is an output instruction.

Since programmers use the same data movement instructions that are used for memory, every input device register and every output device register must be uniquely identified in the same way that memory locations are uniquely identified. To do this, each device register is assigned an address from the memory address space of the ISA. That is, the I/O device registers are *mapped* to a set of addresses that are allocated to I/O device registers rather than to memory locations. Hence, the name *memory-mapped I/O*.

The original PDP-11 ISA had a 16-bit address space. All addresses wherein bits $[15:13] = 111$ were allocated to I/O device registers. That is, of the 2^{16} addresses, only 57,344 corresponded to memory locations. The remaining 2^{13} were memory-mapped I/O addresses.

The LC-2 uses memory-mapped I/O. Table A.1 lists the memory-mapped addresses of all LC-2 device registers.

8.1.3   Asynchronous Versus Synchronous

Most I/O is carried out at speeds very much slower than the speed of the processor. A typist, typing on a keyboard, loads an input device register with one ASCII code every time he/she types a character. A computer can read the contents of that device register every time it executes a load instruction, where the operand address is the memory-mapped address of that input device register.

Many of today's microprocessors execute instructions under the control of a clock that operates well in excess of 300 MHz. Even for a microprocessor operating at only

300 MHz, a clock cycle lasts only 3.3 nanoseconds. Suppose a processor executed one instruction at a time (as the LC-2 does), and it took the processor 10 clock cycles to execute each instruction. At that rate, the processor could read the contents of the input device register once every 33 nanoseconds, **if** it could be supplied at that rate. Unfortunately, people do not type at the rate of 300 million words/minute. *Question:* If the processor reading characters at the rate of one every 33 nanoseconds can keep up with a typist typing at the rate of 300 million words/minute, what is the maximum average number of characters in a word?

We could mitigate this speed disparity by designing hardware that would accept typed characters at some slower fixed rate. For example, we could design a piece of hardware that accepts one character every 30 million cycles. This would require a typing speed of 100 words/minute, which is certainly doable. Unfortunately, it would also require that the typist work in lockstep with the computer's clock. That is not acceptable since the typing speed (even of the same typist) varies from moment to moment.

What's the point? The point is that I/O devices frequently operate at speeds very different from that of a microprocessor, and not in lockstep. This latter characteristic we call *asynchronous.* Most interaction between a processor and I/O is asynchronous. To control processing in an asynchronous world requires some protocol or *handshaking* mechanism. So it is with our keyboard and monitor display. In the case of the keyboard, we will need a one-bit status register, called a *flag*, to indicate if someone has or has not typed a character. In the case of the monitor, we will need a one-bit status register to indicate whether or not the most recent character sent to the monitor has been displayed.

These flags are the simplest form of *synchronization.* A single flag, called the *Ready bit*, is enough to synchronize the output of the typist who can type characters at the rate of 100 words/minute with the input to a processor that can accept these characters at the rate of 300 million characters/second. Each time the typist types a character, the Ready bit is set. Each time the computer reads a character, it clears the Ready bit. By examining the Ready bit before reading a character, the computer can tell whether it has already read the last character typed. If the Ready bit is clear, no characters have been typed since the last time the computer read a character, and so no additional read would take place. When the computer detects that the Ready bit is set, it could only have been caused by a **new** character being typed, so the computer would know to again read a character.

The single Ready bit provides enough handshaking to ensure that the asynchronous transfer of information between the typist and the microprocessor can be carried out accurately.

If the typist could type at a constant speed, and we did have a piece of hardware that would accept typed characters at precise intervals (for example, one character every 30 million cycles), then we would not need the Ready bit. The computer would simply know, after 30 million cycles of doing other stuff, that the typist had typed exactly one more character, and the computer would read that character. In this hypothetical situation, the typist would be typing in lockstep with the processor, and no additional synchronization would be needed. We would say the computer and typist were operating *synchronously*, or the input activity was synchronous.

8.1.4 Interrupt-Driven Versus Polling

The processor, which is computing, and the typist, who is typing, are two separate entities. Each is doing its own thing. Still, they need to interact, that is, the data that is typed has to get into the computer. The issue of *interrupt-driven* versus *polling* is the issue of who controls the interaction. Does the processor do its own thing until being interrupted by an announcement from the keyboard, "Hey, a key has been struck. The ASCII code is in the input device register. You need to read it." This is called *interrupt-driven I/O*, where the keyboard controls the interaction. Or does the processor control the interaction, specifically by interrogating (usually, again and again) the Ready bit until it (the processor) detects that the Ready bit is set. At that point, the processor knows it is time to read the device register. This second type of interaction is called *polling*, since the Ready bit is polled by the processor, asking if any key has been struck.

Section 8.2.2 describes how the polling method works. Section 8.5 further explains interrupt-driven I/O.

8.2 INPUT FROM THE KEYBOARD

8.2.1 Basic Input Registers (the KBDR and the KBSR)

We have already noted that in order to handle character input from the keyboard, we need two things: a data register that contains the character to be input, and a synchronization mechanism to let the processor know that input has occurred. The synchronization mechanism is contained in the status register associated with the keyboard.

These two registers are called the *keyboard data register* (KBDR) and the keyboard *status register* (KBSR). They are assigned addresses from the memory address space. As shown in Table A.1, KBDR is assigned to xF401; KBSR is assigned to xF400.

Even though a character needs only eight bits and the synchronization mechanism needs only one bit, it is easier to assign 16 bits (like all memory addresses in the LC-2) to each. In the case of KBDR, bits [7:0] are used for the data, and bits [15:8] contain x00. In the case of KBSR, bit [15] contains the synchronization mechanism, that is, the Ready bit.

Figure 8.1 shows the two device registers needed by the keyboard. If you look back at the overall structure of the LC-2 data path (shown in Figure 5.9), you can see how KBSR and KBDR fit within the overall scheme of things.

8.2.2 The Basic Input Service Routine

KBSR[15] controls the synchronization of the slow keyboard and the fast processor. When a key on the keyboard is struck, the ASCII code for that key is loaded into

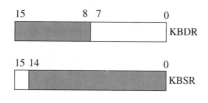

Figure 8.1   Keyboard device registers

KBDR[7:0] and the electronic circuits associated with the keyboard automatically set KBSR[15] to 1. When the LC-2 reads KBDR, the electronic circuits associated with the keyboard automatically clear KBSR[15], allowing another key to be struck. If KBSR[15] = 1, the ASCII code corresponding to the last key struck has not yet been read, and so the keyboard is disabled.

If input-output is controlled by the processor (i.e., via polling), then a program can repeatedly test KBSR[15] until it notes that the bit is set. At that point, the processor can load the ASCII code contained in KBDR into one of the LC-2 registers. Since the processor only loads the ASCII code if KBSR[15] is 1, there is no danger of reading a single typed character multiple times. Furthermore, since the keyboard is disabled until the previous code was read, there is no danger of the processor missing characters that were typed. In this way, KBSR[15] provides the mechanism to guarantee that each key typed will be loaded exactly once.

The following input routine loads R0 with the ASCII code that has been entered through the keyboard, and then moves on to the NEXT_TASK in the program.

```
01    START  LDI    R1, A        ; Test for
02           BRzp   START        ; character input
03           LDI    R0, B
04           BR     NEXT_TASK    ; branch to next task
05    A      .FILL  xF400        ; Address of KBSR
06    B      .FILL  xF401        ; Address of KBDR
```

As long as KBSR[15] is 0, no key has been struck since the last time the processor read the data register. Lines 01 and 02 comprise a loop that tests bit [15] of KBSR. Note the use of the LDI instruction, which loads R1 with the contents of xF400, the memory-mapped address of KBSR. If the Ready bit, bit [15], is clear, BRzp will branch to START and another iteration of the loop. When someone strikes a key, KBDR will be loaded with the ASCII code of that key and the Ready bit of KBSR will be set. This will cause the branch to fall through and the instruction at line 03 to be executed. Again, note the use of the LDI instruction, which this time loads R0 with the contents of xF401, the memory-mapped address of KBDR. The input routine is now done, so the program branches unconditionally to its NEXT_TASK.

8.3   OUTPUT TO THE MONITOR

8.3.1   Basic Output Registers (the CRTDR and the CRTSR)

Output works in a way very similar to input, with CRTDR and CRTSR replacing the roles of KBDR and KBSR, respectively. The letters *CRT* are used in deference to the cathode ray tube, an old electronic device used in monitor displays. In the LC-2, CRTDR is assigned address xF3FF. CRTSR is assigned address xF3FC.

As is the case with input, even though an output character needs only eight bits and the synchronization mechanism needs only one bit, it is easier to assign 16 bits (like all memory addresses in the LC-2) to each output device register. In the case of CRTDR, bits [7:0] are used for data, and bits [15:8] contain x00. In the case of CRTSR, bit [15] contains the synchronization mechanism, that is, the Ready bit.

Figure 8.2 shows the two device registers needed by the monitor. Figure 5.9 shows how CRTSR and CRTDR fit within the overall structure of the LC-2 data path.

8.3.2   The Basic Output Service Routine

CRTSR [15] controls the synchronization of the fast processor and the slow monitor display. When the LC-2 transfers an ASCII code to CRTDR [7:0] for outputting, the electronics of the monitor automatically clear CRTSR [15] as the processing of the contents of CRTDR [7:0] begins. When the monitor finishes processing the character on the screen, it (the monitor) automatically sets CRTSR [15]. This is a signal to the processor that it (the processor) can transfer another ASCII code to CRTDR for outputting. As long as CRTSR [15] is clear, the monitor is still processing the previous character, so the monitor is disabled as far as additional output from the processor is concerned.

If input-output is controlled by the processor (i.e., via polling), then a program can repeatedly test CRTSR [15] until it notes that the bit is set, indicating that it is okay to write a character to the screen. At that point, the processor can store the ASCII code for the character it wishes to write into CRTDR [7:0], setting up the transfer of that character to the monitor's display.

The following routine causes the ASCII code contained in R0 to be displayed on the monitor:

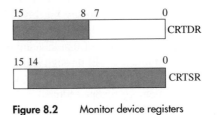

Figure 8.2   Monitor device registers

```
01      START   LDI     R1, A           ; Test if output
02              BRzp    START           ; register ready
03              STI     R0, B
04              BR      NEXT_TASK
05      A       .FILL   xF3FC           ; Address of CRTSR
06      B       .FILL   xF3FF           ; Address of CRTDR
```

Like the routine for KBDR and KBSR in Section 8.2.2, lines 01 and 02 repeatedly poll
CRTSR [15] to see if the monitor electronics is finished yet with the last character
shipped by the processor. Note the use of LDI and the indirect access to xF3FC,
the memory-mapped address of CRTSR. As long as CRT [15] is clear, the monitor
electronics is still processing this character, and BRzp branches to START for another
iteration of the loop. When the monitor electronics finishes with the last character
shipped by the processor, it automatically sets CRTSR [15] to 1, which causes the
branch to fall through and the instruction at line 03 to be executed. Note the use of the
STI instruction, which stores R0 into xF3FF, the memory-mapped address of CRTDR.
The write to CRTDR also clears CRTSR [15], disabling for the moment CRTDR from
further output. The monitor electronics takes over and writes the character to the
screen. Since the output routine is now done, the program unconditionally branches
(line 04) to its NEXT_TASK.

8.3.3 Example: Keyboard Echo

When typing at the keyboard, it is desirable to know exactly what characters one has
typed. We can get this echo capability easily (without any sophisticated electronics)
by simply combining the above two routines, as shown below. The key typed at the
keyboard is displayed on the monitor.

```
START   LDI     R1, KBSR        ; Test for character input
        BRzp    START
        LDI     R0, KBDR
ECHO    LDI     R1, CRTSR       ; Test output register ready
        BRzp    ECHO
        STI     R0, CRTDR
        BR      NEXT_TASK
KBSR    .FILL   xF400           ; Address of KBSR
KBDR    .FILL   xF401           ; Address of KBDR
CRTSR   .FILL   xF3FC           ; Address of CRTSR
CRTDR   .FILL   xF3FF           ; Address of CRTDR
```

8.4   A MORE SOPHISTICATED INPUT ROUTINE

In the example of Section 8.2.2, the input routine would be a part of a program being
executed by the computer. Presumably, the program requires character input from
the keyboard. But how does the person sitting at the keyboard know when to type

a character! Sitting there, the person may wonder whether or not the program is actually running, or if perhaps the computer is busy off doing something else.

To let the person sitting at the keyboard know that the program is waiting for input from the keyboard, the computer typically prints a message on the monitor. Such a message is often referred to as a *prompt*. The symbol that is displayed by your operating system (for example, **%** or **C:**) or by your editor (for example, **:**) are examples of prompts.

The program fragment shown in Figure 8.3 obtains keyboard input via polling as we have shown in Section 8.2.2 already, and also includes a prompt to let the person sitting at the keyboard know when it is time to type a key. Let's examine this program fragment in parts.

You are already familiar with lines 13 through 19 and lines 25 through 28, which correspond to the code in Section 8.3.3 for inputting a character via the keyboard and echoing it on the monitor. Lines 01 through 03, lines 1D through 1F, and lines 22 through 24 recognize that this input routine needs to use general purpose registers R1, R2, and R3. Unfortunately, they most likely contain values that will still be needed after this routine has finished. In order to not lose those values, the ST instructions in lines 01 through 03 save them in memory locations SaveR1, SaveR2, and SaveR3, before the input routine starts its business. These three memory locations have been allocated by the .FILL pseudo-ops in lines 22 through 24. After the input routine is finished and before the program branches unconditionally to its NEXT_TASK (line 20), the LD instructions in lines 1D through 1F restore them to their rightful locations in R1, R2, and R3.

This leaves lines 05 through 08, 0A through 11, 1A through 1C, 29 and 2A. These lines serve to alert the person sitting at the keyboard that it is time to type a character.

Lines 05 through 08 write the ASCII code x0A to the monitor. This is the ASCII code for a *new line*. Most ASCII codes correspond to characters that are visible on the screen. A few, like x0A, are control characters. They cause an action to occur. Specifically, the ASCII code x0A causes the cursor to move to the far left of the next line on the screen. Thus, the name *Newline*. Before attempting to write x0A, however, as is always the case, CRTSR [15] is tested (line 6) to see if CRTDR can accept a character. If CRTSR [15] is clear, the monitor is busy, and the loop (lines 06 and 07) is repeated. When CRTSR [15] is 1, the conditional branch (line 7) is not taken, and x0A is written to CRTDR for outputting (line 8).

Lines 0A through 11 cause the prompt **Input a character>** to be written to the screen. The prompt is specified by the **.STRINGZ** pseudo-op on line 2A and is stored in 19 memory locations—eighteen ASCII codes, one per memory location, corresponding to the 18 characters in the prompt, and the terminating sentinel x0000.

Line 0C iteratively tests to see if the end of the string has been reached (by detecting x0000), and if not, once CRTDR is free, line 0F writes the next character in the input prompt into CRTDR. When x0000 is detected, the program knows that the entire input prompt has been written to the screen and branches to the code that handles the actual keyboard input (starting at line 13).

After the person at the keyboard has typed a character and it has been echoed (lines 13 to 19), the program writes one more new line (lines 1A through 1C) before branching to its NEXT_TASK.

```
01   START    ST      R1,SaveR1      ; Save registers needed
02            ST      R2,SaveR2      ; by this routine
03            ST      R3,SaveR3
04   ;
05            LD      R2,Newline
06   L1       LDI     R3,CRTSR
07            BRzp    L1             ; Loop until Monitor is ready
08            STI     R2,CRTDR       ; Move cursor to new clean line
09   ;
0A            LEA     R1,Prompt      ; Starting address of prompt string
0B   Loop     LDR     R0,R1,#0       ; Write the input prompt
0C            BRz     Input          ; End of prompt string
0D   L2       LDI     R3,CRTSR
0E            BRzp    L2             ; Loop until Monitor is ready
0F            STI     R0,CRTDR       ; Write next prompt character
10            ADD     R1,R1,#1       ; Increment Prompt pointer
11            BR      Loop           ; Get next prompt character
12   ;
13   Input    LDI     R3,KBSR        ;
14            BRzp    Input          ; Poll until a character is typed
15            LDI     R0,KBDR        ; Load input character into R0
16   L3       LDI     R3,CRTSR
17            BRzp    L3             ; Loop until Monitor is ready
18            STI     R0,CRTDR       ; Echo input character
19   ;
1A   L4       LDI     R3,CRTSR
1B            BRzp    L4             ; Loop until Monitor is ready
1C            STI     R2,CRTDR       ; Move cursor to new clean line
1D            LD      R1,SaveR1      ; Restore registers
1E            LD      R2,SaveR2      ; to original values
1F            LD      R3,SaveR3
20            BR      NEXT_TASK      ; Do the program's next task
21   ;
22   SaveR1   .FILL   x0000          ; Allocated space for registers saved
23   SaveR2   .FILL   x0000
24   SaveR3   .FILL   x0000
25   CRTSR    .FILL   xF3FC
26   CRTDR    .FILL   xF3FF
27   KBSR     .FILL   xF400
28   KBDR     .FILL   xF401
29   Newline  .FILL   x000A          ; ASCII code for newline
2A   Prompt   .STRINGZ "Input a character>"
```

Figure 8.3   The input routine for the LC-2 keyboard

8.5   INTERRUPT-DRIVEN I/O

In Section 8.1.4, we noted that interaction between the processor and an I/O device can be controlled by the processor (i.e., polling) or it can be controlled by the I/O device (i.e., interrupt driven). In Sections 8.2, 8.3, and 8.4, we have seen several examples of polling. In each case, the processor tested the Ready bit of the status register, and when it was 1, the processor branched to the instruction that did the input or output operation.

We will not study interrupt-driven I/O in this book in detail. However, we will explain the fundamental enabling mechanism. Two elements are required:

Element 1: A signal from the I/O device indicating that it is ready.

Element 2: A test by the processor during each instruction cycle to see if such a signal is present.

If both elements are present and the executing program so desires, the program does not need to spin its wheels while it again and again checks to see if the Ready bit is set. Instead, the processor can ignore the I/O device and do whatever processing it needs to, until the I/O device lets the processor know that it is ready for interaction. In fact, that is precisely the advantage of interrupt-driven I/O: the processor does not waste time testing the Ready bit but is instead free to do other useful work until being informed by the I/O device that there is I/O activity to deal with.

8.5.1   Element 1: The Interrupt Signal

First, the signal from the I/O device indicates that it is ready for interaction with the processor. If the I/O device is the keyboard, it is ready if someone has typed a character. If the I/O device is the monitor, it is ready if the associated electronic circuits have successfully completed the display of the last character. In both cases, the I/O device is ready when the corresponding Ready bit is set.

In most I/O devices, the status register, in addition to the Ready bit, has an Interrupt Enable (IE) bit, shown as bit [14] in Figure 8.4. The **signal from the I/O device** referred to as Element 1 is the logical AND of the IE bit and the Ready bit. It is also shown in Figure 8.4.

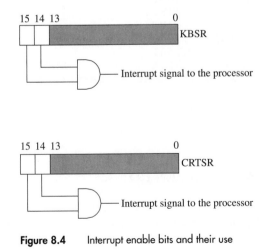

Figure 8.4   Interrupt enable bits and their use

Note that if bit [14] is clear, it does not matter whether the Ready bit is set, Element 1 will not be present, and the I/O device will not be able to interrupt the processor. In that case, the program will have to poll the I/O device to determine if it is ready. Bit [14] can be set or cleared by the processor, depending on whether or not the processor wants polling or interrupt-driven I/O.

If bit [14] is set, then interrupt-driven I/O is enabled. In that case, as soon as someone types a key (or as soon as the monitor has finished processing the last character), bit [15] is set. This, in turn, asserts the output of the AND gate, causing an interrupt signal to the processor.

8.5.2 Element 2: The Test for Interrupts

Second is the test to see if the interrupt signal is present. If bit [14] of the relevant status register is set, interrupt-driven I/O is enabled. This is implemented by a little additional logic to the control unit of the processor. Recall in Chapter 4 that the instruction cycle sequences through the six phases of FETCH, DECODE, EVALUATE ADDRESS, FETCH OPERAND, EXECUTE, and STORE RESULT. Recall further that we said that after the sixth phase, the control unit returns to the first phase, that is, the FETCH of the next instruction.

The additional logic to test for the interrupt signal is to replace that last sequential step of **always** going from STORE RESULT back to FETCH, as follows. The STORE RESULT phase is instead accompanied by a test for the interrupt signal. If the interrupt signal is asserted, then the control unit will not return to the FETCH phase. Instead, it will initiate the execution of a program fragment to carry out the requirements of the I/O device. How it does that is one more thing we will have to leave for some future semester. If the interrupt signal is not asserted, then it is business as usual, with the control unit returning to the FETCH phase to start processing the next instruction.

PROBLEMS

8.1. 1. What is a device register?

2. What is a device data register?

3. What is a device status register?

8.2. Why is a Ready bit not needed if synchronous I/O is used?

8.3. In Section 8.1.1, the statement is made that a typist would have to type at the rate of 3 billion words/minute in order to provide input to a 300 MHz processor at the maximum rate the microprocessor can accept it. This statement makes an assumption about the size of a word. What is that assumption?

8.4.   Are the following interactions usually synchronous or asynchronous?

   1.   Between a remote control and a television set.

   2.   Between the mailman and you, via a mailbox.

   3.   Between a mouse and your PC.

   Under what conditions would each of them be synchronous? Under what conditions would each of them be asynchronous?

8.5.   What is the purpose of bit [15] in the KBSR?

8.6.   What problem could occur if a program does not check the Ready bit of the KBSR before reading the KBDR?

8.7.   Which of the following combinations describe the system in Section 8.2.2?

   1.   Memory mapped and interrupt driven.

   2.   Memory mapped and polling.

   3.   Special opcode for I/O and interrupt driven.

   4.   Special opcode for I/O and polling.

8.8.   Write a program that checks the initial value in memory location x4000 to see if it is a valid ASCII code and if it is a valid ASCII code, prints the character. If the value in x4000 is not a valid ASCII code, the program prints nothing.

8.9.   What problem is likely to occur if the keyboard hardware does not check the KBSR before writing to the KBDR?

8.10.   What problem could occur if the CRT output hardware does not check the CRTSR before writing to the screen?

8.11.   Some computer engineering students decided to revise the LC-2 for their senior project. In designing the LC-3, they decided to conserve on device registers by combining the KBSR and the CRTSR into one status register: the IOSR (the input/output status register). IOSR [15] is the keyboard device Ready bit and IOSR [14] is the CRT device Ready bit. What are the implications for programs wishing to do I/O? Is this a poor design decision?

8.12. Adam H. decided to design a variant of the LC-2 that did not need a keyboard status register. Instead, he created a readable/writable keyboard data and status register (KBDSR), which contains the same data as the KBDR. With the KBDSR, a program requiring keyboard input would wait until a nonzero value appeared in the KBDSR. The nonzero value would be the ASCII value of the last key press. Then the program would write a zero into the KBDSR indicating that it had read the key press. Modify the basic input service of Section 8.2.2 to implement Adam's scheme.

8.13. Which is more efficient, interrupt-driven I/O or polling? Explain.

9

TRAP Routines and Subroutines

9.1 LC-2 TRAP ROUTINES

9.1.1 Introduction

Recall Figure 8.3 of the previous chapter. In order to have the program successfully obtain input from the keyboard, it was necessary for the programmer (in Chapter 8) to know several things:

1. The hardware data registers for both the keyboard and the monitor: the monitor so a prompt could be displayed, and the keyboard so the program would know where to look for the input character.

2. The hardware status registers for both the keyboard and the monitor: the monitor so the program would know when it was okay to display another character in the input prompt, and the keyboard so the program would know when someone had struck a key.

3. The asynchronous nature of keyboard input relative to the executing program.

This is beyond the knowledge of most application programmers. In fact, in the real world, if application programmers (or user programmers, as they are sometimes called) had to understand I/O at this level, there would be much less I/O and far fewer programmers in the business.

In addition, there is another problem with allowing user programs to perform I/O activity by directly accessing KBDR, KBSR, etc. I/O activity involves the use of device registers that are shared by many programs. This means that if a user programmer were allowed to access the hardware registers, and he/she messed up,

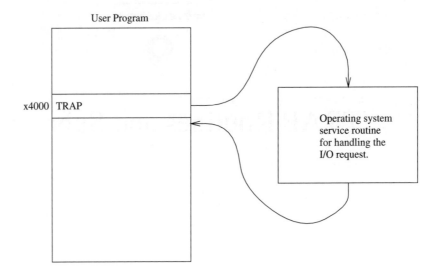

Figure 9.1   Invoking an OS service routine by means of the TRAP instruction

it could create havoc for *other* user programs. Thus, it is ill-advised to give user programmers access to these registers. We say the hardware registers are **privileged** and not accessible to programs that do not have the proper degree of *privilege*.

The notion of privilege introduces a pretty big can of worms. Unfortunately, we cannot do much more than mention it here and leave it for later courses to give it serious treatment. For now, we simply note that there are resources that are not accessible to the user program, and that access to those resources is controlled by endowing some programs with sufficient privilege and other programs without. Having said that, we move on to our problem at hand, a "better" solution for user programs that require input and/or output.

The simpler solution as well as the safer solution to the problem of user programs requiring I/O involves the TRAP instruction and the operating system (which does have the proper degree of privilege). We saw its use in Chapter 5. The user program gets the operating system to do the job by invoking the TRAP instruction. That way, the user program does not have to know the gory details previously mentioned, and other user programs are protected from the consequences of misguided user programmers.

Figure 9.1 shows a user program that, upon reaching location x4000, needs an I/O task performed. The user program requests the operating system to perform the task in behalf of the user program. The operating system takes control of the machine, handles the request specified by the TRAP instruction, and then returns control back to the user program. We often refer to the request made by the user program as a *service call* or a *system call*.

9.1.2 The TRAP Mechanism

The TRAP mechanism involves several elements, as follows:

1. A set of service routines executed on behalf of user programs by the operating system. These are part of the operating system and start at arbitrary addresses in memory. The LC-2 was designed so that up to 256 service routines can be specified.

2. A table of the starting addresses of these 256 service routines. This table is stored in the first 256 addresses in memory (locations x0000 to x00FF). The table is referred to by various companies by various names. One company calls this table the System Control Block. Another company calls it the Interrupt Vector Table. Figure 9.2 provides a snapshot of the System Control Block of the LC-2, with specific starting addresses highlighted, among them the keyboard input service routine (location x04A0), the character output service routine (location x0430), and the machine halt service routine (location xFD70). Note that, for example, the starting address of the keyboard input service routine (location x04A0) is contained in location x0023.

3. The TRAP instruction. When a user program wishes to have the operating system take control of the computer, execute a specific service routine on behalf of the user program, and then return control back to the user program, the user program uses the TRAP instruction.

4. The RET instruction. The RET instruction provides the mechanism for the operating system to return control back to the user program.

9.1.3   The TRAP Instruction

The TRAP instruction causes the service routine to execute by doing two things:

•   It changes the PC to the starting address of the relevant service routine on the basis of its trap vector (to be explained).

•   It provides a way back to the program that initiated the TRAP instruction. The "way back" is referred to as a *linkage*.

The TRAP instruction works as follows. The TRAP instruction is made up of two parts: the TRAP opcode 1111 and the trap vector (bits [7:0]). Bits [11:8] must

x0000	
x0001	
:	:
x0021	x0430
x0022	x0450
x0023	x04A0
x0024	x04E0
x0025	xFD70
:	:

Figure 9.2   The System Control Block

be zero. The trap vector identifies the service routine the user program wants the operating system to perform. In the example below, the trap vector is x23.

15	14	13	12	11	10	9	8	7	6	5	4	3	2	1	0
1	1	1	1	0	0	0	0	0	0	1	0	0	0	1	1

TRAP   trapvector

During the EXECUTE phase of the instruction cycle, the trap vector is zero-extended to 16 bits to form an address. In the preceding case, that address is x0023. The contents at that address, in this case x04A0 (see Figure 9.2), are loaded into the PC. Location x04A0 is the starting address of the TRAP routine to input a character from the keyboard. We say the trap vector "points" to the starting address of the TRAP routine. Thus, TRAP x23 causes the operating system to start executing the keyboard input service routine.

In order to return to the instruction following the TRAP instruction in the user program (after the service routine has completed), there must be some mechanism for saving the address of that next instruction in the user program. The TRAP instruction provides the linkage back by storing the PC in R7 before loading the PC with the starting address of the service routine. This occurs during the EXECUTE phase of the TRAP instruction, so the PC has already been updated (in the FETCH phase) to point to the instruction following the TRAP instruction.

9.1.4 The RET Instruction

The RET instruction is a zero-operand instruction. It consists of the opcode 1101 and no operands. Bits [11:0] of the RET instruction must be zero. The RET instruction is shown below.

15	14	13	12	11	10	9	8	7	6	5	4	3	2	1	0
1	1	0	1	0	0	0	0	0	0	0	0	0	0	0	0

RET

During the EXECUTE phase of the RET instruction, the PC is loaded with the contents of R7. If R7 is not changed during the TRAP routine (i.e., during the time since the TRAP instruction executed), control of the computer will return to the user program at the instruction following the TRAP instruction that initiated the service routine.

Figure 9.3 shows how the LC-2 uses the TRAP instruction and the RET instruction to implement the example of Figure 9.1. The flow of control goes from (A) within a user program that needs a character input from the keyboard, to (B) the operating system service routine that performs that task in behalf of the user program, back to the user program (C) that presumably uses the information contained in the input character.

Recall that the computer continually executes its instruction cycle (FETCH, DE-CODE, etc.) so that the way to change the flow of control is to change the contents of the PC. In that way, the next FETCH will be at a redirected address.

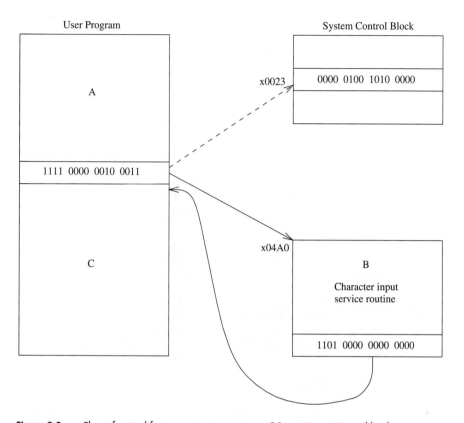

Figure 9.3 Flow of control from a user program to an OS service routine and back

Thus, to request the character input service routine, the TRAP instruction with trap vector x23 is used. Execution of that instruction causes the contents of memory location x0023 (which, in this case, contains x04A0) to be loaded into the PC, and the address of the instruction following the TRAP instruction to be loaded into R7. The dashed lines on Figure 9.3 show the use of the trap vector to obtain the starting address of the trap service routine from the System Control Block.

The next instruction cycle starts with the FETCH of the contents of x04A0, which is the first instruction of the operating system service routine that requests (and accepts) keyboard input. That service routine, as we will see momentarily, is patterned after the keyboard input routine we studied in Section 8.4. Recall that upon completion of that input routine (see Figure 8.3), R0 contains the ASCII code of the key that was typed.

The TRAP service routine executes to completion, ending with the RET instruction. Execution of the RET instruction loads the PC with the contents of R7. If R7 was not changed during execution of the service routine, this would be the address of the instruction following the TRAP instruction in the initiating user program. Thus, the user program resumes execution, with R0 containing the ASCII code of the keyboard character that was typed.

If R7 had been changed during execution of the service routine, we would have a problem returning to the initiating program. To be sure nothing destroys the linkage to the initiating program, we save the contents of R7 in some memory location before starting the service routine. We restore that value to R7 after completing the service routine and just before executing the RET instruction.

9.1.5   An Example

The following program is provided to illustrate the use of the TRAP instruction. It can also be used to amuse the average four year old.

```
01                    .ORIG x3000
02            LD      R2,TERM    ; Load -7
03            LD      R3,ASCII   ; Load ASCII difference
04    AGAIN   TRAP    x23        ; Request keyboard input
05            ADD     R1,R2,R0   ; Test for terminating
06            BRz     EXIT       ; character
07            ADD     R0,R0,R3   ; Change to lowercase
08            TRAP    x21        ; Output to the monitor
09            BRnzp   AGAIN      ; ... and do it again!
0A    TERM    .FILL   xFFC9      ; FFC9 = -7
0B    ASCII   .FILL   x0020
0C    EXIT    TRAP    x25        ; Halt
```

The idea of the program is as follows. A person is sitting at the keyboard. Each time the person types a capital letter, the program outputs the lowercase version of that letter. If the person types a 7, the program terminates.

The program executes as follows. The program first loads constants xFFC9 and x0020 into R2 and R3. The constant xFFC9, which is the negative of the ASCII code for 7, is used to test the character typed at the keyboard. The constant x0020 is the zero-extended difference between the ASCII code for a capital letter and the ASCII code for that letter's lowercase representation. For example, the ASCII code for A is x41; the ASCII code for a is x61. The ASCII codes for Z and z are x5A and x7A respectively.

Then TRAP x23 is executed, which invokes the keyboard input service routine. When control returns to the applicaton program (at line 05), R0 contains the ASCII code of the character typed. The ADD and BRz instructions test for the terminating character 7. If the character typed is not a 7, the ASCII uppercase/lowercase difference is added to the character, storing the result in R0, and a TRAP to the monitor output service routine is called. This causes the lowercase representation of the same letter to be displayed on the monitor. When control returns to the application program (this time at line 09), an unconditional BR to AGAIN is executed, and another request for keyboard input.

Before leaving this example, we note that correct operation of the program assumes that the person sitting at the keyboard only types capital letters and the value 7.

What if the person types a $? A better program would be one that tests the character typed to be sure it really is a capital letter from among the 26 capital letters in the alphabet, and if it is not, takes corrective action. *Question:* Augment the above program to add that test for bad data. That is, write a program that will type the lowercase representation of any capital letter typed and will terminate if anything other than a capital letter is typed.

9.1.6 TRAP Routines for Handling I/O

Using the constructs described above, the input routine described in Figure 8.3 can be slightly modified to be the input service routine shown in Figure 9.4. There are three changes. (1) We add the appropriate .ORIG pseudo-op, which corresponds to the starting address found at location x0023 in the System Control Block, and the terminating .END pseudo-op. (2) We save and restore R7, which contains the linkage back to the initiating program. And (3), we terminate the input routine with the RET instruction, rather than the BR NEXT_TASK, as is done in Figure 8.3, since this service routine is invoked by means of the TRAP x23 instruction, rather than as part of the user program.

The output routine of Section 8.3.2 can be modified in a similar way, as shown in Figure 9.5. The results are input (Figure 9.4) and output (Figure 9.5) service routines that can be invoked simply and safely by the TRAP instruction with the appropriate

```
;   Service Routine for Keyboard Input
;
        .ORIG   x04A0
START   ST      R7,SaveR7       ; Save the linkage back to the program.
        ST      R1,SaveR1       ; Save the values in the registers
        ST      R2,SaveR2       ; that are used so that they
        ST      R3,SaveR3       ; can be restored before RET
;
        LD      R2,Newline
L1      LDI     R3,CRTSR        ; Check CRTDR --  is it free?
        BRzp    L1
        STI     R2,CRTDR        ; Move cursor to new clean line
;
        LEA     R1,Prompt       ; Prompt is starting address
                                ; of prompt string
Loop    LDR     R0,R1,#0        ; Get next prompt character
        BRz     Input           ; Check for end of prompt string
L2      LDI     R3,CRTSR
        BRzp    L2
        STI     R0,CRTDR        ; Write next character of
                                ; prompt string
        ADD     R1,R1,#1        ; Increment Prompt pointer
        BRnzp   Loop
;
```

Figure 9.4   Character input service routine

```
Input       LDI      R3,KBSR              ; Has a character been typed?
            BRzp     Input
            LDI      R0,KBDR              ; Load it into R0
L3          LDI      R3,CRTSR
            BRzp     L3
            STI      R0,CRTDR             ; Echo input character
                                          ; to the monitor
;
L4          LDI      R3,CRTSR
            BRzp     L4
            STI      R2,CRTDR             ; Move cursor to new clean line

            LD       R1,SaveR1            ; Service routine done, restore
            LD       R2,SaveR2            ; original values in registers.
            LD       R3,SaveR3
            LD       R7,SaveR7            ; Restore linkage back prior to RET
            RET                           ; Return to calling program
;
SaveR7      .FILL    x0000                ; Location set aside for saving R7
SaveR1      .FILL    x0000
SaveR2      .FILL    x0000
SaveR3      .FILL    x0000
CRTSR       .FILL    xF3FC
CRTDR       .FILL    xF3FF
KBSR        .FILL    xF400
KBDR        .FILL    xF401
Newline     .FILL    x000A                ; ASCII code for newline
Prompt      .STRINGZ "Input a character>"
            .END
```

Figure 9.4   Character input service routine (*Continued*)


```
            .ORIG    x0430               ; System call starting address
            ST       R7, SaveR7          ; Save R7 so we can RET
                                         ; at the bottom
            ST       R1, SaveR1          ; R1 will be used to poll the CRT
                                         ; hardware
; Write the character
TryWrite    LDI      R1, CRTSR           ; Get status
            BRzp     TryWrite            ; Bit 15 on says CRT is ready
WriteIt     STI      R0, CRTDR           ; Write character

; return from trap
Return      LD       R1, SaveR1          ; Restore registers
            LD       R7, SaveR7          ; Restore jump return R7
            RET                          ; Return from trap

CRTSR       .FILL    xF3FC               ; Address of CRT status register
CRTDR       .FILL    xF3FF               ; Address of CRT data register
SaveR1      .FILL    x0000
SaveR7      .FILL    x0000
            .END
```

Figure 9.5   Character output service routine

trap vector. In the case of input, upon completion of TRAP x23, R0 contains the ASCII code of the keyboard character typed. In the case of output, the initiating program must load R0 with the ASCII code of the character it wishes displayed on the monitor and then invoke TRAP x21.

9.1.7   TRAP Routine for Halting the Computer

Recall in Section 4.4, we discussed the RUN latch that is ANDed with the crystal oscillator to produce the clock that controls the operation of the computer. We noted that if that one-bit latch was cleared, the output of the AND gate would be 0, stopping the clock.

Years ago, most ISAs had a HALT instruction for stopping the clock. Given how infrequently that instruction is executed, it seems wasteful to devote an opcode for it. In many modern computers, the RUN latch is cleared by a TRAP routine. In the LC-2, the RUN latch is bit [15] of memory-mapped location xFFFF. Figure 9.6 shows the TRAP service routine for halting the processor, that is, for stopping the clock.

First, registers R7, R1, and R0 are saved—R7 because it contains the linkage back to the running program, and R1, R0 because they are needed by the service routine. Then (lines 08 through 0D), the banner *Halting the machine* is displayed on the monitor. Finally (lines 11 through 14), the RUN latch (MCR[15]) is cleared by ANDing the MCR with 0111111111111111. That is MCR[14:0] remains unchanged, but MCR[15] is cleared.

Question: What instruction (or TRAP service routine) starts the clock? Table A.3 contains a complete list of the operating system service routines available via the TRAP instruction on the LC-2.

9.1.8   Saving and Restoring Registers

One item we have mentioned in passing that we should emphasize more explicitly is the need to save the value in a register if

1.   Its value will be destroyed by some subsequent action, and
2.   We will need to use the value after that subsequent action.

Consider the following example. Suppose we want to input from the keyboard 10 decimal digits, convert their ASCII codes into their binary representations, and store the binary values in 10 successive memory locations, starting at the address **binary**. We write the program fragment shown at the top of page 180 to do the job.

The first step in the program fragment is initialization. We load R6 with the negative of the ASCII template, in order to subtract x0030 easily from each ASCII code. We load R7 with 10, the initial count. Then we execute the loop 10 times, each time getting a character from the keyboard, stripping away the ASCII template, storing the binary result, and testing if we are done. Only the program does not work! Why?

```
                        . . .
01                      LEA    R3,Binary
02                      LD     R6,ASCII    ; Template for line 05
03                      LD     R7,COUNT    ; Initialize to 10
04      AGAIN           TRAP   x23         ; Get keyboard input
05                      ADD    R0,R0,R6    ; Strip ASCII template
06                      STR    R0,R3,#0    ; Store binary digit
07                      ADD    R3,R3,#1    ; Increment pointer
08                      ADD    R7,R7,#-1   ; Decrement COUNT.
09                      BRp    AGAIN       ; More characters?
0A                      BRnzp  NEXT_TASK   ;
0B      ASCII           .FILL  xFFD0       ; Negative of x0030.
0C      COUNT           .FILL  #10
0D      Binary          .BLKW  #10
                        . . .
```

Answer: The TRAP instruction in line 04 wiped out the value ten that was loaded into R7 in line 03. Therefore, the instructions in lines 09 and 0A did not do what they were intended to do!

Exercise: What will the program fragment in lines 01 to 0D do? The problem is that the TRAP instruction, in addition to loading the PC with the starting address of the service routine, **also** stores in R7 the linkage back to the initiating program. And, because we needed the value we had put in R7 before the TRAP instruction, our program executed incorrectly.

The message is, If a value in a register will be needed after something else is stored in that register, we must *save* it before the something else happens and *restore* it before we can subsequently use it. We save a register value by storing it in memory; we restore it by loading it back into the register. In Figure 9.6, line 02 contains the ST instruction that saves R7, line 1B contains the LD instruction that restores R7, and line 23 sets aside the location in memory for storing R7.

The save/restore problem can be handled either by the initiating program before the TRAP occurs, or by the called program (for example, the service routine) after the TRAP executes. We will see in Section 9.2 that the exact same problem exists for another class of calling/called programs, the subroutine mechanism. But we will get to that in Section 9.2.

We use the term *caller-save* if the calling program handles the problem. We use the term *callee-save* if the called program handles the problem. The appropriate one to handle the problem is the one that knows which registers will be destroyed by subsequent actions.

The callee knows which registers it needs to do its job. Therefore, before it starts, it saves those registers with a sequence of stores. After it finishes, it restores those registers with a sequence of loads. And it sets aside locations to save those register values. In Figure 9.6, the HALT routine needs R0 and R1. So, it saves their values with ST instructions in lines 03 and 04, restores their values with LD instructions in lines 19 and 1A, and sets aside locations for these values in lines 21 and 22.

The caller knows what damage will be done by instructions under its control. Again, in Figure 9.6, the caller knows that each instance of the TRAP instruction will destroy what is in R7. So, before the HALT instruction even starts, it saves R7, and before it finishes, it restores R7.

```
01                         .ORIG    xFD70           ; Where this routine resides
02                 ST      R7, SaveR7       ; Save R7 for subsequent  RET
03                 ST      R1, SaveR1       ; R1: a temp for MC register
04                 ST      R0, SaveR0       ; R0 is used as working space
05
06     ; print message that machine is halting
07
08                 LD      R0, ASCIINewLine
09                 TRAP    x21
0A                 LEA     R0, Message
0B                 TRAP    x22
0C                 LD      R0, ASCIINewLine
0D                 TRAP    x21
0E
0F     ; clear bit 15 at $FFFF to stop the machine
10
11                 LDI     R1, MCR          ; Load MC register into R1
12                 LD      R0, MASK         ; R0 = $7FFF
13                 AND     R0, R1, R0       ; Mask to clear the top bit
14                 STI     R0, MCR          ; Store R0 into MC register
15
16     ; return from HALT routine.
17     ; (how can this routine return if the machine is halted above?)
18     ;
19                 LD      R1, SaveR1       ; Restore registers
1A                 LD      R0, SaveR0
1B                 LD      R7, SaveR7       ; Restore trap return
1C                 RET
1D
1E     ; Some constants
1F
20     ASCIINewLine   .FILL    x000A
21     SaveR0         .FILL    x0000
22     SaveR1         .FILL    x0000
23     SaveR7         .FILL    x0000
24     Message        .FILL    "Halting the machine."
25     MCR            .FILL    xFFFF   ; Address of MCR
26     MASK           .FILL    x7FFF   ; Mask to clear the top bit
27                    .END
```

Figure 9.6   Halt service routine for the LC-2

9.2   SUBROUTINE CALLS/RETURNS

We have just seen how a programmer's productivity can be enhanced if he/she does not have to learn details of the I/O hardware, but can rely instead on the operating system to supply the program fragments needed to perform those tasks. And, we also mentioned in passing that it is kind of nice to have the operating system access these device registers so we do not have to be at the mercy of some other user programmer.

   We have seen that a request for a service routine is invoked in the user program by the TRAP instruction and handled by the operating system. Return to the initiating program is obtained via the RET instruction.

It is often useful to be able to invoke a program fragment multiple times within the same program, without having to retype the program fragment in the source code each time. In addition, it is sometimes the case that one person writes a program that requires such fragments and another person writes the fragments.

Finally, one might require a fragment that has been supplied by the manufacturer as part of the operating system. It is almost always the case that the operating system includes collections of such fragments in order to free the programmer from having to write his/her own. These collections are referred to as *libraries*. An example is the Math Library, which consists of fragments to execute such functions as **square root**, **sine**, and **arctangent**.

Such a program fragment is called a *subroutine* (or alternatively, a *procedure*), or in C terminology, a *function*.

9.2.1   The JSR/RET Mechanism

Figure 9.4 provides a simple illustration of a fragment that must be executed multiple times within the same program. Note the three instructions starting at symbolic address L1. Note also the three instructions starting at addresses L2, L3, and L4. Each of these four 3-instruction sequences do the following:

```
LABEL    LDI      R3,CRTSR
         BRzp     LABEL
         STI      Reg,CRTDR
```

Two of the four program fragments store R0 and the other two store R2, but that is easy to take care of, as we will see. The main point is that, aside from the small nuisance of which register is being stored, the four program fragments do exactly the same thing. The pair of instructions **JSR** and **RET** allows us to execute this one 3-instruction sequence multiple times, while requiring us to include it as a subroutine in our program only once.

The JSR instruction acts very much like the TRAP instruction in that it redirects control to a subroutine, while saving a linkage back to the calling program. The PC is loaded with the starting address of the subroutine, while R7 is loaded with the address of the instruction following the JSR instruction in the initiating program. The last instruction in a subroutine is the RET instruction, which loads PC with the contents of R7, thereby returning control to the instruction following the JSR instruction.

An important difference between the JSR instruction and the TRAP instruction, somewhat beyond the scope of this course, is the nature of the routine that the JSR or TRAP instruction is requesting. In the case of the TRAP instruction (as we saw), these routines (called *service routines*) usually involve hardware resources. Generally, these routines are only available as part of the operating system, which has the required degree of privilege because presumably it knows what it is doing. In the case of the JSR instruction, these routines (called *subroutines*) are either written by the same programmer who wrote the program containing the JSR instruction, or they are written by a colleague, or they are provided as part of a library. In all cases, they involve resources that cannot mess up other people's programs, and so we are not concerned that they are part of a user program.

9.2.2   The JSR and JSRR Instructions

The LC-2 specifies two opcodes for calling subroutines, **JSR** and **JSRR**. The only difference between the two instructions is the addressing mode that is used for evaluating the starting address of the subroutine. JSR evaluates its address in **exactly** the same way that LD and ST do. JSRR evaluates its address in **exactly** the same way that LDR and STR do.

JSR (JMP)   The JSR instruction consists of four parts. Bits [15:12] contain the opcode, 0100. Bits [8:0], as is the case for the LD and ST instructions, contain the pgoffset9, which when concatenated with the page number (PC [15:9]), forms the operand address. In the case of the JSR instruction, this is the starting address of the subroutine. Bit [11], called the L (for **Link**) bit indicates whether the linkage back to the address of the instruction following the JSR instruction will be saved. If bit [11] = 1, that address is saved in R7. If bit [11] = 0, that address is not saved. Bits [10:9] contain zeroes.

If the JSR instruction shown below is stored in location x4200, its execution will cause the PC to be loaded with x43F2, and R7 to be loaded with x4201.

15	14	13	12	11	10	9	8	7	6	5	4	3	2	1	0
0	1	0	0	1	0	0	1	1	1	1	1	0	0	1	0
	JSR			L						pgoffset9					

In the above instruction, if bit [11] had contained a 0, R7 would have remained unchanged. The LC-2 assembly language distinguishes two instructions, depending on whether the linkage back is saved: JSR and JMP. If bit [11] = 1, the linkage back is saved in R7 so a subsequent RET instruction can return control to the instruction following the JSR instruction. The assembly language notes that feature with the acronym *JSR*, for **J**ump**S**ub**R**outine. If bit [11] = 0, the linkage is not saved so the program cannot return to the next instruction. The assembly language notes that with the acronym **Ju**MP, which stands for unconditional jump.

Question: Is there any other instruction in the LC-2 that carries out **exactly** the function of the JMP instruction?

JSRR (JMPR)   The JSRR instruction is exactly like the JSR instruction except for the addressing mode. That is, it forms its operand address in the same way the LDR and STR instructions do, rather than the way the LD and ST do. Bits [15:12] contain the opcode 1100, bit [11] contains the L bit, and bits [10:9] contain zeroes.

The starting address of the subroutine is computed by adding ZEXT (bits [5:0]) to the base register (obtained from bits [8:6]).

If R5 contains x3000, and if the **JSRR** instruction shown below is stored in location x420A, its execution will cause the PC to be loaded with x3002, and R7 to be loaded with x420B.

15	14	13	12	11	10	9	8	7	6	5	4	3	2	1	0
1	1	0	0	1	0	0	1	0	1	0	0	0	0	1	0
	JSRR			L				BaseR				index6			

In the above instruction, if bit [11] had contained a 0, R7 would have remained unchanged. As is the case with JSR and JMP, here too the LC-2 assembly language distinguishes two instructions, depending on whether the linkage back is saved: JSRR and JMPR. If bit [11] = 1, the linkage back is saved in R7 so a subsequent RET instruction can return control to the instruction following the JSRR instruction. If bit [11] = 0, the linkage is not saved so the program has no way to return to the instruction automatically following a JMPR instruction.

Question: What important feature does the JMPR instruction provide that the JMP instruction does not provide?

9.2.3   An Example

Let's look again at the keyboard input service routine of Figure 9.4. In particular, let's look at the three-line sequence that occurs at L1, L2, L3, and L4 :

```
LABEL     LDI     R3,CRTSR
          BRzp    LABEL
          STI     Reg,CRTDR
```

Can the JSR/RET mechanism enable us to replace these four occurrences of the same sequence with a single subroutine. *Answer:* Yes, **almost**.

Figure 9.7, our "improved" keyboard input service routine, contains

```
JSR       WriteChar
```

at lines 05, 0B, 11, and 14, and the four-instruction subroutine

```
WriteChar          LDI     R3,CRTSR
                   BRzp    WriteChar
                   STI     R2,CRTDR
                   RET
```

at lines 1D through 20. Note the RET instruction that is needed to terminate the subroutine.

Note the hedging: *almost.* In the original sequences starting at L2 and L3, the STI instruction forwards the contents of R0 (not R2) to the CRTDR. We can fix that easily enough, as follows.

In line 09 of Figure 9.7, we use

```
LDR       R2,R1,#0
```

instead of

```
LDR       R0,R1,#0.
```

This causes each character in the prompt to be loaded into R2. The subroutine Writechar forwards each character from R2 to the CRTDR.

```
01                      .ORIG    x04A0
02      START   ST      R7,SaveR7
03              JSR     SaveReg
04              LD      R2,Newline
05              JSR     WriteChar
06              LEA     R1,PROMPT
07      ;
08      ;
09      Loop    LDR     R2,R1,#0       ; Get next prompt char
0A              BRz     Input
0B              JSR     WriteChar
0C              ADD     R1,R1,#1
0D              BR      Loop
0E      ;
0F      Input   JSR     ReadChar
10              ADD     R2,R0,#0       ; Move char to R2 for writing
11              JSR     WriteChar      ; Echo to monitor
12      ;
13              LD      R2, Newline
14              JSR     WriteChar
15              JSR     RestoreReg
16              LD      R7,SaveR7
17              RET
18      ;
19      SaveR7  .FILL   x0000
1A      Newline .FILL   x000A
1B      Prompt  .STRINGZ   "Input a character>"
1C      ;
1D      WriteChar LDI   R3,CRTSR
1E              BRzp    WriteChar
1F              STI     R2,CRTDR
20              RET
21      CRTSR   .FILL   xF3FC
22      CRTDR   .FILL   xF3FF
```

Figure 9.7   The LC-2 TRAP service routine for character input

In line 10 of Figure 9.7, we insert the instruction

$$\text{ADD} \qquad \text{R2,R0,\#0}$$

in order to move the keyboard input (which is in R0) into R2. The subroutine Writechar forwards it from R2 to the CRTDR. Note that R0 still contains the keyboard input. Furthermore, since no subsequent instruction in the service routine loads R0, R0 still contains the keyboard input after control returns to the user program.

Finally, in line 13 of Figure 9.7, we insert the instruction

$$\text{LD} \qquad \text{R2,Newline}$$

in order to move the "newline" character into R2. The subroutine Writechar forwards it from R2 to the CRTDR.

Figure 9.7 is the actual LC-2 TRAP service routine provided for keyboard input.

```
23        ;
24        ReadChar        LDI       R3,KBSR
25                        BRzp      ReadChar
26                        LDI       R0,KBDR
27                        RET
28        KBSR            .FILL     xF400
29        KBDR            .FILL     xF401
2A        ;
2B        SaveReg         ST        R1,SaveR1
2C                        ST        R2,SaveR2
2D                        ST        R3,SaveR3
2E                        ST        R4,SaveR4
2F                        ST        R5,SaveR5
30                        ST        R6,SaveR6
31                        RET
32        ;
33        RestoreReg      LD        R1,SaveR1
34                        LD        R2,SaveR2
35                        LD        R3,SaveR3
36                        LD        R4,SaveR4
37                        LD        R5,SaveR5
38                        LD        R6,SaveR6
39                        RET
3A        SaveR1          .FILL     x0000
3B        SaveR2          .FILL     x0000
3C        SaveR3          .FILL     x0000
3D        SaveR4          .FILL     x0000
3E        SaveR5          .FILL     x0000
3F        SaveR6          .FILL     x0000
40                        .END
```

Figure 9.7   The LC-2 TRAP service routine for character input (*Continued*)

9.2.4   Another Subroutine: Writing a Character String to the Monitor

Before we leave the example of Figure 9.7, note the code on lines 09 through 0D. This fragment of the service routine is used to write the sequence of characters *Input a character* to the monitor. A sequence of characters is often referred to as a *string of characters* or a *character string*. This fragment is also present in Figure 9.6, with the result that *Halting the machine* is written to the monitor. In fact, it is so often the case that a user program needs to write a string of characters to the monitor that this function is given its own trap vector in the LC-2 operating system. Thus, if a user program requires a character string to be written to the monitor, it need only provide (in R0) a pointer to the starting address of the character string, and then invoke TRAP x22. In LC-2 assembler this TRAP is called *PUTS*.

Thus, PUTS (or TRAP x22) causes control to be passed to the operating system, and the procedure shown in Figure 9.8 is executed. Note that PUTS is the code of lines 09 through 0D, with a few minor adjustments.

```
; puts.asm
; This service routine writes a NULL-terminated string to the console.
;         It services the PUTS service call (TRAP x22).
; Inputs: R0 is a pointer to the string to print.
; Context Information: R0, R1, and R3 are saved, and R7 is lost
;         in the jump to this routine

                .ORIG   x0450       ; Where this ISR resides
                ST      R7, SaveR7  ; Save R7 for later return
                ST      R0, SaveR0  ; Save other registers that
                ST      R1, SaveR1  ; Are needed by this routine
                ST      R3, SaveR3  ;
;
; Loop through each character in the array
;

Loop            LDR     R1, R0, #0  ; Retrieve the character(s)
                BRz     Return      ; If it is 0, done
L2              LDI     R3,CRTSR
                BRzp    L2
                STI     R1, CRTDR   ; Write the character
                ADD     R0, R0, #1  ; Increment pointer
                BR      Loop        ; Do it all over again

; Return from the request for service call
Return          LD      R3, SaveR3
                LD      R1, SaveR1
                LD      R0, SaveR0
                LD      R7, SaveR7
                RET
;
; Register locations
CRTSR           .FILL   xF3FC
CRTDR           .FILL   xF3FF
SaveR0          .FILL   x0000
SaveR1          .FILL   x0000
SaveR3          .FILL   x0000
SaveR7          .FILL   x0000
                .END
```

Figure 9.8   The LC-2 PUTS service routine

9.2.5 Library Routines

We noted early in this section that there are many uses for the JSR/RET mechanism, among them the ability of a user program to call library subroutines that are provided as part of the operating system. Libraries are provided as a convenience to the user programmer. They are legitimately advertised as "productivity enhancers" since they allow the user programmer to use them without having to know or learn much of their inner details. For example, a user programmer knows what a square root is (we abbreviate **SQRT**), and may need to use sqrt(x) for some value x but does not have a clue as to how to write a program to do it, and probably would rather not have to learn how.

A simple example illustrates the point. We have lost our key and need to get into our apartment. We can lean a ladder up against the wall so that the ladder touches the bottom of our open window, 24 feet above the ground. There is a 10-foot flower bed on the ground along the edge of the wall, so we need to keep the base of the ladder outside the flower bed. How big a ladder do we need so that we can lean it against the wall and climb through the window? Or, stated less colorfully, If the sides of a right triangle are 24 feet and 10 feet, how big is the hypotenuse (see Figure 9.9)?

We remember from high school that Pythagoras answered that one for us:

$$c^2 = a^2 + b^2$$

Knowing a and b, we can easily solve for c by taking the square root of the sum of a^2 and b^2. Taking the sum is not hard—the LC-2 ADD instruction will do the job. The square is also not hard; we can multiply two numbers by a sequence of additions. But how does one get the square root? The structure of our solution is shown in Figure 9.10.

The subroutine SQRT has yet to be written. If it were not for the Math Library, the programmer would have to pick up a math book (or get someone to do it for him/her), check out the Newton-Raphson method, and produce the missing subroutine.

However, with the Math Library, the problem pretty much goes away. Since the Math Library supplies a number of subroutines (including SQRT), the user programmer can continue to be ignorant of the likes of Newton-Raphson. The user still needs to know the label of the target address of the library routine that performs

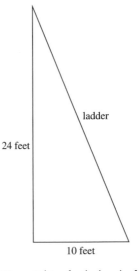

ladder

24 feet

10 feet

Figure 9.9   Solving for the length of the hypotenuse

```
              . . .
              . . .
              LD        R0,SIDE1
              BRz       1$
              JSR       SQUARE
1$            ADD       R1,R0,#0
              LD        R0,SIDE2
              BRz       2$
              JSR       SQUARE
2$            ADD       R0,R0,R1
              JSR       SQRT
              ST        R0,HYPOT
              BRnzp     NEXT_TASK
SQUARE        ADD       R2,R0,#0
              ADD       R3,R0,#0
AGAIN         ADD       R2,R2,#-1
              BRz       DONE
              ADD       R0,R0,R3
              BRnzp     AGAIN
DONE          RET
SQRT          . . .               ; R0 <-- SQRT(R0)
              . . .               ;
              . . .               ; How do we write this subroutine?
              . . .               ;
              . . .               ;
              RET
SIDE1         .BLKW     1
SIDE2         .BLKW     1
HYPOT         .BLKW     1
              . . .
              . . .
```

Figure 9.10   A program fragment to compute the hypotenuse of a right triangle

the square root function, where to put the argument x, and where to expect the result SQRT(x). But these are easy conventions that can be obtained from the documentation associated with the Math Library.

If the library routine starts at addresss SQRT, and the argument is provided to the library routine at R0, and the result is obtained from the library routine at R0, Figure 9.10 reduces to Figure 9.11.

Two things are worth noting:

Thing 1   The programmer no longer has to worry about how to compute the square root function. The library routine does that for him/her.

Thing 2   The pseudo-op .EXTERNAL. We already saw in Section 7.4.2 that this pseudo-op tells the assembler that the label (SQRT) needed to perform the JSRR instruction will be supplied by some other program fragment and will be combined with this program fragment when the *executable image* is produced. The executable image is the binary module that actually executes. The executable image is produced at *link* time.

```
              . . .
              . . .
              .EXTERNAL SQRT
              . . .
              . . .
              LD        R0,SIDE1
              BRz       1$
              JSR       SQUARE
      1$      ADD       R1,R0,#0
              LD        R0,SIDE2
              BRz       2$
              JSR       SQUARE
      2$      ADD       R0,R0,R1
              LD        R4,BASE
              JSRR      R4,#0
              ST        R0,HYPOT
              BRnzp     NEXT_TASK
  SQUARE      ADD       R2,R0,#0
              ADD       R3,R0,#0
  AGAIN       ADD       R2,R2,#-1
              BRz       DONE
              ADD       R0,R0,R3
              BRnzp     AGAIN
  DONE        RET
  BASE        .FILL     SQRT
  SIDE1       .BLKW  1
  SIDE2       .BLKW     1
  HYPOT       .BLKW     1
              . . .
              . . .
```

Figure 9.11   The program fragment of
                   Figure 9.10, using a library
                   routine

This notion of combining multiple modules at link time to produce an executable image is the normal case. You will see concrete examples of this process when we work with the programming language C in the second half of this course.

Most application software requires library routines from various libraries that it would be very inefficient for the typical programmer to produce all of them—assuming the typical programmer could produce such routines in the first place. We have mentioned routines from the Math Library. There are also a number of preprocessing routines for producing "pretty" graphics images. There are other routines for a number of other tasks where it would make no sense at all to have the programmer write the routines from scratch. It is much easier to require only (1) appropriate documentation so that the interface between the library routine and the program that calls that routine is clear, and (2) the use of the proper pseudo-ops such as .EXTERNAL in the source program. The linker can then produce an executable image at link time from the separately assembled modules. Figure 9.12 illustrates the process.

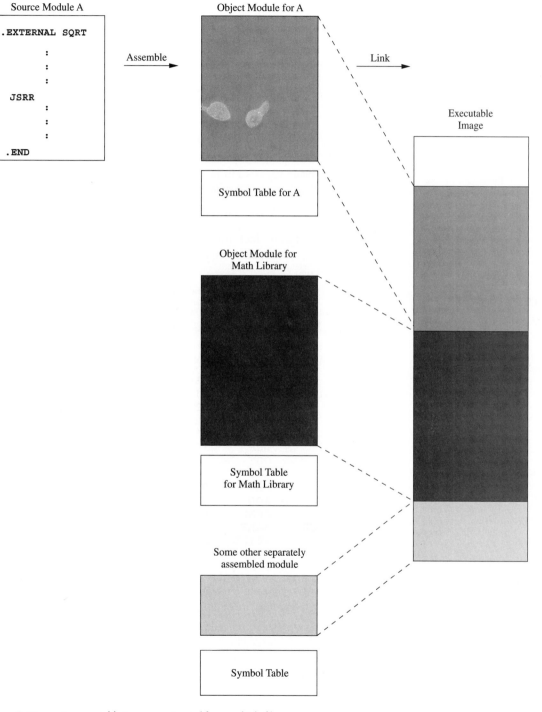

Figure 9.12   An executable image constructed from multiple files

PROBLEMS

9.1. Name some advantages to doing I/O through a trap routine instead of writing the routine yourself each time you would like your program to perform I/O.

9.2. 1. How many TRAP service routines can be implemented in the LC-2? Why?

2. Why must a RET instruction be used to return from a TRAP routine? Why won't a BRnzp (Unconditional BR) instruction work instead?

3. How many accesses to memory are made during the processing of a TRAP instruction? Assume the TRAP is already in the IR.

9.3. Refer to Figure 9.6, the halt service routine.

1. What starts the clock after the machine is HALTed? Hint: How can the halt service routine return after bit 15 of the machine control register is cleared?

2. Which instruction actually halts the machine?

3. What is the first instruction executed when the machine is started again?

4. Where will the RET of the HALT routine return to?

9.4. Consider the following LC-2 assembly language program:

```
            .ORIG    x3000
L1          LEA      R1, L1
            AND      R2, R2, x0
            ADD      R2, R2, x2
            LD       R3, P1
L2          LDR      R0, R1, xC
            OUT
            ADD      R3, R3, -1
            BRZ      GLUE
            ADD      R1, R1, R2
            BRNZP    L2
GLUE        HALT
P1          .FILL    xB
            .STRINGZ "HBoeoakteSmtHaotren!s"
            .END
```

1. After this program is assembled and loaded, what binary pattern is stored in memory location x3005?

2. Which instruction (provide a memory address) is executed after instruction x3005 is executed?

3. Which instruction (provide a memory address) is executed prior to instruction x3006?

4. What is the output of this program?

9.5. Consider the following LC-2 assembly language program:

```
        .ORIG   x3000
        LEA     R0,DATA
        AND     R1,R1,#0
        ADD     R1,R1,#9
LOOP1   ADD     R2,R0,#0
        ADD     R3,R1,#0
LOOP2   JSR     SUB1
        ADD     R4,R4,#0
        BRZP    LABEL
        JSR     SUB2
LABEL   ADD     R2,R2,#1
        ADD     R3,R3,#-1
        BRP     LOOP2
        ADD     R1,R1,#-1
        BRP     LOOP1
        HALT
DATA    .BLKW   10 x0000
SUB1    LDR     R5,R2,#0
        NOT     R5,R5
        ADD     R5,R5,#1
        LDR     R6,R2,#1
        ADD     R4,R5,R6
        RET
SUB2    LDR     R4,R2,#0
        LDR     R5,R2,#1
        STR     R4,R2,#1
        STR     R5,R2,#0
        RET
        .END
```

Assuming that the memory locations at DATA get filled in before the program executes, what is the relationship between the final values at DATA and the initial values at DATA?

9.6. Below is part of a program that was fed to the LC-2 assembler. The program is supposed to read a series of input lines from the console into a buffer, search for a particular character, and output the number of times that character occurs in the text. The input text is terminated by an EOT and is guaranteed to be no more than 1000 characters in length. After the text has been input, the program reads the character to count.

The subroutine labeled COUNT that actually does the counting was written by another individual and is located at address x3500. When called, the subroutine expects the address of the buffer to be in R5 and the address of the character to count to be in R6. The buffer should have a NUL to mark the end of the text. It returns the count in R6.

The OUTPUT subroutine that converts the binary count to ASCII digits and displays them was also written by another individual and is at address x3600. It expects the number to print to be in R6.

Here is the code that reads the input and calls COUNT:

```
            .ORIG   x3000
            LEA     R1,BUFFER
G_TEXT      TRAP    x20         ; Get input text
            ADD     R2,R0,x-04
            BRZ     G_CHAR
            STR     R0,R1,#0
            ADD     R1,R1,#1
            BR      G_TEXT
G_CHAR      STR     R2,R1,#0    ; x0000 terminates buffer
            TRAP    x20         ; Get character to count
            ST      R0,S_CHAR
            LEA     R5,BUFFER
            LEA     R6,S_CHAR
            LD      R4,CADDR
            JSRR    R4,#0       ; Count character
            LD      R4.OADDR
            JSRR    R4,#0       ; Convert R6 and display
            TRAP    x25
CADDR       .FILL   x3500       ; Address of COUNT
OADDR       .FILL   x3600       ; Address of OUTPUT
BUFFER      .BLKW   1001
S_CHAR      .FILL   x0000
            .END
```

There is a problem with this code. What is it, and how might it be fixed? (The problem is *not* that the code for **COUNT** and **OUTPUT** is missing.)

9.7. Recall the machine busy example. Suppose the bit pattern indicating which machines are busy and which are free is stored in memory location x4001. Write subroutines that do the following:

1. Check if no machines are busy, and return 1 if none are busy.

2. Check if all machines are busy, and return 1 if all are busy.

3. Check how many machines are busy, and return the number of busy machines.

4. Check how many machines are free, and return the number of free machines.

5. Check if a certain machine number, passed as an argument in R5 is busy, and return 1 if that machine is busy.

6. Return the number of a machine that is not busy.

9.8. The starting address of the trap routine is stored at the address specified in the trap instruction. Why isn't the first instruction of the trap routine stored at that address instead? Assume each trap service routine requires at most 16 instructions. Modify the semantics of the LC-2 TRAP instruction so that the trap vector provides the starting address of the service routine.

chapter

10

And, Finally . . .

In this chapter, we will complete the ISA-level introduction to computing structures. We have finished our treatment of the ISA of the LC-2. Before moving up in Chapter 11 to programming in C, there are two concepts that we feel it is important to spend some time with: the *stack* and data conversion between ASCII and 2's complement integers. You will find both concepts useful in much of what you do in computer science and engineering, long after this book is just a pleasant memory. After that, we will close out our ISA-level introduction with the design of a calculator, a comprehensive application that makes use of both.

10.1 THE STACK—A VERY IMPORTANT STORAGE STRUCTURE

10.1.1 The Stack—An Abstract Data Type

Throughout your future usage (or design) of computers, you will encounter the storage mechanism known as a *stack*. Stacks can be implemented in many different ways, and we will get to that momentarily. Like everything else in this book, we will attempt to understand how stacks work by building them out of elements we already understand.

But first, it is also important to know that the concept of a stack has nothing to do with how it is implemented. The concept of a stack is the specification of how it is to be *accessed*. That is, the defining ingredient of a stack is that the **last** thing you stored in it is the **first** thing you remove. That is what makes a stack different from everything else in the world. Simply put: Last In, First Out, or LIFO.

In the terminology of computer programming languages, we say the stack is an example of an *abstract data type*. That is, an abstract data type is a storage mechanism that is defined by the operations performed on it and not at all by the specific manner in which it is implemented. In Chapter 19, we will write programs in C that use linked lists, another example of an abstract data type.

10.1.2   Two Example Implementations

A coin holder in the armrest of an automobile is an example of a stack. The first quarter you take to pay the highway toll is the last quarter you previously added to the stack of quarters. As you add quarters, you physically push the earlier quarters down into the coin holder.

Figure 10.1 shows the behavior of a coin holder. Initially, as shown in Figure 10.1a, the coin holder is empty. The first highway toll is 75 cents, and you give the toll collector a dollar. She gives you 25 cents change, a 1995 quarter, which you insert into the coin holder. The coin holder appears as shown in Figure 10.1b.

There are special terms for insertion and removal of elements from a stack. We say we *push* an element onto the stack when we insert it. We say we *pop* an element from the stack when we remove it.

The second highway toll is $4.25, and you give the toll collector $5.00 She gives you 75 cents change, which you insert into the coin holder: first a 1982 quarter, then a 1998 quarter, and finally, a 1996 quarter. Now the coin holder is as shown in Figure 10.1c. The third toll is 50 cents, and you remove (pop) the top two quarters from the coin holder: the 1996 quarter first and then the 1998 quarter. The coin holder is then as shown in Figure 10.1d.

The coin holder is an example of a stack, **precisely** because it obeys the LIFO requirement. Each time you insert a quarter, you do so at the top. Each time you remove a quarter, you do so from the top. The last coin you inserted is the first coin you remove; therefore, it is a stack.

Another implementation of a stack, sometimes referred to as a hardware stack, is shown in Figure 10.2. Its behavior resembles that of the coin holder we just described.

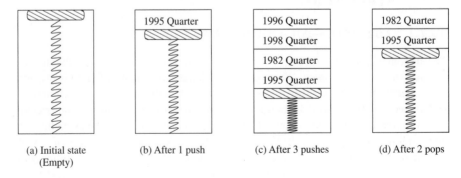

(a) Initial state   (b) After 1 push   (c) After 3 pushes   (d) After 2 pops
(Empty)

Figure 10.1   A coin holder in an auto armrest—example of a stack

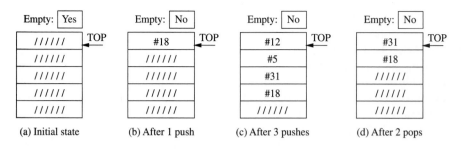

Empty: Yes	Empty: No	Empty: No	Empty: No
////// TOP	#18 TOP	#12 TOP	#31 TOP
//////	//////	#5	#18
//////	//////	#31	//////
//////	//////	#18	//////
//////	//////	//////	//////
(a) Initial state	(b) After 1 push	(c) After 3 pushes	(d) After 2 pops

Figure 10.2   A stack, implemented in hardware—data entries move

It consists of some number of registers, each of which can store an element. The example of Figure 10.2 contains five registers. As each element is added to the stack or removed from the stack, the elements **already** on the stack **move**.

In Figure 10.2a, the stack is initially shown as empty. Access is always via the first element, which is labeled TOP. If the value 18 is pushed on the stack, we have Figure 10.2b. If the three values, 31, 5, and 12, are pushed (in that order), the result is Figure 10.2c. Finally, if two elements are popped from the stack, we have Figure 10.2d. The distinguishing feature of the stack of Figure 10.2 is that, like the quarters in the coin holder, as each value is added or removed, all the values already on the stack move.

10.1.3   Implementation in Memory

By far, the most common implementation of a stack in a computer is as shown in Figure 10.3. The stack consists of a sequence of memory locations along with a mechanism, called the *stack pointer*, that keeps track of the top of the stack, that is, the location containing the most recent element pushed. Each value pushed is stored in one of the memory locations. In this case, the data already stored *does not physically move*.

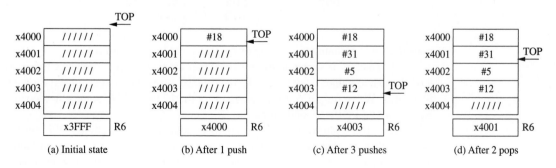

		TOP								
x4000	//////		x4000	#18 TOP		x4000	#18		x4000	#18
x4001	//////		x4001	//////		x4001	#31		x4001	#31 TOP
x4002	//////		x4002	//////		x4002	#5		x4002	#5
x4003	//////		x4003	//////		x4003	#12 TOP		x4003	#12
x4004	//////		x4004	//////		x4004	//////		x4004	//////
	x3FFF	R6		x4000	R6		x4003	R6		x4001	R6
(a) Initial state			(b) After 1 push			(c) After 3 pushes			(d) After 2 pops	

Figure 10.3   A stack, implemented in memory—data entries do not move

In the example shown in Figure 10.3, the stack consists of five locations, x4000 through x4004. R6 is the stack pointer.

Figure 10.3a shows an intially empty stack. Figure 10.3b shows the stack after pushing the value 18, Figure 10.3c shows the stack after pushing the values 31, 5, and 12 in that order. Figure 10.3d shows the stack after popping the top two elements off the stack. Note that those top two elements (the values 5 and 12) are still present in memory locations x4002 and x4003. However, as we will see momentarily, those values 5 and 12 cannot be accessed from the stack.

Push   In Figure 10.3a, R6 contains x3FFF, the address just before the first (BASE) location in the stack. This indicates that the stack is initially empty. We first push the value 18 in the stack, resulting in Figure 10.3b. The stack pointer provides the address of the last value pushed, in this case, x4000, where 18 is stored. Note that the contents of locations x4001, x4002, x4003, and x4004 are not shown. As will be seen momentarily, the contents of these locations are irrelevant since they can never be accessed provided that locations x4000 through x4004 are accessed *only* as a stack.

To push a value on the stack, the stack pointer is incremented, and the value stored. The two-instruction sequence

```
PUSH          ADD      R6,R6,#1
              STR      R0,R6,#0
```

pushes the value contained in R0 onto the stack. Thus, for the stack to be as shown in Figure 10.3b, R0 must have contained the value 18 before the two-instruction sequence was executed.

The three values 31, 5, and 12 are pushed on the stack by loading each in turn into R0, and then executing the two-instruction sequence. In Figure 10.3c, R6 (the stack pointer) contains x4003, indicating that 12 was the last element pushed.

Pop   To pop a value from the stack, the value is read and the stack pointer is decremented. The following two-instruction sequence

```
POP           LDR      R0,R6,#0
              ADD      R6,R6,#-1.
```

pops the value contained in the top of the stack and loads it into R0.

If the stack is as shown in Figure 10.3c and we executed the sequence twice, we would pop two values from the stack. In this case, we would first remove the 12, and then the 5. We would, of course, have to move the 12 from R0 to some other location before calling POP a second time.

Figure 10.3d shows the stack after that sequence of operations. R6 contains x4001, indicating that 31 is now at the top of the stack. Note that the values 12 and 5 are still stored in memory locations x4002 and x4003, respectively. However, since the stack requires that we push by executing the PUSH sequence and pop by executing the POP sequence, we cannot access these two values if we obey the rules. The fancy name for "the rules" is the *stack protocol*.

Underflow   What happens if we now attempt to pop three values from the stack? Since only two values remain on the stack, we would have a problem. Attempting to pop items that have not been previously pushed results in an *underflow* situation. In our example, we can test for underflow by comparing the stack pointer with x3FFF, which would be the contents of R6 if there were nothing left on the stack to pop. If UNDERFLOW is the label of a routine that handles the underflow condition, our resulting POP sequence would be

```
POP       LD        R1,EMPTY        ; EMPTY <-- -3FFF
          ADD       R2,R6,R1        ; Compare stack
          BRz       UNDERFLOW       ; pointer with 3FFF
          LDR       R0,R6,#0
          ADD       R6,R6,#-1
          RET
EMPTY     .FILL     xC001
```

Rather than have the POP routine immediately jump to the UNDERFLOW routine if the POP was unsuccessful, it is often useful to have the POP routine return to the calling program, with the underflow information contained in a register.

A common convention for doing this is to use a register to provide success/failure information. Figure 10.4 is a flowchart showing how the POP routine could be augmented, using R5 to report this success/failure information.

Upon return from the POP routine, the calling program would examine R5 to determine whether the POP completed successfully (R5 = 0), or not (R5 = 1).

Note that since the POP routine reports success or failure in R5, whatever was stored in R5 *before* the POP routine was called is lost. Thus, it is the job of the calling program to save the contents of R5 before the JSR instruction is executed. Recall from Section 9.1.8 that this is an example of a caller-save situation.

The resulting POP routine is shown below. Note that since the instruction immediately preceding the RET instruction sets/clears the condition codes, the calling program can simply test Z to determine whether the POP was completed successfully.

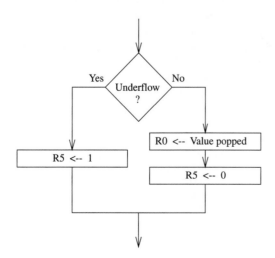

Figure 10.4   POP routine, including test for underflow

```
POP        LD      R1,EMPTY          ; EMPTY <-- -3FFF
           ADD     R2,R6,R1
           BRz     Failure
           LDR     R0,R6,#0
           ADD     R6,R6,#-1
           AND     R5,R5,#0
           RET
Failure    AND     R5,R5,#0
           ADD     R5,R5,#1
           RET
EMPTY      .FILL   xC001
```

Overflow   What happens when we run out of available space, and we try to push a value onto the stack? Since we cannot store values where there is no room, we have an *overflow* situation. We can test for overflow by comparing the stack pointer with (in the example of Figure 10.3) x4004. If they are equal, we have no room to push another value on the stack. If OVERFLOW is the label of a routine that handles the overflow condition, our resulting PUSH sequence would be

```
PUSH       LD      R1,MAX            ; MAX <-- -4004
           ADD     R2,R6,R1
           BRz     OVERFLOW
           ADD     R6,R6,#1
           STR     R0,R6,#0
           RET
MAX        .FILL   xBFFC
```

In the same way that it is useful to have the POP routine return to the calling program with success/failure information, rather than immediately jumping to the UNDERFLOW routine, it is useful to have the PUSH routine act similarly.

We augment the PUSH routine with instructions to store 0 (success) or 1 (failure) in R5, depending on whether or not the push completed successfully. Upon return from the PUSH routine, the calling program would examine R5 to determine whether the PUSH completed successfully (R5 = 0), or not (R5 = 1).

Note again that since the PUSH routine reports success or failure in R5, we have another example of a caller-save situation. That is, since whatever was stored in R5 before the PUSH routine was called is lost, it is the job of the calling program to save the contents of R5 before the JSR instruction is executed.

Also, note again that since the instruction immediately preceding the RET instruction sets/clears the condition codes, the calling program can simply test Z or P to determine whether the POP completed successfully (see PUSH routine below).

```
PUSH       LD      R1,MAX            ; MAX <-- -4004
           ADD     R2,R6,R1
           BRz     Failure
           ADD     R6,R6,#1
           STR     R0,R6,#0
           AND     R5,R5,#0
           RET
Failure    AND     R5,R5,#0
           ADD     R5,R5,#1
           RET
MAX        .FILL   xBFFC
```

10.1.4   The Complete Picture

The POP and PUSH routines allow us to use memory locations x4000 through x4004 as a five-entry stack. If we wish to push a value on the stack, we simply load that value into R0 and execute JSR PUSH. To pop a value from the stack into R0, we simply execute JSR POP. If we wish to change the location or the size of the stack, we adjust BASE and MAX accordingly.

Before leaving this topic, we should be careful to clean up one detail. The subroutines PUSH and POP make use of R1, R2, and R5. If we wish to use the values stored in those registers after returning from the PUSH or POP routine, we had best save them before using them. In the case of R1 and R2, it is easiest to save them in the PUSH and POP routines before using them and then restore them before returning to the calling program. That way, the calling program does not even have to know that these registers are used in the PUSH and POP routines. This is an example of the callee-save situation described in Section 9.1.8. In the case of R5, the situation is different since the calling program does have to know that success or failure is reported in R5. Thus, it is the job of the calling program to save the contents of R5 before the JSR instruction is executed if the calling program wishes to use the value stored there again. This is an example of the caller-save situation.

The final code for our PUSH and POP operations is shown in Figure 10.5.

10.2   ARITHMETIC USING A STACK

10.2.1   The Stack as Temporary Storage

There are computers that use a stack instead of general-purpose registers to store temporary values during a computation. Recall our add instruction

```
ADD      R0,R1,R2
```

takes source operands from R1 and R2 and writes the result of the addition into R0. We call the LC-2 a *three-address machine* because all three locations (the two sources and the destination) are explicitly identified. Some computers use a stack for source and destination operands and explicitly identify *none* of them. The instruction would simply be

```
ADD
```

We call such a computer a stack machine, or a *zero-address machine*. The hardware would know that the source operands are the top two elements on the stack, which would be popped and then supplied to the ALU, and that the result of the addition would be pushed on the stack.

```
;
; Subroutines for carrying out the PUSH and POP functions.  This
; program works with a stack consisting of memory locations x4000
; (BASE) through x4004 (MAX).  R6 is the stack pointer.
;
POP             ST      R2,Save2        ; are needed by POP.
                ST      R1,Save1
                LD      R1,BASE         ; BASE contains -x4000.
                ADD     R1,R1,#1        ; R1 contains -x3FFF.
                ADD     R2,R6,R1        ; Compare stack pointer to x3FFF
                BRz     fail_exit       ; Branch if stack is empty.
                LDR     R0,R6,#0        ; The actual "pop."
                ADD     R6,R6,#-1       ; Adjust stack pointer
                BRnzp   success_exit
PUSH            ST      R2,Save2        ; Save registers that
                ST      R1,Save1        ; are needed by PUSH.
                LD      R1,MAX          ; MAX contains -4004
                ADD     R2,R6,R1        ; Compare stack pointer to x4004
                BRz     fail_exit       ; Branch if stack is full.
                ADD     R6,R6,#1        ; Adjust stack pointer
                STR     R0,R6,#0        ; The actual "push."
success_exit    LD      R1,Save1        ; Restore original
                LD      R2,Save2        ; register values.
                AND     R5,R5,#0        ; R5 <-- success.
                RET
fail_exit       LD      R1,Save1        ; Restore original
                LD      R2,Save2        ; register values.
                AND     R5,R5,#0
                ADD     R5,R5,#1        ; R5 <-- failure.
                RET
BASE            .FILL   xC000           ; BASE contains -x4000.
MAX             .FILL   xBFFC
Save1           .FILL   x0000
Save2           .FILL   x0000
```

Figure 10.5   The stack protocol

To perform an ADD on a stack machine, the hardware would execute two pops, an add, and a push. The two pops would remove the two source operands from the stack, the add would compute their sum, and the push would place the result back on the stack. Note that the pop, push, and add are not part of the ISA of that computer, and therefore not available to the programmer. They are control signals that the hardware uses to make the actual pop, push, and add occur. The control signals are part of the microarchitecture and beyond what we are concentrating on right now. The programmer simply instructs the computer to ADD, and the microarchitecture does the rest.

Sometimes (as we will see in our final example of this chapter), it is useful to process arithmetic using a stack. Intermediate values are maintained on the stack rather than in general-purpose registers, such as the LC-2's R0 through R7. Most general-purpose microprocessors, including the LC-2, use general-purpose registers. Most calculators use a stack.

10.2.2   An Example

For example, suppose you wanted to evaluate $(A + B) \cdot (C + D)$, where A contains 25, B contains 17, C contains 3, and D contains 2, and store the result in E. If the LC-2 had a multiply instruction (we would probably call it MUL), we could use the following program:

```
LD    R0,A
LD    R1,B
ADD   R0,R0,R1
LD    R2,C
LD    R3,D
ADD   R2,R2,R3
MUL   R0,R0,R2
ST    R0,E
```

With a calculator, you could execute the following eight operations:

```
(1)   push      25
(2)   push      17
(3)   add
(4)   push      3
(5)   push      2
(6)   add
(7)   multiply
(8)   pop       E
```

with the final result popped being the result of the computation, that is, 210. Figure 10.6 shows a snapshot of the stack after each of the eight operations.

In Section 10.4, we write a program to cause the LC-2 (with keyboard and monitor) to act like such a calculator. We say the LC-2 simulates the calculator when it executes that program.

But first, let's examine the subroutines we need to conduct the various arithmetic operations.

10.2.3   OpAdd, OpMult, and OpNeg

The calculator we simulate in Section 10.4 has the ability to enter values, add, subtract, multiply, and display results. To add, subtract, and multiply, we need three subroutines:

1. OpAdd, which will pop two values from the stack, add them, and push the result on the stack.

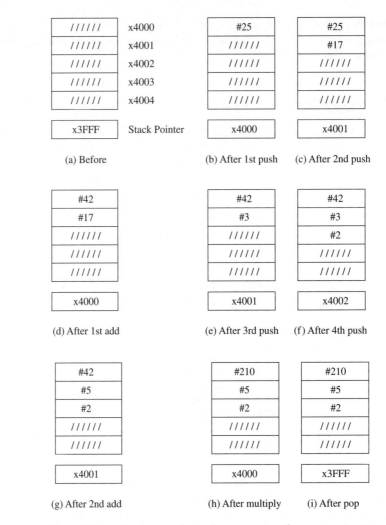

Figure 10.6   Stack usage during the computation of $(25 + 17) \cdot (3 + 2)$

2. OpMult, which will pop two values from the stack, multiply them, and push the result on the stack.

3. OpNeg, which will pop the top value, form its 2's complement negative value, and push the result on the stack.

The OpAdd Algorithm   Figure 10.7 shows the flowchart of the OpAdd algorithm. Basically, the algorithm attempts to pop two values off the stack and, if successful, add them. If the result is within the range of acceptable values (that is, an integer between -999 and $+999$), then the result is pushed on the stack.

There are three things that could prevent the OpAdd algorithm from completing successfully. Each is indicated by a 1 in R5. In each case, the stack is put back to how it was at the start of the OpAdd algorithm. If the first pop is unsuccessful, nothing

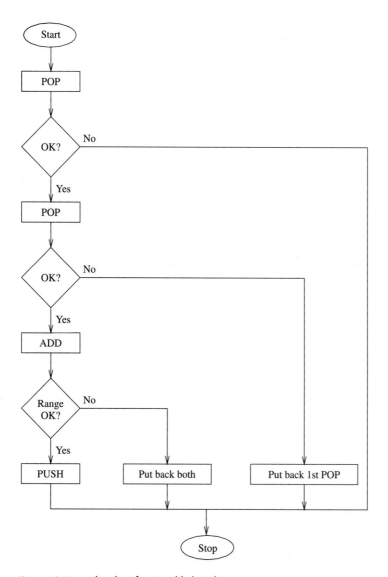

Figure 10.7   Flowchart for OpAdd algorithm

needs to be done since the POP routine leaves the stack as it was. If the second of the two pops reports back unsuccessfully, the stack pointer is incremented, which effectively returns the first value popped to the top of the stack. If the result is outside the range of acceptable values, then the stack pointer is incremented twice, returning both values to the top of the stack.

The OpAdd algorithm is shown in Figure 10.8.

Note that the OpAdd algorithm calls the RangeCheck algorithm. This is a simple test to be sure the result of the computation is within what can be successfully stored in a single stack location. For our purposes, suppose we restrict values to be integers

```
;
;
;       Routine to pop the top two elements from the stack,
;       add them, and push the sum onto the stack.   R6 is
;       the stack pointer.
;
OpAdd        JSR      POP            ; Get first source operand.
             ADD      R5,R5,#0       ; Test if POP was successful.
             BRp      Exit           ; Branch if not successful.
             ADD      R1,R0,#0       ; Make room for second operand
             JSR      POP            ; Get second source operand.
             ADD      R5,R5,#0       ; Test if POP was successful.
             BRp      Restore1       ; Not successful, put back first.
             ADD      R0,R0,R1       ; THE Add.
             JSR      RangeCheck     ; Check size of result.
             BRp      Restore2       ; Out of range, restore both.
             JSR      PUSH           ; Push sum on the stack.
             RET                     ; On to the next task...
Restore2     ADD      R6,R6,#1       ; Increment stack pointer.
Restore1     ADD      R6,R6,#1       ; Increment stack pointer.
Exit         RET
```

Figure 10.8   The OpAdd algorithm

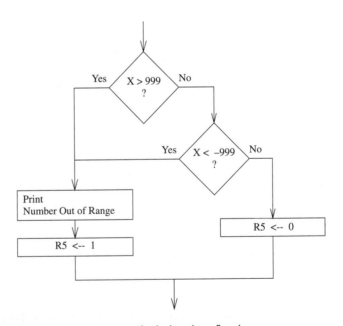

Figure 10.9   The RangeCheck algorithm—flowchart

in the range −999 to +999. This will come in handy in Section 10.4 when we design our home-brew calculator. The flowchart for the RangeCheck algorithm is shown in Figure 10.9. The LC-2 program that implements this algorithm is shown in Figure 10.10.

```
;
;       Routine to check that the magnitude of a value is
;       between -999 and +999.
;
RangeCheck      LD          R5,Neg999
                ADD         R4,R0,R5    ; Recall that R0 contains the
                BRp         BadRange    ; result being checked.
                LD          R5,Pos999
                ADD         R4,R0,R5
                BRn         BadRange
                AND         R5,R5,#0    ; R5 <-- success
                RET
BadRange        ST          R7,Save     ; R7 is needed by TRAP/RET
                LEA         R0,RangeErrorMsg
                TRAP        x22         ; Output character string
                LD          R7,Save
                AND         R5,R5,#0    ;
                ADD         R5,R5,#1    ; R5 <-- failure
                RET
Neg999          .FILL       #-999
Pos999          .FILL       #999
Save            .FILL       x0000
RangeErrorMsg   .FILL       x000A
                .STRINGZ    "Error: Number is out of range."
```

Figure 10.10   The RangeCheck algorithm

The OpMult Algorithm   Figure 10.11 shows the flowchart of the OpMult algorithm, and Figure 10.12 shows the LC-2 program that implements that algorithm. Similar to the OpAdd algorithm, the OpMult algorithm attempts to pop two values off the stack and, if successful, multiplies them. Since the LC-2 does not have a multiply instruction, multiplication is performed as we have done in prior situations as a sequence of adds. Lines 17 to 19 of Figure 10.12 contain the crux of the actual multiply. If the result is within the range of acceptable values, then the result is pushed on the stack.

If the second of the two pops reports back unsuccessfully, the stack pointer is incremented, which effectively returns the first value popped to the top of the stack. If the result is outside the range of acceptable values, which as before will be indicated by a 1 in R5, then the stack pointer is incremented twice, returning both values to the top of the stack.

The OpNeg Algorithm   We have provided algorithms to add and multiply the top two elements on the stack. To subtract the top two elements on the stack, we can use our OpAdd algorithm if we first replace the top of the stack with its negative value. That is, if the top of the stack contains A, and the second element on the stack contains B, and we wish to pop A, B and push B−A, we can accomplish this by first negating the top of stack and then performing OpAdd.

The algorithm for negating the element on the top of the stack, OpNeg, is shown in Figure 10.13.

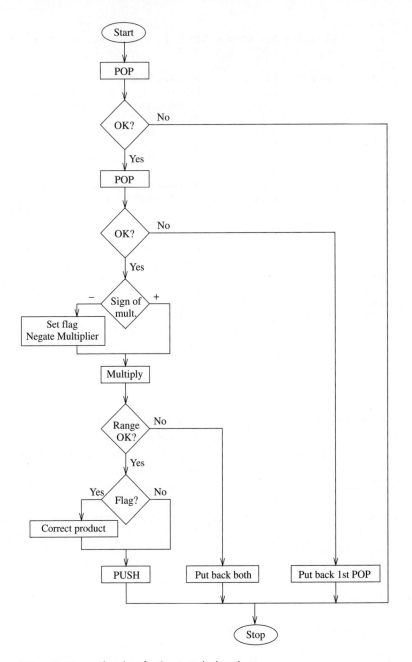

Figure 10.11   Flowchart for the OpMult algorithm

```
01  ;
02  ;      Algorithm to pop two values from the stack, multiply them
03  ;      and if their product is within the acceptable range, push
04  ;      the result on the stack.  R6 is stack pointer.
05  ;
06  OpMult          AND     R3,R3,#0        ; R3 holds sign of multiplier.
07                  JSR     POP             ; Get first source from stack.
08                  ADD     R5,R5,#0        ; Test for successful POP
09                  BRp     Exit            ; Failure
0A                  ADD     R1,R0,#0        ; Make room for next POP
0B                  JSR     POP             ; Get second source operand
0C                  ADD     R5,R5,#0        ; Test for successful POP
0D                  BRp     Restore1        ; Failure; restore first POP
0E                  ADD     R2,R0,#0        ; Moves multiplier, tests sign
0F                  BRzp    PosMultiplier
10                  ADD     R3,R3,#1        ; Sets FLAG: Multiplier is neg
11                  NOT     R2,R2
12                  ADD     R2,R2,#1        ; R2 contains -(multiplier)
13  PosMultiplier   AND     R0,R0,#0        ; Clear product register
14                  ADD     R2,R2,#0
15                  BRz     PushMult        ; Multiplier = 0, Done.
16  ;
17  MultLoop        ADD     R0,R0,R1        ; THE actual "multiply"
18                  ADD     R2,R2,#-1       ; Iteration Control
19                  BRp     MultLoop
1A  ;
1B                  JSR     RangeCheck
1C                  ADD     R5,R5,#0        ; R5 contains success/failure
1D                  BRp     Restore2
1E  ;
1F                  ADD     R3,R3,#0        ; Test for negative multiplier
20                  BRz     PushMult
21                  NOT     R0,R0           ; Adjust for
22                  ADD     R0,R0,#1        ; sign of result
23  PushMult        JSR     PUSH            ; Push product on the stack.
24                  RET
25  Restore2        ADD     R6,R6,#1        ; Adjust stack pointer.
26  Restore1        ADD     R6,R6,#1        ; Adjust stack pointer.
27  Exit            RET
```

Figure 10.12   The OpMult algorithm

```
;
;      Algorithm to pop the top of the stack, form its negative,
;      and push the result on the stack.
;
OpNeg        JSR     POP          ; Get the source operand
             ADD     R5,R5,#0     ; test for successful pop
             BRp     Exit         ; Branch if failure
             NOT     R0,R0
             ADD     R0,R0,#1     ; Form the negative of the source.
             JSR     PUSH         ; Push the result on the stack.
Exit         RET
```

Figure 10.13   The OpNeg algorithm

10.3 DATA TYPE CONVERSION

It has been a long time since we talked about data types. Recall our definition in Section 2.1.2, a data type is a representation of information such that the ISA provides instructions that operate on that representation. We have been exposed to several data types: unsigned integers for address arithmetic, 2's complement integers for integer arithmetic, 16-bit binary strings for logical operations, floating point numbers for scientific computation, and ASCII codes for interaction with input and output devices.

It is important that every instruction be provided with source operands of the data type that the instruction requires. For example, **ADD** requires operands that are 2's complement integers. If the ALU were supplied with floating point operands, the computer would produce garbage results.

It is not uncommon in high-level language programs to find an instruction of the form $A = R + I$ where R (floating point) and I (2's complement integer) are represented in different data types.

If the operation is to be performed by a floating point adder, then we have a problem with I. To handle the problem, one must first convert the value I from its original data type (2's complement integer) to the data type required by the operation (floating point).

Even the LC-2 has this data type conversion problem. Consider a multiple-digit integer that has been entered via the keyboard. It is represented as a string of ASCII characters. To perform arithmetic on it, you must first convert the value to a 2's complement integer. Consider a 2's complement representation of a value that you wish to display on the monitor. To do so, you must first convert it to an ASCII string.

In this section, we will examine routines to convert between ASCII strings of decimal digits and 2's complement binary integers.

10.3.1 Example: The Bogus Program: $2 + 3 = e$

First, let's examine Figure 10.14, a concrete example of how one can get into trouble if one is not careful about keeping track of the data type of each of the values with which one is working.

Suppose we wish to enter two digits from the keyboard, add them, and display the results on the monitor. At first blush, we write the following simple program:

```
TRAP    x23        ; Input from the keyboard.
ADD     R1,R0,#0   ; Make room for another input.
TRAP    x23        ; Input another character.
ADD     R0,R1,R0   ; Add the two inputs.
TRAP    x21        ; Display result on the monitor.
TRAP    x25        ; Halt.
```

Figure 10.14   ADDITION without paying attention to data types

What happens?

Suppose the first digit entered via the keyboard is a 2 and the second digit entered via the keyboard is a 3. What will be displayed on the monitor before the program

terminates? The value loaded into R0 as a result of entering a 2 is the ASCII code
for 2, which is x0032. When the 3 is entered, the ASCII code for 3, which is x0033,
will be loaded. Thus, the ADD instruction will add the two binary strings x0032
and x0033, producing x0065. When that value is displayed on the monitor, it will be
treated as an ASCII code. Since x0065 is the ASCII code for a lowercase *e*, that is
what will be displayed on the monitor.

The reason why we did not get 5 (which, at last calculation, was the correct
result when adding 2 + 3) was that we didn't (*a*) convert the two input characters
from ASCII to 2's complement integers before performing addition, and (*b*) convert
the result back to ASCII before displaying it on the monitor.

Exercise: Correct Figure 10.14 so that it will add 2 one-digit positive integers
and give a one-digit positive sum. Assume that the two digits being added do in fact
produce a single-digit sum.

10.3.2   ASCII to Binary

It is often useful to deal with numbers that require more than one digit to express
them. Figure 10.15 shows the ASCII representation of the three-digit number 295,
stored as an ASCII string in three consecutive LC-2 memory locations, starting at
ASCIIBUFF. R1 contains the number of decimal digits in the number.

Note that in Figure 10.15, a whole LC-2 word (16 bits) is allocated for each
ASCII character. One can (and, in fact, more typically, one does) store each ASCII
character in a single byte of memory. In this example, we have decided to give each
ASCII character its own word of memory in order to simplify the algorithm.

Figure 10.16 shows the flowchart for converting the ASCII representation of
Figure 10.15 into a binary integer. The value represented must be in the range 0 to
+999, that is, it is limited to three decimal digits.

The algorithm systematically takes each digit, converts it from its ASCII code to
its binary code by stripping away all but the last four bits, and then uses it to index
into a table of 10 binary values, each corresponding to the value of one of the 10
digits. That value is then added to R0. R0 is used to accumulate the contributions of
all the digits. The result is returned in R0.

Figure 10.17 shows the LC-2 program that implements this algorithm.

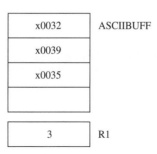

Figure 10.15   The ASCII representation of 295 stored in
consecutive memory locations

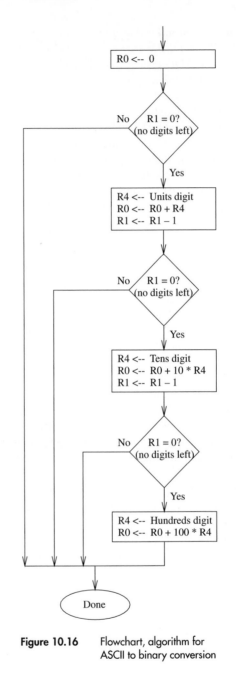

Figure 10.16   Flowchart, algorithm for
ASCII to binary conversion

Exercise: [Very challenging] Suppose the decimal number is arbitrarily long. Rather than store a table of 10 values for the thousands-place digit, another table for the 10 ten-thousands-place digit, and so on, can we design an algorithm to do the conversion without resorting to any tables whatsoever?

```
;
;  This algorithm takes an ASCII string of three decimal digits and
;  converts it into a binary number.  R0 is used to collect the result.
;  R1 keeps track of how many digits are left to process.  ASCIIBUF
;  contains the most significant digit in the ASCII string.
;
ASCIItoBinary   AND     R0,R0,#0          ; R0 will be used for our result
                ADD     R1,R1,#0          ; Test number of digits.
                BRz     DoneAtoB          ; There are no digits
;
                LD      R3,NegASCIIOffset   ; R3 gets xFFD0, i.e., -x0030
                LEA     R2,ASCIIBUFF
                ADD     R2,R2,R1
                ADD     R2,R2,#-1         ; R2 now points to "ones" digit
;
                LDR     R4,R2,#0          ; R4 <-- "ones" digit
                ADD     R4,R4,R3          ; Strip off the ASCII template
                ADD     R0,R0,R4          ; Add ones contribution
;
                ADD     R1,R1,#-1
                BRz     DoneAtoB          ; The original number had one digit
                ADD     R2,R2,#-1         ; R2  now points to "tens" digit
;
                LDR     R4,R2,#0          ; R4 <-- "tens" digit
                ADD     R4,R4,R3          ; Strip off ASCII  template
                LEA     R5,LookUp10       ; LookUp10 is BASE of tens values
                ADD     R5,R5,R4          ; R5 points to the right tens value
                LDR     R4,R5,#0
                ADD     R0,R0,R4          ; Add tens contribution to total
;
                ADD     R1,R1,#-1
                BRZ     DoneAtoB          ; The original number had two digits
                ADD     R2,R2,#-1         ; R2 now points to "hundreds" digit
;
                LDR     R4,R2,#0          ; R4 <-- "hundreds" digit
                ADD     R4,R4,R3          ; Strip off ASCII template
                LEA     R5,LookUp100      ; LookUp100 is hundreds BASE
                ADD     R5,R5,R4          ; R5 points to hundreds value
                LDR     R4,R5,#0
                ADD     R0,R0,R4          ; Add hundreds contribution to total
;
DoneAtoB        RET
NegASCIIOffset  .FILL   xFFD0
ASCIIBUFF       .BLKW   4,x0000
LookUp10        .FILL   #0
                .FILL   #10
                .FILL   #20
                .FILL   #30
                .FILL   #40
                .FILL   #50
                .FILL   #60
                .FILL   #70
                .FILL   #80
                .FILL   #90
;
```

Figure 10.17   ASCII to binary conversion routine

```
LookUp100            .FILL   #0
                     .FILL   #100
                     .FILL   #200
                     .FILL   #300
                     .FILL   #400
                     .FILL   #500
                     .FILL   #600
                     .FILL   #700
                     .FILL   #800
                     .FILL   #900
```

Figure 10.17   ASCII to binary conversion routine
                    (Continued)

10.3.3   Binary to ASCII

Similarly, it is useful to convert the 2's complement integer into an ASCII string so that it can be displayed on the monitor. Figure 10.18 shows the algorithm for converting a 2's complement integer stored in R0 into an ASCII string stored in four consecutive memory locations, starting at ASCIIBUFF. The value initially in R0 is restricted to be in the range -999 to $+999$. After the algorithm completes execution, ASCIIBUFF contains the sign of the value initially stored in R0. The following three locations

```
;
;   This algorithm takes the 2's complement representation of a signed
;   integer, within the range -999 to +999, and converts it into an ASCII
;   string consisting of a sign digit, followed by three decimal digits.
;   R0 contains the initial value being converted.
;
BinarytoASCII   LEA     R1,ASCIIBUFF    ; R1 points to string being generated
                ADD     R0,R0,#0        ; R0 contains the binary value
                BRN     NegSign         ;
                LD      R2,ASCIIplus    ; First store the ASCII plus sign
                STR     R2,R1,#0
                BR      Begin100
NegSign         LD      R2,ASCIIminus   ; First store ASCII minus sign
                STR     R2,R1,#0
                NOT     R0,R0           ; Convert the number to absolute
                ADD     R0,R0,#1        ; value; it is easier to work with.
;
Begin100        LD      R2,ASCIIoffset  ; Prepare for "hundreds" digit
;
                LD      R3,Neg100       ; Determine the hundreds digit
Loop100         ADD     R0,R0,R3
                BRN     End100
                ADD     R2,R2,#1
                BR      Loop100
;
```

Figure 10.18   Binary to ASCII conversion routine

```
End100          STR     R2,R1,#1    ; Store ASCII code for hundreds digit
                LD      R3,Pos100
                ADD     R0,R0,R3    ; Correct R0 for one-too-many subtracts
;
                LD      R2,ASCIIoffset ; Prepare for "tens" digit
;
Begin10         LD      R3,Neg10    ; Determine the tens digit
Loop10          ADD     R0,R0,R3
                BRN     End10
                ADD     R2,R2,#1
                BR      Loop10
;
End10           STR     R2,R1,#2    ; Store ASCII code for tens digit
                ADD     R0,R0,#10   ; Correct R0 for one-too-many subtracts
;
Begin1          LD      R2,ASCIIoffset ; Prepare for "ones" digit
                ADD     R2,R2,R0
                STR     R2,R1,#3
                RET
;
ASCIIplus       .FILL   x002B
ASCIIminus      .FILL   x002D
ASCIIoffset     .FILL   x0030
Neg100          .FILL   xFF9C
Pos100          .FILL   x0064
Neg10           .FILL   xFFF6
```

Figure 10.18   Binary to ASCII conversion routine *(Continued)*

contain the three ASCII codes corresponding to the three decimal digits representing its magnitude.

The algorithm works as follows. First, the sign of the value is determined, and the appropriate ASCII code is stored. The value in R0 is replaced by its absolute value. The algorithm determines the hundreds-place digit by repeatedly subtracting 100 from R0 until the result goes negative. This is next repeated for the tens-place digit. The value left is the ones digit.

Exercise: This algorithm always produces a string of four characters independent of the sign and magnitude of the integer being converted. Devise an algorithm that eliminates unnecessary characters in common representations, that is, an algorithm that does not store leading 0s nor a leading + sign.

10.4   OUR FINAL EXAMPLE: THE CALCULATOR

We conclude Chapter 10 with the code for a comprehensive example: the simulation of a calculator. The intent is to demonstrate the use of many of the concepts discussed thus far, as well as to show an example of well-documented, clearly written code, where the example is much more complicated than what can fit on one or two pages. The calculator simulation consists of 11 separate routines. You are encouraged to study this example before moving on to Chapter 11 and the next topic, High-Level Language Programming.

The calculator works as follows: We use the keyboard to input commands and decimal values. We use the monitor to display results. We use a stack to perform arithmetic operations as described in Section 10.2. Values entered and displayed are restricted to three decimal digits, that is, only values between −999 and +999, inclusive. The available operations are

X Exit the simulation.

D Display the value at the top of the stack.

C Clear all values from the stack.

+ Replace the top two elements on the stack with their sum.

* Replace the top two elements on the stack with their product.

- Negate the top element on the stack.

Enter Push the value typed on the keyboard onto the top of the stack.

Figure 10.19 is a flowchart that gives an overview of our calculator simulation. Simulation of the calculator starts with initialization, which includes setting R6, the stack pointer, to an empty stack. Then the user sitting at the keyboard is prompted for input.

Input is echoed, and the calculator simulation systematically tests the character to determine the user's command. Depending on the user's command, the calculator simulation carries out the corresponding action, followed by a prompt for another command. The calculator simulation continues in this way until the user presses X, signaling that the user is done using the calculator.

Eleven routines comprise the calculator simulation. Figure 10.20 is the main algorithm. Figure 10.21 takes an ASCII string of digits typed by a user, converts it to a binary number, and pushes the binary number on the top of the stack. Figure 10.17 provides the ASCII to binary conversion routine. Figure 10.22 pops the entry on the top of the stack, converts it to an ASCII string, and displays the ASCII string on the monitor. Figure 10.18 provides the binary to ASCII conversion routine. Figures 10.8 (OpAdd), 10.12 (OpMult), and 10.13 (OpNeg) supply the basic arithmetic algorithms using a stack. Figures 10.23 and 10.24 contain versions of the POP and PUSH routines tailored for this application. Finally, Figure 10.25 clears the stack.

Note that a few changes are needed if the various routines are to work with the main program of Figure 10.15. For example, OpAdd, OpMult, and OpNeg must all terminate with

BRnzp NewCommand

instead of RET. Also, some labels are used in more than one subroutine. If the subroutines are assembled separately and certain labels are identified as .EXTERNAL (see Section 9.2.5), then the use of the same label in more than one subroutine is not a problem. However, if the entire program is assembled as a single module, then duplicate labels are not allowed. In that case, one must rename some of the labels (e.g., Restore1, Restore2, Exit, and Save) so that all labels are unique.

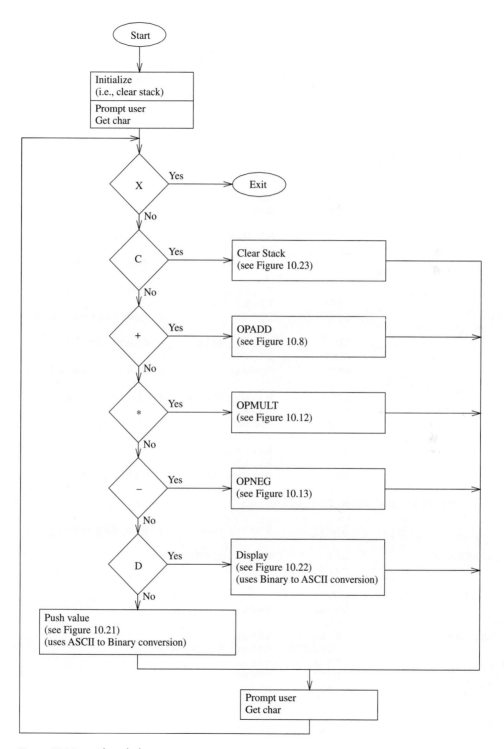

Figure 10.19   The calculator, overview

```
;
;    The Calculator, Main Algorithm
;
                    LEA         R6,StackBase    ; Initialize the Stack.
                    ADD         R6,R6,#-1       ; R6 is stack pointer
                    LEA         R0,PromptMsg
                    PUTS
                    GETC
                    OUT
;
; Check the command
;
Test                LD          R1,NegX         ; Check for X
                    ADD         R1,R1,R0
                    BRz         Exit
;
                    LD          R1,NegC         ; Check for C
                    ADD         R1,R1,R0
                    BRz         OpClear         ; See Figure 10.23
;
                    LD          R1,NegPlus      ; Check for +
                    ADD         R1,R1,R0
                    BRz         OpAdd           ; See Figure 10.8
;
                    LD          R1,NegMult      ; Check for *
                    ADD         R1,R1,R0
                    BRz         OpMult          ; See Figure 10.12
;
                    LD          R1,NegMinus     ; Check for -
                    ADD         R1,R1,R0
                    BRz         OpNeg           ; See Figure 10.13
;
                    LD          R1,NegD         ; Check for D
                    ADD         R1,R1,R0
                    BRz         OpDisplay       ; See Figure 10.22
;
; Then we must be entering an integer
;
                    BRnzp       PushValue       ; See Figure 10.21
;
NewCommand          LEA         R0,PromptMsg
                    PUTS
                    GETC
                    OUT
                    BRnzp       Test
Exit                HALT
PromptMsg           .FILL       x000A
                    .STRINGZ "Enter a command:"
NegX                .FILL       xFFA8
NegC                .FILL       xFFBD
NegPlus             .FILL       xFFD5
NegMinus            .FILL       xFFD3
NegMult             .FILL       xFFD6
NegD                .FILL       xFFBC
```

Figure 10.20   The calculator's main algorithm

```
; This algorithm takes a sequence of ASCII digits typed by the user,
; converts it into a binary value by calling the ASCIItoBinary
; subroutine and pushes the binary value onto the stack.
;
PushValue           LEA         R1,ASCIIBUFF    ; R1 points to string being
                    LD          R2,MaxDigits    ; generated
;
ValueLoop           ADD         R3,R0,xFFF6     ; Test for carriage return
                    BRz         GoodInput
                    ADD         R2,R2,#0
                    BRz         TooLargeInput
                    ADD         R2,R2,#-1       ; Still room for more digits
                    STR         R0,R1,#0        ; Store last character read
                    ADD         R1,R1,#1
                    GETC
                    OUT                         ; Echo it
                    BRnzp       ValueLoop
;
GoodInput           LEA         R2,ASCIIBUFF
                    NOT         R2,R2
                    ADD         R2,R2,#1
                    ADD         R1,R1,R2        ; R1 now contains no. of char.
                    JSR         ASCIItoBinary
                    JSR         PUSH
                    BRnzp         NewCommand
;
TooLargeInput       GETC                        ; Spin until carriage return
                    OUT
                    ADD         R3,R0,xFFF6
                    BRnp        TooLargeInput
                    LEA         R0,TooManyDigits
                    PUTS
                    BRnzp       NewCommand
TooManyDigits       .FILL       x000A
                    .STRINGZ    "Too many digits"
MaxDigits           .FILL       x0003
```

Figure 10.21 The calculator's PushValue routine

```
; This algorithm calls BinarytoASCII to convert the 2's complement
; number on the top of the stack into an ASCII character string, and
; then calls PUTS to display that number on the screen.
;
OpDisplay           JSR         POP             ; R0 gets the value to be displayed
                    ADD         R5,R5,#0
                    BRp         NewCommand      ; POP failed, nothing on the stack.
;
                    JSR         BinarytoASCII
                    LD          R0,NewlineChar
                    OUT
                    LEA         R0,ASCIIBUFF
                    PUTS
                    ADD         R6,R6,#1        ; Push displayed number back on stack
                    BRnzp       NewCommand
NewlineChar         .FILL       x000A
```

Figure 10.22 The calculator's display routine

```
;   This algorithm POPs a value from the stack and puts it in
;   R0 before returning to the calling program.  R5 is used to
;   report success (R5=0) or failure (R5=1) of the POP operation.
;
POP             LEA     R0,StackBase
                NOT     R0,R0
                ADD     R0,R0,#2        ; R0 = -(addr.ofStackBase -1)
                ADD     R0,R0,R6        ; R6 = StackPointer
                BRz     Underflow
                LDR     R0,R6,#0        ; The actual POP
                ADD     R6,R6,#-1       ; Adjust StackPointer
                AND     R5,R5,#0        ; R5 <-- success
                RET
Underflow       ST      R7,Save         ; TRAP/RET needs R7
                LEA     R0,UnderflowMsg
                PUTS                    ; Print error message.
                LD      R7,Save         ; Restore R7
                AND     R5,R5,#0
                ADD     R5,R5,#1        ; R5 <-- failure
                RET
Save            .FILL   x0000
StackBase       .BLKW   9, x0000
StackMax        .FILL   x0000
UnderflowMsg    .FILL   x000A
                .STRINGZ "Error: Too Few Values on the Stack."
```

Figure 10.23   The calculator's POP routine

```
;   This algorithm PUSHes on the stack the value stored in R0.
;   R5 is used to report success (R5=0) or failure (R5=1) of
;   the PUSH operation.
;
PUSH            ST      R1,Save1        ; R1 is needed by this routine
                LEA     R1,StackMax
                NOT     R1,R1
                ADD     R1,R1,#1        ; R1 = - addr. of StackMax
                ADD     R1,R1,R6        ; R6 = StackPointer
                BRz     Overflow
                ADD     R6,R6,#1        ; Adjust StackPointer for PUSH
                STR     R0,R6,#0        ; The actual PUSH
                BR      Success_exit
Overflow        ST      R7,Save
                LEA     R0,OverflowMsg
                PUTS
                LD      R7,Save
                LD      R1, Save1       ; Restore R1
                AND     R5,R5,#0
                ADD     R5,R5,#1        ; R5 <-- failure
                RET
Success_exit    LD      R1,Save1        ; Restore R1
                AND     R5,R5,#0        ; R5 <-- success
                RET
Save            .FILL   x0000
Save1           .FILL   x0000
OverflowMsg     .STRINGZ "Error: Stack is Full."
```

Figure 10.24   The calculator's PUSH routine

```
;
; This routine clears the stack by resetting the stack pointer (R6).
;
OpClear      LEA      R6,StackBase   ; Initialize the Stack.
             ADD      R6,R6,#-1      ; R6 is stack pointer
             BRnzp    NewCommand
```

Figure 10.25   The OpClear routine

PROBLEMS

10.1.   What are the defining characteristics of a stack?

10.2.   What is an advantage to using the model in Figure 10.3 to implement a stack versus the model in Figure 10.2?

10.3.   Write a function that implements another stack function, peek. Peek returns the value of the first element on the stack without removing the element from the stack. Peek should also do underflow error checking. (Why is overflow error checking unnecessary?)

10.4.   How would you check for underflow and overflow conditions if you implemented a stack using the model in Figure 10.2? Rewrite the Push and Pop routines (in Figure 10.5) to model a stack implemented as in Figure 10.2, that is, one in which the data entries move with each operation.

10.5.   Rewrite the Push and Pop routines such that the stack on which they operate holds elements that take up two memory locations each.

10.6.   Rewrite the Push and Pop routines to handle stack elements of arbitrary sizes.

10.7.   The following operations are performed on a stack:

PUSH A, PUSH B, POP, PUSH C, PUSH D, POP, PUSH E,
POP, POP, PUSH F

1.   What does the stack contain after the **PUSH F**?

2.   At which point does the stack contain the most elements? Without removing the elements left on the stack from the previous operations, we perform:

PUSH G, PUSH H, PUSH I, PUSH J, POP, PUSH K,
POP, POP, POP, PUSH L, POP, POP, PUSH M

3.   What does the stack contain now?

10.8.   The input stream of a stack is a list of all the elements we pushed onto the stack, in the order that we pushed them. The input stream from Problem 10.7 was

ABCDEFGHIJKLM

The output stream is a list of all the elements that are popped off the stack, in the order that they are popped off.

1. What is the output stream from Problem 10.7? *Hint:* BDE . . .

2. If the input stream is ZYXWVUTSR, create a sequence of pushes and pops such that the output stream is YXVUWZSRT.

3. If the input stream is ZYXWVUTSR, how many different output streams can be created?

10.9. Describe, in your own words, how the Multiply step of the OpMult algorithm in Figure 10.11 works. Is there a way to make the Multiply step work faster, that is, to have it compute the product using fewer total instructions?

10.10. Correct Figure 10.14 so that it will add 2 one-digit positive integers and produce a one-digit positive sum. Assume that the two digits being added do in fact produce a single-digit sum.

10.11. Modify Figure 10.14, assuming that the input numbers are one-digit positive hex numbers. Assume that the two hex digits being added together do in fact produce a single hex-digit sum.

10.12. The code in Figure 10.17 converts a decimal number represented as ASCII digits into binary. Extend this code to also convert a hexadecimal number represented in ASCII into binary. If the number is preceded by an x, then the subsequent ASCII digits (three at most) represent a hex number, otherwise it is decimal.

10.13. Refer to the flowchart in Figure 10.16 and the code in Figure 10.17. Suppose the decimal number is arbitrarily long. Rather than store a table of 10 values for the thousands-place digit, another table of 10 values for the ten-thousands-place digit, and so on, can we design an algorithm to do the conversion without resorting to any tables whatsoever?

10.14. The code in Figure 10.18 always produces a string of four characters, independent of the sign and magnitude of the integer being converted. Modify the code such that it eliminates unnecessary characters in common representations, that is, leading 0s and a leading + sign.

chapter
11

Introduction to Programming in C

11.1 OUR OBJECTIVE

Congratulations, and welcome to the second half of the book! You have now completed an introduction to the basic underlying structure of computer systems. With this foundation solidly in place, you are now well prepared to move upwards in the levels of transformation, and to deal with the high-level computer programming language called C.

In the second half of this book, we will cover C from a unique perspective. We will rely on your understanding of the low-level computing hardware to teach you high-level programming in C. At every step, with every new high-level concept, we will be able to make a connection to the lower levels of the computer system. From this perspective, nothing will be mysterious. We approach the computer system from the bottom-up in order to reveal that there indeed is no magic going on when you execute the programs you write. It is our belief that with this mystery removed, you will comprehend programming concepts more quickly and deeply and in turn become better programmers.

Let's begin with a quick overview of the first half. In the first 10 chapters, we described the LC-2, a simple computer that has all the important characteristics of a more complex, real computer. A basic idea behind the design of the LC-2 (and indeed, behind all modern computers) is that simple elements are systematically combined to form more sophisticated devices. MOS transistors are connected together to build logic gates. Logic gates are used to build the memory and datapath elements, and these elements are combined to create the LC-2. This systematic connection of simple elements to create something more sophisticated is an important concept that is pervasive throughout computing. You will continue to see many examples of it in this half of the book.

After describing the hardware of the LC-2, we described how to program it in the 1s and 0s of its native machine language. Having gotten a taste of the error-prone and unnatural process of programming in 1s and 0s, we quickly moved to the more user-friendly LC-2 assembly language. We learned how to decompose a programming problem systematically into pieces that could be easily coded on the LC-2. We examined how low-level TRAP subroutines perform commonly needed tasks on behalf of the programmer, tasks such as input and output. The concepts of systematic decomposition and subroutines are important not only for low-level programming but when using high-level languages as well. You will continue to see examples of these concepts many times before the end of the book.

In this half of the book, we go through the major components of the C programming language. The parts of the language not described within the the main body of the text are covered in the C reference manual in Appendix D. Our primary objectives are to introduce fundamental high-level programming constructs—variables, control structures, functions, arrays, pointers, recursion, simple data structures—and instill a good problem-solving methodology for attacking programming tasks. Along the way, we discuss C syntax and programming style often relying on many examples of C code to convey these points.

In this chapter, we dive head first into C by looking at a simple example program. Using this example, we point out some important details that you will need to know in order to start programming in C. But before we look at this example, let's examine why high-level languages are important in the first place and let's look at the techniques by which high-level programs are converted into machine language.

11.2 BRIDGING THE GAP

As computing hardware becomes faster and more powerful, software applications become more complex and sophisticated. New generations of computer systems spawn new generations of software that can do more powerful things than previous generations. As the software gets more sophisticated, the job of developing it becomes more difficult. To keep the programmer from being quickly overwhelmed, it is critical that the process of programming be kept as simple as possible. Automating any part of this process (i.e., having the computer do part of the work) is a welcome enhancement.

As we made the transition from LC-2 machine language in Chapters 5 and 6 to LC-2 assembly language in Chapter 7, you no doubt noticed and appreciated how assembly language greatly simplified programming the LC-2. The 1s and 0s became mnemonics and memory addresses became symbolic labels. The assembler filled some of the *gap* between the algorithm level and the ISA level in the levels of transformation (see Figure 1.6). It would be desirable for the language level to fill more of that gap. High-level languages do just that. Let's look at some ways in which they help.

• **High-level languages allow us to give symbolic names to values.** When programming in machine language, if we want to keep track of the iteration count of a loop, we need to set aside a memory location or a register in which to store the counter value. To access the counter, we need to remember the spot where we last stored it. The process is easier in assembly language because we can assign a meaningful label to the counter's memory location. In a higher level language such as C, the programmer simply assigns the value a name (and, as we will see later, provides the *type* and indicates the *scope*) and the programming language takes care of allocating storage for it and performing the appropriate data movement operations whenever the programmer refers to it. Since most programs contain many values, having such a convenient way to handle values is a critically useful enhancement.

• **High-level languages provide an abstraction of the underlying hardware**. In other words, high-level languages provide a uniform interface independant of underlying ISA or hardware. For example, often a programmer will want to do an operation that is not naturally supported by the instruction set. In the LC-2, there is no one instruction that performs an integer multiplication. Instead, an LC-2 assembly language programmer must write a small piece of code to perform multiplication. The set of operations supported by a high-level language is usually larger than the set supported by the ISA. The language will generate the necessary code to carry out the operation whenever the programmer uses it. The programmer can concentrate on the actual programming task knowing that these high-level operations will be performed correctly and without having to deal with the low-level implementation.

• **High-level languages provide expressiveness**. Because of the systematic way in which programming tasks are broken down (as with systematic decomposition in Chapter 6), several control patterns appear frequently in the code we write. A construct to test a condition and do something if the condition is true or another if the condition is false, for instance, is a very common programming construct. Whenever this construct is needed, the assembly language programmer must generate a sequence of the proper assembly language instructions to carry it out. In high-level languages, these common programming structures have simple expressions fashioned after those we use in English. For example, if we want to **get(Umbrella)** if the condition **isItCloudy** is true, otherwise **get(Sunglasses)** if it is false, then in C we can use the following C *control structure*:

```
if (isItCloudy)
    get(Umbrella);
else
    get(Sunglasses);
```

• **High-level languages enhance code readability**. Since common control structures are expressed using simple, Englishlike statements, the program itself becomes easier to read. One can look at a program in a high-level language and notice loops and decision constructs and understand the code with less effort than with a program written in assembly language. As you will no doubt discover if you have not already, the readability of code is very important in programming. Often as programmers, we are given the task of debugging or building upon someone else's code. If the *syntax* and *semantics* of the language are natural and intuitive to begin with, then understanding code in that language is a much simpler task. The syntax of a programming language defines how its various components must be connected together to form proper code. The semantics of the language specify how the properly formed code behaves.

•   **Many high-level languages provide safeguards against bugs.** By making the programmer adhere to a strict set of rules, the language can make checks as the program is translated or as it is executed. If certain rules or conditions are violated, an error message will direct the programmer to the spot in the code where the bug is likely to exist.

11.3   TRANSLATING HIGH-LEVEL LANGUAGE PROGRAMS

Just as LC-2 assembly language programs need to be translated (or more specifically, assembled) into machine language, so must programs written in a high-level language. After all, the underlying hardware can only execute machine code. How this translation is done depends on the particular high-level language. One translation technique is called *interpretation*. With interpretation, a translation program called an *interpreter* reads in the high-level language program and performs the operations indicated by the programmer. The high-level language program does not directly execute but rather is executed by the interpreter program. The other technique is called *compilation* and the translator, called a *compiler*, completely translates the high-level language program into machine language. The compiled program (i.e., the executable image) can then execute directly on the hardware. Keep in mind that both interpreters and compilers are themselves programs running on the computer system.

11.3.1   Interpretation

With interpretation, a high-level language program is just a set of commands for the interpreter program. The interpreter reads in the commands and carries them out as defined by the language. The high-level language program is not directly executed by the hardware but is in fact just input data for the interpreter. Often, interpreters translate the high-level language program section by section, a single line, command, or subroutine at a time.

For example, the interpreter might read a single line of the high-level language program and directly carry out the effects of that line on the underlying computer system. If the line said, "Take the square root of B and store it into C," then the interpreter will carry out the square root by issuing the correct stream of instructions in the ISA of the computer to perform square root. Once the current line is processed, the interpreter moves on to the next line and executes it. This process continues until the entire high-level language program is done.

High-level languages that are often interpreted include LISP, BASIC, Perl, and Java. Special-purpose languages tend to be interpreted, such as the symbolic math language called Maple, or the numerical math package called Matlab. The LC-2 simulator is also a form of interpreter. Other examples include the UNIX or MS-DOS shells. Both execute your commands as you type them in.

11.3.2   Compilation

With compilation, on the other hand, our high-level language program is translated into machine code that can be directly executed on the hardware. To do this effectively, the compiler must analyze the source program as a larger unit (usually, the entire source file) before producing the translation. A program need only to be compiled once and can be executed many times. Many programming languages including C, C++, and FORTRAN, are typically compiled. The LC-2 assembler is an example of a rudimentary compiler.

In contrast to an interpreter, the compiler *processes* our high-level language program and converts it into machine code. We provide the compiler with a file (or possibly multiple files) containing our program, and it creates a new file containing a machine language version of the code. The compiler does not execute our program (though some sophisticated compilers do execute the program in order to better optimize its performance), but rather only transforms it from the high-level language into the computer's native machine language.

11.3.3   Pros and Cons

There are advantages and disadvantages with either translation technique. With interpretation, developing and debugging a program is usually easier. Interpreters often allow the ability to execute a program one section (single line, for example) at a time. This allows the programmer to examine intermediate results and make code modifications and additions on-the-fly. However, with interpretation, programs take longer to execute as there is an intermediary, the interpreter, which is actually doing the work. With the compiler's assistance, the programmer can produce code that executes more quickly and uses memory more efficiently. Since compilation produces more efficient code, and since it does not require an interpreter, most real-world software, including the software we buy, tends to be produced using compiled languages.

11.4   THE C PROGRAMMING LANGUAGE

The C programming language was developed in 1972 by Dennis Ritchie at Bell Laboratories. C was developed for use in writing compilers and operating systems and, for this reason, the language has a low-level bent to it. The language allows the programmer to manipulate data items at a very low level yet still provides the expressiveness and convenience of a high-level language. It is for these reasons that C is very widely used today as more than just a language to develop compilers and system software.

Because of its low-level approach, C is the correct high-level language for learning about computing systems. C allows us to make clearer connections to the underlying levels in our discussions of basic high-level programming concepts. Learning more advanced concepts, such as object-oriented programming in C++ or Java, is a shorter leap forward once these fundamental, basic concepts are understood.

All the examples and specific details of C presented in this text are based on a standard version of C called ANSI C. As with many programming languages, several variants of C have been introduced throughout the years. In 1989, the American National Standards Institute approved "an unambiguous and machine-independent definition of the language C" in order to standardize the widely popular language. This version is referred to as *ANSI C*. ANSI C is supported by most C compilers. In order to compile and try out the sample code in this text, having access to an ANSI C compiler will be essential.

11.4.1   The C Compiler

The C compiler is the typical mode of translation from a C source program to an *executable image*. Recall from Section 7.4.1 that an executable image is a machine language representation of a program that is ready to be loaded into memory and executed. The entire compilation process involves several components, only one of which is the compiler. Often, the whole mechanism is casually referred to as *the compiler*, because when we use the C compiler, the preprocessor and the linker are often automatically invoked. Figure 11.1 shows how the compilation process is handled by these components.

The Preprocessor   As its name implies, the C preprocessor "preprocesses" the C program before handing it off to the actual compiler. The C preprocessor scans through the source files (the source files contain the actual C program) looking for and acting upon C preprocessor directives. These directives are similar to pseudo-ops in LC-2 assembly language. They instruct the preprocessor to transform the C source file in some controlled manner, for example, by substituting the character string **DAYS_THIS_MONTH** with the string **30** or by inserting the contents of file **stdio.h** into the source file at the current line. All preprocessor directives begin with a pound sign **#** as the first character. All useful C programs rely on the preprocessor. You will soon discover the importance of the preprocessor in C programming. We deal with several important preprocessor directives in detail later in this chapter.

The Compiler   After the preprocessor transforms the input source file, the program is ready to be handed over to the actual compiler. The compiler transforms the preprocessed program into an *object module*. Recall from Section 7.4.2 that an object module is the machine code for one section of the program. There are two major phases of compilation: analysis, where the source program is broken down or *parsed*

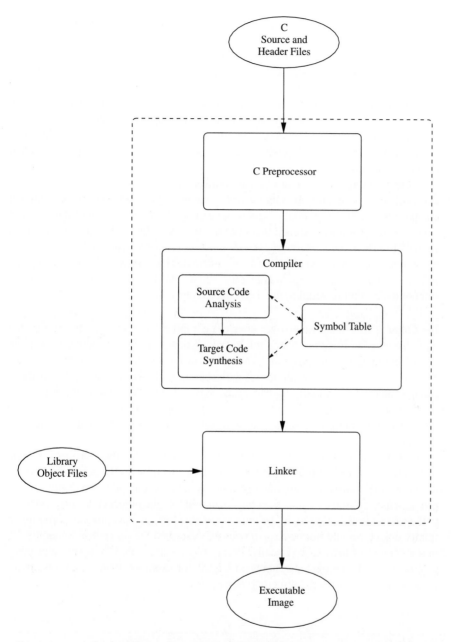

Figure 11.1 The dotted box indicates the overall compilation process—the preprocessor, the compiler, and the linker. This process is often casually referred to as the C compiler, even though the compiler is only one part of it. The inputs are C source and header files and library object files. The output is an executable image.

into it constituent parts, and synthesis, where a machine code version of the program is generated. Often, the two portions of a compiler corresponding to these two phases are called the compiler's front end and the compiler's back end. It is the job of the front end to read in, parse, and build an internal representation of the original program. The back end generates machine code and, if directed, attempts to optimize this code to run more quickly and efficiently on the particular computer for which it is targeted. Each of these two phases is typically divided into subphases where a specific task, such as parsing, register allocation, or instruction scheduling, is accomplished. Some compilers generate assembly code and use an assembler to complete the translation to machine code.

One of the most important internal bookkeeping mechanisms the compiler uses in translating a program is the *symbol table*. A *symbol table* is the compiler's internal mapping between the symbolic names appearing in the program and the items to which the programmer assigned them (items such as variables and functions, which we will discuss in the next few chapters). The C compiler's symbol table is similar to the symbol table maintained by the LC-2 assembler (see Section 7.3.3), but slightly different information is kept within each entry. We'll examine the C compiler's symbol table in more detail in the next chapter.

The Linker   The linker takes over after the compiler has translated the source file into object code. It is the linker's job to link together all object modules to form an executable image of the program. The output of the linker is an executable image. The executable image is a version of the program that can be loaded into memory and executed by the underlying hardware. When you click on the icon for the web browser on your computer, you are instructing the operating system to read the web browser executable image from your hard drive and load it into memory and start executing it.

Often, C programs rely upon library routines. Library routines perform common and useful tasks (such as I/O) and are prepared for general use by the programmers who developed the system software (the operating system and compiler, for example). If a program uses a library routine, then the linker will find the object code corresponding to the routine and link it within the final executable image. This process of linking in library objects should not be new to you; we described the process in Section 9.2.5 in the context of the LC-2. Usually, library objects are stored in a particular place depending on the computer system. In UNIX, for example, many common library objects can be found in the directory `/usr/lib`.

11.5   A SIMPLE EXAMPLE

We are now ready to start our exploration of the C programming language. Many of the new C concepts we present will be coupled with LC-2 code generated by an LC-2 C compiler. In some cases, we will describe what actually happens when this code is

```
/*
 *
 *    Program Name : countdown, our first C program
 *
 *    Description  : This program prompts the user to type in a
 *    positive number and counts down from that number to 0,
 *    displaying each number along the way.
 *
 */

/* The next two lines are preprocessor directives */
#include <stdio.h>
#define STOP 0

/* Function    : main                                             */
/* Description : prompts user for input, then display countdown   */
main()
{
    /* Variable declarations */
    int counter;                    /* Hold intermediate count values */
    int startPoint;                 /* Starting point for count down  */

    /* Prompt the user for input */
    printf("===== Countdown Program =====\n");
    printf("Enter a positive number: ");
    scanf("%d", &startPoint);

    /* Count down from the input number to 0 */
    for (counter = startPoint; counter >= STOP; counter--)
        printf("%d\n", counter);
}
```

Figure 11.2   A program prompts the user for a decimal number and counts down from that number to 0

executed. Keep in mind that you are not likely to be using an LC-2–based computer but rather one based on a real ISA. For example, if you are using a Windows machine, then it is likely that your compiler will generate IA-32 code, not LC-2 code.

Although many of the examples and specific details will be for C, we will point out things that are fundamental to most high-level programming languages. Many of the examples are complete programs you can compile and execute. When examples are not complete programs, we refer to them as *code segments*.

Let's begin by diving head first into a simple C example. Figure 11.2 shows its *source code*. We will use this example to point out some important structural features of C and to jump-start the process of learning C. The example is a simple one: It prompts the user to type in a number and then counts down from that number to 0.

You are encouraged to compile, execute, and test out this program. At this point, it is not important to understand completely what each individual line of code does. There are, however, several aspects of this program that are useful to understand now. Understanding these aspects will help you in writing your first few C programs and help you better comprehend the examples that will be presented in the subsequent chapters. We'll focus on four aspects: the function **main**, the code's comments and programming style, preprocessor directives, and the I/O function calls.

11.5.1   The Function **main**

The function **main** begins at the line containing **main()** and ends at the closing brace on the last line of the source listing. These lines of the source code consitute a *function definition* for a function named **main**. What were called subroutines in LC-2 assembly language programming (which we discussed in Chapter 9) are referred to as *functions* in C. Functions are a very important part of C, and we will devote all of Chapter 14 to them. In C, the function **main** serves a special purpose: It is where execution of the program begins. Every C program, therefore, requires a function named **main**.

In this example, the code for function **main** can be broken down into two components. The first component contains the variable *declarations* for the function. Two variables, one called **counter** and the other **startPoint**, are created for use within the function **main**. Variables are a very useful high-level programming device, giving us a way to symbolically name the values we use within our programs. More on variables in the next chapter.

The second component contains the *statements* of the function. These statements express the actions the program is to perform. For all C programs, execution starts in **main** and progresses, statement by statement, until the last statement in **main** is completed.

In this example, the first grouping of statements displays a message and prompts the user to input a positive number. The output generated by this section looks as follows:

```
===== Countdown Program =====
Enter a positive number:
```

Once the user enters a number, the program enters the last statement, which is a **for** loop (a type of iteration construct that we will discuss in Chapter 13). The loop counts downward from the number typed by the user to 0. For example, if the user entered the number 5, the program's output would look as follows:

```
===== Countdown Program =====
Enter a positive number: 5
5
4
3
2
1
0
```

Notice in this example that many lines of the source code are terminated by semicolons, **;** . In C, semicolons are used to terminate declarations and statements and are necessary for the compiler to break the program down unambiguously into its constituent components. More on C syntax in the next chapter.

11.5.2   Formatting, Comments, and Style

C is a generally free-format language. The amount of spacing between words and between lines within a program does not change the meaning of the program. The programmer is free to structure the program in whatever manner he/she sees fit while obeying the syntactic rules of C. Programmers use this freedom to format the code in a manner that makes it easier to read. In the example program, the **for** loop is indented in such a manner that the statement being iterated is easier to identify. Also in the example, notice the use of blank lines to separate different regions of code in the function **main**. These blank lines are not necessary but are used to provide visual separation of the code. Often, statements that together accomplish a larger task are grouped together into a visually identifiable unit. The C code examples throughout this book use a conventional indentation style typical for C.

Commenting code in C is different than in LC-2 assembly language. Comments in C begin with **/*** and end with ***/**. They can span multiple lines. Notice that this example program contains several lines of comments, some on a single line, some spanning multiple lines. Comments are expressed differently from one programming language to another (for example, comments in C++ begin with the sequence **//** and extend to the end of the line), yet their purpose is always the same: They provide a way for the programmer to describe what his/her code does.

Properly commenting code is an important part of the programming process. Good comments enhance code readability, allowing someone not familiar with the code to understand it more quickly (and someone once familiar with the code to recall it sooner). Since programming tasks often involve working in teams, code very often gets shared or borrowed between programmers. In order to work effectively on a programming team, or to write code that is worth sharing, it is important to adopt a good commenting style early on.

A good commenting style involves providing information at the beginning of each source file that describes the code contained within it, the date it was last modified, and by whom. Furthermore, each function (see function **main** in the example) should have a brief description of what the function accomplishes, along with a description of its inputs and outputs. Also, comments are usually interspersed within the code to explain the intent of the various sections of the code. Too many comments, in particular ones that provide no additional information beyond what is obvious, can clutter up the program and make it harder to read.

11.5.3   The C Preprocessor

We have briefly mentioned the C preprocessor in Section 11.4.1. Recall that it transforms the original C program before it is handed off to the compiler. Our simple example contains two commonly used preprocessor directives: **#define** and **#include**.

The C examples in this book rely only on these two directives; Appendix D describes several others.

The **#define** directive is a simple yet powerful directive. It instructs the C preprocessor to replace occurrences of any text that matches X with text Y, a process formally referred to as *macro substitution*. In the example, the **#define** causes the text **STOP** to be substituted with the text **0**. So the following source line

```
for (counter = startPoint; counter >= STOP; counter--)
```

is transformed (internally, only between the preprocessor and compiler) into

```
for (counter = startPoint; counter >= 0; counter--)
```

Often, the **#define** directive is used to create fixed values within a program. Below are several examples.

```
#define NUMBER_OF_STUDENTS 25
#define MAX_LENGTH      80
#define LENGTH_OF_GAME 300
#define PRICE_OF_GASOLINE 1.49
#define COLOR_OF_EYES  brown
```

With **#define**, we can symbolically refer to the price of gasoline as **PRICE_OF_GASOLINE**. No surprise that **PRICE_OF_GASOLINE** is referred to as a *symbolic constant*. If the price of gasoline were to change, we simply modify the value that substitutes for the macro **PRICE_OF_GASOLINE**. This often proves to be very convenient—the value can be used multiple times within the program, yet only one spot in the code needs to be modified if the value changes. Notice that the last example is slightly different. In this example, one string of characters **COLOR_OF_EYES** is being substituted for another, **brown**. The common programming style is to use uppercase for the symbolic name. More examples and a more precise description of **#define** can be found in Appendix D.

The **#include** directive instructs the preprocessor literally to insert another file into the source file. Essentially, the **#include** directive itself is replaced by the contents of another file. At this point, the usefulness of this command may not be completely apparent, but as we progress deeper into the C language, you will understand how *C header files* can be used to contain **#defines** and declarations that are useful among multiple source files.

For instance, all programs that use the C I/O functions must include the I/O library's header file **stdio.h**. This file defines some relevant information about the I/O functions in the library. The preprocessor directive, **#include <stdio.h>** is used to insert the header file before compilation begins.

There are two variations of the **#include** directive:

```
#include <stdio.h>
#include "program.h"
```

The first variation uses angle brackets (< >) around the filename. This tells the preprocessor that the header file can be found in a predefined directory, usually determined by the configuration of the system and which contains many system-related and library-related header files, such as **stdio.h**. Often, we want to include headers files we have created ourselves. The second variation, using double quotes (**" "**) around the filename, instructs the preprocessor that the header file can be found in the same directory as the C source file.

More information about the **#include** command can be found in Appendix D.

Notice that none of the preprocessor macros end with a semicolon. Since **#define** and **#include** are preprocessor directives and not C statements, they are required to be terminated by semicolons.

11.5.4   Input and Output

We close this chapter by pointing out how to perform input and output from a C program. We describe these functions at a high level now and save the details for Chapter 18, when we introduce enough background material to understand C I/O down to a low level. Since all useful programs perform some form of I/O, learning the I/O capabilities of C is an important first step. In C, I/O is performed by library functions, similar to the IN and OUT trap routines provided by the LC-2 system software.

Three lines of the example program perform output using the C library function **printf**. The function **printf** performs output to the standard output device, which is typically defined to be the monitor. It requires a *format string* in which we can provide two things: (1) text to print out and (2) specifications on how to print out values. The text is simply the text we want output to the standard output device when the **printf** is executed. For example, the statement

```
printf("43 is a prime number");
```

prints out the following text to the output device.

```
43 is a prime number.
```

In addition to text, it is often useful to print out values generated within a program. The specifications within the format string indicate how we want these values to be printed out. Let's examine a few examples:

```
printf("%d is a prime number.", 43);

printf("43 plus 59 as a character is %d.", 43 + 59);
printf("43 plus 59 in hexadecimal is %x.", 43 + 59);
printf("43 plus 59 as a character is %c.", 43 + 59);

printf("The wind speed is %d km/hr.", windSpeed);
```

The first example contains the format specification **%d** in its format string. It causes the value listed after the format string to be *embedded* in the output as a decimal number in place of the **%d**. So the output of the first example would be

```
43 is a prime number.
```

The subsequent examples show other variants of **printf**. In the second **printf**, the format specification causes the value 102 to be embedded in the text. In the third example, the format specification **%x** causes 66 (because 102 equals x66) to be embedded in the message. Similarly, in the fourth example, the format specification of **%c** displays the value interpreted as an ASCII character which, in this case, would be lowercase **f**. The output of this statement would be

```
43 plus 59 as a character is f.
```

What is important to notice is that the binary pattern being supplied to **printf** after the format string is the same for all three statements. Here, **printf** interprets the binary pattern 0110 0110 first as a decimal number, then as a hexadecimal number, and finally as an ASCII character. The C output function **printf** manages the process of converting the bit pattern into the proper sequence of ASCII characters based on the format sepecifications we provide it. Table E.1 contains a list of format specifications that can be used with **printf**—all format specifications begin with the percent sign, **%**.

The final example demonstrates a very commonly used form of **printf**. Here, a value generated during the execution of the program, in this case the variable **windSpeed**, is output as a decimal number. The value displayed depends on the value of **windSpeed** when this particular line of code is executed. More on variables in the next chapter.

If you were to execute a program containing the five preceding **printf** statements, you would notice that they are all displayed on one single line, in other words, without any line breaks. If we want line breaks to appear, we must put them explicitly within the format string in the places we want them to occur. New lines, tabs, and other special characters require the use of a special backslash \ sequence. For example, to print a new line character (and thus cause a line break), we use the special sequence **\n**. We can rewrite the **printf** statements above as such:

```
printf("%d is a prime number.\n", 43);
printf("43 plus 59 in decimal is %d.\n", 43 + 59);
printf("43 plus 59 in hexadecimal is %x.\n", 43 + 59);
printf("43 plus 59 as a character is %c.\n", 43 + 59);

printf("The wind speed is %d km/hr.\n", windSpeed);
```

Notice that each format string ends by printing the new line character **\n**. Each subsequent **printf** will begin on a new line. Table D.1 contains a list of other special characters that are useful when generating output. The output generated by these five statements would look as follows. Of course, we are assuming that it is not a very windy day.

```
43 is a prime number.
43 plus 59 in decimal is 102.
43 plus 59 in hexadecimal is 66.
43 plus 59 as a character is f.
The wind speed is 2 km/hr.
```

In our sample program in Figure 11.2, `printf` appears three times in the source. The first two versions display only text and no values (thus, they have no format specifications). The third version prints out the value of variable `counter`. Generally speaking, we can display as many values as we like within a single `printf`. The number of format specifications (for example, `%d`) must equal the number of values that follow the format string.

Question: What happens if we replaced the third `printf` in the sample program with the following? The expression "`startPoint - counter`" calculates the value of `startPoint` minus the value of `counter`.

```
printf("%d %d\n", counter, startPoint - counter);
```

Modify the source code, compile, and execute the program and you will notice that the program now counts both up and down.

Having dealt with output, we now turn to the corresponding input function `scanf`. The function `scanf` performs input from the standard input device, which is the keyboard by default. It requires a format string (similar to the one required by `printf`) and a list of variables into which the values retrieved from the input device will be stored. The function `scanf` reads input from this device and, according to the conversion characters in the format string, converts the input and assigns the converted values to the variables listed. Let's look at an example.

In the sample program, we use `scanf` to read in a single decimal number using the format specification `%d`. Recall from our discussion on LC-2 keyboard input, the value received via the keyboard is in ASCII. The format specification `%d` informs `scanf` to expect a sequence of *numeric* ASCII keystrokes (i.e., the digits 0 to 9). This sequence is interpreted as a decimal number and converted into an integer. The resulting binary pattern will be stored in the variable called `startPoint`. The function `scanf` automatically performs type conversions (in this case, from ASCII to integer) for us! The format specification `%d` is one of several that can be used with `scanf`. Table E.2 lists them all. There are specifications to read in a single character, a floating point value, an integer expressed as a hexadecimal value, and so forth.

A very important thing to remember about `scanf` is that variables that are being modified by the `scanf` function (for example, `startPoint`) must be preceded by an `&` character. This may seem a bit mysterious, but we discuss the reason for this notation in Chapter 17. As we see in that chapter, not all variables require the `&`. We make the distinction between which variables require the ampersand and which do not once we have covered the concept of pointers.

Below are several more examples of `scanf` including one that reads in two decimal numbers. Notice that the variables being modified by `scanf` are all preceded by an ampersand.

```
/* Reads in a character and stores it in nextChar */
scanf("%c", &nextChar);

/* Reads in a floating point number and stores it in
   variable radius */
scanf("%lf", &radius);

/* Reads two decimal numbers and stores them in variables
   length and width */
scanf("%d %d", &length, &width);
```

PROBLEMS

11.1. Describe some problems or inconveniences you found when programming in lower level languages.

11.2. How do higher level languages help reduce the tedium of programming in lower level languages?

11.3. What are some disadvantages to programming in a higher level language?

11.4. What is the difference between interpretation and compilation?

11.5. What is the primary advantage to writing in a compiled language?

11.6. Another advantage of compilation over interpretation is that a compiler can perform "global" optimizations. Since a compiler can examine the entire program when generating machine code, it can reduce the amount of computation by analyzing what the program is attempting to do.

The following algorithm performs some very straightforward arithmetic based on value typed at the keyboard. It outputs a single result.

1. Get W from the keyboard
2. $X \leftarrow W + W$
3. $Y \leftarrow X + X$
4. $Z \leftarrow Y + Y$
5. Print Z to the screen

1. An interpreter would execute the program statement by statement. In total, five statements would execute. At least how many arithmetic operations would the interpreter perform on behalf of this program? State what the operations would be.

2. A compiler would analyze the entire program before generating machine code, and possibly optimize the code. If the underlying ISA were capable of all arithmetic operations (i.e., addition, subtraction, multiplication, division), at least how many operations would be needed to carry out this program? State what the operations would be.

11.7. Is the LC-2 simulator a compiler or an interpreter?

11.8. For this question refer to Figure 11.1.

1. Describe the input to the C preprocessor.

2. Describe the input to the C compiler.

3. Describe the input to the linker.

11.9. What happens if we changed the second-to-last line of the program in Figure 11.2 from:

1. `printf("%d\n", counter);`

2. `printf("%c\n", counter + 'A');`

3. `printf("%d\n%d\n", counter, startPoint + counter);`

11.10. The following lines of C code appear in a program. What will be the output of each `printf` statement?

```
#define LETTER '1'
#define ZERO    0
#define NUMBER 123

printf("%c", 'a');

printf("x%x", 12288);

printf("$%d.%c%d\n", NUMBER, LETTER, ZERO);
```

11.11. The function **scanf** reads in a character from the keyboard and the function **printf** prints it out. What do the following two statements accomplish?

```
scanf("%c", &nextChar);
printf("%d\n", nextChar);
```

11.12. Describe a program (at this point we do not expect you to be able to write working C code) that reads a decimal number from the keyboard and prints out its hexadecimal equivalent.

chapter

12

Variables and Operators

12.1 INTRODUCTION

In this chapter, we cover two basic concepts of programming, variables and operators. *Variables* hold the values upon which a program acts, and *operators* are the programming devices for manipulating these values. Variables and operators together allow the programmer to more easily express the computation that constitutes the real work done by a program.

Let's look at an example that contains both. The following line of C code increments the value of **score** by 3. The addition operator **+** is used to add 3 to the value of the variable **score**. This new value is then assigned using the assignment operator **=** back to **score**.

```
score = score + 3;
```

We closely examine many more examples of variables and operators throughout this chapter. The first part of this chapter is devoted to variables. Here we cover the basic types of variables available in C and how they are declared and used. In the second part, we cover C's rich set of operators. Along the way, we go through several complete programming examples.

12.2 VARIABLES

A value is any data item upon which a program performs an operation. Examples of values include the iteration counter for a loop, or an input value entered by a user, or the partial sum of a series of numbers that are being added together. Managing these values is a central concept in programming. When programming in LC-2 assembly language, we explicitly stored these values in memory or in a register and wrote code to move them from place to place in order to operate on them.

Because values are such an important and elementary programming concept, high-level languages attempt to make the process of managing them easier on the programmer. High-level languages allow the programmer to refer to values *symbolically*, by a name rather than its storage location. LC-2 assembly language allows labeling of memory locations, giving us a way to refer symbolically to values we placed in memory. High-level languages go a step further—they automatically find a place in memory to store these symbolically named values and generate the proper sequence of data movement operations whenever we refer to them. The programmer can then focus on writing the program and need not worry about where in memory to store a value or about juggling the value between memory and the registers. In high-level languages, these symbolically named values are called *variables*.

In order to manage the process of tracking our variables for us, the high-level language translator (the C compiler, for instance) needs to know several characteristics about each variable in the program. It needs to know, obviously, the symbolic name with which we will refer to the variable. It needs to know what type of information the variable will contain, where in the program the variable will be used, and how long the value of the variable will persist. In most languages, C included, this information is provided by the variable's *declaration*.

Let's look at an example. The following declares a variable called **echo** that will contain an integer value.

```
int echo;
```

The compiler then reserves an integer's worth of memory for **echo** (sometimes, the compiler can optimize the program such that **echo** is stored in a register and therefore does not require a memory location, but that is a subject for later). Whenever **echo** is referred to in the subsequent C code, the compiler will generate the appropriate machine code to access it.

In C, all variables must be declared before they can be used. In fact, most variables must be declared at the beginning of the *block* in which they appear (global variables are the exception to this rule. We will deal with them momentarily). In C, a *block* is any subsection of a program beginning with the open brace character { and ending with the closing brace character }. If a block is to contain any local variables, they must be declared immediately following the block's open brace.

For example, in the C program in Figure 12.1, the integer variable **echo** is declared within the block that contains the code for function **main**. Typically, most nonglobal variables are declared at the beginning of the function in which they are used (such as **echo** in the example). This program gets a number from the keyboard and displays it on the screen.

As we mentioned, a variable's declaration assists the compiler in managing the storage of that variable. In C, a variable's declaration conveys three pieces of information to the compiler: the variable's *identifier*, its *type*, and its *scope*. The first two of these, the C compiler, gets explicitly from the variable's declaration. In the case

```
#include <stdio.h>

main()
{
    int echo;

    scanf("%d", &echo);
    printf("%d\n", echo);
}
```

Figure 12.1   A simple C program that *echos* a number typed at the keyboard back to the screen.

of the example declaration `int echo;`, the identifier is `echo`, and the variable is of integer type, as indicated by the `int` preceding its name. The third piece of information is the variable's scope. The scope of a variable is the region of the program in which the variable is accessible. It is implicitly specified by the place in the code where the declaration occurs.

Before we take a look at identifiers, type, scope in more detail, we note a fourth attribute called *storage class*. C variables can be either of automatic or static storage class. The storage class of a variable determines whether or not a variable loses its value when the block that contains it has been completed. Automatic variables lose their values when their block completes; static variables retain their values between invocations. In C, global variables are of static storage class, that is, they retain their value until the program completes. Nonglobals (variables declared within a block) are by default of automatic storage class. We will say a little more on storage class shortly, but for the most part, we leave a more complete treatment of this topic for the Appendix D.3.4

12.2.1   Three Basic Data Types: `int`, `char`, `double`

By now, you should be very familiar with the following concept: the meaning of a particular pattern of bits depends on the data type imposed on the pattern. For example, the binary pattern `0110 0110` might represent the lowercase **f** or it might represent the decimal number 102. What it represents depends on whether we treat the pattern as an ASCII data type or as a 2's complement integer data type.

A variable's declaration informs the compiler about the variable's type. The compiler uses a variable's type information to allocate it a proper amount of storage for the variable. Also, its type indicates how operations on the variable are to be performed at the lower levels. For instance, performing an addition on two integer variables can be done on the LC-2 with one ADD instruction. If the two variables were double-precision floating-point numbers, then our LC-2 compiler would have to generate a small sequence of instructions to perform the addition because no single LC-2 instruction performs a floating-point addition.

In C are three commonly used data types: signed integers, floating-point numbers, and characters. Variables of these types can be created with the type specifiers `int`, `char`, and `double` (which is short for *double*-precision floating point).

int

The `int` type specifier declares a signed integer value. The internal representation and range of values of an `int` depends on the ISA of the computer and the specifics of the compiler being used. In the LC-2, for example, an `int` is a 16-bit 2's complement integer that can represent numbers between −32,768 and −32,767. If you use an IA-32-based PC, then on your computer, an `int` is a 32-bit 2's complement number that can represent numbers between −2,147,483,648 and +2,147,483,647. In most cases, an `int` is a 2's complement integer in the word length of the underlying ISA.

We've seen several examples of integers in C already. Here's another. The following line of code declares an integer variable called **numberOfSeconds**. When the compiler sees this declaration, the compiler sets aside enough storage (in the case of the LC-2, one memory location) for this variable.

```
int numberOfSeconds;
```

It should be no surprise that variables of integer type appear frequently in programs. They often conveniently represent the real world data we want our programs to process. For example, in an application that tracks whale migration, we can use an integer to represent the sizes of pods of grey whales seen off the California coast. Integers are also useful for program control. An integer can be useful as the iteration counter for a counter-controlled loop.

char

The `char` type specifier declares a variable whose data value represents a character.

Below are two examples. The first declaration creates a variable named **lock**. The second one declares **key**. The second declaration is slightly different; it also contains an **initializer**. In C, variables can be set to an initial value as they are declared using an optional initializer in the declaration. In this example, the variable **key** will have the initial value of the ASCII code for uppercase *Q*. Also notice that the uppercase *Q* is surrounded by single quotes ' '. In C, characters that are to be interpreted as ASCII *literals* are surrounded by single quotes.

What initial value will the variable **lock** have? We'll address this issue shortly.

```
char lock;
char key  = 'Q';
```

The following C program (Figure 12.2) shows a particularly tedious way to print the message "July 4" on the screen.

```
#include <stdio.h>

main()
{
    char monthChar1 = 'J';
    char monthChar2 = 'u';
    char monthChar3 = 'l';
    char monthChar4 = 'y';

    int  day = 4;

    printf("%c%c%c%c %d\n", monthChar1, monthChar2,
                            monthChar3, monthChar4, day);
}
```

Figure 12.2   A tedious way to display a message to the output device

Although eight bits are sufficient to hold an ASCII character, for purposes of making the examples in this textbook less cluttered, all **char** variables will be allocated 16 bits by our LC-2 C compiler.

double

The type specifier **double** allows us to declare variables of the floating-point type we examined in Section 2.7.1. Floating-point numbers allow us to conveniently deal with numbers that have fractional components or numbers that are very large or very small. Recall from our previous discussion in Section 2.7.1 that floating-point numbers have three parts: a sign, a fraction, and an exponent.

Here are three example declarations of variables of type **double**:

```
double costPerLiter;
double electronsPerSecond;
double averageTemp;
```

As with **int**s and **char**s, we can also optionally initialize a floating-point number along with its declaration. Before we can completely describe how to initialize floating-point variables, we must first discuss how to represent floating-point *literals* in C. Floating-point literals are represented containing either a decimal point or an exponent, or both, as demonstrated in the example code below. The exponent is signified by the character *e* or *E* and can be positive or negative. It represents the power of 10 by which the fractional part (the part that precedes the *e* or *E*) is multiplied. Note that the exponent must be an integer value. For more information on floating-point literals, see Appendix D.2.4.

```
double onePointOne = 1.1;          /* This is 1.1    */
double oneHundredTen = 1.1E2;      /* This is 110.0  */
double oneHundred = 1E2;           /* This is 100.0  */
double oneTenth = 1E-1;            /* This is 0.1    */
double minusOneTenth = -1E-1;      /* This is -0.1   */
```

Another floating-point type specifier in C is called **float**. It declares a single-precision floating-point variable; **double** creates one that is double-precision. Recall from our previous discussion on floating-point numbers in Chapter 2 that the precision of a floating-point number depends on the number of bits of the representation allocated to the fraction. In C, depending on the compiler and the ISA, a **double** may have more bits allocated for the fraction than a **float**, but never fewer. However, unlike the name implies, the **double** does not necessarily have twice the number of bits of precision than a **float**. The size of the **double** type is dependent upon the ISA and the compiler. Usually, a **double** is 32 bits long, in compliance with the IEEE 754 floating point standard.

Variations of These Three Types   C gives the programmer the ability to specify larger or smaller sizes for these three basic type. The modifiers **long** and **short** can be attached to **int** with the intent of extending or shortening the default size. For example, a **long int** can declare an integer that has twice the number of bits as a regular **int**, thereby allowing us to represent a larger range of numbers. Similarly, the specifier **long** can be attached to the **double** type to create a larger floating-point type (if supported by the particular system) with greater range and precision.

Likewise, the modifier **short** can be used to create variables that are smaller than the default size. The **short** modifier can be useful when trying to conserve on memory space when handling data that does not require the full range of the default data type. The following example demonstates how the variations are declared:

```
long double particlesInUniverse;
long int worldPopulation;
short int ageOfStudent;
```

Because the size of the three basic C types is closely tied to the types supported by the underlying ISA, many compilers only support these modifiers **long** and **short** if the computer's ISA supports these size variations. Even though a variable can be declared as a **long int**, it may be equivalent to a regular **int** if the underlying ISA has no support for longer versions of the integer data type. See Appendix D.3.3 for more examples and additional information on **long** and **short**.

Another useful variation of the basic **int** data type is the unsigned integer. We can declare an unsigned integer using the **unsigned** type modifier. With unsigned integers, all bits are used to represent nonnegative integers (i.e., postive numbers and zero). In the LC-2 for instance, which has 16-bit integers, an unsigned integer has a value between 0 and 65535.

The following is an example of an unsigned integer:

```
unsigned int numberOfDays;
```

12.2.2   Identifiers

Most high-level languages have flexible rules for the variable names (more generally known as *identifiers*) that can be chosen within a program. C allows you to create identifiers composed of upper- and lowercase letters of the alphabet, digits, and the underscore character _. Only letters and the underscore character, however, can begin an identifier. An identifier can be of any length, but only the first 31 characters are used by C compiler to differentiate variables—only the first 31 characters matter to the compiler.

Here are several tips on standard C naming conventions: Variables beginning with an underscore (e.g., `__index__`) conventionally are used only in special library code. Variables are almost never declared in all uppercase letters. The convention of all uppercase is used solely for symbolic values created using the preprocessor directive `#define`. See Section 11.5.3 for examples of symbolic constants. Programmers like to visually partition variables that consist of multiple words. In this book, we use uppercase (e.g., `wordsPerSecond`). Other programmers prefer underscores (e.g., `words_per_second`).

Giving variables meaningful names is important for writing good code. Variable names should be chosen to reflect a characteristic of the value they represent, allowing the programmer to recall more easily what the value is used for. For example, a value used to count the number of words the person at the keyboard types per second could be called `wordsPerSecond`.

There are certain *keywords* in C, which have special meaning and are therefore restricted from being used as identifiers. A list of C keywords can be found in Appendix D.2.6. One keyword we have encountered already is `int`, and therefore we cannot use `int` as a name. Having a variable named `int` would not only be confusing to someone trying to read through the code but possibly to the compiler as well. The compiler may not be able to determine whether a particular `int` refers to the variable or to the type specifier.

12.2.3   Scope: Globals and Locals

The third piece of information the compiler gleans from a variable's declaration is its scope. The scope of a variable defines the region of the program in which the variable is accessible. Some variables can be accessed throughout the program; these are referred to as *global variables*. Some variables can only be accessed in smaller regions of a program. These variables are local to the region in which they are accessible.

In C, the programmer does not explicitly state the scope of a variable. Instead the compiler infers the scope from the place in the program a variable is declared. Scope in C is a fairly simple matter. Either a variable is *local* if it is declared within a block or it is *global* because it is declared outside of all blocks. Recall from our previous discussion of blocks in C that a block is a section of code beginning with an open brace { and ending with a closing brace }.

Local variables are accessible only within the block in which they are declared. In C, by default, local variables are of the automatic storage class, meaning they lose their storage (and thus their value) once the block they are local to completes execution. More on this later.

Global variables, on the other hand, can be accessed and modified from any block within the program. They retain their storage throughout the duration of the program. Globals can be extremely helpful in certain programming situations. Because they can be modified from anywhere within the program, they can add complications later when debugging or changing the code. They should therefore be used with caution. For this reason, novice programmers are often instructed not to use global variables.

The following program contains both a global variable and a variable local to the function **main**:

```
#include <stdio.h>

int itsGlobal = 0;       /* This variable is global */

main()
{
  int itsLocal = 1;      /* This is local to main */

  printf("Global %d Local %d\n", itsGlobal, itsLocal);
}
```

Now that we have discussed globals and locals, let's answer the question we asked earlier: What initial value will a variable have if it has no initializer? In C, by default, local variables start up with an unknown value, that is, the storage location they are assigned is not cleared and thus contains whatever last value was stored there. More generally, in C, variables of the automatic storage class are uninitialized. Local variables by default are of the automatic storage class. Global variables are initialized to 0 when the program starts execution. More generally, all variables of the static storage class (globally declared variables are always static) are initialized to 0.

Even with these simple scoping rules, more complex situations are possible in C. Variables declared at the beginning of a function are local to the function, and they can be accessed only within the body of the function. But also, a programmer can create a sub-block of C code anywhere within a function (we will see how sub-blocks are useful in the next chapter). Variables declared within a sub-block are local to that sub-block.

It is possible, and sometimes useful, to declare two different variables with the same name within different blocks of the same function. For instance, it might be convenient to use the name **count** for the counter variable for several different loops within the same program. C allows this, as long as the different variables sharing the same name are declared in seperate blocks.

Let's look at an example. The C program in Figure 12.3 is similar to the previous program except we have added a sub-block within **main**. Within this sub-block, we have declared a new variable **itsLocal**. It has the same name as the local variable declared at the beginning of **main**. Execute this program and you will notice that when the sub-block is executing the prior version of **itsLocal** is hidden. It becomes visible again once the sub-block is done executing, which is at the third **printf**.

```
#include <stdio.h>

int itsGlobal = 0;        /* This variable is global */

main()
{
  int itsLocal = 1;       /* This variable is local to main */

  printf("Global %d Local %d\n", itsGlobal, itsLocal);

  {
    int itsLocal = 2;     /* This is local to this sub-block */

    printf("Global %d Local %d\n", itsGlobal, itsLocal);
  }

  printf("Global %d Local %d\n", itsGlobal, itsLocal);
}
```

Figure 12.3   A C program that demonstrates C's scoping rules

12.2.4   More Examples

Let's examine a couple more examples of variable declarations in C.

The following examples demonstrate declarations of the three basic types discussed in this chapter. Some declarations have no initializers; some do. Note how floating point and character literals are expressed in C.

```
double width;
double pType = 9.44;
double mass = 6.34E2;
double verySmallAmount = 9.1094E-31;
double veryLargeAmount = 7.334553E102;
int average = 12;
int windChillIndex = -21;
int unknownValue;
int mysteryAmount;
char car    = 'A';
char number = '4';
```

In C, it is also possible to have literals that are hexadecimal values. A literal that has the prefix `0x` will be treated as a hexademical number. In the following examples, both integer variables are initialized using hexadecimal literals.

```
int programCounter = 0x3000;
int sevenBits = 0xA1234;
```

Shown below are some sample variations of the three basic types:

```
long int ounces;
short int gallons;
long double veryVeryLargeNumber = 4.12936E361;
unsigned int sizeOfClass = 900;
float oType = 9.24;
float tonsOfGrain = 2.998E8;
```

For the sake of a more complete coverage of C syntax, we present the following example. In this line of code, four integer variables are declared on a single line. Each different variable is separated by a comma and the complete declaration ends with a semicolon. Though this form of declaration is legal in C, such style is typically discouraged. Instead, the preferred style is to declare each variable on a separate line.

```
int i, j, k, l;
```

12.2.5   Symbol Table

In Chapter 7, we examined how the assembler systematically keeps track of labels within an assembly program by using a symbol table. Like the assembler, the C compiler keeps track of variables through a symbol table in order to translate the original program into machine code. Whenever the compiler reads a variable declaration, it creates a new entry in its symbol table corresponding to the variable being declared. The entry contains enough information for the compiler to manage the storage allocation for the variable and generation of the proper sequence of machine code whenever the variable is used in the program. Each symbol table entry for a variable contains (1) its name, (2) its type, (3) the place in memory the variable has been allocated storage, and (4) an identifier to indicate the block in which the variable is declared (i.e., the scope of the variable). Over the next few chapters, we will reveal how the compiler uses this information to manage variables.

Figure 12.4 shows the symbol table entries corresponding to the variables declared in the example program from the previous chapter. The declarations from this program are shown below. There are two variables declared, thus two entries are added to the symbol table for them. Both have a scope local to **main**. The variable **i** is an integer variable and is stored at offset 3. The variable **start** is also of type **int** and is stored at offset 4. More on what these offsets mean in a moment.

```
int counter;
int startPoint;
```

12.2.6   Allocating Space for Variables

There are two regions of memory in which C variables are allocated storage: the *global data section* and the *run-time stack*.[1] The global data section is where all global

---

[1] For examples in this textbook, all variables will be assigned a memory location. However, real compilers perform code optimizations that attempt to allocate variables in registers. Since registers take less time to access than memory, the program will run faster if frequently accessed values are put into registers. Compilers can sometimes even remove unused variables altogether.

Symbol Table

Name	Type	Offset	Scope
counter	int	3	main

Name	Type	Offset	Scope
startPoint	int	4	main

Figure 12.4   The compiler's symbol table when it compiles the program from Chapter 11

variables are stored. More generally, it is where variables of the static storage class are allocated. The run-time stack is where local variables (of the default automatic storage class) are allocated storage.

The offset field in the symbol table provides the precise information about where in memory variables are actually stored. The offset field simply indicates how many locations from the beginning of the section a variable is allocated storage.

For instance, if a global variable **earth** has an offset of 4 and the global data section started at memory location 0x8000, then **earth** would be stored in location 0x8004. For all our examples in this text, we use R5 to contain the address of the beginning of the global data section. Loading the variable **earth** into R3, for example, can be accomplished with the following LC-2 instruction:

LDR   R3, R5, #4

If **earth** were, instead, a local variable with an offset of 5, then it would be stored five locations from the top of the run-time stack. For all our examples in this text, we use R6 to contain the address of the top of the run-time stack. Said another way, R6 is the stack pointer for the run-time stack. To load the value of **earth** into R4, we would use the following LC-2 instruction:

LDR   R4, R6, #5

A preview of things to come: since the run-time stack is a stack as we described in Chapter 10, items will get pushed on and popped off as different functions are called during execution. Because of this, our stack pointer R6 will change. We go through the whole mechanism of how R6 get properly updated when we discuss functions in Chapter 14. For now, let's assume that R6 always contains the correct top of stack.

Figure 12.5 shows the organization of memory when a program is running. The program itself occupies a region of memory, so does the run-time stack and the global data section. There is another region as well which we will describe in upcoming chapters. Notice that R5 is anchored. It always contain the same address. It "points" to the beginning of the global data section. R6 points to the current top of the run-time stack, and the PC points to the current instruction in the executable image.

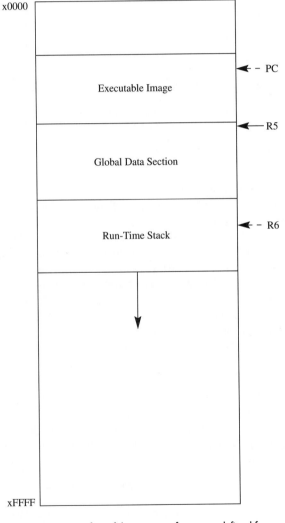

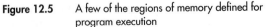

Figure 12.5   A few of the regions of memory defined for program execution

```
#include <stdio.h>

#define RADIUS  15.0                    /* This value is in centimeters */

main()
{
  /* Variable declarations */
  const double pi = 3.14159;
  double area;
  double circumference;

  /* Calculations */
  area = pi * RADIUS * RADIUS;          /* area of a circle = pi*r^2  */

  circumference = 2 * pi * RADIUS;  /* circumference of a        */
                                    /* circle = 2*pi*r           */

  /* Output */
  printf("The area of a circle with radius %f cm is %f cm^2\n",
         RADIUS, area);

  printf("The circumference of a circle with radius %f cm is %f cm^2\n",
         RADIUS, circumference);
}
```

Figure 12.6   A C program that computes the area and circumference of a circle with a radius of 15 cm

12.2.7 Literals, Constants, and Symbolic Values

In C, variables can also be declared as *constants* by adding the **const** qualifier before the type specifier. These constants are really variables whose values do not change during the execution of a program. For example, in writing a program that calculates the area and circumference of a circle of a given radius, it might be useful to create a floating point constant called **pi** initialized to the value 3.14159. Figure 12.6 contains an example of such a program.

You might be able to tell by quickly scanning this code that it calculates the area and circumference of a circle. We have not covered the C multiplication ***** and assignment operators **=** yet (we cover them in the next section of this chapter), however, the actions carried out by this code are very straightforward. The statement

$$\text{area = pi * RADIUS * RADIUS;}$$

causes the value of **pi** times **RADIUS** times **RADIUS** to be stored in the variable **area**. Similarly the statement

$$\text{circumference = 2 * pi * RADIUS;}$$

causes the value of 2 times **pi** times **RADIUS** to be stored in the variable **circumference**. In the **printf** function calls, these values, which are floating-point values, are printed out using the **%f** format specification.

We use this example to point out a distinction between three types of constant values that often appear in C code. *Literal* constants are unnamed values that appear *literally* in the source code. In the circle example, the values **2** and **3.14159** are examples of *literal* constants. An example of the second type of constant value is **pi**, which is declared as a constant value using a variable declaration with the **const** qualifier. The third type of constant value is created using the preprocessor directive **#define**, an example of which is the symbolic value **RADIUS**. All three types create values that do not change during the execution of a program.

When and where to use a literal or a constant or a symbolic value is an important matter of programming style. All three can be used interchangeably, but each has a specific use.

Literals are used only in situations where the resulting code is more clear with the values explicitly stated. For example, in the statement that calculates the circumference in the code in Figure 12.6, the literal value **2** is a part of the equation because we are accustomed to seeing the formula for a circle's circumference as $2\pi r$. Another example is a statement to increment a counter variable (e.g., **i = i + 1;**). The amount of the increment appears literally in the source code.

The more important distinction is between declared constants and symbolic values. Declared constants are used for things we traditionally think of as constant values, which are values that never change. The constant **pi** is an example. Physical constants such as the speed of light, or the number of days in a week, are conventionally represented by declared constants.

Values that stay constant during a single execution of the program but which might be different from user to user, or possibly from invocation to invocation, are represented by symbolic values using **#define**. Such values can be thought of as parameters for the program. For example, **RADIUS** in the program above can be changed and the program recompiled, then reexecuted.

12.3 OPERATORS

All high-level languages have a set of operators that allow the programmer to manipulate variables. Some operators perform arithmetic, some perform logic functions, and others perform comparisons between values. These operators allow the programmer to express a computation in a more natural, convenient, and compact way than by expressing it as a sequence of assembly-language instructions.

The first thing to realize is that even with a small set of operate instructions, the LC-2 can be programmed to do any computation that we can do by hand. The LC-2 supports only ADD, AND, and NOT instructions, but these operations are complete enough for it to do other, more complex operations. Programmers can, if they are so inclined, have the LC-2 calculate the square root of a value. In a process similar to the construction of the LC-2 datapath from very simple logic gates, one can perform sophisticated operations using the simple ones natively supported by the LC-2.

To help illustrate this point, we introduce the C multiplication operator, *. We have declared three unsigned integer variables, **x**, **y**, and **z** in the following code segment. The last line is a statement that performs a multiplication of **x** and **y** and *assigns* the result to **z**.

```
unsigned int x = 7;
unsigned int y = 5;
unsigned int z;

z = x * y;
```

Our LC-2 C compiler generates LC-2 code that first initializes the values of **x** to 7 and **y** to 5, and then performs the multiplication by repeatedly adding the value of **x** to itself a total of **y** times. This code is similar to the code we saw in the calculator example in Chapter 10. Figure 12.7 lists the resulting LC-2 code generated by our hypothetical compiler. Keep in mind that R6 contains the address of the top of the run-time stack where all local variables are allocated storage.

```
            AND   R4, R4, #0    ;    zero out R4
            ADD   R4, R4, #7    ;    R4 <- 7
            STR   R4, R6, #3    ;    x = 7;
                                ;    x has offset 3

            AND   R4, R4, #0    ;    zero out R4
            ADD   R4, R4, #5    ;    R4 <- 5
            STR   R4, R6, #4    ;    y = 3;
                                ;    y has offset 4

            AND   R4, R4, #0    ;    zero out R4
            LDR   R2, R6, #3    ;    load the value of x into R2
            LDR   R3, R6, #4    ;    load the value of y into R3
  LOOP      BRZ   DONE
            ADD   R4, R4, R2    ;    The multiply loop
            ADD   R3, R3, #-1   ;    The result is in R2
            BR    LOOP

  DONE:     STR   R4, R6, #5    ;    z = x * y;
                                ;    z has offset 5
```

Figure 12.7   The LC-2 code for C multiplication

12.3.1 Expressions and Statements

Before proceeding, let's take a moment to define a little C syntax. At this point, we have covered variables and constants. We can combine variables and constants with operators, such as the multiply operator from the previous example, to form a C *expression*. In the previous example, **x * y** is an expression.

Expressions can be grouped to form a *statement*. Again from the previous example, `z = x * y;` is a statement. Statements in C are like complete sentences in English. Just as a sentence captures a complete thought or action, a C statement expresses a complete unit of work to be carried out by the computer. All simple statements in C end with a semicolon character, `;`. The semicolon terminates the end of a statement in much the same way a punctuation mark terminates a sentence in English.

In C it is possible to create statements that do not express any computation but are syntactically considered statements. The null statement is simply a semicolon, as shown in the example below:

```
z = x * y;   /* This statement accomplishes some work */
;            /* Null statement -- no work done here    */
5;           /* also, no work done here                */
```

One or more simple statements can be grouped together to form a compound statement, or *block*, by enclosing the simple statements within braces, `{ }`. Syntactically, compound statements are equivalent to simple statements. We shall see examples of compound statements in the next chapter. By the end of this chapter, you will be familiar not only with variables and operators but with using variables and operators to form expressions and simple C statements.

12.3.2   The Assignment Operator

The first C operator we formally introduce is the C assignment operator. Its symbol is simply the equal sign, `=`. The operator works as follows. First, the right-hand side of the assignment operator is evaluated. Second, the left-hand side is set to the value of the right-hand side. Let's take a look at a C code segment that uses the assignment operator and its LC-2 translation.

```
int x = 9;

x = x + 4;   /* We now expect the value of x to be 13 */
```

The LC-2 code looks like

```
                    ;    initialize x
        AND  R2, R2, #0   ;    Clear out R2
        ADD  R2, R2, #9   ;    R2 contains the value 9
        STR  R2, R6, #3   ;    x = 9;
                    ;    notice, x has offset 3

        LDR  R2, R6, #3   ;    Get the value of x
        ADD  R2, R2, #4   ;    calculate x + 4
        STR  R2, R6, #3   ;    x = x + 4;
```

The LC-2 translation includes an instruction to reload the value of **x** into R2 (the LDR instruction), even though this reloading is not necessary. The compiler could have removed that instruction and the program would still work (in fact, it would run faster). For the sake of making the examples clearer, in all the LC-2 code presented in this half of the book, we include the translation corresponding to each individual

C statement. Keep in mind that a real compiler will attempt to eliminate unnecessary instructions when generating optimized machine code, but that is a subject for a more advanced course in compiler construction.

Notice that even though the arithmetic symbol for equality is the same as the C symbol for assignment, they have different meanings. In mathematics, by using the equal sign = one is making the assertion that the right-hand and left-hand expressions are equivalent. In C, using the = operator causes the compiler to generate code that will make the left-hand side change its value to equal the value of the right-hand side. In other words, the left-hand side is *assigned* the value of the right.

In C, all expressions evaluate to a value of particular type. From the previous example, the expression **x + 4** evaluates to the integer value of 13. This integer value of 13 is then assigned to the integer variable **x**. What would happen if we constructed an expression of mixed type, for example **x + 4.3**? The general rule is that the mixed expressions like the one shown will be *promoted* from integer to floating point. If an expression contains both integer and character types, it will be promoted to integer type. Shorter types are converted to longer types. What if we attempted to assign an expression of one type to a variable of another, for example **x = x + 4.3**? The type of a variable remains immutable in C, so the expression is converted to the type of the variable. In this case, the expression is converted to integer, and the fractional part is dropped.

The fact that all C expressions evaluate to a value is an important concept to keep in mind; some programmers tend to rely on this fact heavily. Expressions containing the assignment operator evaluate to the value being assigned. For example, the expression **x = 3** itself has the integer value 3. The following is a valid C statement:

```
y = x = 3;   /* y will get the value 3 because x = 3   */
             /* evaluates to the value 3               */
```

12.3.3 Arithmetic Operators

The arithmetic operators are easy to understand. Many of the operations and corresponding symbols are ones to which we are accustomed, having used them since learning the arithmetic in grade school. For instance, + performs addition, - subtraction, * performs multiplication (which is different from the symbol we are accustomed to for multiplication in order to avoid confusion with the letter *x*), and / performs division. Just as when doing arithmetic by hand, there is an order to which expressions are evaluated. Multiplication and division are evaluated first, followed by addition and subtraction. More on this in the next section.

Below we show several C statements formed using the arithmetic operators:

```
distance = rate * time;

netIncome = income - taxesPaid;

fuelEconomy = milesTraveled / fuelConsumed;

area = 3.14159 * radius * radius;

y = a*x*x + b*x + c;
```

These operators are translated slightly differently depending on the type of the expression in which they are used. For instance, the C compiler generates a different stream of LC-2 instructions if the two operands being added together are of type **double** (recall, values of type **double** are double-precision floating-point numbers) than if the operands are integers. Adding two integers in the LC-2 can be done with an ADD instruction, whereas adding two floating-point values requires a more complex sequence of LC-2 instructions to deal with the different representation.

What happens when we divide two integer values? When performing an integer divide in C, the fractional part is dropped and the integral part is the result. The expression **11/4** evaluates to 2. The modulus operator **%**, can be used to calculate the integer remainder. For example, **11 % 4** evaluates to 3. Said another way, **(11/4) * 4 + (11 % 4)** equals 11. The modulus operator can be used only with integral (**char** and **int**) data types.

```
z = x / y; /* If x and y are integers, the result is the
              integral portion: e.g., 7 / 2 = 3 */

z = x % y; /* The result is x mod y, e.g., 7 % 2 = 1 */
```

Table 12.1 lists all the arithmetic operations and their symbols. Multiplication, division, and modulus have higher precedence than addition and subtraction. Arithmetic operators of equal precedence associate from left to right.

12.3.4 Precedence and Associativity

Before proceeding to the next set of operators, we diverge momentarily to answer an important question. What value is stored in **x** as a result of the following statement?

$$x = 2 + 3 * 4;$$

Just as when doing arithmetic by hand, there is an order to which expressions are evaluated. For instance, when doing arithmetic, multiplication and division have higher *precedence* than addition and subtraction. For operations of equal precedence, evaluation is carried out from left to right, that is, they *associate* left to right. In programming language terms, operators are arranged in terms of *precedence* and *associativity*. For the arithmetic operators, the C precedence rules are the same as we

Table 12.1   Arithmetic operators in C

Operator Symbol	Operation	Example Usage
*	multiplication	x * y
/	division	x / y
%	modulus	x % y
+	addition	x + y
-	subtraction	x - y

were taught in grade-school arithmetic. In the preceding statement, **x** is assigned the value 14 because the multiplication operator has higher precedence than addition.

Here is an example of associativity. What is the value of **x** after this statement executes?

```
x = 2 + 3 - 4 + 5;
```

The operators + and - are of equal precedence, but they associate left to right. The value of 6 is assigned to **x**.

The complete set of precedence and associativity rules for all operators is provided in Table 12.6 at the end of this chapter and also in Appendix D.5.10. Attempting to memorize this table is counterproductive to learning C. Instead, it is important to realize that the precedence rules exist and to roughly comprehend the logic behind them. Refer to the table whenever you are unsure. There is a safeguard, however: parentheses.

Parentheses override the evaluation rules by specifying explicitly which operations are to be performed ahead of others. Evaluation always begins at the innermost set of parentheses. We can surround a subexpression with parentheses if we want that subexpression to be evaluated first. So in the example below, say the variables **a**, **b**, **c**, and **d** are all equal to 4. The statement

```
x = a * b + c * d / 2;
```

could be written equivalently as

```
x = (a * b) + ((c * d) / 4);
```

For both statements, **x** is set to the value of 20. Here the program will always evaluate the innermost subexpression first and move outward before falling back on the precedence rules. What value would the expression below evaluate to if **a**, **b**, **c**, **d** equal 4? The answer 32 should not surprise you.

```
x = a * (b + c) * d / 4;
```

Parentheses help make code more readable since most of the people reading the code are unlikely to have memorized C's precedence rules. For this reason, for long or complex expressions, it is often stylistically preferable to use parentheses, even if the code works fine without them.

12.3.5 Bitwise Operators

Now, we cover C's bitwise operators. The C operator corresponding to the LC-2 instruction AND is **&**. The **&** operator performs an AND *bitwise* (bit by bit) across the two input operands. The C operator | performs a bitwise OR. The operator ~ performs a bitwise NOT and takes only one operand (i.e., it is a unary operator). The operator ^ performs a bitwise XOR. Examples of expressions using these operators are given below.

Recall that in C, hexadecimal constants are preceded by a **0x**.

```
0x1234 | 0x5678    /* equals 0x567C */
0x1234 & 0x5678    /* equals 0x1230 */
0x1234 ^ 0x5678    /* equals 0x444C */
~0x1234            /* equals 0xEDCB */
1234 & 5678        /* equals 1026.  */
```

C has two shift operators: `<<` and `>>`. They accomplish a left shift and right shift respectively. They are both binary operators, meaning they require two operands. The second operand, which must be an integer or character type, indicates the number of bit positions to shift the value of the first operand. The resultant value is the value of the expression; neither of the two original operand values are modified. Examples of expressions using the shift operators follow:

```
0x1234 << 3        /* equals 0x91A0 */
0x1234 >> 2        /* equals 0x048D */
1234 << 3          /* equals 9856.  */
1234 >> 2          /* equals 308.   */
```

The operand to be shifted can be of any type. The programmer, if he/she wants, could shift a **char** variable or a **double** variable. This is an example of the flexibility of C that has helped make it so popular. A programmer can manipulate the bits of an arbitrary variable in whatever fashion he/she thinks is necessary. However, this flexibility also allows programmers to shoot themselves in the foot and spend countless hours tracking down and fixing bugs.

Below, we show several C statements formed using the bitwise operators.

```
int f = 7;
int g = 8;
int h = 0;

h = f & g;      /* h will equal 0     */

h = f | g;      /* h will equal 15    */

h = ~f | ~g;    /* h will equal -1    */

h = f << 1;     /* h will equal 14    */

h = g << f;     /* h will equal 1024. */
```

Table 12.2 lists all the bitwise operations and their symbols. The operators are listed in order of precedence, the NOT operator having highest precedence, and the left and right shift operators having equal precedence, followed by AND, then XOR, then OR. They all associate from left to right. See Table 12.6 for a complete listing of operator precedence.

12.3.6   Logical Operators

Next, we examine C's logical operators. Before we begin, we need to mention C's concept of logically true and logically false values. C adopts the notion that a nonzero

Table 12.2   Bitwise operators in C

Operator Symbol	Operation	Example Usage
~	bitwise NOT	~x
<<	left shift	x << y
>>	right shift	x >> y
&	bitwise AND	x & y
^	bitwise XOR	x ^ y
|	bitwise OR	x | y

value (i.e., a value other than zero) is logically true. Anything with a value of zero is logically false. It is an important concept to remember, and we will see it surface many times as we go through the various components of the C language.

C supports three logical operators: **&&**, **||**, and **!**. The **&&** operator performs a logical AND of its two operands; it evaluates to an integer value of 1 (which is logically true) if both of its operands are logically true. Said another way, the **&&** evaluates to a 1 if both of its operands are nonzero. For example, 3 **&&** 4 evaluates to a 1. The expression **x && y** evaluates to a 1 only if **x** AND **y** are both not zero. It evaluates to 0 otherwise.

The **||** operator is C's logical OR operator. The expression **x || y** evaluates to a 1 if either **x** OR **y** are nonzero. The negation operator **!** changes the logical state of its operand. So **!x** is 1 only if **x** equals 0. It evaluates to 0 otherwise.

Here are some examples of the logical operators, with several previous examples of bitwise operators included to highlight the difference.

```
int f = 7;
int g = 8;
int h = 0;

h = f & g;      /* bitwise operator: h will equal 0  */

h = f && g;     /* h will equal 1                     */

h = f | g;      /* bitwise operator: h will equal 15 */

h = f || g;     /* h will equal 1                     */

h = ~f | ~g;    /* bitwise operator: h will equal -1 */

h = !f && !g    /* h will equal 0                     */

h = 29 || -52   /* h will equal 1                     */
```

Table 12.3   Logical operators in C

Operator Symbol	Operation	Example Usage
!	logical NOT	!x
&&	logical AND	x && y
||	logical OR	x || y

Table 12.3 lists logical operators in C and their symbols. The logical NOT operator has highest precedence, then logical AND, then logic OR. See Table 12.6 for a complete listing of operator precedence.

12.3.7   Relational Operators

C has several operators to test the relationship between two values. As we will see in the next chapter, these operators are often used in C to generate conditional constructs (recall conditional constructs from our discussion of systematic decomposition in Chapter 5).

An example of a relational operator is the equality operator, ==. This operator tests if two values are equal. If they are equal, the expression evaluates to a 1, and if they are not, the expression evaluates to 0. The following shows two examples:

```
q = (312 == 83);   /* q will equal 0 */
z = (x == y);      /* z will equal 1 if x equals y */
```

In the second example, the right-hand side of the assignment operator = is the expression $x == y$, which evaluates to a 1 or a 0. Once evaluated, the right-hand side is assigned to the left-hand side. The parentheses are not required since the == operator has higher precedence than the = operator.

Like the equality operator, the inequality != operator evaluates to a 1 if the operands are not equal. Other relational operators test for greater than, less than, and so on, as described below.

```
int f = 7;
int g = 8;
int h = 0;

h = f == g; /* Equal To operator.  h will equal 0 */

h = f > g;  /* Greater Than operator. h will equal 0  */

h = f != g; /* Not Equal To operator. h will equal 1  */

h = f <= g; /* Less Than Or Equal To. h will equal 1 */

h = f == (g - 1);   /* What will h equal here? */

h = f == g - 1;     /* What about here? */
```

The next example is a preview of coming attractions. The C relational operators are very useful for performing tests on variables in order to change the flow of the program. In the next chapter, we describe the C **if** statement in more detail. However, the concept of an **if** construct is not a new one—we have been dealing with decision constructs ever since learning how to program the LC-2 in Chapter 5.

```
if (tankLevel == 0)
    printf("Warning: Tank Empty!!\n");
```

Here, a warning message is printed only if the variable **tankLevel** is equal to zero.

Table 12.4 lists all the relational operators and provides a simple example of each. The first four operators have higher precedence than the last two. Both sets associate from left to right.

Table 12.4   Relational operators in C

Operator Symbol	Operation	Example Usage
>	greater than	x > y
>=	greater than or equal	x >= y
<	less than	x < y
<=	less than or equal	x <= y
==	equal	x == y
!=	not equal	x != y

12.3.8   A Simple Example

At this point, we have covered enough C operators to go through a simple example in C (see Figure 12.8). Say we want to create a program that performs a simple network task: It calculates the amount of time required to transfer some data across a network. We need to know how much data there is to be transferred and the transfer rate of the network. We also want the result to be displayed in hours, minutes, seconds format. We can decompose this larger task into three smaller ones: first, get values for transfer amount and transfer rate from the keyboard; second, calculate the transfer time; and third, print out the results. Printing out the results involves converting the calculated time into hours, minutes, and seconds, and displaying it in the proper format on the screen.

12.3.9   C's Special Operators

The C programming language has a collection of unusual operators, which have become a trademark of C programming. Most of these operators are combinations of operators we have already seen. The combinations are such that they make expressing commonly used expressions even simpler. However, to someone who is not accustomed to the shorthand notation of these operators, reading and trying to understand C code that contains these operators can be difficult.

++ and --   The **++** operator *increments* a variable to the next higher value. The **--** operator *decrements* it. For example, the expression **x++** increments the value of integer variable **x** by 1. The expression **x--** decrements the value of **x** by 1.

```
#include <stdio.h>

main()
{
    int amount;          /* The number of bytes to be transferred  */
    int rate;            /* The average network transfer rate       */
    int time;            /* The time, in seconds, for the transfer  */

    /* These vars are used to convert time into hours, mins, secs */
    int hours;           /* The number of hours for the transfer   */
    int minutes;         /* The number of mins for the transfer    */
    int seconds;         /* The number of secs for the transfer    */

    /* Prompt, then read amount to be transferred */
    printf("How many bytes of data to be transferred?  ");
    scanf("%d", &amount);

    /* Prompt, then read transfer rate */
    printf("What is the average transfer rate (in bytes/sec)?  ");
    scanf("%d", &rate);

    time = amount / rate;

    /* Convert time into hours, minutes, seconds               */
    hours = time / 3600;              /* 3600 seconds in an hour   */

    minutes = (time % 3600) / 60;    /* 60 seconds in a minute    */

    seconds = ((time % 3600) % 60);  /* remainder is seconds      */

    /* Output results */
    printf("The expected time for transfer is : %dh %dm %ds\n",
            hours, minutes, seconds);
}
```

Figure 12.8   A C program that performs a simple network rate calculation

The ++ and -- operators can be used on either side of a variable. The expression ++**x** operates in a slightly different order than **x**++. If the expression **x**++ is part of a larger expression, then the value of the expression is the value of **x** prior to the increment; with the expression ++**x**, the value of the expression is the incremented value of **x**. If the operator ++ appears before the variable, then it is used in *prefix* form. If it appears after the variable, it is in *postfix* form. The prefix forms are often referred to as *preincrement* and *predecrement*, whereas the postfix are *postincrement* and *postdecrement*.

Let's examine a couple of examples:

$$x = 4;$$
$$y = x++;$$

Here, assuming both **x** and **y** are integers, the variable **x** is incremented. However, the original value of **x** is assigned to the variable **y** (i.e., the value of **x**++ evaluates to the original value of **x**). After this code executes, the variable **y** will have the value 4, and **x** will be 5.

Similarly, the following code increments **x**.

```
x = 4;
y = ++x;
```

With this code, the expression **++x** evaluates to the value after the increment. In this case, the value of both **y** and **x** will be 5.

This subtle distinction between the postfix and prefix forms is not too important to understand for now. For most of the examples we present in this book, the prefix and postfix forms of these operators can be used interchangeably. You can find a precise description of this difference in Appendix D.5.6.

C also allows certain arithmetic and bitwise operators to be combined with the assignment operator. For instance, if we wanted to add 29 to variable **x**, we could use the shorthand operator **+=** as follows:

```
x  += 29;
```

This code is equivalent to

```
x = x + 29;
```

Table 12.5 lists some of the special operators provided by C. The postfix operators have highest precedence, followed by prefix. The assignment operators have lowest precedence. Each group associates from right to left.

Table 12.5   Special operators in C

Operator Symbol	Operation	Example Usage
++	increment (postfix)	x++
--	decrement (postfix)	x--
++	increment (prefix)	++x
--	decrement (prefix)	--x
+=	add and assign	x += y
-=	subtract and assign	x -= y
*=	multiply and assign	x *= y
/=	divide and assign	x /= y
%=	modulus and assign	x %= y
&=	and and assign	x &= y
|=	or and assign	x |= y
^=	xor and assign	x ^= y
<<=	left-shift and assign	x <<= y
>>=	right-shift and assign	x >>= y

More examples are as follows:

```
int f = 7;
int g = 8;
int h = 0;
h += g;          /* h will equal 8                */

h %= f;          /* Equivalent to h = h % f;    */
                 /* Initially, h = 8, f = 7.    */
                 /* Afterwards, h will equal 1 */

h <<= 3;         /* Equivalent to h = h << 3;   */
                 /* Initially, h equals 1.      */
                 /* Afterwards, h will equal 8 */
```

Conditional expressions   Conditional expressions are a unique feature of C that allow for simple decisions to be made with a simple expression. The symbols for the conditional expression are the question mark and colon, **?** and **:**. The best way to describe how conditional expressions work is to jump into an example:

$$x = a ? b : c;$$

Here variable **x** will get either the value of **b or** the value of **c** based on the value of **a**. If **a** is nonzero (logically true), then **x** will be assigned the value of **b**. Otherwise, **x** will be assigned the value of **c**. The operation of the C conditional expression is very similar to the operation of the multiplexor, or MUX, that we discussed in Chapter 3. Figure 12.9 pictorially describes the equivalence: The output of the MUX, x, will equal either b or c, depending on the value of the select, a.

Figure 12.10 is a complete program, which uses the conditional expression to calculate the maximum of two integers. The example program prompts the user for two integers and stores them in the variables **input1** and **input2**. The maximum of these two values is determined by a conditional expression and is assigned to the variable **maxValue**. The value of **maxValue** is output using **printf**.

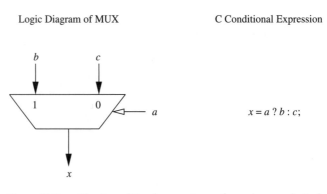

Figure 12.9 are labels: Logic Diagram of MUX   C Conditional Expression, with $x = a ? b : c;$

Figure 12.9   The C conditional expression performs the same logical function as a multiplexor

```
#include <stdio.h>

main()
{
    int maxValue;
    int input1, input2;

    printf("Input an integer: ");
    scanf("%d", &input1);
    printf("Input another integer: ");
    scanf("%d", &input2);

    maxValue = (input1 > input2) ? input1 : input2;
    printf("The larger number is %d\n", maxValue);
}
```

Figure 12.10   A C program that uses a conditional expression

12.3.10   Tying It Together

We can combine various operators and operands to form complex expressions. The following example demonstrates a peculiar blend of operators forming a complex expression.

$$y = x \& z + 3 \;||\; 9 - w\text{--} \% 6;$$

Table 12.6 lists all the C operators (including some that we have not yet covered but will cover in later chapters) and their order of evaluation. Using the information presented in the table, we can evaluate the complex expression previously presented. According to the rules of evaluation, this statement is equivalent to the following:

$$y = (x \& (z + 3)) \;||\; (9 - ((w\text{--}) \% 6));$$

Another more useful expression that consists of multiple operators is given below. In this example, if the value of the variable **age** is between 18 and 25, the expression evaluates to 1. Otherwise it is 0. Notice that even though the parentheses are not required to make the expression evaluate as we described, they do help make the code easier to read.

$$(18 <= age) \;\&\&\; (age <= 25)$$

Table 12.6   Operator precedence, from highest to lowest

Precedence Group	Associativity	Operators
1	l to r	*function call* `()` `[ ]` `.` `->`
2	r to l	*postfix* `++` *postfix* `--`
3	r to l	*prefix* `++` *prefix* `--`
4	r to l	*indirection* `*` *address* `&`
		unary `+` *unary* `-`
		`~` `!` `sizeof`
5	r to l	*cast* `(type)`
6	l to r	*multiply* `*` `/` `%`
7	l to r	`+` `-`
8	l to r	`<<` `>>`
9	l to r	`<` `>` `<=` `>=`
10	l to r	`==` `!=`
11	l to r	`&`
12	l to r	`^`
13	l to r	`|`
14	l to r	`&&`
15	l to r	`||`
16	l to r	`?:`
17	r to l	`=` `+=` `-=` `*=` etc.

12.4   A MORE COMPREHENSIVE EXAMPLE

Figure 12.11 is a complete C program that performs some simple operations on integer variables and then outputs the results of these operations. There is one global variable, **inGlobal**, and three local variables, **inLocal**, **outLocalA**, and **outLocalB**, which are local to the function main.

The program starts off by assigning initial values to **inLocal** and **inGlobal**. Alternatively, we could have assigned initial values to these variables using an initializer in their declarations. After the initialization step, the variables **outLocalA** and **outLocalB** are updated based on two calculations performed using **inLocal** and **inGlobal**. After the calculation step, the values of **outLocalA** and **outLocalB** are output using the **printf** library function. Notice because we are using **printf**, we must include the Standard I/O library header file, **stdio.h**.

When analyzing this code, the LC-2 C compiler will assign the global variable **inGlobal** the first available spot in the global data section, which is at offset 0. When analyzing the function **main**, it will assign **inLocalA** to offset 3, **outLocalA** to offset 4, and **outLocalB** to offset 5 on the top of the run-time stack. A snapshot of the compiler's symbol table corresponding to this program is shown in Figure 12.12.

Offsets 0, 1, and 2 off the top of the stack contain bookkeeping information needed to help maintain the stack. They, therefore, are not used for variables. We will describe what these bookkeeping values are when we discuss functions in Chapter 14. For now, keep in mind that the first variable is allocated into offset 3 off the top of the stack.

The resulting assembly code generated by the LC-2 C compiler is listed in Figure 12.13. Execution starts at the instruction labeled **main**.

```
/* Include the standard I/O header file */
#include <stdio.h>

int inGlobal;        /* Variable inGlobal is a global variable    */
                     /* because is declared outside of all blocks */

main()
{
  int inLocal;       /* Variables inLocal, outLocalA, outLocalB */
  int outLocalA;     /* are all local to main                   */
  int outLocalB;

  /* Initialize */
  inLocal  = 5;
  inGlobal = 3;

  /* Perform calculations */
  outLocalA = inLocal++ & ~inGlobal;
  outLocalB = (inLocal + inGlobal) - (inLocal - inGlobal);

  /* Print out results */
  printf("The results are : outLocalA = %d, outLocalB = %d\n",
 outLocalA, outLocalB);
}
```

Figure 12.11   A C program that performs simple operations

Symbol Table

Name	Type	Offset	Scope
inGlobal	int	0	global

Name	Type	Offset	Scope
inLocal	int	3	main

Name	Type	Offset	Scope
outLocalA	int	4	main

Name	Type	Offset	Scope
outLocalB	int	5	main

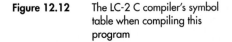

Figure 12.12   The LC-2 C compiler's symbol table when compiling this program

```
main:
    AND   R0, R0, #0
    ADD   R0, R0, #2    ;   The compiler assigns variable a an offset of 3
    STR   R0, R6, #3    ;   inLocal = 2;

    AND   R0, R0, #0
    ADD   R0, R0, #3    ;   inGlobal assigned to offset 0 in the global area
    STR   R0, R5, #0    ;   inGlobal = 3;

    LDR   R0, R6, #3    ;   get value of inLocal : r0 contains original value
    ADD   R1, R0, #1    ;   increment inLocal
    STR   R1, R6, #3    ;   inLocal++

    LDR   R1, R5, #0    ;   get value of inGlobal
    NOT   R1            ;   ~inGlobal
    AND   R2, R0, R1    ;   calculate inLocal & ~inGlobal
    STR   R2, R6, #4    ;   outLocalA = inLocal++ & ~inGlobal;
                        ;   The variable outLocalA is assigned an offset of 4

    LDR   R0, R6, #3    ;   get value of inLocal
    LDR   R1, R5, #0    ;   get value of inGlobal
    ADD   R0, R0, R1    ;   calculate inLocal + inGlobal

    LDR   R2, R6, #3    ;   get value of inLocal
    LDR   R3, R5, #0    ;   get value of inGlobal
    NOT   R3
    ADD   R3, R3, #1    ;   calculate -inGlobal
    ADD   R2, R2, R3    ;   calculate inLocal - inGlobal
    NOT   R2
    ADD   R2, R2, #1    ;   calculate -(inLocal - inGlobal)
    ADD   R0, R0, R2    ;   (inLocal + inGlobal) - (inLocal - inGlobal)
    STR   R0, R6, #5    ;   outLocalB = (inLocal + inGlobal) - (inLocal - inGlobal);
                        ;   The variable outLocalB is assigned an offset of 5
    :
    :
<code for calling the function printf>
    :
    :
```

Figure 12.13   The LC-2 code for the previous C program

12.5   SUMMARY

In this chapter, we covered two basic high-level programming language constructs: variables and operators. All high-level languages provide support for managing the values upon which a program operates. These values are called variables. In C, variables have three major characterisics: type, identifier, and scope. The type of a variable indicates some properties of the values the variable will contain. We covered three basic C types: **int**, **char**, and **double**. A variable's identifier is its symbolic name. We can choose a name to reflect something about the variable, thereby allowing us to more easily recall its purpose. The scope of a variable indicates to the compiler where within the program the variable is accessible.

Operators allow us to quickly and compactly describe the computations we want the computer to perform. In C, there are operators for arithmetic operations, bitwise manipulations, logical operations, relational operations, and well as several commonly needed special operations. We can combine operators and variables to form expressions. Expressions are the basic elements of statements. Operators have precedence and associativity, which help determine the order of evaluation when multiple operators appear in the same expression. Using variables and operators, we covered several complete, yet simple example C programs.

PROBLEMS

12.1. Assuming that space for the variable **ff** is allocated at offset 3, generate the compiler's symbol table for the following code.

```
{
    float ff;
    char cc;
    int ii;
    char dd;

    /* ... */

}
```

12.2. The following variable declaration appears in a program:

```
int r;
```

1. If **r** is a local variable, to what value will it be initialized?
2. If **r** if a global variable, to what value will it be initialized?

12.3. What are the ranges for the following two variables if they are stored as 32-bit quantities?

```
int plusOrMinus;
unsigned int positive;
```

12.4. Evaluate the following floating-point constants. Write their values in standard notation.

1. $111 \, E -11$
2. $-0.00021 \, E \, 4$
3. $101.101 \, E \, 0$

12.5. Write the LC-2 code that would result if the following variable declarations were compiled using the LC-2 C compiler:

```
char c = 'a';
int  x = 3;
int  y;
int  z = 10;
```

12.6. For the code below, state the values that are printed out by each **printf** statement. Assume that the statements are executed in the order A, B, C, D.

```
int t;   /* This variable is global */

{
    int t = 2;

    printf("%d\n", t);       /*  A  */

    {

        printf("%d\n", t);   /*  B  */

        t = 3;
    }

    printf("%d\n", t);       /*  C  */
}

{

    printf("%d\n", t);       /*  D  */
}
```

12.7. Given that **a** and **b** are both integers where **a** and **b** have been assigned the values 6 and 9 respectively, what is the value of each of the following expressions? Also, if the value of **a** or **b** changes, give their new value.

1. `++a + b--`
2. `a | b`
3. `a || b`
4. `a & b`
5. `a && b`
6. `!(a + b)`
7. `a % b`
8. `b / a`
9. `a = b`
10. `a = b = 5`
11. `a = (++b < 3) ?  a :  b`
12. `a <<= b`

12.8. For the following questions, write a C expression to perform the following relational test on the character variable **letter**.

1. Test if **letter** is any alphabetic (lowercase or uppercase) character.
2. Test if **letter** is any alphabetic character or a number.

12.9. 1. What does the following statement accomplish? The variable `letter` is a character variable.

```
letter = ((letter >= 'a' && letter <= 'z') ? '!' : letter);
```

2. Modify the statement above so that it coverts lowercase to uppercase.

12.10. Write a program that reads an integer from the keyboard and displays a *Y* if it is divisible by 3 or an *N* otherwise.

12.11. Explain the difference between the following C statements:

1. `j = i++;`
2. `j = ++i;`
3. `j = i + 1;`
4. `i += 1;`
5. `j = i += 1;`
6. Which statements modify the value of `i`? Which ones modify the value of `j`? If `i = 1` and `j = 0` initially, what will the values of `i` and `j` be after each statement is run separately?

12.12. Say variables **a** and **b** are both declared locally as `long int`.

1. Translate the expression `a + b` into LC-2 code, assuming a `long int` occupies 2 bytes. Assume **a** is allocated at offset 3 and **b** is at offset 4.

2. Translate the same expression, assuming a `long int` occupies 4 bytes, **a** is allocated offset 3, and **b** is at offset 5.

12.13. If initially, `a = 1, b = 1, c = 3`, and `result = 999`, what are the values of the variables after the following C statement is executed?

```
result = ((b+1) | --c) + a;
```

12.14. Recall the machine busy example from previous chapters. Say the integer variable **machineBusy** tracks the busyness of all 16 machines. Recall that a 0 in a particular bit position indicates the machine is busy and a 1 in that position indicates that machine is idle.

1. Write a C statement to make machine 5 busy.
2. Write a C statement to make machine 10 idle.
3. Write a C statement to make machine **n** busy. That is, the machine which has become busy is in integer variable **n**.
4. Write a C expression to check if machine 3 is idle. If it is idle, the expression returns a 1. If it is busy, the expression returns a 0.
5. Write a C expression that evaluates to the number of idle machines. For example, if the binary pattern in **machineBusy** were `1011 0010 1110 1001`, then the expression will evaluate to 9.

12.15. What purpose does the semicolon serve in C?

12.16. Say we are designing a new computer-programming language that includes the operators @, #, $ and U. How would the expression w @ x # y $ z U a get evaluated under the following constraints?

1. The precedence of @ is higher than # is higher than $ is higher than U. Use parentheses to indicate the order.

2. The precedence of # is higher than U is higher than @ is higher than $.

3. Their precedence is all the same, but they associate left to right.

4. Their precedence is all the same, but they associate right to left.

12.17. Notice that the C assignment operators have the lowest precedence. Say we have developed a new programming language called Q that works exactly like C, except that the assignment operator had the highest precedence.

1. How would the following C statement work in Q? In other words, what would the value of **x** be after it executed?

$$x = x + 1;$$

2. How would we change this C statement so that it works the same way in Q?

12.18. Modify the example program in Chapter 11 (Figure 11.2) such that it prompts the user to type a character and then prints every character from that character down to the character ! in the order they appear in the ASCII table.

12.19. Write a C program to calculate the sales tax on a sales transaction. Prompt the user to enter the amount of the purchase and the tax rate. Output the amount of sales tax and the total amount (including tax) on the whole purchase.

12.20. Suppose your program contains the two integer variables **x** and **y** which have values 3 and 4 respectively. Write C statements that will exchange the values in **x** and **y** such that after the statements are executed, **x** is equal to 4 and **y** is equal to 3.

1. First, write this routine using a temporary variable for storage.

2. Now rewrite this routine without using a temporary variable for storage.

chapter

13

Control Structures

In Chapter 6, we introduced the three constructs of systematic decomposition: the sequential construct, the conditional construct, and the iteration construct. We discovered that these constructs are very helpful when transforming a problem into a computer program. We often require the ability to perform a subtask conditionally, or to repeat a subtask within our programs.

Recall that using stepwise refinement, we could break down a large task into one consisting of simpler steps. Once the task was refined to a level where each step was a fairly detailed set of operations, it was then relatively simple to program it in LC-2 instructions.

We want to apply the same systematic decomposition when programming in C. In order to do so, we need the ability to create all three types of constructs within our C programs. Using expressions and statements as covered in the previous chapter, we can create sequential constructs. In this chapter, we cover C's version of conditional and iteration constructs.

We begin this chapter by describing C's conditional constructs: the **if** and **if-else** statements and the slightly more sophisticated **switch** statement. After conditional constructs, we move on to C's iteration constructs: the **for**, **while**, and **do-while** statements. With many of these constructs, we will present the corresponding LC-2 code generated by our hypothetical LC-2 C compiler to help illustrate how these constructs behave. Finally, in this chapter we'll go through some problem solving using the C we've learned in these first three C chapters.

13.1   CONDITIONAL CONSTRUCTS

Conditional constructs allow a programmer to select an action based on some condition. This is a very common programming construct and is supported by every useful programming language. C provides two types of basic conditional constructs: **if** and **if-else**. There is also a special-purpose conditional construct called **switch**.

13.1.1   The **if** Statement

The **if** statement is quite simple. It performs an action if a condition is true. The action is a C statement, and it is executed only if the condition, which is a C expression, evaluates to a nonzero (logically true) value. Let's take a look at an example.

```
if (x <= 10)
    y = x * x + 5;
```

We see that the statement **y = x * x + 5;** is only executed if the expression **x <= 10** is nonzero. Recall from our discussion of the **<=** operator (the less than or equal to operator) that it evaluates to 1 if the relationship is true, 0 otherwise.

Syntactically, the condition we are testing must be surrounded by parentheses. The parentheses allow the compiler to unambiguously separate the condition from the rest of the **if** statement. The statement that follows can be any legal C statement.

The statement following the condition can also be a *compound statement*, or *block*, which is a sequence of statements beginning with an open brace and ending with a closing brace. Compound statements are used in order to group one or more simple statements into a single entity. This entity is itself equivalent to a simple statement. Using compound statements with an **if** statement we can base the execution of several statements on a single condition. For example, in the following code, both **y** and **z** will be modified if **x** is less than or equal to 10.

```
if (x <= 10) {
    y = x * x + 5;
    z = (2 * y) / 3;
}
```

As with all statements in C, the format of the **if** statement is flexible. The indentation used in the preceding example is one form of conventional indentation for an **if** statement. It allows someone reading the code to quickly identify the portion that executes if the condition is true. The format does not affect the behavior of the program. Even though the following code is indented like the code above, it behaves differently. The second statement **z = (2 * y) / 3;** is not associated with **if** and will execute regardless of the condition.

```
if (x <= 10)
    y = x * x + 5;
    z = (2 * y) / 3;
```

Figure 13.1 shows the control flow of an `if` statement using the notation we establish when discussing systematic decomposition in Chapter 6. The diagram corresponds to the following code:

```
if (condition)
    action;
```

The statement labeled *action* can be a compound statement and consist of multiple statements.

Here are more examples of `if` statements:

```
if (0 <= age && age <= 11)
   kids = kids + 1;

if (pattern1 && pattern2)
   value = value / 10;

if (loadMAR & clock)
   regMAR = bus;

if (month == 4 || month == 6 || month == 9 || month == 11)
   printf("The month has 30 days\n");

if (x = 2)    /* This condition is always true.    */
   y = 5;     /* The variable y  will always be 5. */
```

The final example given points out a very common mistake made when programming in C (sometimes expert C programmers even make this mistake). The condition is constructed with the assignment operator = which causes the value of **x** to change to 2. This condition is always true: Recall from our discussion on the assignment

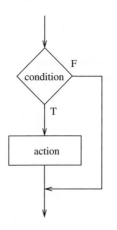

Figure 13.1   The C `if` statement, pictorially represented

operator that it evaluates to the value being assigned (in this case, 2). Since the condition is always nonzero, **y** will always get assigned the value 5 and **x** will always be assigned 2. The preceding code is very different from this (even though they look similar at first glance):

```
if (x == 2)
    y = 5;
```

Here, a test for equality is performed, not an assignment as done in the previous version. If **x** equals 2, then the variable **y** is set to 5. The variable **x** is not modified. Let's look at the LC-2 code that is generated, assuming that **x** and **y** are integers and their offsets on the run-time stack are 3 and 4 respectively.

```
LDR   R0, R6, #3   ; load x into R0
ADD   R0, R0, #-2  ; subtract 2 from x
BRnp  NOT_TRUE     ; If condition is not true,
                     then skip the assignment

AND   R1, R1, #0   ; R1 <- 0
ADD   R1, R1, #5   ; R1 <- 5
STR   R1, R6, #4   ; y = 5;

NOT_TRUE :                ; the rest of the program
         :
```

Notice that it is most straightforward for the LC-2 C compiler to generate code that tests for the opposite of the original condition (**x** not equal to 2) and to branch based on its outcome.

The **if** statement is itself a statement. Therefore, it is legal to *nest* an **if** statement as demonstrated in the following C code. Since the statement following the first **if** is a simple statement (i.e., composed of only one statement), no braces are required.

```
if (x == 3)
    if (y != 6) {
        z = z + 1;
        w = w + 2;
    }
```

The inner **if** statement only executes if **x** is equal to 3. There is an easier way to express the aforementioned code. Can you do it with only one **if** statement? See below for the answer.

```
if ((x == 3) && (y != 6)) {
    z = z + 1;
    w = w + 2;
}
```

13.1.2 The if-else Statement

If we wanted to perform one set of actions if a condition were true and another set if the same condition were false, we could use the following sequence of **if** statements:

```
if (x == y)
    z = 4;

if (x != y)
    z = 9;
```

Here, **z** will be set to 4 if **x** is equal to **y**, otherwise **z** will be assigned the value 9. It turns out that this is a very common programming construct. Since we need express the opposite of the condition everytime we want to use this construct, having to code it this way can get tedious quickly. Fortunately, C provides a more convenient way to express it: the **if-else** statement.

The following code is equivalent to the previous code segment.

```
if (x == y)
    z = 4;
else
    z = 9;
```

As with the **if** statement, each component of an **if-else** can be a compound statement, as in the following example.

```
if (x) {
    y++;
    z--;
}
else {
    y--;
    z++;
}
```

If the variable **x** is nonzero, then the **if** condition is true, **y** is incremented, and **z** decremented. Otherwise, **y** is decremented and **z** incremented. The LC-2 code generated by the LC-2 C compiler is listed in Figure 13.2. We are assuming that **x**, **y**, and **z** are integer variables declared as locals. Their offsets are 3 for **x**, 4 for **y**, and 5 for **z**.

The flow diagram for the **if-else** is shown in Figure 13.3. The figure corresponds to the following code:

```
if (condition)
    action_if;
else
    action_else;
```

The lines **action_if** and **action_else** can correspond to compound statements and thus consist of multiple statements.

```
        LDR   R0, R6, #3    ;   load the value of x
        BRz   ELSE          ;   if x is equal to 0, perform else part

        ; x is not equal to 0
        LDR   R1, R6, #4    ;   load y into R1
        ADD   R1, R1, #1
        STR   R1, R6, #4    ;   y++;

        LDR   R1, R6, #5    ;   load z into R1
        ADD   R1, R1, #-1
        STR   R1, R6, #5    ;   z--;

        BR DONE

        ; The condition is false
ELSE:   LDR   R1, R6, #4    ;   load y into R1
        ADD   R1, R1, #-1
        STR   R1, R6, #4    ;   y--;

        LDR   R1, R6, #5    ;   load z into R1
        ADD   R1, R1, #1
        STR   R1, R6, #5    ;   z++;

DONE:         :
              :
```

Figure 13.2   The LC-2 code generated for an `if-else` statement

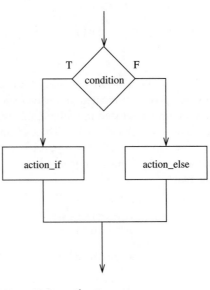

Figure 13.3   The C `if-else` statement,
pictorially represented

```
#include <stdio.h>

main()
{
  int month;

  printf("Enter the number of the month: ");
  scanf("%d", &month);

  if (month == 4 || month == 6 || month == 9 || month == 11)
    printf("The month has 30 days\n");
  else if (month == 1 || month == 3 || month == 5 ||
           month == 7 || month == 8 || month == 10 || month == 12)
    printf("The month has 31 days\n");
  else if (month == 2)
    printf("The month has either 28 days or 29 days\n");
  else
    printf("Don't know that month\n");
}
```

Figure 13.4   A program that determines the number of days in a month

We can connect conditional constructs together to form a longer sequence of conditional tests. The example in Figure 13.4 shows a complex decision structure created using the **if** and **if-else** statements. No other control structures are used.

At this point, we need to mention a C syntax rule for associating *ifs* with *elses*: An **else** is associated with the closest unassociated **if**. The following example points out why this is important.

```
if (x != 10)
    if (y > 3)
        z = z / 2;
    else
        z = z * 2;
```

Without this rule, it would not be clear whether the **else** associates with the *outer* **if** or the *inner* **if**. For this situation, the rule states that the **else** is coupled with the inner **if** because it is closer than the outer **if** and the inner **if** statement has not already been coupled to another **else** (i.e., it is unassociated). The code is equivalent to the following:

```
if (x != 10) {
    if (y > 3)
        z = z / 2;
    else
        z = z * 2;
}
```

Just as parentheses can be used to modify the order of evaluation of expressions, braces can be used to associate statements. If we wanted to associate the **else** with the outer **if**, we could write the code as such:

```
if (x != 10) {
    if (y > 3)
        z = z / 2;
}
else
    z = z * 2;
```

Before we leave the **if-else** statement for bigger things, we present a very common use for the **if-else** construct. The **if-else** statement is very handy for checking for possible bad situations during execution. We can use it for error checking, as shown in Figure 13.5.

This example performs simple division based on two numbers scanned from the keyboard. However, because division by 0 is undefined, if the user enters a divisor equal to 0, we need to display a message indicating the result cannot be generated. The **if-else** statement serves us nicely for that purpose.

A stylistic note: Notice that the nonerror case appears in the **if-else** statement first and the error case second. Although we could have coded either way, having the common, nonerror case first provides a visual cue to someone reading the code that the error case is the uncommon one.

```
#include <stdio.h>

main()
{
    int dividend;
    int divisor;
    int result;

    printf("Enter the dividend: ");
    scanf("%d", &dividend);
    printf("Enter the divisor: ");
    scanf("%d", &divisor);

    if (divisor != 0) {
        result = dividend / divisor;
        printf("The result of the division is %d\n", result);
    }
    else
        printf("A divisor of zero is not allowed\n");
}
```

Figure 13.5   A program that has error-checking code

13.1.3   The switch Statement

Another control structure that often appears in our programs is a series of tests based on the same variable. For example,

```
char keyPress;

if (keyPress == 'a') {
   /* statement A */
}
else if (keyPress == 'b') {
   /* statement B */
}
else if (keyPress == 'x') {
   /* statement C */
}
else if (keyPress == 'y') {
   /* statement D */
}
```

In this code, one (or none) of the statements labeled A, B, C, or D will be executed depending on the value of the character variable **keyPress**. If **keyPress** is equal to the character a, then statement A is performed, if it is equal to the character b, then statement B is performed, and so forth. If **keyPress** does not equal a or b or x or y, then none of the statements are executed.

If there are many of these conditions to check, then many tests will be required in order to find the "matching" one. In order to give the compiler an opportunity to better optimize this code by bypassing some of this testing, C provides the **switch** statement. The following code segment behaves the same as the code in the previous example. It uses a **switch** statement.

```
char keyPress;

switch (keyPress) {
case 'a':
  /* statement A */
  :
  break;

case 'b':
  /* statement B */
  :
  break;

case 'x':
  /* statement C */
  :
  break;

case 'y':
  /* statement D */
  :
  break;
}
```

Notice that the **switch** statement contains several lines beginning with the keyword **case**, followed by a label. The program evaluates **keyPress** first. Then it determines which of the following **case** labels matches the value of **keyPress**. If any label matches, then the statements following it are executed.

Let's go through it piece by piece. The **switch** keyword precedes the expression on which to base the decision. This expression must be of integral type, which means it must be either an **int** or a **char**. If the value of the expression matches one of the **case** labels, the code following the **case** keyword is executed. Each **case** consists of a sequence of zero or more statements similar to a compound statement, however, no delimiting braces are required. Conceptually, each **case** label is an entry point into the compound statement of the **switch**. The place within this compound statement to start executing is determined by which **case** matches the value of the **switch** expression. Each **case** label within a **switch** statement must be different; identical labels are not allowed.

Furthermore, each **case** label must be a constant expression. It cannot be based on a value that changes as the program is executing. The following is not a legal **case** label (assuming **i** is a variable):

```
case i:
```

In the preceding **switch** example, each **case** ends with a **break** statement. The **break** exits the **switch** construct and changes the flow of control directly to the statement after the closing brace of the **switch**. The **break** statements are optional. If they are not used, then control will go from the current **case** to the next. For example, if the **break** after statement C were omitted, then a match on **case** **'x'** would cause statement C *and* statement D to be executed. However, in practice, **case**s almost always end with a **break**.

We can also include a **default** case. This case is selected if the **switch** expression matches none of the **case** constants. If no **default** case is given, and the expression matches none of the constants, then none of the **case**'s within the **switch** are executed.

A stylistic note: The last **case** of a **switch** does not need to end with a **break**, since execution of the **switch** completes there anyway. However, including a **break** for the final **case** is good programming practice. If another **case** is ever added to the end of the **switch**, then you will not have to remember to also add the **break** to the previous **case**. Just a bit of good, defensive programming.

For further description of the **switch** statement, see Appendix D.7.3.

13.1.4 An Example Program

The program in Figure 13.6 performs a function similar to the calculator example from Chapter 10. The user is prompted for three items: an integer operand, an operation to perform, and another integer operand. The program then performs the operation on the two input values and displays the results on the screen. The program makes use of a **switch** to decide which operation the user has selected.

```
#include <stdio.h>

main()
{
  int operand1, operand2;    /* Input values upon which to operate */
  int result = 0;            /* Result of the operation            */
  char operation;            /* operation to perform               */

  /* Get the input values */
  printf("Enter first operand: ");
  scanf("%d", &operand1);
  printf("Enter operation to perform (+, -, *, /): ");
  scanf("\n%c", &operation);
  printf("Enter second operand: ");
  scanf("%d", &operand2);

  /* Perform the calculation */
  switch(operation) {
  case '+':
    result = operand1 + operand2;
    break;

  case '-':
    result = operand1 - operand2;
    break;

  case '*':
    result = operand1 * operand2;
    break;

  case '/':
    if (operand2 != 0)                /* Notice the error-checking code. */
      result = operand1 / operand2;
    else
      printf("Divide by 0 error!\n");
    break;

  default:
    printf("Invalid operation!\n");
    break;
  }

  /* Print out the result */
  printf("The answer is %d\n", result);
}
```

Figure 13.6   Calculator program in C

13.2   ITERATION CONSTRUCTS

Iteration constructs repeat a sequence of code in a controlled manner. In C, there
are three iteration constructs: the **while** statement, the **for** statement, and the
do-while statement.

13.2.1   The `while` Statement

We begin by describing C's simplest iteration statement: the **while**. A **while** loop repeatedly executes a statement *while* a condition is true. Before each iteration of the statement, the condition is checked. If the condition evaluates to a logical true (nonzero) value, then the statement is executed again.

In the example program in Figure 13.7, the loop keeps iterating while the value of x is less than 10. It produces the following output:

```
0  1  2  3  4  5  6  7  8  9
```

The **while** statement breaks down into two components:

```
while (test)
   loop_body;
```

The **test** component is an expression used to determine whether or not to continue executing the loop. It is tested before each execution of the **loop_body**. The statement **loop_body** expresses the work to be done within the loop. It can be a compound statement. In other words, the loop executes the **loop_body** *while* the **test** is true.

Figure 13.8 shows the control flow using the notation of systematic decomposition. Two branches are required: one conditional branch to exit the loop and one unconditional branch to loop back to the test to determine whether or not to execute another iteration.

The LC-2 code generated by the compiler for the **while** example in Figure 13.7 is listed in Figure 13.9.

The **while** statement is useful for coding loops where the iteration process involves testing for a *sentinel* condition. When the sentinel is encountered, the loop terminates. For example, when we wrote the character counting program in Chapters 5 and 7, we created a loop that terminated when the sentinel EOT character (a character with ASCII code 4) was detected.

```
#include <stdio.h>

main()
{
    int x = 0;

    while (x < 10) {
        printf("%d ", x);
        x = x + 1;
    }
}
```

Figure 13.7   A program containing a simple `while` loop

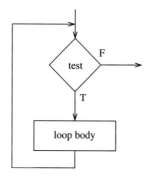

Figure 13.8   The C `while` statement pictorially represented

```
        AND   R0, R0, #0    ;    clear out R0
        STR   R0, R6, #3    ;    x = 0;

        ; while (x < 10)

        ; test
LOOP:   LDR   R0, R6, #3    ;    perform the test
        ADD   R0, R0, #-10
        BRpz  DONE           ;    x is not less than 10

        ; loop body
        LDR   R0, R6, #3    ;    get x
        :
        <code for calling the function printf>
        :
        ADD   R0, R0, #1    ;    x + 1
        STR   R0, R6, #3    ;    x = x + 1;
        BR    LOOP           ;    another iteration?

DONE:   :
        :
```

Figure 13.9   The LC-2 code generated for a `while` statement

The program in Figure 13.10 uses the **while** statement to test for a sentinel condition. Can you determine what this program does without running it on a computer?[1]

---

[1] This program behaves slightly differently than you might expect. You might expect it to print out each input character, as the user types it in. However, because of the way C deals with keyboard I/O, the program does not get any input until the user hits the Enter key. We explain why this is when dealing with the low-level issues surrounding I/O in Chapter 18.

```
#include <stdio.h>

main()
{
  char echo = 'A';    /* Initialize char variable echo */

  while (echo != '\n') {
    scanf("%c", &echo);
    printf("%c", echo);
  }
}
```

Figure 13.10   Another program with a simple **while** loop

We end our treatment of the **while** statement by pointing out a common mistake when using **while** loops. The program below will never terminate because the loop body (which consists of a simple statement) does not change the looping condition. In this case, it always remains true. Such loops (which are often the result of a programming mistake) that never terminate are called *infinite loops*.

```
x = 0;
while (x < 10)
    printf("%d ", x);
```

13.2.2   The **for** Statement

The syntax for the C **for** statement may look a little intimidating at first. After analyzing its syntax and examining the resulting LC-2 code, the notation begins to make sense.

In its most straightforward form, the **for** statement allows us to repeat a statement a specified number of times. For example,

```
for (i = 0; i < 10; i++)
    printf("%d ", i);
```

will produce the following output. It loops exactly 10 times.

```
0 1 2 3 4 5 6 7 8 9
```

The **for** statement is composed of four components, broken down as follows:

```
for (init; test; reinit)
    loop_body;
```

The three components within the parentheses, **init**, **test**, and **reinit**, control the behavior of the loop and must be separated by semicolons. The final component, **loop_body**, specifies the actual computation to be performed within the loop. As always, if the work to be performed within the loop cannot be stated with a single simple statement, then a compound statement can be used by enclosing several simple statements with braces.

Let's take a look at each component of the **for** loop in detail. The **init** component is an expression that is evaluated before the **first** iteration. It is typically used to initialize variables in preparation for executing the loop.

The **test** component is an expression that gets evaluated before *every* iteration to determine if another iteration should be executed. If the **test** expression evaluates to zero, then the **for** terminates and the control flow is passed to the next statement. If the expression is nonzero, then another iteration of the **loop_body** is performed. Therefore, in the previous code example, the test component $i < 10$ causes the loop to keep repeating as long as i is less than 10.

The **reinit** component is an expression that is evaluated at the end of *every* iteration. It is used to prepare (or reinitialize) for the next iteration. In the previous code example, the variable i is incremented before each repetition of the loop body.

The **loop_body** is a statement that defines the work to be performed in each iteration. It can be a compound statement.

Figure 13.11 shows the flow diagram of the **for** statement. There are four blocks, one for each of the four components of the **for** statement. There is a conditional branch that determines whether to exit the loop based on the outcome of the **test** expression or to proceed with another iteration. An unconditional branch loops back to the **test** at the end of each iteration, after the **reinit** expression is evaluated.

Even though the syntax of a **for** statement allows it to be very flexible, most of the **for** loops you will encounter (or will write) are of a standard form. They are almost always used to execute a body of code for a certain number of iterations. In

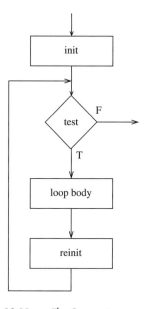

Figure 13.11   The C **for** statement

the example at the beginning of this section, we used the **for** loop to execute the loop body 10 times.

Below are some examples of code with **for** loops. The indentation used for these loops is stylistic; the indentation does not affect their behavior. The convention is to indent loop bodies so they can be quickly identified by someone scanning through the code.

```
/* --- What is the output of loop? --- */
for (i = 0; i <= 10; i++)
    printf("%d ", i);

/* --- What does this one output?  --- */
letter = 'a';

for (c = 0; c < 26; c++)
    printf("%c ", letter+c);


/* --- What does this loop do?     --- */
numberOfOnes = 0;

for (bitNum = 0; bitNum < 16; bitNum++) {
    if (inputValue & (1<<bitNum))
        numberOfOnes++;
}
```

Let's take a look at the LC-2 translation of a simple **for** loop. Assume **i** is a local integer variable whose offset is 3 off the top of the run-time stack. The loop body is a simple one: the local variable **x** (offset 4) is incremented by the current value of **i**.

```
int x = 0;

for (i = 0; i < 10; i++)
    x += i;
```

The LC-2 code generated by the compiler is shown in Figure 13.12.

Here is a common mistake made when using **for** loops within C code.

```
x = 0;
for (i = 0; i < 10; i++);
    x = x + 1;

printf("x = %d\n", x);
printf("i = %d\n", i);
```

What gets output by the first **printf**? The answer is **x** = **1**. Why? The second **printf** outputs **i** = **10**. Why? See Problem 13 in the exercises at the end of this chapter.

A **for** loop can be constructed using a **while** loop (actually, vice versa as well). In programming, they can be used interchangeably, to a degree. When to use which

```
        AND  R0, R0, #0    ;    clear out R0
        STR  R0, R6, #4    ;    x = 0;

        ; init
        AND  R0, R0, #0    ;    clear out R0
        STR  R0, R6, #3    ;    init (i = 0)

        ; test
LOOP:   LDR  R0, R6, #3    ;    perform the test
        ADD  R0, R0, #-10
        BRpz DONE          ;    i is not less than 10

        ; loop body
        LDR  R0, R6, #4    ;    get x
        LDR  R1, R6, #3    ;    get i
        ADD  R0, R0, R1    ;    x + i
        STR  R0, R6, #4    ;    x += i;

        ; reinit
        LDR  R0, R6, #3
        ADD  R0, R0, #1
        STR  R0, R6, #3    ;    i++
        BR   LOOP

DONE:   :
        :
```

Figure 13.12   The LC-2 code generated for a `for` statement

looping construct may seem confusing at first. Using one instead of the other in a particular situation depends on several factors, such as programming style and taste, but there are certain tasks which lend themselves to a particular type of loop. As we have seen, **while** loops are particularly useful for sentinel loops, whereas **for** loops are useful for counter-controlled loops.

Nested Loops   Figure 13.13 contains another example of a **for** where the loop body is composed of another **for** loop. This construct is referred to as a *nested loop* because the inner loop is nested within the outer. In this example, the program prints out a multiplication table for the numbers 0 through 9. Each iteration of the inner loop prints out a single product in the table. An entire row is printed for each iteration of the outer loop. Notice that the **printf** function call contains a special character sequence in its format string. The **\t** sequence cause a tab character to be printed out. The tab helps align the columns of the multiplication table so the output looks neater.

Figure 13.14 contains a slightly more complex example. The number of iterations of the inner loop depends on the value of i as determined by the outer loop. Notice that braces are not required for the outer loop because its loop body (the inner loop) consists of only a single **for** statement. For a challenging exercise based on this example, take a look at problem 10 at the end of this chapter.

```
#include <stdio.h>

main()
{
  int multiplicand;    /* Contains the first operand of each multiply  */
  int multiplier;      /* Contains the second operand of each multiply */

  for (multiplicand = 0; multiplicand < 10; multiplicand++) {
    for (multiplier = 0; multiplier < 10; multiplier++) {
      printf("%d\t", multiplier * multiplicand);
    }
    printf("\n");
  }
}
```

Figure 13.13   A program that prints out a multiplication table

```
#include <stdio.h>

main()
{
  int sum = 0;          /* Initial the result variable */
  int input;            /* Holds user input            */
  int inner, outer;     /* Iteration variables         */

  /* Get input */
  printf("Input an integer: ");
  scanf("%d", &input);

  /* Perform calculation */
  for (outer = 1; outer <= input; outer++)
    for (inner = 0; inner < outer; inner++) {
      sum += inner;
    }

  /* Output result */
  printf("The result is %d\n", sum);
}
```

Figure 13.14   A program with a nested `for` loop

13.2.3 The `do-while` Statement

With a `while` loop, the condition is always evaluated *before* an iteration is performed. Therefore, it is possible for the `while` loop to execute zero iterations (i.e., when the condition is false from the start). There is a slight variant in C of the `while` statement called `do-while`, which always performs at least one iteration. In a `do-while` loop, the condition is evaluated *after* an iteration is performed. The operation of the `do-while` is demonstrated in the following example:

```
x = 0;
do {
    printf("%d \n", x);
    x = x + 1;
} while (x < 10);
```

Here, the conditional test, **x < 10**, is evaluated at the end of each iteration. Thus, the loop body will execute at least once. The next iteration is performed only if the test evaluates to a nonzero value. This code produces the following output (it has the same output as the code in Figure 13.7):

```
0 1 2 3 4 5 6 7 8 9
```

Syntactically, a **do-while** is composed of two components:

```
do
    loop_body;
while (test);
```

The **loop_body** component is a statement (simple or compound) that describes the computation to be performed by the loop. The **test** is an expression that determines whether another iteration is to be performed.

Figure 13.15 shows the control flow using the systematic decomposition notation. Notice the slight change from the flow of a **while** loop. The loop body and the test are interchanged. A conditional branch loops back to the top of the loop body, initiating another iteration. Notice that one iteration is always executed.

To further highlight the difference between **while** and **do-while**, we revisit a previous example. Figure 13.10 contains a simple program with a **while** loop. In case you have not figured it out already, this program simply reads the user's keyboard

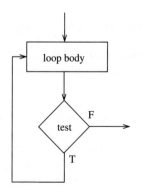

Figure 13.15   The C **do-while** statement

```
#include <stdio.h>

main()
{
  char echo;

  do {
    scanf("%c", &echo);
    printf("%c", echo);
  }
  while (echo != '\n');
}
```

Figure 13.16   The echo program, revisited

input a single character at a time, and displays it to the output device character by character. In Figure 13.16, we show how this loop would be coded with a **do-while** instead. Notice that because at least one iteration of the loop executes, we no longer need to initialize the variable **echo**. See Problem 15 at the end of the chapter for a question regarding a slight, subtle difference between the **while** version and the **do-while** version of this program.

At this point, the differences between the three types of C iteration constructs may seem very subtle, but once you become comfortable with them and build up experience using these constructs, you will begin to appreciate their differences. To a large degree, these constructs can be used interchangeably. Three flavors of iteration were provided as a convenience to the programmer. However, stylistically, there are times when one construct makes more sense to use than another—often the type of loop you choose will convey information about the intent of the loop to someone reading your code. As you build experience with programming, you discover that the decision of which construct to use when becomes much clearer.

13.2.4 The **break** and **continue** Statements

In this section, we describe two constructs that are sometimes used in conjunction with the C iteration constructs. The **break** statement causes the compiler to generate code which will prematurely exit the current block (i.e., compound statement). We have already seen the **break** statement in the context of the C **switch** statement. When used within a loop body, the **break** causes the loop to end by causing control to jump out of the iteration statement altogether. The **continue** statement causes the compiler to generate code which will end the current iteration and start the next. These statements can occur within the loop body and apply to the iteration construct immediately enclosing them. Essentially, the **break** and **continue** statements cause the compiler to generate an unconditional branch instruction somewhere in the loop body. Below are two example code segments that use **break** and **continue**. The output generated by each is also given. See D.7.7 and D.7.8 in Appendix D for additional information.

```
/* This code segment produces the output: 0 1 2 3 4 */
for (i = 0; i < 10; i++) {
   if (i == 5)
      break;
   printf("%d ", i);
}
```

The following example is similar, except it uses a **continue** statement:

```
/* This code produces the output: 0 1 2 3 4 6 7 8 9 */
for (i = 0; i < 10; i++) {
   if (i == 5)
      continue;
   printf("%d ", i);
}
```

13.3   COMPLETING THE PICTURE: C SYNTAX

Up until this point, we have mentioned bits and pieces of C syntax in passing. Here, we summarize what we have learned and put C syntax into a more logical framework. C syntax is fairly straightforward and regular (i.e., there are not many special cases), however, it is filled with opportunities for shooting oneself in the foot. Keep in mind that the point of the syntax of any high-level language is to remove ambiguity. The programming language is a connection between our human languages, which are riddled with ambiguity, and the precise mechanical language of the machine.

We have seen two broad categories of constructs in the C programming language: declarations and statements. We use declarations to inform the compiler of variables we intend on using within the program. Statements, on the other hand, describe the work we wish to perform.

13.3.1   Declarations

The variable declarations we have discussed have a very simple form, which is shown below. The brackets [ ] are used to indicate an optional portion: A variable's declaration can contain an optional initial value for the variable.

type identifier [= initializer];

The type designates the data type for the variable and can be one of the standard types supported by C (**int**, **char**, **double**, for example) or a type defined by the programmer. See Appendix D.3.5 for information on programmer-defined types. Identifiers can be almost any sequences of upper- and lowercase letters, digits, and the underscore character. They cannot begin with a digit. The initializer is optional, and is specified with an = followed by a expression that is typically a constant. As a matter of convenience, variables of the same type can be declared together in a single declaration, separated by commas. Here, three integer variables are declared. The variable **y** is initialized to 3. As stated, this form of declaration is discouraged.

int x, y = 3, z;

13.3.2 Statements

Statements are composed of expressions. An *expression* is a sequence of variable identifiers, constants, and operators used in a legal fashion. An expression ending in a semicolon signifies a simple statement. A statement can also be combined with other statements and declarations to form a compound statement or *block*. A compound statement is syntactically equivalent to a single statement; anyplace a statement is required, a compound statement can be used. The control constructs (**if**, **if-else**, **switch**, **for**, **while**, **do-while**) create statements, which execute conditionally, partially, or iterate.

A block can also contains variable declarations. They must appear before any statements. Any variables declared within a block are local to that block—they are accessible only within the block. For example,

```
int i, k;

for (i = 0; i < 10; i++) {
  for (k = 0; k < 20; k++) {
    int i = 10;
    :
    :
  }
}
```

The variable **i** declared within the loop body of the inner **for** statement is different than the **i** declared at the outermost level. The inner **i** is only accessible within the loop body in which it is defined. The outer **i** is accessible everywhere except in the inner loop body. Each **i** will be allocated to a different memory location, thus they are essentially different variables sharing the same name.

13.4   PROBLEM SOLVING USING C

We have now covered enough C at this point to dive into solving some substantial programming problems. In this section, we examine three problems. We approach the first two problems using the systematic decomposition methodology described in Chapter 6, refining the problem until we are able to write a C program for it.

13.4.1   Problem 1: Approximating the Value of π

For the first programming problem, we want to calculate the value of π using its series expansion. The series is the following:

$$\pi = 4 - \frac{4}{3} + \frac{4}{5} - \frac{4}{7} + \cdots + (-1)^{n-1}\frac{4}{2n+1} + \cdots$$

Since the series deals with fractional numbers, we use the **double** floating-point type for any variables directly involved in the calculation. The series is an infinite series, and the more terms we evaluate, the more accurate our approximation of π. After initializing some variables, we ask the user to input the number of term of the series to evaluate. Then, we evaluate the series. Finally, we print out the result. We have defined the problem as a sequence of sequential constructs. Figure 13.17 shows the decomposition we have done so far.

Most of the sequential constructs in Figure 13.17 are very straightforward. Converting them into C code should be quite simple. One of the constructs in the figure, however, requires some additional refinement. We need to put a little thought into the subtask labeled *Evaluate Series*. For this subtask, we essentially want to *iterate* through the series, term by term, until we evaluate exactly the number of terms the user indicates. We want to use a counter-controlled iteration construct. Figure 13.18 shows the decomposition. We maintain a counter for the current loop iteration. If the counter is less than the limit indicated by the user, then we evaluate another term. Notice that the refined version of the subtask looks like the flow diagram for a **for** loop.

We are almost done. The only nontrivial subtask remaining is "Evaluate another term." Notice that all even terms in the series are subtracted, and all odd terms

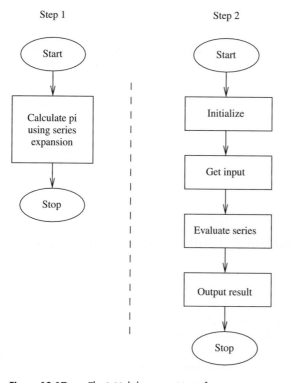

Figure 13.17   The initial decomposition of a program that evaluates the series expansion for π for a given number of terms

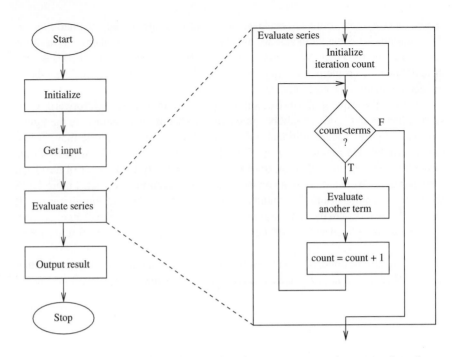

Figure 13.18   The refinement of the subtask Evaluate Series into one that iterates "limit" for a given number of times. Within this loop, we evaluate terms within the series expansion for π.

are added. Within this subtask, we need to determine if the particular term we are evaluating is an odd or an even term, and then accordingly factor it into the current value of the approximation. This involves using a decision contruct as shown in Figure 13.19. The complete code resulting from this stepwise refinement is shown in Figure 13.20.

13.4.2   Problem 2: Finding Prime Numbers Less than 100

This problem involves finding all the prime numbers that are less than 100. Recall that a number is prime if the only two numbers that evenly divide it are 1 and itself. We can approach this problem by first stating it as a single task. We can refine this single task into two separate sequential subtasks: Initialize and then perform the calculation.

Performing the calculation subtask is the brunt of the programming effort. Essentially, the calculation subtask can be stated as such: We want to check every integer between 2 and 100 to determine if it is prime. If it is prime, we want to print it out. We want to iterate from 2 through 100, determining if each number is prime—a counter-controlled loop should work just fine for this purpose. We can further refine the calculation subtask into smaller subtasks, as shown in Figure 13.21. Notice that the flow diagram has the look of a **for** loop.

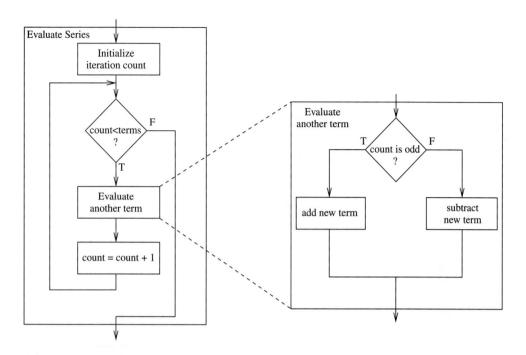

Figure 13.19   Add or subtract the current term depending on if it is odd or even.

```
#include <stdio.h>

main()
{
  int count;                    /* Iteration variable          */
  int numOfTerms;               /* Number of terms to evaluate */
  double pi = 0;                /* approximation of pi         */

  printf("Number of terms (must be 1 or larger) : ");
  scanf("%d", &numOfTerms);

  for (count = 1; count <= numOfTerms; count++) {
    if (count % 2)
      pi = pi + (4.0 / (2.0 * count - 1));        /* Odd terms added */
    else
      pi = pi - (4.0 / (2.0 * count - 1)); /* Even terms subtracted */
  }

  printf("The approximate value of pi is %f\n", pi);
}
```

Figure 13.20   A program to calculate π

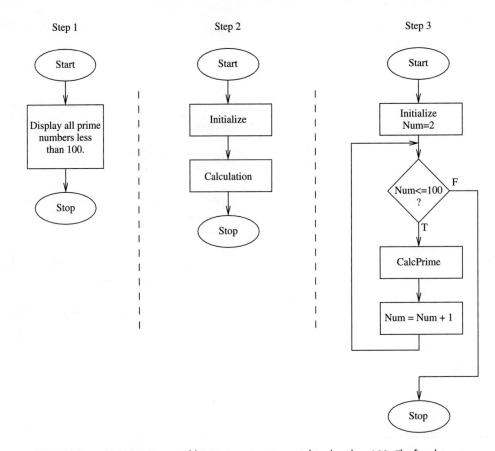

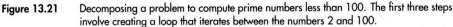

Figure 13.21   Decomposing a problem to compute prime numbers less than 100. The first three steps involve creating a loop that iterates between the numbers 2 and 100.

The problem is beginning to take shape, and we can already start mapping portions of it into C code. We still need to refine the CalcPrime subtask. In this subtask, we need to actually determine if the current number is prime or not. Here, we rely on the fact that any number between 2 and 100 that is *not* prime will have at least one divisor between 2 and 10 that is not itself. We can refine this subtask as shown in Figure 13.22.

Finally, we need to detail out the "Divide number by integers 2 through 10" subtask. It involves dividing the current number by all integers between 2 and 10 and determining if any of them evenly divide it. To do this, we can either use many sequential constructs or use an iteration construct to cycle through all the integers between 2 and 10. Figure 13.23 shows the decomposition using the iteration construct.

Now, coding this problem into a C program is a small step forward. The program is listed in Figure 13.24. There are two **for** loops within the program, one of which is nested within the other. The outer loop sequences through all the integers between 2 and 100; it corresponds to the loop created when we decomposed the calculation subtask. An inner loop determines if the number generated by the outer loop has any

Step 3

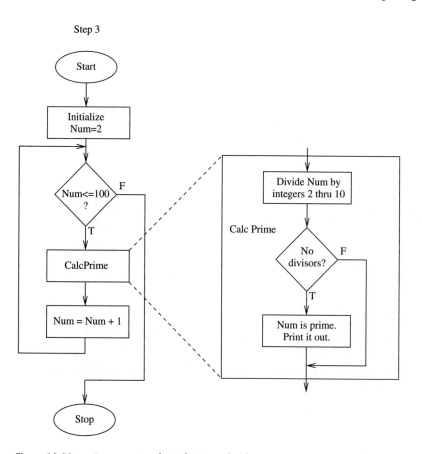

Figure 13.22   Decomposing the CalcPrime subtask

divisors; it corresponds to the loop created when we decomposed the "Divide number by integers 2 through 10" subtask. One item of note: If a divisor between 2 and 10 is found, then a flag variable called **prime** is set to *false*. It is set to *true* before the inner loop begins. If it remains *true*, then the particular number generated by the outer loop has no divisors and is therefore prime.

To do this, we are utilizing the C preprocessor's macro substitution facility. We have defined, using **#define**, two symbolic names, **FALSE**, which maps to the value 0 and **TRUE**, which maps to 1. The preprocessor will simply replace each occurrence of the word **TRUE** in the source file with 1 and each occurrence of **FALSE** with 0.

13.4.3 Problem 3: Detecting a Sequence of Text

For this problem, we want to develop a program that reads in a line of input from the keyboard, up until the first new line character is typed. Within the entire line of input, the program determines the number of occurrences of the character sequence *the*.

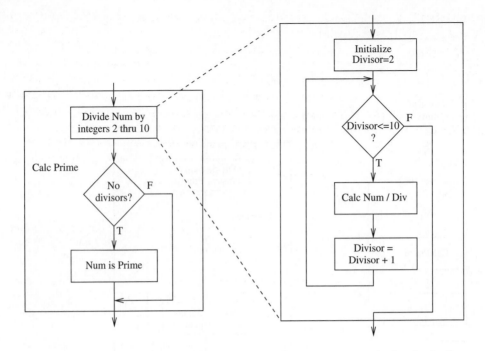

Figure 13.23   Determining if a number less than or equal to 100 is prime can be done by dividing it by integers between 2 and 10

```
#include <stdio.h>
#define FALSE 0
#define TRUE  1

main()
{
  int num, divisor, prime;

  /* Start with 2 and go until 100  */
  for (num = 2; num <= 100; num++) {

    prime = TRUE;   /* Assume the number is prime */
    /* Test if the candidate number is a prime */
    for (divisor = 2; divisor <= 10; divisor++)
      if (((num % divisor) == 0) && num != divisor)
        prime = FALSE;

    if (prime)
      printf("The number %d is prime\n", num);
  }
}
```

Figure 13.24   A program that finds all primes between 2 and 100

For this problem, we dive right into the source code, which is shown in Figure 13.25. The program makes use of a C standard I/O function called **getchar**. The function **getchar** is very much like the LC-2 TRAP routine IN (except no banner requesting input is displayed on the screen). It receives input from the keyboard and *returns* the ASCII value of the key that was typed. In C, a function can also return a value (a concept we will explore in the next chapter). The function call **getchar()** returns the ASCII value of the keypress. In this program, this value is assigned to the variable **key**. The expression `((key = getchar()) != '\n')`

```c
#include <stdio.h>

main()
{
  char key;                 /* Holds the current input character       */
  int count = 0;            /* Number of "the" encountered             */
  int match = 0;            /* Number of previous characters that match */

  /* When the user types a newline, the program will end               */
  while ((key = getchar()) != '\n') {
    switch (match) {

    case 0:                 /* Starting point                          */
      if (key == 't')
        match++;
      else
        match = 0;
      break;

    case 1:                 /* Got a 't' already. If this character    */
      if (key == 'h')       /* is an 'h', then proceed to 'e'.         */
        match++;
      else if (key == 't')  /* If it is a 't', start from match = 1    */
        match = 1;
      else                  /* otherwise start over                    */
        match = 0;
      break;

    case 2:                 /* Got 'th' already                        */
      if (key == 'e') {     /* if we get an 'e', increment             */
        count++;            /* and start over.                         */
        match = 0;
      }
      else if (key == 't')  /* If we get a 't' start from match = 1    */
        match = 1;
      else                  /* else start over.                        */
        match = 0;
      break;
    }
  }
  printf("The number of times 'the' was detected: %d\n", count);
}
```

Figure 13.25   A program that counts the occurrences of *the* in the input stream

controls the **while** loop. To explain what this expression accomplishes, we dissect it into its constituent parts. Because of the parentheses, the first subexpression that is evaluated is **(key = getchar())**. As mentioned, the value returned by the **getchar** function is assigned to the variable **key**. Since the assignment operator **=** is used, this subexpression then evaluates to the value assigned to **key**, so **(key = getchar())** equals whatever keystroke was detected by **getchar**. The subexpression is an operand to the relational operator **!=**, the "not equal to" operator. The other operand is the ASCII constant **'\n'** or newline. The entire expression evaluates to 1 if the ASCII value assigned to **key** is not the ASCII value of the newline character. Otherwise it is zero.

With each character read in from the keyboard, the program evaluates whether the character is part of the sequence *the*. The variable named **match** records the *state* of the current sequence. It indicates if the previous characters in the input stream were part of the sequence *the*. For example, if the previous input character was a *t*, then **match** is set to 1. Then, if the next character is an *h*, we can advance **match** to 2; otherwise we reset it to 0 or 1. Why 1? If the letter we see is a *t*, then we need to prepare for seeing *the*. If the previous two characters were *th*, then **match** equals 2—now, if we see that the next character is an *e*, then we have detected the sequence *the* and we can increment our sequence counter. If **match** equals 2 and we do not see an *e*, then we reset **match** back to 0 or 1—we had a close call, but not quite a full match.

PROBLEMS

13.1.   Re-create the LC-2 compiler's symbol table when it compiles the calculator program listed in Figure 13.6.

13.2.   1.   Write what the following code looks like after it is processed by the preprocessor.

```
#define VERO -2

if (VERO)
    printf("True!");
else
    printf("False!");
```

2.   What is the output produced when this code is run?

3.   If we modified the code to the following, does the code behave differently? If so, how?

```
#define VERO -2

if (VERO)
    printf("True!");
else if (!VERO)
    printf("False!");
```

13.3. An `if-else` statement can be used in place of the C conditional operator (see Section 12.3.9). Rewrite the following statement using an `if-else` rather than the conditional operator.

```
x = a ? b : c;
```

13.4. Describe the behavior of the following statements for the case when **x** equals 0 and when **x** equals 1.

1.
```
if (x = 0)
    printf("x equals 0\n");
else
    printf("x does not equal 0\n");
```

2.
```
if (x == 0)
    printf("x equals 0\n");
else
    printf("x does not equal 0\n");
```

3.
```
if (x == 0)
    printf("A\n");
else if (x != 1)
    printf("B\n");
else if (x < 1)
    printf("C\n");
else if (x)
    printf("D\n");
```

4.
```
int x;
int y;

switch (x) {

case 0:
    y = 3;

case 1:
    y = 4;
    break;

default:
    y = 5;
    break;
}
```

5. What happens if **x** is not equal to 0 or 1 for part 4?

13.5. What will the LC-2 code for the `switch` statement in part 4 of the previous problem look like?

13.6. Figure 13.14 contains a C program with a nested `for` loop.

1. Mathematically state the series that this program calculates.

2. Write a program to calculate the following function:

$$f(n) = f(n - 1) + f(n - 2)$$

with the following initial conditions,

$$f(0) = 1, \quad f(1) = 1$$

13.7. Can the following `if-else` statement be converted into a **switch**? If yes, convert it. If no, why not?

```
if (x == 0)
    y = 3;
else if (x == 1)
    y = 4;
else if (x == 2)
    y = 5;
else if (x == y)
    y = 6;
else
    y = 7;
```

13.8. At least how many times will the statement called **loopBody** execute the following constructs?

1.
```
while(condition)
    loopBody;
```
2.
```
do
    loopBody;
while(condition);
```
3.
```
for(init; condition; reinit)
    loopBody;
```
4.
```
while(condition1)
    for(init; condition2; reinit)
        loopBody;
```
5.
```
do
    do
        loopBody;
    while(condition1);
while(condition2);
```

13.9. What is the output of each of the following code segments?

1.
```
a = 2;
while(a > 0) {
    a--;
}
printf("%d", a);
```
2.
```
a = 2;
do {
    a--;
} while(a > 0)
printf("%d", a);
```
3.
```
b = 0;
for (a = 3; a < 10; a += 2)
    b = b + 1;
printf("%d %d", a, b);
```

13.10. Convert the program in Figure 13.4 into one that uses a **switch** statement instead of `if-else`.

13.11. The following is an incomplete C program. Below the C program is its LC-2
translation. Based on the LC-2 code, re-create the C program.

```
/* The C program */
main() {
    int a, b;

/* The LC-2 translation */
.ORIG    x3000
LEA      R6, STACK
AND      R0, R0, #0
ADD      R0, R0, #10
STR      R0, R6, #4
AND      R0, R0, #0
ADD      R0, R0, #5
STR      R0, R6, #3
LDR      R0, R6, #4
LDR      R1, R6, #3
NOT      R1, R1
ADD      R1, R1, #1
ADD      R0, R1, R0
STR      R0, R6, #3
LDR      R0, R6, #3
ADD      R0, R0, R0
STR      R0, R6, #4
LDR      R0, R6, #3
BRp      Print
HALT
Print    LD       R0, Value
OUT
HALT
Value    .FILL x31
```

13.12. For the following questions, **x** is an integer with the value 4.

1. What output is generated by the following code segment?

```
if (7 > x > 2)
    printf("True.");
else
    printf("False.");
```

2. Does the following code cause an infinite loop?

```
while(x > 0)
    x++;
```

3. What is the value of **x** after the following code has executed?

```
for (x = 4; x < 4; x--) {
    if (x < 2)
        break;
    else if (x == 2)
        continue;
    x = -1;
}
```

13.13. The following code:

```
x = 0;
for (i = 0; i < 10; i++);
    x = x + 1;

printf("x = %d\n", x);
printf("i = %d\n", i);
```

has the following output:

```
x = 1
i = 10
```

Why?

13.14. Change this program so that it uses a **do-while** loop instead of a **for** loop.

```
main() {
    int i;
    int sum;

    for(i = 0; i <= 100; i++) {
        if (i % 4 == 0)
            sum = sum + 2;
        else if (i % 4 == 1)
            sum = sum - 6;
        else if (i % 4 == 2)
            sum = sum * 3;
        else if (i % 4 == 3)
            sum = sum / 2;
    }
    printf("%d\n", sum);
}
```

13.15. The echo program in Figure 13.10 and Figure 13.16 are very similar. However, they have a very slight difference in behavior. Can you identify it?

13.16. Write a C program that accepts as input a single integer **k**, then writes a pattern consisting of a single 1 on the first line, two 2s on the second line, three 3s on the third line, and so forth, until it writes **k** occurrences of **k** on the last line.

For example, if the input is 5, the output should be the following:

```
1
2   2
3   3   3
4   4   4   4
5   5   5   5   5
```

13.17. 1.   Convert the following **while** loop into a **for** loop.

```
while (condition)
    loopBody;
```

2. Convert the following **for** loop into a **while** loop.

```
for (init; condition; reinit)
    loopBody;
```

13.18. What is the output of the following code?

```
int r = 0;
int s = 0;
int w = 12;
int sum = 0;

for (r = 1; r <= w; r++)
    for (s = r; s <= w; s++)
        sum = sum + s;

printf("sum =%d\n", sum);
```

chapter

14

Functions

14.1 INTRODUCTION

Functions are the soul of C programming. Functions—called subroutines or procedures in other programming languages—allow the programmer to create a program from smaller, simpler subcomponents. We've seen this concept already. We built larger things from simpler building blocks when building gates out of transistors, and logic structures out of gates, and the LC-2 datapath out of logic structures. In a similar fashion, functions provide *abstraction* when building a program; they allow low-level details to be buried deeper within a program, giving the program a clearer, high-level structure.

Functions are useful for a variety of other reasons, too. For instance, if the same bit of work needs to be done at multiple spots within a program, then using a function to do this work proves to be quite useful. The function gets *called* from the various spots where the work is required. Functions that perform subtasks common enough to be required by many programs can be put into a collection of functions called a *library*. Most C programmers heavily utilize C's standard library functions, examples of which include the I/O functions `printf`, `scanf`, and `getchar`.

We have seen examples of functions when we programmed in LC-2 assembly language. All of Chapter 9 was devoted to LC-2 subroutines and traps. Traps (for example, the IN and OUT system traps) are highly specialized, system functions—functions written by the system designers that perform common, useful tasks that require low-level manipulation of the hardware.

The C programming language is oriented around functions. A C program is essentially a collection of functions. Every statement belongs to one (and only one) function. All C programs start and finish execution in the function **main**. The function **main** may call other functions along the way, and they may, in turn, call more functions. As we saw when dealing with the LC-2 equivalent of functions, after a function completes, control returns to the point where the function was called. Control eventually returns to the function **main**, and when **main** completes, the program completes (provided something did not cause the program to terminate prematurely).

In this chapter, we cover C functions. Along the way we examine some substantive examples, and we go through a problem-solving exercise involving functions. We also describe, again using the LC-2 as a model, the low-level mechanics of functions in C in order to deepen our appreciation for them.

14.2 HIGH-LEVEL PROGRAMMING STRUCTURE

Functions give our programs high-level structure. That is, we can look at a well-crafted program that uses functions and quickly discern something about its operation without getting mired by the details of it.

Below is an example of how functions give a program structure. The example is the function **main** of a chess program. The program is organized such that the functions **SetUpBoard**, **DetermineSides**, **WhitesTurn**, **BlacksTurn**, and **NoOutcomeYet** perform the major subtasks.

```
main()
{
    /* Set up the chess board */
    SetUpBoard();

    /* Determine who is black, who is white */
    DetermineSides();

    /* Play the game! */
    do {
        WhitesTurn();
        BlacksTurn();
    } while(NoOutcomeYet());
}
```

Whereas the internal workings of the algorithm are not apparent, this structured programming style reveals the flow and organization of the program. The details of the algorithm are hidden within the functions, whose names reveal the jobs they do.

We can treat each function as a small program that performs a well-defined subtask. The first function, **SetUpBoard**, sets up the chessboard. This function will initialize the internal representation for the chessboard and place the pieces in the correct initial spots. Once the code is written, it can be tested independently of the other functions. Functions are good places to divide a large programming task among several programmers. For example, one programmer can work on the **SetUpBoard** function while another works on the **DetermineSides** function.

By treating functions as individual subprograms, the whole programming process is made easier to manage, by simplifying coding and reducing the amount of time needed to get a complex program debugged and running.

14.3   FUNCTIONS IN C

We begin with a simple example. Figure 14.1 is a program that simply prints a message using a function named *PrintBanner*. This is a C function in its simplest form. Program execution begins at the function **main**, which calls the function **PrintBanner**. The function **PrintBanner** calls the function **printf**, which, as we know, is a C library function. Once the message is printed, the flow of control returns to **main**. The function **main** calls **printf** and then **PrintBanner** again before terminating.

This program contains the simplest form of function call: **PrintBanner** requires no input from **main** to do its subtask. It simply does its thing and returns control back to **main**. It provides **main** with no output data (not counting the banner printed to the screen). In other words, no arguments are passed from **main** to **PrintBanner** and no values are returned from **PrintBanner** to **main**.

Another stylistic note: If we wanted to change the banner from being composed of the equal sign character = to something else, then we need only to change one line regardless of the number of spots within the program from where the banner is printed. This can be an important time-saving and bug-reducing technique, particularly for programs with lots of lines of code.

```c
#include <stdio.h>

void PrintBanner();              /* Function declaration */

main()
{
   PrintBanner();
   printf("A simple C program.\n");
   PrintBanner();
}

void PrintBanner()
{
   printf("=============================\n");
}
```

Figure 14.1   A C program that uses a function to print a banner message

```
#include <stdio.h>

/* This is the declaration (or prototype) for the function factorial.  */
int Factorial(int n);                                    /* -- A -- */


/* The function main --- all C programs must contain a function main    */
main()
{
  int number;                   /* Number from user                   */
  int answer;                   /* Answer calculated by factorial     */

  printf("Input a number: ");   /* Function call to a library function */
                                /* -- where is its prototype?         */
  scanf("%d", &number);         /* Function call to a library function */

  answer = Factorial(number);   /* Function call to factorial  -- B -- */

  printf("The factorial of %d is %d\n", number, answer);  /* Output    */
}

/* The function definition for factorial.                    -- C -- */
int Factorial(int n)
{
  int i;                        /* Iteration count                    */
  int result = 1;               /* Initialized result                 */

  for (i = 1; i <= n; i++)      /* This loop calculates factorial     */
    result = result * i;

  return result;                /* Return to caller         -- D -- */
}
```

Figure 14.2   A C program to calculate factorial

Now we move to a slightly more sophisticated example. Figure 14.2 lists an example C program that contains two functions, **main** and **Factorial**. This example is different from the previous in that it requires some communication between the two functions.

The high-level structure of the program is apparent from the code in **main**. A message is printed, a decimal number is scanned from the keyboard, a function named **Factorial** is called, and the value of the variable **answer** is displayed on the screen.

The function **Factorial** performs a calculation based on an input value it receives from the function that called it, which in this case is the value in *n*. The calculation can be stated as multiplying all positive integers less than or equal to *n* together. This calculation is called *factorial* and is algebraically stated as:

$$\text{factorial}(n) = n! = 1 \times 2 \times 3 \times \ldots \times n$$

The value calculated by this function is called *result*. Its value is returned (using the **return** statement) to the function that is called **Factorial**, which in this case is **main**. The function **Factorial** requires an *argument*, and it *returns* a value.

Within this program, the flow of control goes from statement to statement in the function **main**. However, each of the statements in **main** causes another function to be invoked. The first statement in **main**, **printf("Input a number: ");** prints out a query. The second statement **scanf("%d", &number)** calls the function **scanf** to read the user's input and assign it the variable **number**. The third statment in **main** calls the function **Factorial**. When control returns back to **main**, the return value from **Factorial** is assigned to the variable **answer**. It is then displayed using a call to **printf**.

In Figure 14.2, there are four lines of code marked with a capital letter in the right-hand margin of the code. These lines correspond to key components of the function **Factorial**. They are its *declaration* (also known as the *prototype*), its *definition*, which contains the source code for the function, its *call*, which invokes the function, and its *return*.

14.3.1   The Declaration

In the example above, the source code line marked -- **A** -- is the function declaration for **Factorial**. A function's declaration informs the compiler about the function in a fashion similar to how a variable's declaration informs the compiler about a variable. Sometimes called a *function prototype*, a function declaration contains the name of the function, the type of value it returns, and a list of input values it expects. The function declaration ends with a semicolon.

The first item appearing in a function's declaration is the type of the value the function returns. The type can be any C data type (e.g., **int**, **char**, **double**). This type describes the type of the single output value that the function produces. Not all functions return values. For example, the function **PrintBanner** from the previous example did not return a value. If a function does not return a value, then its return type must be declared as **void**.

A function's name can be any legal C identifier. Often, programmers choose function names somewhat carefully to reflect the action the function performs. Programmers sometimes differentiate the names of functions from the names variables; often, we do this by having the first character of a function's name in uppercase.

Finally, a function's declaration also describes the number and type of the input *parameters* required by the function. A declaration also conveys the order in which the function expects to receive its input parameters. Often the names of the parameters are also included but are not required. Some functions may not require any input. The function **PrintBanner** required no input parameters. Its parameter list was empty.

In the previous example, the function **Factorial** takes one integer parameter (called *n* within the function) and returns an integer value.

14.3.2   The Call

The line marked -- **B** -- is the actual function call to **Factorial**. In this statement, the function **Factorial** is initiated to perform its task. The values that are to be transmitted to the function, called *arguments*, are enclosed within parentheses immediately following the name of the function being called. Arguments can be any legal expression, as long as they match the type expected by the function being called. In this example, we want the function **Factorial** to compute the factorial of the integer value in the variable called **number**. The value returned by **Factorial** is then assigned to the integer variable **answer**.

14.3.3   The Definition

The code beginning at the line marked -- **C** -- indicates the beginning of the function definition of **Factorial**. Notice that this first line matches the function declaration (however, minus the semicolon). Within the parentheses after the name of the function is the function's *formal parameter list*. The formal parameter list is a list of variable declarations, where each variable will contain a value passed to the function from the calling function. From every place in the program this function is called, the actual arguments appearing in the call should match the type and ordering of the formal parameter list.

The actual function's body appears in the braces following the parameter list. A function's body consists of declarations and statements that define the computation the function performs. Any variable declared within these braces is local to the function. Notice that a function's body is precisely a compound statement.

14.3.4   The Return Value

The line marked -- **D** -- is where control passes back from **Factorial** to whichever function called it, which in this case is the function **main**. Since **Factorial** is returning a value, then an expression must follow the **return** keyword and the type of this expression must match the return type declared for the function. In the case of **Factorial**, the statement **return result;** transmits the calculated factorial stored in **result** back to the caller. In general, functions that return a value must include at least one **return** statement in their body. Functions that do not return a value—functions declared as type **void**—do not require a **return** statement; the **return** is optional. For these functions, control passes back to the caller after the last statement has been executed.

You might notice that the information contained within a function's declaration is also contained within its definition. Why do we need to declare a function when a compiler can glean the same information once we define it? Examine closely the source code of the factorial program in Figure 14.2 and you might notice that the function call to **Factorial** appears before its definition. Without the declaration (all declarations typically appear at the top of a source file), the compiler would not know anything about the function **Factorial** when it sees the function call. It may not be able to generate the proper code for the function call. Therefore, either we define the functions before we call them in the source (which is not always possible to do), or we declare all functions beforehand. If all functions are declared properly beforehand, then the ordering of functions within a source file has no bearing on program behavior. We can define functions in any order we please. The convention we will follow is that the function **main** will be defined first and all other functions will follow.

Let's summarize: A function declaration (or prototype) informs the compiler of a function, indicating the number and types of parameters the function expects and indicating what type of value the function returns. A function definition is the actual source code for the function. The formal parameter list of the definition indicates the names of the function's parameters and in which order they will be passed by the caller. And finally, a function is invoked via a function call. Input values, or arguments, for the function to act upon are listed within the parentheses of the function call. Literally, the value of each argument listed in the function call will be assigned to each parameter in the parameter list, the first argument assigned to the first parameter, the second argument to the second parameter, and so forth. The return value is the output of the function and is passed back to the caller function.

14.4   ANOTHER EXAMPLE

Figure 14.3 lists a program that uses a function to convert a given amount of foreign currency into dollars using a given exchange rate. The function, **ValueInDollars**, takes as input two **double**s, and returns a **double**.

This function is called from the the function **main** twice. The first time, it is used to convert francs into dollars. The number of francs to convert is read from the keyboard using **scanf** (notice that the format specification to read a **double** value is **%lf**). The conversion rate between francs and dollars is specified as a preprocessor macro. The symbol **DOLLARS_PER_FRANC** will be substituted by the value **0.16** by the preprocessor. The value returned by **ValueInDollars** is assigned to the variable **total**. This process is repeated again to convert yen into dollars.

14.5   THE RUN-TIME STACK

Before we finish our discussion of functions, we need to understand a mechanism central to their execution: the run-time stack. As we shall see, the run-time stack is necessary to enable functions to call themselves, a programming technique called *recursion* to which we devote all of Chapter 16. To understand functions (or subroutines, or procedures) well, you must understand the underlying stack mechanism that implements them.

```
/* This program calculates the dollar value of your foreign currency */

#define DOLLARS_PER_FRANC   0.16
#define DOLLARS_PER_YEN     0.01

#include <stdio.h>

/* Function declarations */
double ValueInDollars(double amount, double rate);

main()
{
    double francs, dollarsOfFrancs;        /* francs, value of francs */
    double yen, dollarsOfYen;              /* yen, value of yen       */
    double total = 0.00;                   /* total amount of currency */

    printf("Enter amount of Francs : ");
    scanf("%lf", &francs);

    dollarsOfFrancs = ValueInDollars(francs, DOLLARS_PER_FRANC);
    printf("You have $%f dollars worth of Francs\n", dollarsOfFrancs);

    printf("Enter amount of Yen    : ");
    scanf("%lf", &yen);

    dollarsOfYen = ValueInDollars(yen, DOLLARS_PER_YEN);
    printf("You have $%f dollars worth of Yen\n", dollarsOfYen);

    total = dollarsOfFrancs + dollarsOfYen;
    printf("You have $%f dollars worth of Francs and Yen\n", total);
}

/* Convert currency into dollars, given an exchange rate */
double ValueInDollars(double amount, double rate)
{
    double value;

    value = amount * rate;
    return value;
}
```

Figure 14.3   A C program that converts francs and yen into dollars

14.5.1   The Activation Record

While analyzing the code of a function, the LC-2 compiler first creates entries in its symbol table (see Section 12.2.5) for parameters and variables declared within the function. Within the symbol table, the compiler keeps track of where each variable is allocated storage in memory. Recall that variables are assigned offsets beginning at a region of memory whose base address is in R6. Each function's local variables are allocated storage in this manner. But in order for this to work properly, as different functions are called, we need a systematic means of changing R6 as control passes from one function to another. Each C function is translated into LC-2 instructions assuming that R6 contains the base address of a region of memory allocated for its local variables.

In order to make this happen, the compiler creates a memory template of all the local variables within a function while processing the source code for that function. This template is called the *activation record*. The activation record is essentially a systematic means of organizing the memory in which a function's local variables are stored. We also keep bookkeeping information within the activation record—this bookkeeping information is used to assist in pushing and popping items to the stack and returning back to the caller function during execution.

An activation record has a very simple structure, which we describe using the following code. Figure 14.4 shows the activation record for this function, called **NoName**. The function **NoName** has three local variables and two parameters, as shown below:

```
int NoName(int a, int b)
{
    int w, x, y;

    /* Function body */
    :
    :
    return y;
}
```

The first three entries of all LC-2 activation records for all functions are reserved for bookkeeping information. The first entry is reserved for the return value, regardless

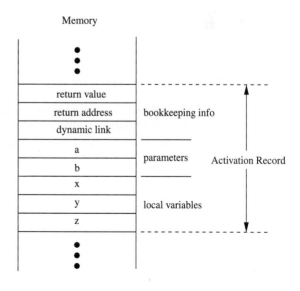

Figure 14.4   The activation record and symbol table entries for the function **NoName**

of whether a function returns a value or not. The function **NoName** returns an integer value. The **return** statement at the end of the function body causes the value of integer variable *y* to be written into the space reserved for the return value in the activation record. This happens just before control is passed back to the caller function.

The second entry in the activation record is the return address. This is the address of the instruction to execute after the function **NoName** has completed execution. In LC-2 terms, it is the same as the link address of a **JSR** instruction. As we shall see, function calls and returns in C are implemented using LC-2 **JSR** and **RET** instructions.

The final bookkeeping entry is called the *dynamic link*. It is the memory address of the activation record of the function that called **NoName**. More on the dynamic link later.

Each of the formal parameters are given entries in the activation record immediately following the three bookkeeping entries. In this case, there are two parameters each requiring one memory location. Local variables are allocated in the entries following the parameters. In this case, three entries are allocated for local variables. The compiler is able to determine the structure of any function's activation record as it analyzes the function's definition.

When the function **NoName** executes, the *stack pointer* R6, which points to the top of the run-time stack, will point to the beginning of **NoName**'s activation record. In other words, when function **NoName** is called, its activation record is *pushed* on top of the run-time stack.

The layout of a function's activation record allows the compiler to determine the memory address of each of the parameters and local variables when generating the machine code for the function. The offsets from the top of the activation record indicate where in memory, starting from the stack pointer, each variable and parameter is stored. For example, in order to load the value of local variable **x** into register R3, the compiler simply generates an **LDR R3, R6, #5**.

14.5.2 Activation Records During Execution

Each time a function is called, we want to give it the same execution environment: R6 should contain the beginning of a region of memory that contains the function's activation record. A simple approach is to have the compiler assign each function a spot in memory where it can place its activation record. So, for example, function **main** gets location x1000, function **NoName** gets location x1020, and so forth. Here, the compiler would simply ensure that activation records did not overlap. However, since we need the ability of functions to call themselves, this scheme will not work—when a function calls itself, it will overwrite the values stored from its previous invocation. We will examine this extensively in the next chapter when we discuss recursion.

A simple approach that solves this problem and allows a function to call itself is to allocate the activation records at run time on a stack. Recall from Chapter 10, that a stack is a fundamental data structure in which *Push* and *Pop* are the two data manipulation operations. The Push operation adds an item to the top of the stack, and Pop removes the item last added to the stack, that is, off the top of the stack. In the case of the run-time stack, the items that are pushed and popped are activation records.

When a program is executed, a region of memory is reserved for the stack. During execution, as a function is called, an activation record for that function is pushed onto the stack. When the function completes, the function's activation record is popped off the stack, and control is passed back to the caller function. Let's look at an example of this process:

```
main()
{
  int a;
  int b;

  :
  b = NoName(a, 10);
  :
}

int NoName(int a, int b)
{
  int w, x, y;

  /* Function body */
  :
  return y;
}
```

Figure 14.5 shows the run-time stack at several points during the execution of this program. The run-time stack begins at some fixed point in memory and grows toward higher numbered memory addresses. In this figure, since higher numbered addresses are at the bottom of the diagram, the stack grows downward. The point where the stack begins is determined by the designers of the operating system and varies from one computer system to another. In the LC-2, the stack begins at 0x4000.

Execution begins with a call by the LC-2 operating system to the function **main**. At this point, the activation record of **main** (which is similar in format to any other activation records) is pushed onto the run-time stack, and R6 contains the address of the beginning of **main**'s activation record. This is shown in Figure 14.5(a). Once the call to function **NoName** is encountered, the LC-2 code associated with the call manipulates the stack in such a way that once **NoName** begins execution, the activation record for **NoName** is on top of the stack and R6 contains the address for it. This is shown in Figure 14.5(b). When **NoName** completes, its activation record is popped off the stack and **main**'s record is once again at the top, as shown in Figure 14.5(c). The mechanism to make all this happen is done by LC-2 code generated by the compiler. In translating a function call, the compiler generates LC-2 code to push a record onto the stack. When translating a function return, the compiler generates LC-2 code to pop a record off the stack. Let's look at how this is done.

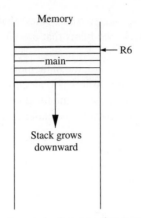

(a) Run-time stack when execution starts

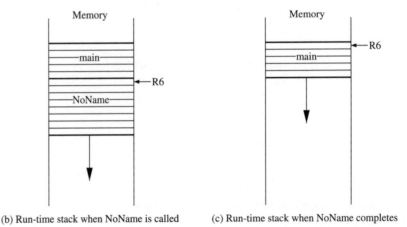

(b) Run-time stack when NoName is called   (c) Run-time stack when NoName completes

Figure 14.5   Several snapshots of the run-time stack while the NoName program
executes.

14.6 IMPLEMENTING FUNCTIONS IN C

In this section we describe the mechanics of function calls in C. There are four
segments of code that carry out the process of Pushing and Popping activation records:
First, code in the *caller* function (the function in which the call occurs) performs the
push of an activation record onto the stack. Second, the code at the beginning of the
callee function (the function to which the call was made) saves some bookkeeping
information so that control can be successfully passed back to the caller function
when the callee function completes. Third, when the callee function has completed
its job, a code in the callee function pops its activation record off the stack and returns
control back to the caller function. Finally, once control is back in the caller function,
code is executed to retrieve the callee function's return value.

In the next few sections, we present the actual LC-2 code for carrying out these operations. We do so by closely examining the statement **b** = **NoName(a, 10);** from the code in the previous code segment.

14.6.1   The Call

In the statement **b** = **NoName(a, 10);**, the function **NoName** is called with two arguments. The value returned by the function is then assigned to the local integer variable **b**. In translating this function call, the compiler generates LC-2 code which does the following:

1. Transmits the value of the two arguments to the function **NoName** by writing the values in the parameter fields of a *new* activation record.

2. Stores the value of R6 into the dynamic link field of this new activation record.

3. Modifies R6 to contain the address of this new activation record. This effectively pushes a new activation record on the stack.

4. Transfers control to **NoName** via the **JSR** instruction.

The LC-2 code to perform this function call looks as follows:

```
LDR   R0, R6, #3   ; load a
STR   R0, R6, #8   ; store the first argument to NoName
AND   R0, R0, #0   ; R0 <- 0
ADD   R0, R0, #10  ; R0 <- 10
STR   R0, R6, #9   ; store the second argument to NoName

STR   R6, R6, #7   ; store R6 into the dynamic link of rec
                   ; we pushed a new record on the stack
ADD   R6, R6, #5   ; Move R6 to point to start of record.
JSR   NoName
```

The first seven LC-2 instructions accomplish the task of transmitting the argument values. When generating the code to accomplish this, the compiler needs to be aware only of the size of the activation record of the caller function. The caller function in this case is the function **main**, and it has an activation record size of five (three bookkeeping entries plus two local variables). The compiler knows that the new activation record will begin *immediately* after the activation record for **main**. It needs to know very little about the function being called aside from the number, order, and type of the parameters.

The sixth instruction (**STR R6, R6, #7**) stores the current value of R6 into the dynamic link field of the new activation record. The dynamic link is used, as we shall see, to correctly pop a record off the stack. It stores the value of the old top of stack. The seventh instruction increments R6 just beyond the current activation record and points it to the activation record for **NoName**. Finally, a **JSR** instruction initiates the execution of the callee function. Recall that the LC-2 **JSR** instruction places the return address in R7.

Figure 14.6 shows the layout in memory of these two activation records after this code has executed. Some values have not been generated, such as the return value for **main**. These values are marked with a - -.

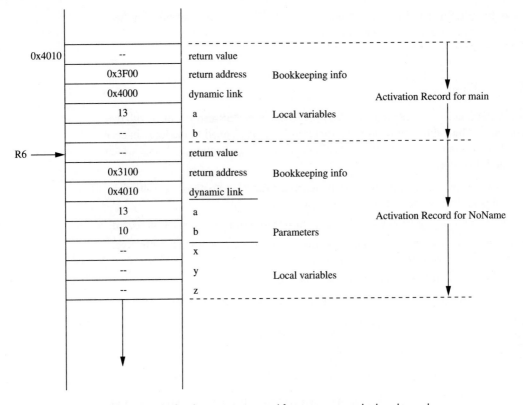

Figure 14.6   The run-time stack after the activation record for **NoName** is pushed on the stack.

14.6.2   Starting the Callee Function

The instruction executed after the **JSR** is the first instruction in the callee function **NoName**. Before the compiler can generate the code corresponding to the statements within a function, it must take care of some bookkeeping due to the function call. All functions in C (including **main**) are called from somewhere, thus all functions must start off by saving the value of R7 (it contains the return address of where they need to return control) into the return address entry in the activation record. The LC-2 code to do this is quite simple:

```
NoName:
        STR R7, R6, #1    ; store return address
```

When the **JSR** in the caller function executes, the address of the instruction following the **JSR** in the code is put into R7. The first task of the callee function is to store the value in a safe place in memory—losing the return address would leave no way to return control to the caller function. For this reason, each activation record contains a spot where we can safely store the return address.

14.6.3   Ending the Callee Function

Once the callee function has completed its work, several things need to be performed to return control back to the caller function. Firstly, a function that returns a value needs a mechanism for the return value to be transmitted properly back to the caller function. This transmission happens via the activation record. Secondly, all functions must pop the current activation record. To enumerate,

1. If there is a return value, it is written into the return value entry of the activation record.

2. The return address is loaded into R7.

3. The value of the dynamic link entry is loaded into R6. The activation is effectively popped from the stack.

4. The **RET** instruction returns control back to the caller function.

    The LC-2 instructions corresponding to this for **NoName** are

```
LDR   R0, R6, #6   ; load the value of y
STR   R0, R6, #0   ; store it into the return value entry
LDR   R7, R6, #1   ; load the return address
LDR   R6, R6, #2   ; load the dynamic link

RET
```

The first two instructions write the return value, which in this case is the local variable *y*, into the first entry of the activation record. The second instruction copies the value of the return address into R7. It was written into the activation record when the callee function started execution. The third instruction copies back the dynamic link (the old top of stack) into R6. This effectively pops the activation record off the stack. Even though the activation record is popped off the stack, the values still remain in memory (a fact that should not be surprising, having dealt with the physical operation of memory in Chapter 3). Once control is passed back to the caller function, it reads the return value from the activation record that was just popped.

14.6.4   Returning to the Caller Function

After the callee function executes the **RET** instruction, control is passed back to the caller function. In some cases, there is no return value (if the callee is declared of type **void**) and, in some cases, the caller function ignores the return value. Again, from our previous example, the return value is assigned to local variable *b*. The code after the **JSR** looks as follows:

```
JSR   NoName

LDR   R0, R6, #5   ; load the return value
                   ; (just beyond actrec for main)
STR   R0, R6, #4   ; b = NoName(a, 10);
  :
```

```
main:
        :
        LDR   R0, R6, #3   ; load a
        STR   R0, R6, #8   ; store the first argument to NoName
        AND   R0, R0, #0   ; R0 <- 0
        ADD   R0, R0, #10  ; R0 <- 10
        STR   R0, R6, #9   ; store the third argument to NoName

        STR   R6, R6, #7   ; store R6 into the dynamic link of rec
                           ; we pushed a new record on the stack
        ADD   R6, R6, #5   ; move R6 to point to start of record
        JSR   NoName

        LDR   R0, R6, #5   ; load the return value
                           ; (just beyond actrec for main)
        STR   R0, R6, #4   ; b = NoName(a, 10);
        :

NoName:
        STR R7, R6, #1     ; store return address

        :
        :                  ; the body of NoName
        :
        LDR   R0, R6, #6   ; load the value of y
        STR   R0, R6, #0   ; store it into the return value entry
        LDR   R7, R6, #1   ; load the return address
        LDR   R6, R6, #2   ; load the dynamic link

        RET
```

Figure 14.7   The LC-2 code corresponding to a C function call and return

The **LDR** instruction loads the callee function's return value from the activation record that was just popped off the stack. The act of popping a record moves only the stack pointer R6; the values in memory from the popped record persist until they are overwritten (i.e., after a new record is pushed on the stack) or the computer is halted and powered down.

14.6.5 Tying It All Together

The code for the call location in **main** and the beginning and end of **NoName** is listed in Figure 14.7. Here, the LC-2 code segments presented in the previous sections are all combined, showing the overall structure of the code.

14.7   PROBLEM SOLVING: CASE CONVERSION

In this section, we go through the development of a program that reads input from the keyboard and echos it back to the screen. We have already seen an example of a program that does just this in the previous chapter (see Figure 13.16). However, this time, we throw in a slight twist: We want the program to convert lowercase characters into uppercase before echoing them on the screen.

Our approach to solving this problem is to use the previous echo program from Figure 13.16. To avoid having to restructure the original echo code, we use a function to perform the conversion. This function is called after each character is scanned from the keyboard and before it is displayed to the screen. The conversion function requires a single character as a parameter, and returns either the same character (in the case that the character is already uppercase, or if it is not a character of the alphabet), or it will return an uppercase version of the character. Figure 14.8 shows the flow of this program. The flowchart of the original echo program is shaded in gray. To this original flowchart, we are adding a function call to perform the conversion.

Figure 14.9 shows an example C program that takes input from the keyboard, converts each input character into uppercase, and prints out the result. When the input

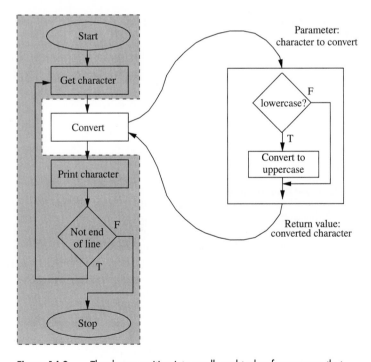

Figure 14.8   The decomposition into smaller subtasks of a program that converts input characters into uppercase

```c
#include <stdio.h>

/* Function declarations */
char ToUpper(char inchar);

/* Function main:                                                    */
/* Prompt for a line of text, Read one character, uppercase it,      */
/* print it out, then get another                                    */
main()
{
  char echo;                            /* Input character           */
  char upcase;                          /* Converted character       */

  printf("Input a line of text : ");

  do {
    scanf("%c", &echo);
    upcase = ToUpper(echo);
    printf("%c%", upcase);
  }
  while (echo != '\n');
}


/* Function ToUpper:                                                 */
/* If the parameter is lower case return its uppercase ASCII value   */
char ToUpper(char inchar)
{
  int outchar;

  outchar = inchar;

  if ('a' <= inchar && inchar <= 'z')
    outchar = inchar - ('a' - 'A');

  return outchar;
}
```

Figure 14.9   A program with a function to convert lowercase letters to uppercase

character is the new line character, the program terminates. The conversion process from lowercase to uppercase is done by the function **ToUpper**.

The corresponding LC-2 code for this example is shown in Figure 14.10. Because the LC-2 ISA is not byte-addressable, a character variable occupies a full word of memory to make this example easier to understand.

```
main:
        STR   R7, R6, #1   ;   even main needs to store return address
        :
        :                  ;   call to printf, test for the while loop
        :
        LDR   R0, R6, #3   ;   load value of echo
        STR   R0, R6, #8   ;   store echo as first parameter
        STR   R6, R6, #7   ;   store current top of stack as dynamic link
        ADD   R6, R6, #5   ;   move top of stack to new activation record
        JSR   ToUpper      ;   the call
        LDR   R0, R6, #5   ;   load return value and stick it into upcase
        STR   R0, R6, #4   ;   upcase = ToUpper(echo);
        :
        :                  ;   code for call putchar
ToUpper:
        STR   R7, R6, #1   ;   store away the return address
        LDR   R0, R6, #3   ;   load the parameter inchar
        STR   R0, R6, #4   ;   outchar = inchar;

        LD    R1, ASCII_a  ;   load the ascii value of 'a'
        NOT   R1
        ADD   R1, R1, #1   ;   R1 contains -'a'
        ADD   R1, R0, R1   ;   inchar - 'a'
        BRn   FALSE        ;   inchar is less than 'a'
        LD    R1, ASCII_z  ;   load the ascii value of 'z'
        NOT   R1
        ADD   R1, R1, #1   ;   R1 contains -'z'
        ADD   R1, R0, R1   ;   inchar - 'z'
        BRn   FALSE        ;   inchar is greater than 'z'

        ;   The condition is true ('a'<= inchar && inchar <= 'z')
        LD    R1, neg_ASCII_a_minus_A   ; load ascii value of -('a'-'A')
        LDR   R0, R6, #3   ;   load inchar
        ADD   R0, R1, R0   ;   calculate inchar - ('a' - 'A')
        STR   R0, R6, #4   ;   outchar = inchar - ('a' - 'A');

FALSE:
        LDR   R0, R6, #4   ;   load outchar
        STR   R0, R6, #0   ;   store it into the return value entry
        LDR   R7, R6, #1   ;   load the return address
        LDR   R6, R6, #2   ;   load the dynamic link
        RET                ;   return outchar;
ASCII_a:              .FILL #97
ASCII_z:              .FILL #122
neg_ASCII_a_minus_A:  .FILL #-32
```

Figure 14.10   LC-2 version of the C uppercase program

PROBLEMS

14.1.   What is the significance of the function **main**? Why must all programs contain this function?

14.2.   Refer to the structure of an activation record for this question.

1.   What is the purpose of the dynamic link?

2.   What is the purpose of the return address?

3.   What is the purpose of the return value?

14.3.   Refer to the C syntax of function for this question.

1.   What is a function declaration? What is its purpose?

2.   What is a function prototype?

3.   What is the function definition?

4.   What are arguments?

5.   What are parameters?

14.4.   For each of the items below, identify whether the caller function or the callee function performs the action.

1.   Writing the arguments into the activation record.

2.   Writing the return value.

3.   Writing the dynamic link.

4.   Modifying the value in R6 to contain the address of the called function's activation record.

14.5.   What is the output of the program below? Explain.

```
void MyFunc(int z);

main()
{
    int z = 2;

    MyFunc(z);
    MyFunc(z);
}

void MyFunc(int z)
{
    printf("%d ", z);
    z++;
}
```

14.6. What is the output of the following program?

```
#include <stdio.h>

int Multiply(int d, int b);

int d = 3;

main()
{
  int a, b, c;
  int e = 4;

  a = 1;
  b = 2;

  c = Multiply(a, b);
  printf("%d %d %d %d %d\n", a, b, c, d, e);
}

int Multiply(int d, int b)
{
  int a;
  a = 2;
  b = 3;

  return (a * b);
}
```

14.7. Below is the code for a C function named **Bump**.

```
int Bump(int x)
{
    int a;

    a = x + 1;

    return a;
}
```

1. Draw the activation record for **Bump**.

2. Write one of the following in each entry of the activation record to indicate what is stored there.
   (*a*) Local variable
   (*b*) Argument
   (*c*) Address of an instruction
   (*d*) Address of data
   (*e*) Other

3. Some of the entries in the activation record for **Bump** are written by the function that calls **Bump**; some are written by **Bump** itself. Identify the entries written by **Bump**.

14.8. Are the arguments to a function placed on the stack before or after the JSR to that function? Why?

14.9.   A C program containing the function **food** has been compiled into LC-2 assembly language. The translation of the function looks like the following:

```
food      STR      R7, R6, #1
          STR      R6, R6, #12
          ADD      R6, R6, #10
          JSR      pizza
          LDR      R7, R6, #1
          LDR      R6, R6, #2
          RET
```

1. How many entries does the activation record for **food** have?
2. If the function **pizza** takes no arguments, then how many local variables must it have?

14.10.   Modify the example in Figure 14.9 to *also* convert each character to lowercase. The new program should print out both the lower- and uppercase versions of each input character.

14.11.   Write a function to print out an integer value in base 4 (using only the digits 0, 1, 2, 3). Use this function to write a program that reads two integers from the keyboard, displays both numbers and their sum in base 4 on the screen.

14.12.   Write a function that returns a 1 if the first integer input parameter is evenly divisible by the second. Using this function, write a program to find the smallest number that is evenly divisible by all integers less than 10.

14.13.   Below is a function written in C and its translation into LC-2 assembly code. Unfortunately, the compiler that made the translation had a bug and made two mistakes (some compilers really make mistakes). Identify and correct the mistakes, and explain why they are mistakes.

```
int Smaller(int x, int y)
{
   if (x <= y)
      return x;
   else
      return y;
}
```

```
Smaller  STR      R7, R6, #1
         LDR      R0, R6, #3
         LDR      R1, R6, #4
         NOT      R2, R1
         ADD      R2, R2, #1
         ADD      R2, R0, R2
         BRz      LABEL1
         LDR      R0, R6, #3
         STR      R0, R6, #0
         BR       LABEL2
LABEL1   LDR      R0, R6, #4
         STR      R0, R6, #0
LABEL2   LDR      R6, R6, #2
         LDR      R7, R6, #1
         RET
```

14.14. The following C program is compiled into LC-2 machine language and loaded into address x3000 before execution. Not counting the JSRs to library routines for I/O, the object code contains 3 JSRs (one to function **f**, one to **g**, and one to **h**). Suppose the addresses of the three JSR instructions are x3102, x3301, and x3304. And suppose the user provides **4 5 6** as input values. Draw a picture of the run-time stack, providing the contents of locations if possible when the program is about to return from function **f**. Assume the stack starts at location x4000.

```c
#include <stdio.h>

main()
{
    int a,b,c;

    printf("Type three numbers: ");
    scanf("%d %d %d", &a, &b, &c);
    printf("%d", f(a,b,c));
}

int f(int x, int y, int z)
{
    int x1;

    x1 = g(x);
    return h(y,z) * x1;
}

int g(int arg)
{
    return arg*arg;
}

int h(int arg1, int arg2)
{
    return arg1/arg2;
}
```

14.15. Referring once again to the machine-busy example from previous chapters, remember that we represent the busyness of a set of 16 machines with a bit pattern. Recall that a 0 in a particular bit position indicates the corresponding machine is busy and a 1 in that position indicates that machine is idle.

1. Write a function to count the number of busy machines for a given busyness pattern. The input to this function will be a bit pattern (which can be represented by an integer variable), and the output will be an integer corresponding to the number of busy machines.

2. Write a function to take two busyness patterns and determine which machines have changed state, that is, gone from busy to idle, or idle to busy. The output of this function is simply another bit pattern with a 1 in each position corresponding to a machine that has changed its state.

3. Write a program that reads a sequence of 10 busyness patterns from the keyboard and determines the average number of busy machines and the average number of machines that change state from one pattern to the next. The user signals the end of busyness patterns by entering a pattern of all 1s (all machines idle). Use the functions you developed for parts 1 and 2 to write your program.

14.16.   1. Write a C function that mimics the behavior of a 4-to-1 multiplexor. See Figure 3.13 for a description of a 4-to-1 mux.

2. Write a C function that mimics the behavior of the LC-2 ALU.

14.17.   Notice that on a telephone keypad, the keys labeled 2, 3, 4, . . . , 9 also have letters associated with them. The key, for example, labeled 2 corresponds to the letters *A*, *B*, and *C*. Write a program that will map a seven-digit telephone number into all possible character sequences that the phone number can represent. For this program, use a function that performs the mapping between digits and characters. The digits 1 and 0 map to nothing.

chapter
15

Debugging

15.1 INTRODUCTION

Programmers often spend more time debugging their programs than they spend writing them. The C programming language is particularly notorious for bugs because of the large amount of flexibility given to the programmer. Because of the sheer amount of time required for debugging, effective debugging skills are critically important for the proficient programmer.

As we mentioned before, debugging is applied common sense. Using information about a program and its execution, a programmer can deduce (using common sense) where things are going wrong. Debugging a program is a bit like solving a puzzle. The available clues logically lead to the solution. Often there is a critical piece of information, which when found, immediately reveals the bug.

In this chapter, we describe some techniques you can use to find the bugs within a program. The simple techniques we describe, such variable tracing and error-checking code, go a long way. They are not practical for all debugging jobs, however; larger programs require more sophisticated debugging techniques. For larger tasks, a source-level debugger is invaluable. A source-level debugger is a tool that allows the programmer to monitor a program interactively during its execution. Different computer systems, Windows NT or UNIX, for example, support different specific debuggers. However, almost all debuggers support a set of core operations that are required for any debugging task. We will describe these core operations.

15.2   TYPES OF ERRORS

With programming in general, be it at a high level or low level, several types of errors frequently make their way into our programs. *Syntactic errors* are the easiest to deal with because they are caught by the translation mechanism. The translator notifies us of such errors when we attempt to translate the program, often pointing out exactly where the error occurred. *Semantic errors*, on the other hand, are problems that can often be very difficult to find. They occur when we program something that is syntactically correct but not exactly what we intended. Once they are found, they are often easy to fix. Both syntactic and semantic errors are typographic errors: these occur when we type something we did not mean to type. *Algorithmic errors* are errors where our approach to solving a problem is wrong. They are often hard to detect and once detected can be very hard to fix. This classification of errors is based on broad strokes and intended to clarify how errors get into our programs. There are many errors that are not clearly of a single type.

15.2.1   Syntactic Errors

In C, syntactic errors (often casually called *syntax errors*) are always caught by the compiler. These occur when we ask the compiler to translate code that is not legal. For instance, the code listed in Figure 15.1 contains a syntax error which the compiler will flag when the code is compiled.

The declaration for the variable *i* is missing a semicolon. Often, missing semicolons and missing variable declarations account for a significant number of syntax errors you will encounter. It is hard to write a complete program without missing a semicolon somewhere. The good news is that these types of errors are easy to detect (because the compiler detects them for us) and easy to fix. Some compilers attempt to keep analyzing a program beyond the first syntax error it encounters, and thereby detect other syntax errors past the first with a single compilation. However, the compiler sometimes cannot gracefully recover from the first syntax error, and the

```
#include <stdio.h>

main()
{
   int i
   int j;

   for (i = 0; i <= 10; i++) {
       j = i * 7;
       printf("%d x 7 = %d\n", i, j);
   }
}
```

Figure 15.1   This program contains a syntactic error

first error causes an avalanche of other errors triggered by the first. Fixing the first one can sometimes remove many subsequent ones.

15.2.2   Semantic Errors

Semantic errors are similar to syntactic errors because they occur for the same reason: Our minds and our fingers are not completely coordinated when typing in a program. Semantic errors, however, do not involve incorrect syntax; therefore, the program gets translated and we are able to execute it. It is not until we analyze the output that we discover that the program is not doing what we expected. Figure 15.2 lists an example of the same program as above, with a simple semantic error (the original syntax error is fixed). The program should print out a multiplication table for the number 7.

Here, a single execution of the program reveals the problem. Only one entry of the multiplication table is printed. You should be able to deduce, given your knowledge of C programming, why this program behaves incorrectly. Why is $11 \times 7 = 70$ printed out? This program demonstrates something called a *control flow* error. Here, the program's control flow, or the order in which statements are executed, is different than we intended.

A common semantic error involving local variables is listed in Figure 15.3. This example uses the factorial program we encountered in Section 14.3.

The program in Figure 15.3 calculates the sum of all integers less than or equal to the number input from the keyboard (i.e., it calculates $1 + 2 + 3 + \ldots + n$). The program keeps repeating, prompting for input and calculating the result of the function **AllSum**, until the user enters a number less than or equal to 0, in which case it stops. Try executing this program on several numbers. Why doesn't it work properly? Hint: Draw out the run-time stack for an execution of this program and you will notice that a variable within **AllSum** should be initialized.

Semantic errors are particularly troubling because they often go undetected by both the compiler *and* the programmer until a particular set of inputs triggers the error. Again referring to the **AllSum** program from Figure 15.3 with the previous semantic error fixed (the variable **result** should be initialized to 0), notice that if the

```
#include <stdio.h>

main()
{
  int i;
  int j;

  for (i = 0; i <= 10; i++)
    j = i * 7;
    printf("%d x 7 = %d\n", i, j);
}
```

Figure 15.2   A program with a semantic error

```
#include <stdio.h>

int AllSum(int n);

int main()
{
  int in;                         /* Input value              */
  int sum;                        /* Value of 1+2+3+..+n      */

  do {
    printf("Input a number: ");
    scanf("%d", &in);

    if (in > 0) {
      sum = AllSum(in);
      printf("The AllSum of %d is %d\n", in, sum);
    }
  } while (in > 0);
}


int AllSum(int n)
{
  int i;                          /* Iteration count          */
  int result;                     /* Result to be returned    */

  for (i = 1; i <= n; i++)        /* This loop calculates sum */
    result = result + i;

  return result;                  /* Return to caller         */
}
```

Figure 15.3   A program with a bug involving local variables

value passed to **AllSum** is too large, then **AllSum** may return an erroneous result because it has exceeded the range of the integer variable **result**. Fix the previous bug, compile the program, and input a number larger than 65,536 and you will notice the bug.

Some are caught during execution because an illegal action is performed by the program. Almost all computer systems have safeguards that prevent a program from doing certain things, one of which is reading or writing certain parts of memory. For instance, it is undesirable for a user's program to modify the memory that stores the operating system. When such an illegal action is performed by a program, the operating system terminates its execution and prints out a *run-time error* message. Often, these types of illegal actions are inadvertently put into programs due to poor programming. Here is an example. Let's modify the **scanf** statement from the previous example to the following:

$$\text{scanf("\%d", in);}$$

The ampersand character, **&**, as we shall see in Chapter 17, is a special operator in the C language. Omitting it here causes a run-time error message to be displayed when the program is executed. Here, the program has requested that an unmodifiable memory location be written. We shall look at this particular example in more detail in Chapter 18.

15.2.3   Algorithmic Errors

The final type of major programming error is the *algorithmic error*. Here, due to improper design, the program does not correctly perform the intended task. These types of errors can be hidden, as they may not appear until many trials of the program have been run. Once detected and isolated, they can be very hard to repair. The good news is that these types of errors can be eliminated by proper planning before you sit in front of a computer to type in the program. A good example of this sort of bug is the Year 2000 computer bug, or Y2K bug. Many computer programs minimize the amount of memory required to store dates. They use enough bits to store only the last two digits of the year, and no more. Thus, the year 2000 is indistinguishable from the year 1900 (or 1800 or 2100 for that matter). This presents a problem whenever a century crossover rolls around. Say, for example, you had checked out a book from the university library in late 1999 and it was due back sometime in early 2000. If the library's computer system had the Y2K bug, you would have gotten an overdue notice in the mail with some hefty fines listed on it. As a consequence, a lot of money and effort were devoted to tracking down Y2K-related bugs before January 1st, 2000 rolled around.

15.3   DEBUGGING TECHNIQUES

Because bugs are a significant issue in developing computer software, very sophisticated systems for detecting and repairing them are often used. Complex software may behave correctly with a certain set of input but fail with another. Often, it is hard to find the right set of input to make it fail. Once that certain input case is found, then isolating the cause of the bug is yet another hard task.

Clearly, good techniques for finding and fixing errors are necessary. For the process of detecting bugs, most programmers resort to brute-force testing, using random permutations of the inputs in the hope of finding a case that causes the software to break. Once a failure is detected, a variety of techniques are used to isolate its source.

But perhaps the best solution is to adopt a programming discipline that prevents bugs from being introduced in the first place. Programming practices such as structured programming enforce an orderliness that results in the program to have less complexity than it would otherwise. Programs that are unstructured—spaghetti code, as it is often referred to, because the program's control flow is a tangled mess—provide plenty of opportunity for bugs to creep in and create extra debugging hurdles.

The best programming methodology also incorporates easy ways to test the program. Writing a program module by module allows it to be tested modularly. Once a function is written, be sure the function is behaving as you expect by testing it separately from the rest of the program. This is not always possible, but is highly recommended when it is. A benefit of writing shorter and simpler functions is that it not only better modularizes the programming, but simplifies testing.

15.3.1 Ad-hoc Techniques

The simplest thing to do once you realize that there is a problem with your program is to visually inspect the source code. Sometimes the nature of the failure tips you off to the region of the code where the bug is likely to exist. This technique is fine if the region of source code is small, and you are very familiar with that region.

Another simple technique is to insert statements within the code to print out information during execution. You might dump out, or trace, the values of critical variables or any information that you think will be useful in finding the bug. You can also add **printf** statements to monitor a program's control flow, thereby checking for control flow errors. If the program is easy to compile and the bug appears quickly during execution, this technique is reasonable to use.

Several techniques of defensive programming allow you to identify error conditions before they propagate too far from their source. *Assertions* and *error checks* are statements added to the source code which flag a condition that the programmer knows should not exist. For example, below we have added the following error check to the **Factorial** function from the previous chapter (see Figure 14.2). Now the function prints a warning message and returns a −1 if its parameter is out of the correct operating range.

```
int Factorial(int n)
{
  int i;                   /* Iteration count       */
  int result = 1;          /* Initialized result    */

  /* Check for legal parameter values */
  if (n < 1 || n > 31) {
    printf("Bad input. Input must be >= 1 and <= 31.\n");
    return -1;
  }

  for (i = 1; i <= n; i++)   /* Calculates factorial */
    result = result * i;

  return result;             /* Return to caller     */
}
```

Assertions can be added to check if a function returns a value within an expected range. If the return value is out of this range, an error message is displayed. In the following example, we are checking that the calculation performed by the function **IncomeTax** is within reasonable bounds. As you can guess, this function calculates the income tax based on a particular income provided as a parameter to it. We do not pay more tax than we collect in income (fortunately!), and we never pay a negative tax. Here if the calculation within **IncomeTax** is botched, then it will be caught.

```
tax = IncomeTax(income);
if (tax < 0 || tax > income)
    printf("Error in function IncomeTax!\n");
```

When and where to add such assertion statements require deep familiarity with the program. Wantonly placed assertions are not helpful. They may even trigger a warning message when nothing is wrong.

15.3.2 The Source-level Debugger

Sometimes the ad-hoc techniques cannot deliver enough information to uncover the source of a bug quickly. In these cases, programmers often turn to a *source-level debugger* to find problem spots. A source-level debugger is a tool that allows a program to be executed one statement at a time. A debugger allows us to monitor variables and control flow as the program is executing. It is very similar to the LC-2 debugger, except it deals with code generated from high-level source code.

In order to use the source-level debugger on a program, the program must be compiled in a special way. The compiler must *annotate* the executable image with enough additional information so the debugger can map a machine language instruction to its corresponding statement in the source program. Also, information about variable names and their allocated locations (i.e., the symbol table) must be included so that a programmer can examine the value of any variable within the program.

Many new debuggers are interactive; they have *graphical user interfaces* (GUIs, pronounced *gooey*). Interactive debuggers simplify the debugging process by providing a visual interface in which you can see the source code, monitor values, set breakpoints, and perform commonly used commands more conveniently than with their command-driven counterparts. Despite better interfaces, all debuggers, whether interactive or command-driven, support a core set of debugging operations. We now describe those operations.

Breakpoints We have already discussed breakpoints when dealing with the LC-2. Breakpoints allow us to specify points during the execution of a program when the program should stop execution. Once the program has stopped, we can examine the values of variables, or memory, and even modify their values.

We can select any line within the program at which to set a breakpoint. Most interactive debuggers allow you to set a breakpoint by simply clicking on the line.

Sometimes it is useful to stop at a line only if a certain condition is true. For example, we might want to stop at the following line only if the variable x is equal to 16:

```
for (x = 0; x < 100; x++)
```

Most debuggers have ways of specifying conditional breakpoints.

Single-stepping Once a breakpoint is set, it is often useful to proceed through the execution one source line at time—a process referred to as *single-stepping*. The LC-2 debugger has a command that executes a single LC-2 instruction of the program.

Similarly, source-level debuggers allow execution to proceed one source line at a time. The step command executes the current source line and then pauses the program again. Single-stepping through a program is very useful, particularly when stepping through the region of a program where the bug is suspected to exist. We can set a breakpoint near the suspected region and then check the values of variables as we single-step through. Since interactive debuggers indicate which line in the source is the current line being executed, single-stepping is a very good technique for detecting control flow errors.

Displaying Values   While execution is paused at a particular spot, examining the values within variables can be useful for tracking down a suspected bug. How this is done depends on the particular debugger being used. Some debuggers allow you to point to a variable in the source code and thereby cause its current value to pop up in a separate window. Some debuggers require you to type in a command indicating the name of the variable you want to examine. Regardless, all debuggers in some way allow you to probe the state of the program at any breakpoint.

PROBLEMS

15.1.   The following programs each have a single error which prevents them from operating as specified. With as few changes as possible, correct the programs. All of the programs should output a single number that is the sum of the integers from 1 to 10, inclusive.

1.
```c
#include <stdio.h>
main()
{
    int i = 1;
    int sum = 0;

    while (i < 11)
    {
        sum = sum + i;
        ++i;
        printf("%d\n", sum);
    }
}
```

2.
```c
#include <stdio.h>
main()
{
    int i;
    int sum = 0;

    for (i = 0; i >= 10; ++i)
        sum = sum + i;
    printf("%d\n", sum);
}
```

3.
```
          #include <stdio.h>
          main()
          {
              int i = 0;
              int sum = 0;

              while (i <= 11)
                  sum = sum + i++;
              printf("%d\n", sum);
          }
```

4.
```
          #include <stdio.h>
          main()
          {
              int i = 0;
              int sum = 0;

              for (i = 0; i <= 10;)
                  sum = sum + ++i;
              printf("%d\n", sum);
          }
```

15.2. The following program fragments have syntax errors and therefore will not compile. Assume that all variables have been properly declared. Fix the errors so that the fragments will not cause compiler errors.

1.
```
          i = 0;
          j = 0;
          do {
              j = j + 1;
              while (i < 5);
          }
```

2.
```
          if (cont == 0)
              a = 2;
              b = 3;
          else
              a = -2;
              b = -3;
```

3.
```
          #define LIMIT 5;

          if (LIMIT)
              printf("True");
          else
              printf("False");
```

15.3. The following C code was written to find the minimum of a set of positive integers that a user enters from the keyboard. The user signifies the end of the set by entering the value −1. Once all the numbers have been entered and processed, the program outputs the minimum. However, the code contains a serious error. Identify and suggest ways to fix the error. Use a source-level debugger, if needed, to find it.

```
#include <stdio.h>

main()
{
    /* Initialize variables */
    int smallestNumber = 0;
    int nextInput;

    /* Get the first input number */
    scanf("%d", &nextInput);

    /* Keep reading inputs until user enters -1 */
    while (nextInput != -1) {
        if (nextInput < smallestNumber)
            smallestNumber = nextInput;
        scanf("%d", &nextInput);
    }

    printf("The smallest number is %d\n", smallestNumber);
}
```

15.4. The following program reads in a line of characters from the keyboard and echos only the alphabetic characters within the line. For example, if the input were "Let's meet at 6:00pm.", then the output should be "Lets meet at 6pm." However, the program has a bug. Can you identify and fix the bug?

```
#include <stdio.h>

main()
{
    char echo;

    do {
        scanf("%c", &echo);
        if ((echo > 'a' || echo < 'z') &&
            (echo > 'A' || echo < 'Z'))
            printf("%c", echo);
    }
    while (echo != '\n');
}
```

15.5. Use a source-level debugger to monitor the execution of the following code:

```
#include <stdio.h>

int IsDivisibleBy(int divisor, int quotient);

main()
{
    int i;  /* Iteration variable                */
    int j;  /* Iteration variable                */
    int f;  /* The number of factors of a number */


    for (i = 2; i < 1000; i++) {
```

```
        f = 0;
        for (j = 2; j < i; j++) {
            if (IsDivisibleBy(i, j))
                f++;
        }
        printf("The number %d has %d factors\n", i, f);
    }
}

int IsDivisibleBy(int divisor, int quotient)
{
    if (divisor % quotient == 0)
        return 1;
    else
        return 0;
}
```

1. Set a breakpoint at the beginning of function **IsDivisibleBy** and examine the parameter values for the first 10 calls. What are they?

2. What is the value of *f* after the inner **for** loop completes and the value of *i* equals 660.

3. Can this program be written more efficiently? Hint: Monitor the value of the arguments when the return value of **IsDivisibleBy** is 1.

15.6. Using a source-level debugger, determine for what values of parameters the function **Mystery** return a 0.

```
#include <stdio.h>

int Mystery(int a, int b, int c);

main()
{
    int i;            /* Iteration variable      */
    int j;            /* Iteration variable      */
    int k;            /* Iteration variable      */
    int sum = 0;      /* running sum of Mystery  */

    for (i = 100; i > 0; i--) {
        for (j = 1; j < i; j++) {
            for (k = j; k < 100; k++)
                sum = sum + Mystery(i, j, k);
        }
    }
}

int Mystery(int a, int b, int c)
{
    static max = 1000;
    int out;

    out = 3*a*a + 7*a - 5*b*b + 4*b + 5*c ;

    return out;
}
```

15.7. The following program manages flight reservations for a small airline that has only one plane that has **SEATS** number seats for passengers. This program processes ticket requests from the airline's Web site. The command *R* requests a reservation. If there is a seat available, the reservation is approved. If there are no seats, the reservation is denied. Subsequently, a passenger with a reservation can purchase a ticket using the *P* command. This means that for every *P* command, there must be a preceding *R* command; however, not every *R* will materialize into a purchased ticket. The program ends when the *X* command is entered. Below is the program, but it contains serious design errors. Identify the errors. Propose and implement a correct solution.

```
#define SEATS 10

#include <stdio.h>

main()
{
  int seatsAvailable = SEATS;
  char request;

  do {
    scanf("%c", &request);

    if (request == 'R') {
      if (seatsAvailable)
        printf("Reservation Approved!\n");
      else
        printf("Sorry, flight fully booked.\n");
    }

    if (request == 'P') {
      seatsAvailable--;
      printf("Ticket purchased!\n");
    }
  }
  while (request != 'X');

  printf("Done! %d seats not sold\n", seatsAvailable);
}
```

chapter
16

Recursion

16.1 INTRODUCTION

The idea behind recursion is simple. A recursive function is one that performs its task by calling itself on smaller pieces of the task. A recursive function, in the process of generating its result, makes a call to itself to solve a subcomponent of the result.

Here is a recursive procedure with which you might be familiar. Suppose we want to find a particular student's exam in a set of exams that are already in alphabetical order. We might pick an exam about halfway through the set and examine the name on the exam at that halfway point. If it is not the exam we are looking for, then we search the appropriate half (depending on the student's name and the name on the exam at the halfway point) using the same technique. For example, say we are looking for the exam of Babe Ruth and, at the halfway point, we find Mickey Mantle's exam. Since we are not looking for Mickey's exam, we repeat the process on the bottom half (i.e., the half containing Mantle through Yastrzemski). Fairly quickly, we close in on and locate Babe Ruth's exam if it exists in the set. This technique of searching through an alphabetized set of exams is recursive because we are applying the same searching algorithm to continually smaller and smaller subsets of exams.

When applied correctly, recursion can simplify certain programming tasks considerably. We shall see many examples of this as we progress through this chapter. Recursion is similar to iteration, and often the two can be used interchangeably. There are programming situations, however, where using recursion leads to a much simpler program.

16.2   WHAT IS RECURSION?

A function that calls itself is said to be a recursive function, as in the function
RunningSum in the example below.

```
int RunningSum(int n)
{
  if (n == 1)
     return 1;
  else
     return (n + RunningSum(n-1));
}
```

This function calculates the running sum of all the integers between its input
parameter n and 0. For example, **RunningSum(4)** calculates $4 + 3 + 2 + 1 + 0$.
However, it does this calculation recursively. The function body of **RunningSum**
contains a function call to itself. Notice that the running sum of 4 is really 4 plus the
running sum of 3. Likewise, the running sum of 3 is 3 plus the running sum of 2.
This *recursive* definition is the basis for a recursive algorithm. In other words,

$$\text{RunningSum}(n) = n + \text{RunningSum}(n - 1)$$

You might have already encountered recursion in mathematics. Sometimes,
we express a function as a function of smaller values. These are called *recurrence
equations*. The equation previously given is a recurrence equation for **RunningSum**.

With recurrence equations, we must also supply an initial case. So in addition to
the formula above, we need to state

$$\text{RunningSum}(1) = 1$$

Now, we can evaluate

$$
\begin{aligned}
\text{RunningSum}(4) &= 4 + \text{RunningSum}(3) \\
&= 4 + 3 + \text{RunningSum}(2) \\
&= 4 + 3 + 2 + \text{RunningSum}(1) \\
&= 4 + 3 + 2 + 1
\end{aligned}
$$

During execution of the function call **RunningSum(4)**, **RunningSum** makes a
function call to itself, this time with an argument of 3 (i.e., **RunningSum(3)**).
However, before **RunningSum(3)** completes, it makes a call to **RunningSum(2)**.
And before **RunningSum(2)** completes, it makes a call to **RunningSum(1)**.
RunningSum(1), however, makes no additional recursive calls and returns the
value 1 back to **RunningSum(2)**. Now **RunningSum(2)** can complete, and
it passes the value $2 + 1$ back to **RunningSum(3)**. Now, **RunningSum(3)**
completes and passes control back to **RunningSum(4)** along with the return value
of $3 + 2 + 1$. Figure 16.1 pictorially shows this flow of control.

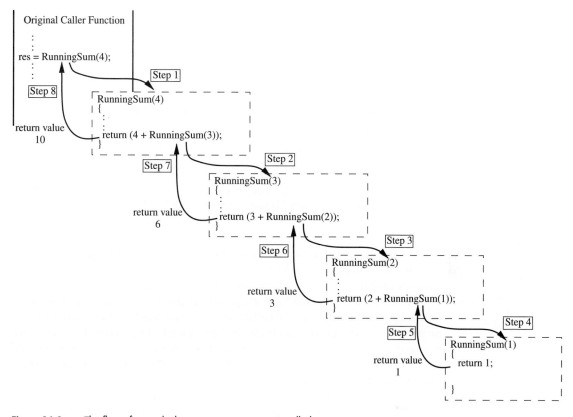

Figure 16.1   The flow of control when `RunningSum(4)` is called

16.3   A HIGH-LEVEL EXAMPLE: BINARY SEARCH

In this chapter we present several examples of recursion to help you better grasp the concept. We also delve into the inner workings of a recursive function to demonstrate how the run-time stack makes it all happen.

In the introduction to this chapter, we described a recursive technique for finding an exam in set of exams in alphabetical order. The technique is called *binary search*. Here we express the binary search algorithm using *pseudocode*. Pseudocode is short-hand notation of C code. It is not as detailed as C code (for instance, no types are specified). Its intent is to capture the flow of an algorithm.

In order to express the algorithm properly, we need to describe a set of exams as two numbers. Assume the exams are sequentially numbered after they are sorted. The first of the two numbers indicates the the exam number at the top of the pile and the second number the exam at the bottom. So if we have 100 exams when we start, the exam at the top will be numbered 1, and the bottom exam will be numbered 100.

```
FindExam(studentName, start, end)
{
  halfWayPoint = (end + start)/2
  /* Error case: exam doesn't exist in the set */
  if (end < start)
    ExamNotFound();
  /* We found the exam! */
  if (studentName == NameOfExam(halfWayPoint))
    ExamFound(half_way_point);
  /* Search the top half */
  else if (studentName < NameOfExam(half_way_point))
    FindExam(studentName, start, halfWayPoint-1);
  else
    /* Search the bottom half */
    FindExam(studentName, halfWayPoint+1, end);
}
```

The function **FindExam** is called with three arguments: the name we are searching for, the exam number at the top of the set, and the exam number at the bottom. Each time the function is called, we first calculate the halfway point through the set. If the exam we are searching for is at the halfway point, we are done. If it is not, we search the top half or the bottom half depending on the whether the student's name is greater than or less than the name on the exam at the halfway point. For this we use a recursive call to **FindExam**. Notice that the recursive function has two terminal cases—one where the exam is found and one where the exam is determined not to exist in the set.

16.4   TOWERS OF HANOI

There is a classic puzzle known as the Towers of Hanoi, and the recursive solution to it is the simplest solution. The puzzle involves a platform with three posts. On one of the posts sit a number of wooden disks, each smaller than the one below it. The objective is to move all the disks from their current post to another post. There are two rules for moving disks: only one disk can be moved at a time, and a larger disk can never be placed upon a smaller disk. Figure 16.2 shows the initial configuration of the puzzle.

As the legend associated with the puzzle goes, when the world was created, the priests at the Temple of Brahma were given the task of moving 64 disks from one post to another. When they completed their task, the world would end.

Now how would we go about writing a computer program to solve this puzzle? If we view the problem from the end first, we can make the following observation: the last sequence of moves **must** involve moving the largest disk from post 1 to the target post, say post 3, and then moving the other disks back on top of it. Conceptually, we need to move all $n - 1$ disks off the largest disk and onto the intermediate post, then we move the largest disk from its post onto the target post. Then we move all $n - 1$

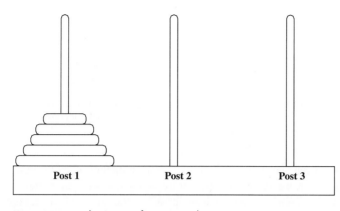

Figure 16.2   The Towers of Hanoi puzzle

disks from the intermediate post onto the target post. And we are done! Actually, we are not done because moving $n - 1$ disks in one move is not legal. However, we have stated the problem in such a manner that we can solve it if we can solve the two smaller subproblems of it. Once the largest disk is on the target post, we do not need to deal with it any further. Now the $n - 1$ disk becomes the largest disk, and the subobjective becomes to move it to the target pole. We can therefore apply the same technique. We now have a recursive definition of the problem. Below is a recursive C function of this algorithm.

```
/*
   Move disk 'diskNumber' from startPost to endPost using
   midPost for temporary storage.  Disk 1 is the smallest disk.
*/
MoveDisk(diskNumber, startPost, endPost, midPost)
{
   if (diskNumber > 1) {

      /* Move n-1 disks off the current disk (on startPost) and
         put them on the intermediate post (midPost)         */
      MoveDisk(diskNumber-1, startPost, midPost, endPost); /* -- A -- */

      /* Move the largest disk.                              */
      printf("Move disk number %d from post %d to post %d.\n",
             diskNumber, startPost, endPost);

      /* Move all n-1 disks onto the end post                */
      MoveDisk(diskNumber-1, midPost, endPost, startPost); /* -- B -- */
   }
   else
      printf("Move disk number 1 from post %d to post %d.\n",
             diskNumber, startPost, endPost);
}
```

Like with recurrence equations in mathematics, all recursive functions require a terminal case (also called *base case*), which ends the recursion. Here, we have stated that moving disk 1 (smallest disk) requires no other disks be moved since it is always on top and can be moved directly from one post to another.

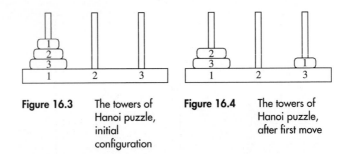

Figure 16.3   The towers of Hanoi puzzle, initial configuration

Figure 16.4   The towers of Hanoi puzzle, after first move

Let's see what happens when we play a game with three disks. Below is an initial function call to **MoveDisk**. We start off by saying that we want to move disk 3 (the largest disk) from post 1 to post 3, using post 2 as the intermediate storage post, i.e., we want to solve a three-disk Towers of Hanoi puzzle. See Figure 16.3.

```
/* diskNumber 3; startPost 1; endPost 3; midPost 2 */
MoveDisk(3, 1, 3, 2)
```

This call invokes another call to **MoveDisk** to move disks 1 and 2 off of disk 3 and onto post 2 using post 3 as intermediate storage. The call happens at the call site labeled - - - **A** - - - in the source code.

```
/* diskNumber 2; startPost 1; endPost 2; midPost 3 */
MoveDisk(2, 1, 2, 3)
```

To move disk 2 from post 1 to post 2, we must first move disk 1 off disk 2 and onto post 3 (the intermediate storage). So this triggers another call to **MoveDisk** again from the call site labeled - - - **A** - - -.

```
/* diskNumber 1; startPost 1; endPost 3; midPost 2 */
MoveDisk(1, 1, 3, 2)
```

Since disk 1 can always be moved, the (second) **printf** statement is executed; we actually move a disk. See Figure 16.4.

```
Move disk number 1 from post 1 to post 3.
```

This invocation of the function returns back to its caller. The caller function was the call **MoveDisk(2, 1, 2, 3)**. Recall that we were waiting for all disks on top of disk 2 to be moved to post 3. That having been completed, we can now move disk 2 from post 1 to post 2. The **printf** is the next statement to execute, signaling another disk to be moved. See Figure 16.5.

```
Move disk number 2 from post 1 to post 2.
```

Next, a call is made to move all disks that were on disk 2, back onto disk 2. This call happens at the call site labeled - - - **B** - - -.

```
/* diskNumber 1; startPost 2; endPost 3; midPost 1 */
MoveDisk(1, 2, 3, 1)
```

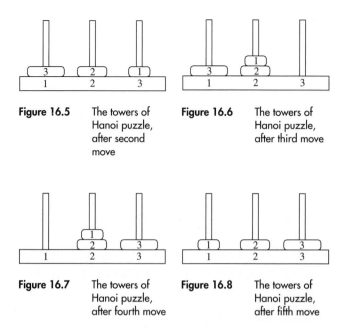

Figure 16.5   The towers of Hanoi puzzle, after second move

Figure 16.6   The towers of Hanoi puzzle, after third move

Figure 16.7   The towers of Hanoi puzzle, after fourth move

Figure 16.8   The towers of Hanoi puzzle, after fifth move

Again, since disk 1 has no disks on top of it, we see the move printed. See Figure 16.6.

Move disk number 1 from post 3 to post 2.

Now control passes back to the call **MoveDisk(2, 1, 2, 3)** which, having completed its task of moving disk 2 (and all disks on top of it) from post 1 to post 2, returns to its caller. Its caller is **MoveDisk(3, 1, 3, 2)**. Now, all disks have been moved off of disk 3 and onto post 2. Disk 3 can be moved from post 1 onto post 3. The **printf** is the next statement executed. See Figure 16.7.

Move disk number 3 from post 1 to post 3.

The next subtask remaining is to move disk 2 (and all disks on top of it) from post 2 onto post 3. We can use post 1 for intermediate storage. The following call is made from call site `--- B ---`.

```
/* diskNumber 2; startPost 2; endPost 3; midPost 1 */
MoveDisk(2, 2, 3, 1)
```

In order to do so, we must first move disk 1 from post 2 onto post 1. This call is made from call site `--- A ---`.

```
/* diskNumber 1; startPost 2; endPost 1; midPost 3 */
MoveDisk(1, 2, 1, 3)
```

The move requires no submoves. See Figure 16.8.

Move disk number 1 from post 2 to post 1.

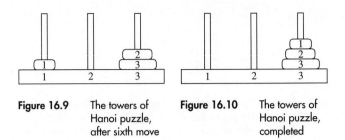

Figure 16.9   The towers of
                 Hanoi puzzle,
                 after sixth move

Figure 16.10   The towers of
                  Hanoi puzzle,
                  completed

Return passes back to the caller **MoveDisk(2, 2, 3, 1)**, and disk 2 is moved onto post 3. See Figure 16.9.

Move disk number 2 from post 2 to post 3.

The only thing remaining is to move all disks that were on disk 2 back on top.

```
/* diskNumber 1; startPost 1; endPost 3; midPost 2 */
MoveDisk(1, 1, 3, 2)
```

The move is done immediately. See Figure 16.10.

Move disk number 1 from post 1 to post 2.

and the puzzle is completed!

16.5   A DETAILED EXAMPLE IN C

The following recurrence equations generates a well-known sequence of numbers.

$$f(n) = f(n-1) + f(n-2)$$
$$f(0) = 1$$
$$f(1) = 1$$

This function generates a mathematically significant sequence of numbers known as the *Fibonacci numbers*. If we wanted to write a C function to generate the nth Fibonacci number, we could simply take the relationship and directly code it into a recursive function, as shown in Figure 16.11. The function **Fibonacci** performs the calculation.

We are stating that calculating the nth Fibonacci number can be done by calculating the $n-1$ number and the $n-2$ number and adding them together. The *terminal condition* must be supplied in order for this relationship to have a definite termination point. Notice in the previous example, a terminal condition caused the recursion to eventually terminate.

Whenever the function **Fibonacci** is called, whether from itself or another function, a new copy of its activation record is pushed on the run-time stack. Each invocation of the function gets a new, private copy of all variables declared within the function. Each copy is different than any other copy. They are essentially different

```
#include <stdio.h>

int Fibonacci(int n);

main()
{
   int in;
   int number;

   printf("Which Fibonacci number? ");
   scanf("%d", &in);

   number = Fibonacci(in);
   printf("That Fibonacci number is %d\n", number);
}

int Fibonacci(int n)
{
   if (n == 0 || n == 1)
      return 1;
   else
      return (Fibonacci(n-1) + Fibonacci(n-2));
}
```

Figure 16.11   Fibonacci is a recursive C function to calculate the *n*th Fibonacci number

variables that share a common name and are defined within the same function. The essence of making recursion work is the run-time stack. If the variables of this function were statically allocated in memory, then each recursive call to **Fibonacci** would overwrite the values of the previous call.

Let's see what happens when we call the function **Fibonacci** with the parameter 3, **Fibonacci(3)**. We start off with the activation record for **Fibonacci(3)** on top of the run-time stack. Figure 16.12 shows the progression of the stack as the original function call is evaluated.

Since the parameter *n* which equals 3 does not meet the terminal condition (i.e., it does not equal 1 or 0), the function will calculate **Fibonacci(3-1)** first, as the expression **Fibonacci(n-1) + Fibonacci(n-2)** is evaluated left to right. A call is made to **Fibonacci(2)**, and an activation record for **Fibonacci(2)** is pushed onto the run-time stack (see Figure 16.12, step 2).

For **Fibonacci(2)**, the parameter **n** equals 2 and does not meet the terminal condition, therefore a call is made to **Fibonacci(1)** (see Figure 16.12, step 3). This call is made in the course of evaluating **Fibonacci(2-1) + Fibonacci(2-2)**.

The call **Fibonacci(1)** results in no more recursive calls because the parameter **n** meets the terminal condition. The value 1 is returned back to **Fibonacci(2)**, which now can complete the evaluation of **Fibonacci(1) + Fibonacci(0)** by calling **Fibonacci(0)** (see Figure 16.12, step 4). The call **Fibonacci(0)** immediately returns a 1.

Now, the call **Fibonacci(2)** can complete and return its subcalculation (its result is 2) back to its caller, **Fibonacci(3)**. Having completed the left-hand component of the expression **Fibonacci(2) + Fibonacci(1)**, **Fibonacci(3)**

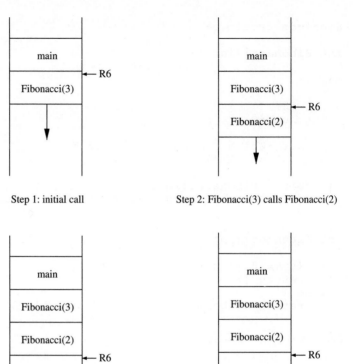

Step 1: initial call   Step 2: Fibonacci(3) calls Fibonacci(2)

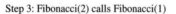

Step 3: Fibonacci(2) calls Fibonacci(1)   Step 4: Fibonacci(2) calls Fibonacci(0)

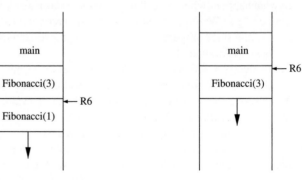

Step 5: Fibonacci(3) calls Fibonacci(1)   Step 6: back to the starting point

Figure 16.12   Snapshots of the run-time stack for the function call
                     Fibonacci(3)

calls **Fibonacci(1)** (see Figure 16.12, step 5), which immediately returns the value 1. Now **Fibonacci(3)** is done—its result is 3 (Figure 16.12, step 6).

The trace of all function calls made is listed:

```
Fibonacci(3)
Fibonacci(2)
Fibonacci(1)
Fibonacci(0)
Fibonacci(1)
```

We could state the recursion of **Fibonacci(3)** algebraically, as follows:

```
Fibonacci(3) = Fibonacci(2) + Fibonacci(1)
             = (Fibonacci(1) + Fibonacci(0)) + Fibonacci(1)
             = 1 + 1 + 1 = 3
```

Try tracing the execution of **Fibonacci(4)**. You may notice that the trace of **Fibonacci(3)** is a component of the trace of **Fibonacci(4)**. No surprise, since **Fibonacci(4) = Fibonacci(3) + Fibonacci(2)**.

The LC-2 C compiler generates the following code for this program, listed in Figure 16.13. Now, notice that the compiler determined that a temporary variable

```
Fibonacci:
        STR   R7, R6, #1    ;   store away the return address
        LDR   R0, R6, #3    ;   load the parameter n
        BRZ   FIB_END       ;   n==0
        ADD   R0, R0, #-1   ;
        BRZ   FIB_END       ;   n==1

        LDR   R0, R6, #3    ;   load the parameter n
        ADD   R0, R0, #-1   ;   calculate n-1
        STR   R0, R6, #8    ;   store input as first parameter
        STR   R6, R6, #7    ;   store top of stack as the dynamic link
        ADD   R6, R6, #5    ;   move the top of stack to new act record
        JSR   Fibonacci     ;   the call back to itself: Fibonacci(n-1)

        LDR   R0, R6, #5    ;   read the return value
        STR   R0, R6, #4    ;   store it to compiler generated temp value
        LDR   R0, R6, #3    ;   load the parameter n
        ADD   R0, R0, #-2   ;   calculate n-2
        STR   R0, R6, #8    ;   store input as first parameter
        STR   R6, R6, #7    ;   store top of stack as the dynamic link
        ADD   R6, R6, #5    ;   move top of stack to new act record
        JSR   Fibonacci     ;   the call back to itself: Fibonacci(n-2)

        LDR   R0, R6, #5    ;   read the return value
        LDR   R1, R6, #4    ;   read the temporary value: Fibonacci(n-1)
        ADD   R0, R0, R1    ;   Fibonacci(n-1) + Fibonacci(n-2)
        STR   R0, R6, #0    ;   write the return value
        LDR   R6, R6, #2    ;   load the dynamic link
        RET
FIB_END:
        AND   R0, R0, #0    ;   clear R0
        ADD   R0, R0, #1    ;   R0 = 1

        STR   R0, R6, #0    ;   write the return value
        LDR   R6, R6, #2    ;   load the dynamic link
        RET
```

Figure 16.13   Fibonacci in LC-2

was required in order to translate the function **Fibonacci** properly. Most compilers will do this when compiling an expression that is composed of many subexpressions. Such temporary values are given storage in the activation record below the space for the programmer-declared local variables. This temporary variable is allocated in the activation record of **Fibonacci** at offset 4. The total length of the record is five locations.

16.6   ANOTHER DETAILED EXAMPLE IN C

Figure 16.14 lists a recursive C function which takes a positive integer value and converts each digit of the value into ASCII and displays the resulting characters.

The recursive function **IntToAscii** works as follows: to print out a number, say 21,669, for example (i.e., we are making the call **IntToAscii(21669)**), the function will subdivide the problem into two parts. First 2166 must be printed out via a recursive call back to **IntToAscii**, and once the call is done, the 9 will be printed. Said another way, the recursive call causes a smaller number—the original

```
#include <stdio.h>

void IntToAscii(int i);

main()
{
  int in;

  printf("Input number: ");
  scanf("%d", &in);

  IntToAscii(in);
  printf("\n");
}

void IntToAscii(int num)
{
  int prefix;
  int currDigit;

  if (num < 10)                   /* The terminal case -            */
    putchar(num + '0');           /* only one digit to convert      */
  else {
    prefix = num / 10;            /* First convert the number,      */
    IntToAscii(prefix);           /* without least significant digit */
    currDigit = num % 10;         /* Now, convert and display       */
    putchar(currDigit + '0');     /* least significant digit        */
  }
}
```

Figure 16.14   **IntToAscii** is a recursive function that converts integers to ASCII

number minus the last digit—to be processed. Eventually, a recursive call is made with an argument that has only one digit. This causes the number to be displayed, and the call stack starts to unwind.

The details of the function are as such: First, remove the least significant digit of the parameter **num** by shifting it to the right one digit by dividing by 10. With this new (and smaller) value, we make a recursive call. If the input value **num** is only a single digit, it is converted to ASCII and displayed to the screen—no recursive calls necessary for this case.

The output in this program is performed using the C standard output function **putchar**. It works like the LC-2 OUT TRAP routine. It outputs the ASCII character passed to it.

Once control is passed back after a recursive call, the digit that was removed is converted to ASCII and displayed. To clarify, we present a trace of calls for the original call of **IntToAscii(12345)**:

IntToAscii(12345)	
IntToAscii(1234)	
IntToAscii(123)	
IntToAscii(12)	
IntToAscii(1)	
putchar('1')	See Figure (a).
putchar('2')	
putchar('3')	See Figure (b).
putchar('4')	
putchar('5')	

Figure 16.15 (page 360) shows two snapshots of the run-time stack during this call.

PROBLEMS

16.1. For this question, refer to the examples that appear in the chapter.

1. How many calls to **RunningSum** (see Section 16.2 in the chapter) are made for the call **RunningSum(10)**?

2. How about for the call **RunningSum(n)**? Give your answer in terms of n.

3. How many calls to **MoveDisk** are made in the Towers of Hanoi problem if the initial call is **MoveDisk(4, 1, 3, 2)**. This call plays out a four-disk game.

4. How many calls are made for an n-disk game?

5. How many calls to **Fibonacci** (see Figure 16.11) for the initial call **Fibonacci(10)**?

6. How many calls are required for the nth Fibonacci number?

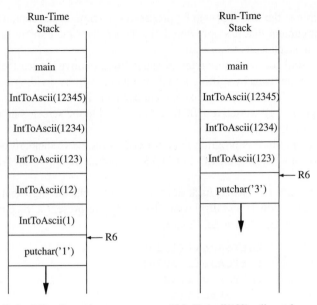

(a) IntToAscii(1) calls putchar   (b) IntToAscii(123) calls putchar

Figure 16.15   Two snapshots of the run-time stack during
                     IntToAscii(12345).

16.2.   Compile the following C function into an LC-2 assembly code fragment.
You may assume that the address of the stack is in R6 and the return address
is in R7 when your code begins.

```
int count(int arg)
{
   if (arg < 1)
      return 0;

   /*
    * Hint: x % y is the remainder of x divided by
    * y. In this case, the condition will be true
    * if and only if arg is odd. How can you test
    * whether arg is odd or even in LC-2 without
    * doing any division?
    */

   else if (arg % 2)
      return(1 + count(arg - 2));
   else
      return(1 + count(arg - 1));
}
```

16.3.   Is the return address for a recursive function always the same at each function
call? Why or why not?

16.4.   What would happen if we reversed the **putchar** call and the recursive call
in the code for **IntToAscii** in Figure 16.14?

16.5.   Consider the following C program:

```c
#include <stdio.h>

int Power(int a, int b);

int main(void)
{
    int x, y, z;

    printf("Input two numbers: ");
    scanf("%d %d", &x, &y);

    if (x > 0 && y > 0)
      z = Power(x,y);
    else
      z = 0;

    printf("The result is %d.\n", z);
}

int Power(int a, int b)
{
    if (a < b)
        return 0;
    else
        return 1 + Power(a/b, b);
}
```

1. State the complete output if the input is
   (*a*) **4 9**
   (*b*) **27 5**
   (*c*) **−1 3**

2. What does the function **Power** compute?

3. Figure 16.16 is a snapshot of the stack after a call to the function **Power**. Two activation records are shown, with some of the entries filled in. Assume the snapshot was taken just before execution of one of the **return** statements in **Power**. What are the values in the entries marked with a question mark? If an entry contains an address, use an arrow to indicate the location the address refers to.

16.6.   Take the following C function:

```c
int Sigma( int k )
{
    int l;

    l = k -1;

    if (k==0)
        return 0;
    else
        return (k + Sigma(l));
}
```

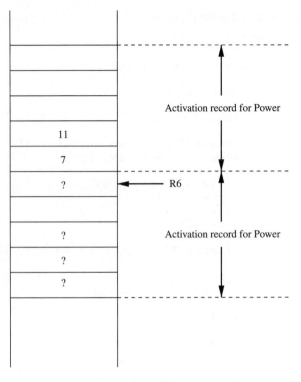

Figure 16.16   Two snapshots of the run-time stack during
`IntToAscii(12345)`

1. Convert the following recursive function into a nonrecursive function. Assume **Sigma()** will always be called with a nonnegative argument.

2. Exactly 1KB of contiguous memory is available exclusively for the run-time stack of the recursive function, and addresses and integers are 16 bits wide. How many recursive function calls can be made before the program runs out of memory? Assume no storage is needed for temporary values.

16.7. The following C program is compiled and executed on the LC-2. When the program is executed, the run-time stack starts at memory location xC000 and grows toward xFFFF (the stack can occupy up to 32 pages of memory).

```
SevenUp(int x)
{
    if (x == 1)
        return 7;
    else
        return (7 + sevenUp(x - 1));
}

main()
{
```

```
    int a;

    printf("Input a number \n");
    scanf("%d", &a);

    a = SevenUp(a);

    printf("%d is 7 times the number\n", a);
}
```

1. What is the largest input value for which this program will run correctly? Explain your answer.

2. If the run-time stack starts at x4000, what is the largest input value for which this program will run correctly? (In this case, the stack can occupy up to 96 pages of memory.) Explain your answer.

16.8. What is the returned value of the call **ea(110, 24)** where **ea** is the following C function?

```
int ea(int x, int y)
{
    int a;

    if (y == 0)
        return x;
    else {
        a = x % y;
        return (ea(y, a));
    }
}
```

16.9. Write a program without recursive functions equivalent to the following C program.

```
main()
{
    printf("%d", M());
}

void M()
{
    int num, x;

    printf("Type a number: ");
    scanf("%d", &num);
    if (num <= 0)
        return 0;
    else {
        x = M();
        if (num > x)
            return num;
        else
            return x;
    }
}
```

16.10. Consider the following recursive function:

```
int func (int arg)
{
    if (arg % 2 != 0)
        return func(arg - 1);
    if (arg <= 0)
        return 1;

    return func(arg/2) + 1;
}
```

1. Is there a value of **arg** that causes an infinite recursion? If so, what is it?

2. Suppose that the function **func** above is part of a program whose main function is given below. How many functions calls are made to **func** when the program is executed?

```
main()
{
    printf("The value is %d\n", func(10));
}
```

3. What value is output by the program?

16.11. What is the output of the following C program?

```
#include <stdio.h>

void Magic(int in);
int Even(int n);

int main()
{
    Magic(10);
}

void Magic(int in)
{
    if (in == 0)
        return;
    if (Even(in))
        printf("%i\n", in);
    Magic(in - 1);
    if (!Even(in))
        printf("%i\n", in);
    return;
}

int Even(int n)
{
    /* even, return 1; odd, return 0 */
    return (n % 2) == 0 ? 1 : 0;
}
```

17

Pointers and Arrays

17.1 INTRODUCTION

In this chapter, we introduce two simple but powerful programming constructs: pointers and arrays. Neither pointers nor arrays are completely new topics to us. We have dealt with the basic concepts behind them when writing assembly code for the LC-2. Now, we examine them in the context of C.

A pointer is simply the address of a variable in memory. With pointers, we can *indirectly* access variables. The ability to access memory indirectly enables some useful capabilities. With pointers, we can create functions that modify the arguments passed by the caller function. With pointers, we can create sophisticated ways of organizing data into structures that grow and shrink (like the run-time stack) during a program's execution. We will see examples of both of these uses for pointers over the next few chapters.

Arrays are simply lists of data arranged sequentially in memory. For example, an itemized list of all the telephone calls you've made over the past month might be arranged in memory as an array in the phone company's computer system. To access a particular item in an array, we need to specify which element we want. As we'll see, an expression like **a[4]** will access the fifth element in the array named **a**. Arrays enable many things, allowing us to conveniently process groups of data such as vectors, matrices, lists, and characters strings.

17.2   POINTERS

In the C program in Figure 17.1, the function **Swap** is designed to switch the value of its two arguments. The function **Swap** is called from **main** with the arguments **valueA** which equals 3 and **valueB** which equals 4. Once, **Swap** returns control to **main** we want **valueA** and **valueB** to have their values swapped. However, compile and execute the code and you will notice that the arguments passed to **Swap** remain unchanged.

Let's examine the run-time stack during the execution of **Swap** to try to figure out why. Figure 17.2 shows that the function **Swap** modifies the local copies of the parameters **firstVal** and **secondVal**. However, when **Swap** completes and control returns to **main**, the modified values are lost when the activation record for **Swap** is popped off the stack.

The problem here is that C always passes these arguments from the caller function to the callee function *by value*. C simply evaluates each argument that appears in a function call as an expression and places the value of the expression in the appropriate place in the activation record for the function being called. In order for **Swap** to modify the actual arguments the caller function passes to it, it must have access to the caller function's activation record—it must access the locations at which the arguments are stored in order to modify their values. The function **Swap** needs the *addresses* of **valueA** and **valueB** in **main** in order to change their values. As we shall see next few sections, pointers and their associated operators enable this to happen.

```c
#include <stdio.h>

void Swap(int firstVal, int secondVal);

main()
{
  int valueA = 3;
  int valueB = 4;

  printf("Before Swap: valueA = %d and valueB = %d\n", valueA, valueB);
  Swap(valueA, valueB);
  printf("After Swap : valueA = %d and valueB = %d\n", valueA, valueB);
}

void Swap(int firstVal, int secondVal)
{
  int tempVal;                 /* Needed to hold firstVal when swapping */

  tempVal = firstVal;
  firstVal = secondVal;
  secondVal = tempVal;
}
```

Figure 17.1   The function **Swap** attempts to swap the values of its two parameters

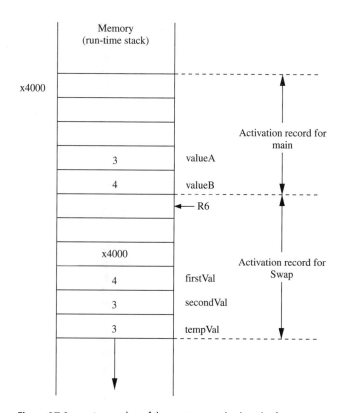

Figure 17.2   A snapshot of the run-time stack when the function
Swap is about to return control

17.2.1 Declaring Pointer Variables

Pointer variables contain memory addresses of variables. The pointer is said to *point* to the variable whose address it contains. Associated with a pointer variable is the *type* of value to which it points. So, for instance, an integer pointer variable points to an integer value. To declare a pointer variable in C, we use the following syntax:

```
int *ptr;
```

Here we have declared a variable named **ptr** that points to an integer. The asterisk (*****) indicates that the identifier that follows is a pointer variable. C programmers will often say that **ptr** is of type **int** *star*. Pointer variables are initialized in C similar to all other variables. If this pointer variable is locally declared, it will not be initialized automatically. Similarly, we can declare

```
char *cp;
double *dp;
unsigned *ip;
```

The variable **cp** points to a character, and **dp** points to a double-precision floating point number and **ip** to a unsigned integer. This syntax of using * may seem a bit odd at first, but once we have gone through the pointer operators, the rationale behind the syntax will be clear.

17.2.2   Operators for Pointers

Now that we can declare pointer variables, let's take a look at how they can be used. C has two operators for pointer-related manipulations, the address operator **&**, and indirection operator *.

The Address Operator &   The address operator, whose symbol is an ampersand **&**, generates the memory address of its operand. Its operand must be something that is stored in memory (more precisely stated, a memory object). A variable, for instance, is a proper operand for the **&** operator; the number **3**, for example, is not. In the following code sequence, the pointer variable **ptr** will point to the integer variable **i**. The expression on the right-hand side of the second assignment statement generates the memory address of **i**.

```
int i;
int *ptr;

i = 4;
ptr = &i;
```

Let's examine the LC-2 code for this sequence. Both declared variables are locals and allocated on the stack. The variable **i** is allocated offset 3 and **ptr** offset 4.

```
AND   R0, R0, #0    ;    clear R0
ADD   R0, R0, #4    ;    R0 = 4
STR   R0, R6, #3    ;    i = 4;

AND   R0, R0, #0    ;    clear R0
ADD   R0, R6, #3    ;    generate the memory address of i
STR   R0, R6, #4    ;    ptr = &i;
```

Figure 17.3 shows the top of the run-time stack after the statement **ptr = &i;** has executed. The current top-of-stack is at memory location x4011. Notice that **i** contains the integer value 4 and **ptr** contains the memory address of **i**.

The Indirection Operator *   The second pointer operator is called the *indirection*, or *dereferencing*, operator and its symbol is the asterisk * (pronounced *star* in this context). It allows us to indirectly manipulate the value to which a pointer is pointing. In literal terms, the indirection operator * means the "value pointed to by" the variable (or expression) that follows. The expression ***x** refers to the value pointed to by **x**. In the previous example, ***ptr** refers to the value stored in variable **i**. Here, ***ptr** and **i** can be used interchangeably. Adding to the previous C code example,

Run-time stack

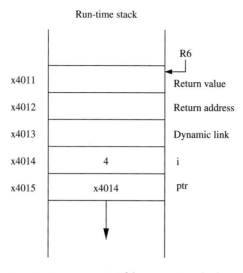

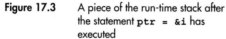

Figure 17.3 A piece of the run-time stack after the statement **ptr** = **&i** has executed

```
int i;
int *ptr;

i = 4;
ptr = &i;
*ptr = *ptr + 1;
```

Essentially, ***ptr = *ptr + 1;** is another way of saying **i = i + 1;**. Just as with other types of variables we have seen, the ***ptr** means different things depending on which side of the assignment operator it appears. On the right-hand side of the assignment operator, it refers to the value that appears at that location (in this case the value 4). On the left-hand side, it indicates the location that gets modified (in this case, the address of **i**). Notice that this interpretation is the same as with an integer variable. Let's examine the LC-2 code for the final statement.

```
LDR  R0, R6, #4   ;   R0 contains the value of ptr
LDR  R1, R0, #0   ;   load *ptr into R1
ADD  R1, R1, #1   ;   add 1 to *ptr
STR  R1, R0, #0   ;   *ptr = *ptr + 1;
```

Notice that this code is different from what would get generated if the final C statement had been **i = i + 1;**. With the pointer dereference, the compiler generates two **LDR** instructions for the indirection operator on the right-hand side, one to load the memory address contained in **ptr** and another to get the value stored at that address. With the dereference on the left-hand side, the compiler has generated a **STR R1, R0, #0**. Had the statement been **i = *ptr + 1;**, the compiler would have generated a **STR R1, R6, #3**.

One of the hallmarks of C is the flexibility the programmer is given when dealing with pointer variables. Pointers values can be manipulated using a subset of C operators. For example, addition and subtraction between a pointer and an integer is allowed. For more information on other types of legal operations involving pointers, see Section D.3.5. Adding to the previous C code example is the following:

```
int i;
int *ptr;

i = 4;
ptr = &i;
*ptr = *ptr + 1;
ptr = ptr + 1;
```

The new statement `ptr = ptr + 1` modifies the memory address stored in `ptr`. Now `ptr` is incremented to point to the next memory location. The amount that `ptr` is incremented depends on the type of object to which it points. If the variable occupies two locations of memory (say, for example, a double-precision floating-point number) then `ptr` is actually incremented by 2 by the LC-2 compiler. Here, since `ptr` points to an integer, the `ptr` will point to the next memory location after the last statement completes. Once incremented, `ptr` will point to itself—see the activation record in Figure 17.3. Even though `ptr` is no longer pointing to an integer, the compiler will not complain and will generate code treating the value at `*ptr` is an integer assuming the programmers know what they are doing.

What would happen if the following line were added to the end of the previous code example?

```
*ptr = *ptr + 1;
```

17.2.3 Some Examples Using Pointer Variables

Having described the operations of the two C pointer operators, we can now repair the `Swap` function that did not quite accomplish the swap of its arguments. We will use the two new operators to assist. Figure 17.4 lists the same program with a revised version of `Swap` called `NewSwap`.

The first modification we have made is that the parameters of `NewSwap` are no longer integers but are now pointers to integers (`int *`). The two parameters are now the memory addresses of the two items we want swapped. Within the function `NewSwap`, we have added the indirection operator `*` to signify that the values pointed to by these parameters are to be modified. These values themselves are in the activation record for `main`. Finally, when we call `NewSwap` from `main`, we need to supply the proper memory addresses for the two values to be swapped. The `&` operator does the trick. Figure 17.5 shows the run-time stack when the function `NewSwap` is called and when the function `NewSwap` completes.

We have now seen examples of the two most commonly used methods of passing arguments to a function. By design, C passes information from the caller to the callee by evaluating each argument expression in the call statement and placing its value in the callee's activation record. Most types of arguments (e.g., `int`, `char`, `double`) are passed by *by value*. However, we have just seen an example (`NewSwap`) where

```c
#include <stdio.h>

void NewSwap(int *firstVal, int *secondVal);

main()
{
  int valueA = 3;
  int valueB = 4;

  printf("Before NewSwap: valueA = %d and valueB = %d\n", valueA, valueB);
  NewSwap(&valueA, &valueB);
  printf("After NewSwap : valueA = %d and valueB = %d\n", valueA, valueB);
}

void NewSwap(int *firstVal, int *secondVal)
{
  int tempVal;                    /* Needed to hold firstVal when swapping */

  tempVal = *firstVal;
  *firstVal = *secondVal;
  *secondVal = tempVal;
}
```

Figure 17.4   The function **NewSwap** swaps the values of its two parameters

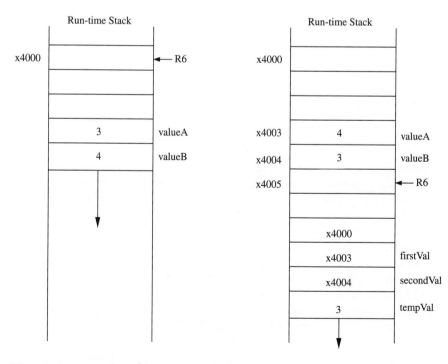

Figure 17.5   Snapshots of the run-time stack when the function **NewSwap** is called and when it completes

```c
#include <stdio.h>

main()
{
    int dividend;              /* The number to be divided      */
    int divisor;               /* The number to divide by       */
    int quotient;              /* Integer result of division    */
    int remainder;             /* Integer remainder of division */
    int error;                 /* Did something go wrong?       */

    printf("Input dividend: ");
    scanf("%d", &dividend);
    printf("Input divisor: ");
    scanf("%d", &divisor);

    error = IntDivide(dividend, divisor, &quotient, &remainder);

    if (!error)                /* if error is zero, !error is non-zero */
      printf("Answer: %d remainder %d\n", quotient, remainder);
    else
      printf("Something is awry...\n");
}

int IntDivide(int x, int y, int *quoPtr, int *remPtr)
{
    if (y != 0) {
      *quoPtr = x / y;         /* Modify the value pointed to by quoPtr */
      *remPtr = x % y;         /* Modify the value pointed to by remPtr */
      return 0;
    }
    else
      return -1;
}
```

Figure 17.6   The function `IntDivide` calculates the integer portion and remainder of an integer divide; it returns a −1 if the divisor is 0.

a *call by reference* is emulated using the address and indirection operators. When an argument is passed by reference, its **address** is passed to the callee function. The called function then can use the indirection operator to access (and modify) the original value in the caller's activation record.

Let's take another look at a passing by reference in C. The program in Figure 17.6 contains a function **IntDivide**, which takes four arguments, two of which are passed by value, two of which are passed by reference. The function **IntDivide** divides the first parameter **dividend** by the second parameter **divisor**. The integer portion of the quotient is written into the third parameter **quotient**, and the integer remainder is written into the fourth parameter **remainder** since both **quotient** and **remainder** need to be modified by the function, they are passed by reference.

Notice that the function **IntDivide** also returns a value: It returns a −1 if the **divisor** is zero, indicating that an error has occurred. It returns zero otherwise. The function **main** checks the return value to determine if anything went wrong

```c
#include <stdio.h>

int *ModSwap(int *firstVal, int *secondVal);

main()
{
  int valueA = 3;
  int valueB = 4;
  int *valueMax;

  printf("Before ModSwap: valueA = %d and valueB = %d\n", valueA, valueB);
  valueMax = ModSwap(&valueA, &valueB);
  printf("After ModSwap : valueA = %d and valueB = %d\n", valueA, valueB);
  printf("The larger value is %d\n", *valueMax);
}

int *ModSwap(int *firstVal, int *secondVal)
{
  int tempVal;                    /* Needed to hold firstVal when swapping */

  tempVal = *firstVal;
  *firstVal = *secondVal;
  *secondVal = tempVal;

  if (*firstVal >= *secondVal)
   return firstVal;
  else
   return secondVal;
}
```

Figure 17.7   The function ModSwap returns a pointer

during the function call to **IntDivide**. If so, it displays a message. Using the return value to signal a problem during a function call between caller and callee is a great programming practice. It is highly encouraged whenever possible.

It is now time to revisit some notation that we introduced in Chapter 11. Now that we know how to pass by an argument by reference, let's reexamine the I/O library function **scanf**:

$$scanf("\%d", \&input);$$

Since function **scanf** needs to update the variable **input** with the decimal value read from the keyboard, we must pass the address of **input**. Thus, the address operator **&** is required.

Functions can also return pointer values. The function must be declared as returning a pointer type. The code from Figure 17.7 contains a modified version of the function **NewSwap** called **ModSwap**: It is modified not only to swap the values of the two original arguments but to return the address of the argument with the larger value after swapping.

17.2.4   The Syntax Demystified

Before we complete our introduction to pointers, let's attempt to make sense of the pointer declaration and dereference * operator syntax. We have seen that to declare a pointer variable, we use a declaration of the following form:

```
type *ptr;
```

where **type** can be any of the predefined (or programmer defined) types such as **int**, **char**, **double**, and so forth, and **ptr** is simply any legal variable identifier. Here we are declaring a variable, which when the * (dereference) operator is applied to it, generates a variable of type **type**. That is, ***ptr** is of type **type**. Similarly, when we declare a function to return a pointer type, like **int *ModSwap** in the previous example, we are specifying the type of the value pointed to by the returned memory address.

The operator * can be applied to any valid pointer expression (unlike **&**, which must only be applied to memory object such as variables). We can create something that looks strange but which can be meaningful in certain contexts. The following example involves evaluating a pointer to a pointer:

```
q = **j;
```

Whereas statements like this one are uncommon, they do occur, and you should be aware of and comfortable with their syntax.

As with all other operators, the address and indirection operator are evaluated according to the C precedence and associativity rules. The precedence and associativity of these and all other operators is listed in Table 12.6. Notice that both of these pointer operators have very high precedence.

17.3   ARRAYS

Arrays are similar to pointers in the sense that they give the programmer the ability to specify a variable location indirectly. With pointers, we could specify a variable by referencing it via a pointer variable. With arrays, we can specify a particular value within a contiguous sequence of values by specifying an offset from the beginning of the sequence. We have seen examples of arrays already when programming the LC-2 (although we never referred to them as *arrays*). Most programming languages directly support arrays. In this section, we will describe how arrays work in C.

Arrays are most useful when the data upon which the program operates is naturally expressed as a contiguous sequence of values. For instance, if we wanted to write a program to take a sequence of 100 numbers entered from the keyboard and *sort* them into ascending order, then an array would be the natural choice for storing these numbers in memory. The program would be almost impossible to write using the simple variables we have been using so far.

17.3.1   Declaring Arrays and Accessing Elements

First, let's examine how to declare an array. Like all other variables, arrays must have
a type associated with them. The type indicates the properties of the values stored in
the array. Following is an example of a declaration for an array of 10 integers:

```
int grid[10];
```

The keyword **int** indicates that we are declaring something of type integer. The
name of the array is **grid**. We can choose any legal identifier for the name of an
array—the rules are the same as those for any variable. The brackets indicate we
are declaring an array and the 10 indicates that the array is to contain 10 integers,
all of which will be sequentially located in memory. Figure 17.8 shows a pictorial
representation of memory allocated to **grid**. If the array **grid** were a local variable,
then its memory space would be allocated in its function's activation record.

Having declared the array **grid**, let's examine how to access different values in
this array. Notice in Figure 17.8 that the array's first element is actually number 0,
which means the last element is numbered 9. To access a particular element, we use
an *index* within brackets. For example,

```
x = grid[3] + 1;

grid[6] = 5;
```

The first statement reads the value stored in the fourth (remember, we start numbering with 0) element of **grid**, adds 1 to it, and stores the result into variable **x**.

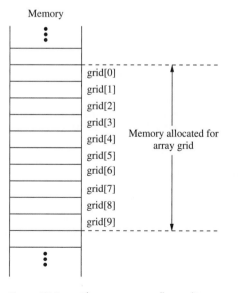

Figure 17.8   The array **grid** allocated in
memory

The second statement sets the seventh element of grid equal to 5. Let's look at the LC-2 code for this example. Let's say that **x** is a local variable allocated slot 3 in the activation record and **grid** is a local variable occupying slots 4 through 13.

```
ADD  R0, R6, #4    ; put the base address of grid into R0
ADD  R1, R0, #3    ; calculate address of grid[3]
LDR  R2, R1, #0    ; grid[3]
ADD  R2, R2, #1    ; grid[3] + 1
STR  R2, R6, #3    ; x = grid[3] + 1;

AND  R2, R2, #0    ;
ADD  R2, R2, #5    ; R2 = 5
ADD  R0, R6, #4    ; put the base address of grid into R0
ADD  R1, R0, #6    ; calculate address of grid[6]
STR  R2, R1, #0    ; grid[6] = 5;
```

Notice that the first and eighth instructions calculate the base address of the array and put it into R0. This address corresponds to the location of the first element (element 0) or expressed another way, **&grid[0]**. We can access any element in the array by adding the index of the desired element to the base address.

The power of arrays comes from the fact that an array's index can be any legal C expression of integer type. The example below demonstrates

$$\text{grid[x+1]} = \text{grid[x]} + 2;$$

Let's look at the LC-2 code for the statement above. Assume **x** is at offset 3 in the current activation record and **grid** starts at entry 4 and ends on entry 13.

```
LDR  R0, R6, #3    ; load the value of x
ADD  R1, R6, #4    ; put the base address of grid into R1
ADD  R1, R0, R1    ; calculate address of grid[x]
LDR  R2, R1, #0    ; grid[x]
ADD  R2, R2, #2    ; grid[x] + 2

LDR  R0, R6, #3    ; load the value of x
ADD  R0, R0, #1    ; x+1
ADD  R1, R6, #4    ; put the base address of grid into R1
ADD  R1, R0, R1    ; calculate address of grid[x+1]
STR  R2, R1, #0    ; grid[x+1] = grid[x] + 2;
```

17.3.2   Examples Using Arrays

First, we start off with a simple C program that uses integer arrays. This program adds two *vectors* by adding the corresponding elements from each vector together to form the sum. Said another way, **sum[i] = a[i] + b[i]**, or element 3 of the sum is produced by taken element 3 of the first vector and adding it to element 3 of the second. So if we add a 10 element vector with another 10 element vector, the result will be another 10 element vector. The natural representation for a vector in a C program is an integer array. Figure 17.9 contains the C code to read in two 10 element vectors, add them together, and print out their sum vector.

```c
#include <stdio.h>

#define VECTOR_SIZE 10

main()
{
  int i;
  int j;
  int VectorA[VECTOR_SIZE];
  int VectorB[VECTOR_SIZE];
  int VectorSum[VECTOR_SIZE];

  /* Input Vector A */
  printf("Enter %d numbers for Vector A.\n", VECTOR_SIZE);
  for (i = 0; i < VECTOR_SIZE; i++) {
    printf("Input VectorA[%d] : ", i);
    scanf("%d", &VectorA[i]);
  }
  printf("\n");

  /* Input Vector B */
  printf("Enter %d numbers for Vector B.\n", VECTOR_SIZE);
  for (i = 0; i < VECTOR_SIZE; i++) {
    printf("VectorB[%d] : ", i);
    scanf("%d", &VectorB[i]);
  }
  printf("\n");

  /* Calculate VectorSum */
  for (i = 0; i < VECTOR_SIZE; i++) {
    VectorSum[i] = VectorA[i] + VectorB[i];
  }

  /* Output Sum */
  printf("The sum of VectorA and VectorB is \n");
  for (i = 0; i < VECTOR_SIZE; i++) {
    printf("VectorSum[%d] = %d \n", i, VectorSum[i]);
  }
}
```

Figure 17.9   A C program that calculates the sum of two 10 element vectors

Another stylistic note: Notice the use of the preprocessor macro **VECTOR_SIZE** to represent a constant value of the size of the input set. This is a common use for preprocessor macros, which are usually found at the beginning of the source file (or within C header files). Now, if we want to increase the size of the vectors, we simply change the definition of the macro (one change) and recompile the program. If we did not use the macro, changing the vector size would require multiple changes to the code in multiple spots. The changes could be potentially difficult to track down, and forgetting to do one would likely result in a program that did not work correctly. Using preprocessor macros for such constant values is good programming practice.

```
#include <stdio.h>

#define MAX_NUMS 10

main()
{
  int index;                      /* Loop iteration variable        */
  int copyIndex;                  /* Loop variable for copy loop     */
  int numbers[MAX_NUMS];          /* Original input numbers          */
  int copies[MAX_NUMS];           /* Num times each input is repeated */

  /* Get input */
  printf("Enter %d numbers.\n", MAX_NUMS);
  for (index = 0; index < MAX_NUMS; index++) {
    printf("Input number %d : ", index);
    scanf("%d", &numbers[index]);
  }

  /* Copy loop -- scan through entire array, counting number of    */
  /* duplicates each input value has within the original array     */
  for (index = 0; index < MAX_NUMS; index++) {
    copies[index] = 0;
    for (copyIndex = 0; copyIndex < MAX_NUMS; copyIndex++) {
      if (numbers[copyIndex] == numbers[index])
        copies[index]++;
    }
  }

  /* Print the results */
  printf("\nThe input set, along with number of copies:\n");
  for (index = 0; index < MAX_NUMS; index++)
    printf("Original number %d.  Number of copies of it %d\n",
           numbers[index], copies[index]);
}
```

Figure 17.10   A C program that determines the number of repeated values in an input sequence

Now onto a slightly more complex example. Figure 17.10 lists a C program which reads in a sequence of **MAX_NUMS** decimal numbers from the keyboard and determines the number of times each input number is repeated within the sequence. The program then prints out each number, along with the number of times it repeats.

In this program, we use two arrays, **numbers** and **copies**. Both are declared to contain **MAX_NUMS** integer values. The array **numbers** stores the input sequence. The array **copies** is calculated by the program and holds the number of copies of the corresponding element in **numbers**. For example, if **numbers[3]** equals 115, and there are a total of four 115s in the input sequence (i.e., there are four 115s in the array **numbers**), then **copies[3]** will equal 4.

This program consists of three loops, of which the middle loop is actually a *nested loop* (see Section 13.2.2) consisting of two loops. The first **for** loop reads in the sequence from the keyboard, storing each number into an element of the array **numbers**.

The second **for** loop contains the nested loop. This body of code determines how many copies of each element exist within the entire array. The outer loop iterates the variable **index** from 0 through **MAX_NUMS**; we use **index** to scan through the array from the first element **numbers[0]** through the last element **numbers[MAX_NUMS]**. The inner loop also iterates from 0 through **MAX_NUMS**; we use this loop to scan through the array again, this time determining how many of the elements match the element selected by the outer loop (i.e., **numbers[index]**). Each time a copy is detected (i.e., **numbers[CopyIndex] == numbers[index]**), the corresponding element in the copies is incremented (i.e., **copies[index]++**).

The final **for** loop simply prints out the original sequence, and the number of copies of each number in the original sequence.

17.3.3   Arrays as Parameters

Passing arrays between functions is a useful thing. Say we want to create a set of functions that calculates the mean and median on an array of integers. We would need either (1) to pass the entire array from one function to another or (2) the pass a reference to the array. If the array contains a large number of elements, copying each element from one activation record onto another could be very costly in execution time and run-time stack space. Fortunately, C naturally passes arrays by reference. Figure 17.11 is a C program that contains a function **Average** whose single parameter is an array of integers.

When calling the function **Average** from **main**, we pass to it the value associated with the array identifier **numbers**. Notice that we are not using the brackets **[ ]** of standard array notation here. In C, an array's name refers to the address of the base element of the array. The name **numbers** is therefore equivalent to **&numbers[0]**. The type **numbers** is similar to **int ***. It is an address of memory location containing an integer.

In using **numbers** as the argument to the function **Average**, we are causing the address of the array **numbers** to be put onto the stack. Within the function **Average**, the parameter **inputValues** is assigned the address of the array. Within **Average** we can access the elements of the original array using standard array notation. Figure 17.12 on page 381 shows the run-time stack after **Average** has been called.

Since arrays are passed by reference in C, any modifications to the array values made by the called function will be visible to the caller once control returns to it. How would we go about passing only a single element of an array by value? By reference?

```
#define MAX_NUMS 10

int Average(int input_values[MAX_NUMS]);

main()
{
  int index;                /* Loop iteration variable  */
  int numbers[MAX_NUMS];    /* Original input numbers    */
  int mean;                 /* average of numbers        */

  /* Get input */
  printf("Enter %d numbers.\n", MAX_NUMS);
  for (index = 0; index < MAX_NUMS; index++) {
    printf("Input number %d : ", index);
    scanf("%d", &numbers[index]);
  }

  mean = Average(numbers);

  printf("The average of these numbers is %d\n", mean);
}

int Average(int inputValues[MAX_NUMS])
{
  int index;
  int sum = 0;

  for (index = 0; index < MAX_NUMS; index++) {
    sum = sum + inputValues[index];
  }

  return (sum / MAX_NUMS);
}
```

Figure 17.11   An example of an array as a parameter to a function

17.3.4   Strings in C

Arrays in C can be used to create *strings*. Strings are sequences of characters and are useful for representing text. Strings are nothing more than character arrays, with each subsequent element containing the next character of the string. For example,

<code>char word[10];</code>

declares an array capable of storing a string of 10 characters. Longer strings require a larger array. What if we wanted to store a word with fewer than 10 characters within this array? In C, the convention is to use the character whose ASCII value is 0 as a sentinel to identify the end of the string. Such strings are also called *null-terminated strings*. '\0' is the special character corresponding to the end of a string. Continuing with our previous declaration,

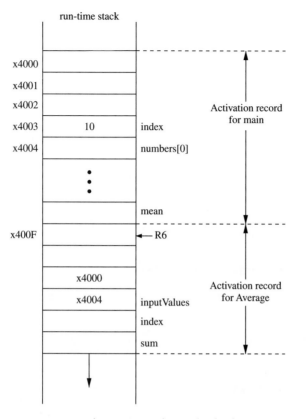

Figure 17.12   The run-time stack immediately after
Average has been called

```
char word[10];

word[0] = 'H';
word[1] = 'e';
word[2] = 'l';
word[3] = 'l';
word[4] = 'o';
word[5] = '\0';
```

```
printf("%s", word);
```

Here, we are assigning the elements of the array individually. The array will contain the string Hello. Because we need a spot for the end-of-string character, we can store only nine characters or fewer in the array **word**. We have also used a new **printf** format specification **%s**, which prints out a string of characters, starting with the character pointed to by the corresponding parameter and ending at the end-of-string character '\0'.

ANSI C compilers also allow strings to be initialized within their declarations. For instance, the above example can be rewritten to the following. Make note of two things: First, character strings are distinguished from single characters with double quotes **" "**. Single quotes are used for single characters, such as, **'A'**. Second,

```
#include <stdio.h>

#define MAX_STRING 20

void CharSwap(char *firstVal, char *secondVal);
void Reverse(char string[MAX_STRING]);

main()
{
  char input[MAX_STRING];     /* Input string, read from the keyboard  */

  printf("Input a word (less than 20 characters) :");
  scanf("%s", input);

  Reverse(input);

  printf("The word reversed is %s.\n", input);
}

void CharSwap(char *firstVal, char *secondVal)
{
  char tempVal;                /* Needed to hold firstVal when swapping  */

  tempVal = *firstVal;
  *firstVal = *secondVal;
  *secondVal = tempVal;
}

void Reverse(char string[MAX_STRING])
{
  int index;
  int length = 0;

  /* Calculate the string length */
  while ((string[length] != '\0') && (length < MAX_STRING))
    length++;

  /* Reverse it! */
  for (index = 0; index < (length / 2); index++)
    CharSwap(&string[index], &string[length - (index + 1)]);
}
```

Figure 17.13   A program that gets a string from the keyboard and prints it with its characters reversed

notice that the compiler automatically adds the termination character to the end of the string.

```
char word[10] = "Hello";

printf("%s", word);
```

Let's examine a slightly more complex example involving strings. In this example, listed in Figure 17.13, we read an input string from the keyboard using **scanf**, then call a function to reverse the string. The reversed string is printed to the screen.

Notice that we are using the format specification **%s** in the **scanf** statement. Here, a string of characters ending with *white space* is read from the keyboard. In C, any space, tab, new line, carriage return, vertical tab, or form-feed character is considered white space. So for the statement **scanf("%s", input)**, if the user typed (from *The New Colossus*, by Emma Lazarus)

```
Not like the brazen giant of Greek fame,
With conquering limbs astride from land to land;
```

only the word *Not* will be stored in the string **input**. The rest of the text line will **not** be discarded but is retained for subsequent **scanf** calls to read. We examine this I/O behavior very closely in Chapter 18. Notice that the maximum word size is 20 characters. What happens if the first word is longer? The **scanf** function has no information on the size of the array **input** and will keep storing characters to the array address it was provided until white space is encountered. So what then happens if the first word is longer than 20 characters? Any local variables that are allocated after the array **input** in the function **main** will be overwritten. Draw out the activation record before and after the call to **scanf** to see why.

The function **Reverse** performs two tasks in order to reverse the string properly. The first loops calculate the length of the string (the length of the string is necessary to determine where the last character is). The second loop performs the reversal by swapping the first character with the last, the second character with the second to last, the third character with the third to last, and so on.

The condition on the **while** loop may seem a little mysterious. There are two parts connected using the AND logical operator **&&**. If either part evaluates to zero, then the loop terminates. The first part of the condition, **string[length] != '\0'**, detects the end-of-string character (**\0**). If the character **string[length]** is '\0', then the first part of the logical AND will be false. The second part of the logical AND, **length < MAX_STRING**, causes the loop to terminate when there are no more array elements left to check.

The second loop calls the function **CharSwap** on pairs of characters within the string. First, **CharSwap** is called on the first and last character, then on the second and second to last character, and so forth. The function **CharSwap** (as we saw with similar versions previously in the chapter) exchanges the value of the two input parameters.

The C standard library provides many prewritten functions for strings. For example, functions to copy strings, concatenate strings, compare strings, or calculate string lengths can be found in the C standard library, and the declarations for these functions can be included via the **<string.h>** header file. More information on some of these string functions can be found in Appendix D.8.2.

17.3.5 The Relationship Between Arrays and Pointers

We have mentioned in passing the similarity between an array's name and a pointer variable to an element of the same type. For instance,

```
char word[10];
char *cptr;

cptr = word;
```

is a legal, and sometimes useful, sequence of code. Here, we have assigned the pointer variable **cptr** to point to the base address of the array **word**. Because they are both pointers to characters, **cptr** and **word** can be used interchangeably. For example, we can access the fourth character within the string, either by using **work[3]** or ***(cptr + 4)**.

One difference between the two, though, is that **cptr** is a variable and can be reassigned. The array identifier **word**, on the other hand, cannot be. For example, the following statement is illegal: **word = newArray**. The identifier is actually a **constant** expression of type **const char *** and always points to a spot chosen by the compiler. Once it has been allocated an initial location, it cannot be moved.

Table 17.1 shows the equivalence of several expressions involving pointer notation and array notation. Each row in the table is a group of expressions with the same meaning.

Table 17.1   The relationship between pointers and arrays

cptr	word	&word[0]
(cptr + n)	word + n	&word[n]
*cptr	*word	word[0]
*(cptr + n)	*(word+n)	word[n]

17.3.6 More Examples

The next example program is one we have used in other parts of the textbook. We have now seen enough of the C programming language to comprehend fully the C version of the character-counting program initially described in Chapter 5. It is listed in Figure 17.14.

In this program, we have used an external function called **GetFile**, for which we have not provided the source code. This function is part of another source file, which can be compiled separately and linked in to create an executable image. For the purpose of this example, the function **GetFile** is not necessary. **GetFile** performs the task of initializing the array **text** to contain the series of characters that constitute the sequence of text to analyze.

The main loop of the program is trivial. We simply check each character of the array until we encounter the end-of-file sentinel character, which, like for strings, is also equal to the character '\0'. Every array element that matches the character for which we are searching increments the counter variable **count**. After the end-of-file character is detected, the value of **count** is displayed.

```
#include <stdio.h>

#define MAX_SIZE 1000

void GetFile(char text[MAX_SIZE]);

main()
{
   int index = 0;              /* Index through the entire file */
   int count = 0;              /* Holds the number of matches   */
   char find;                  /* Character to search for       */
   char text[MAX_SIZE];        /* Input character file          */

   GetFile(text);

   printf("Please input a character to search for :");
   scanf("%c", &find);

   /* Scan the file */
   while (text[index] != '\0') {
      if (text[index] == find)
         count++;
      index++;
   }

   /* Print out the results */
   printf("The number of occurrences of %c is %d\n", find, count);
}
```

Figure 17.14   The character-counting program in C

The next example in Figure 17.15 (page 386) is a simple sorting program. This program starts off by reading 10 integers from the keyboard into an array and then arranges them in increasing order—a process known as *sorting*. This array is passed to the function **InsertionSort**, which arranges them using a very straightforward technique called the *insertion sort*.

Insertion sort is best described by an example. Say you wanted to sort your music collection into alphabetical order by artist. If you were sorting your compact discs using insertion sort, you would split the CDs into two groups, the sorted group and the unsorted group. Initially, the sorted group would be empty as all your CDs would be yet unsorted. You would sort by taking a CD from the unsorted group and *inserting* it into the proper position amongst the sorted CDs. For example, if the sorted group contained three CDs, one by John Coltrane, one by Charles Mingus, and one by Thelonious Monk, then inserting the Miles Davis CD would mean inserting it between the Coltrane CD and the Mingus CD. You keep doing this until all CDs in the unsorted group have been inserted into the sorted group.

It turns out that an insertion sort is not only easy to do by hand, by rather simple to do by computer. Instead of CDs, the following program sorts a sequence of numbers stored in an array. The process of insertion sorting is very much what was described above: We take each element of this array and insert it into the proper spot within an already sorted subcomponent of the array.

```c
#include <stdio.h>

#define MAX_NUMS 10

void InsertionSort(int list[MAX_NUMS]);

main()
{
  int index;                        /* iteration variable          */
  int numbers[MAX_NUMS];            /* list of number to be sorted */

  /* Get input */
  printf("Enter %d numbers.\n", MAX_NUMS);
  for (index = 0; index < MAX_NUMS; index++) {
    printf("Input number %d : ", index);
    scanf("%d", &numbers[index]);
  }

  InsertionSort(numbers);           /* Call sorting routine        */

  /* Print sorted list */
  printf("\nThe input set, in ascending order:\n");
  for (index = 0; index < MAX_NUMS; index++)
    printf("%d\n", numbers[index]);
}

void InsertionSort(int list[MAX_NUMS])
{
  int unsorted;       /* Used to iterate thru unsorted list items */
  int sorted;         /* Used to iterate thru sort items          */
  int unsortedItem;   /* Current item we're trying to insert      */

  /* This loop iterates from 1 thru MAX_NUMS */
  for (unsorted = 1; unsorted < MAX_NUMS; unsorted++) {
    unsortedItem = list[unsorted];

    /* This loop iterates from unsorted thru 0, unless
       we hit an element smaller than current item */
    for (sorted = unsorted - 1;
         (sorted >= 0) && (list[sorted] > unsortedItem);
         sorted--)
      list[sorted + 1] = list[sorted];

    list[sorted + 1] = unsortedItem; /* Insert item               */
  }
}
```

Figure 17.15   Insertion sort program

We need to represent two groups of items, the sorted items and the unsorted items. It turns out that it is convenient to represent both groups within the original array. The initial part of the array contains the sorted items and the remainder of the array contains the unsorted items. We pick the next unsorted item and insert it into the sorted part at the correct point. We keep doing this until we have gone through the entire array.

The actual **InsertionSort** routine (shown in Figure 17.15) contains two loops, which are nested within each other. The outer loops scans through all the unsorted items (analogous to going through the unsorted CDs, one by one). The inner loop scans through the already sorted items scanning for the proper place at which to insert the new item. Once we have detected an already sorted element that is larger than the one we are inserting, we insert the new element between the larger and the one before it.

Let's take a closer look by examining what happens during a pass of the insertion sort. Say the array **list** contains the 10 numbers:

```
2 16 69 92 15 37 92 38 82 19
```

During this pass, the variable **unsorted** equals 4, meaning the first four items within the array are already sorted, and we are in the process of inserting **list[4]**, or 15.

The inner loop iterates the variable **sorted** through the list of already sorted elements. It does this from the highest numbered element down to 0 (i.e., starting at 3 down to 0). Notice that the condition on the **for** loop terminates the loop once a list item *less* than the current item, 15, is found.

In each iteration of this inner loop, we copy the largest sorted item to the next highest element. So after the first iteration of the inner loop, the array **list** contains

```
2 16 69 92 92 37 92 38 82 19
```

Notice that we have overwritten 15 (**list[4]**). That is okay because we have a copy of it in the variable **unsortedItem**. After the second iteration, **list** contains

```
2 16 69 69 92 37 92 38 82 19
```

After the third iteration, **list** contains:

```
2 16 16 69 92 37 92 38 82 19
```

Now the **for** loop terminates because the condition is no longer true because the current sorted list item **list[0]**, which is 2, is not larger than the current unsorted item **unsortedItem**, which is 15. Now the inner loop terminates, and the statement following it **list[sorted + 1] = unsortedItem;** executes. Now **list** contains, and the sorted group contains one more element.

```
2 15 16 69 92 37 92 38 82 19
```

17.3.7   Common Pitfalls with Arrays in C

Exceeding the size (or bounds) of an array is one of the most common errors made with arrays in C programming. Unlike some programming languages, C provides no support for ensuring that an array index is actually within an array. The compiler

```
#include <stdio.h>

main()
{
  int array[10];
  int i;

  for(i=0; i <= 10; i++)
    array[i] = 0;
}
```

Figure 17.16   This C program contains a
serious flaw

blindly generates code for the expression **a[i]**, even if the index **i** accesses a memory location beyond the end of the array. This is part of C's "surrender control to the programmer" philosophy. Even though this philosophy has contributed greatly to the success of the language, it adds to the effort required to get a C program working. Figure 17.16 lists an example of how an innocent semantic mistake can lead to a serious debugging effort.

Analyze this program by drawing out the activation record for **main** with **array** at offset 3 and **i** at offset 13. What happens? One note: If you compiled this program using a real compiler, the behavior you see will be different because different compilers arrange variables differently in the activation record. There is no C standard on activation record formats.

C does not support array declarations with variable expressions. The following code in C is illegal. The size of array **temp** must be known when the compiler analyzes the source code.

```
void SomeArrayFunction(int array, int num_elements)
{
  int temp[num_elements];   /* Generates a syntax error */

  :
}
```

To deal with limitation, most C programmers make assumptions about the size of the data set the program will operate on and then allocate arrays with extra space. Error-checking code is sometimes added to detect the situation of when the allocated space does not suffice. Another option is to use dynamic memory allocation to allocate the array at run-time. More on this later.

PROBLEMS

17.1. Write a C function that takes as a parameter a character string of unknown length, containing a single word. Your function should translate this string from English into Pig Latin. This translation is performed by removing the first letter of the string, appending onto the end, and concatenating the letters *ay*. You can assume that the array contains enough space for you to add the extra characters.

For example, if your function is passed the string "Hello", after your function returns, the string should have the value "elloHay". The first character of the string should be "e".

17.2. Write a C program that accepts a list of numbers from the user until a number is repeated (i.e., is the same as the number preceding it). The program then prints out the number of numbers entered (excluding the last) and their sum. When the program is run, the prompts and responses will look like the following:

```
Number: 5
Number: -6
Number: 0
Number: 45
Number: 45
4 numbers were entered and their sum is 44
```

17.3. Write the LC-2 code that gets generated for the statement `q = **j`, where `q` and `j` are both local variables dealing with integers.

17.4. What is the output when the following code is compiled and run?

```
int x;

main()
{
    int *px = &x;
    int x = 7;

    *px = 4;
    printf("x = %d\n", x);
}
```

17.5. Create a string function that returns a 0 if both strings are the same, a 1 if **stringA** appears before **stringB** in the sorted order of a dictionary, or a 2 if **stringB** appears before **stringA**.

17.6. Using the function developed for Exercise 5, modify the Insertion Sort program so that it operates upon strings instead of integers.

17.7.   For this question, examine the following program:

```
#include <stdio.h>

main()
{
    int apple;
    int *ptr;
    int **ind;

    ind = &ptr;
    *ind = &apple;
    **ind = 123;

    ind++;
    *ptr++;
    apple++;

    printf("%x %x %d\n", ind, ptr, apple);
}
```

Assuming the activation record for **main** begins at location x4000 on the run-time stack, what gets printed out by the program?

17.8.   Translate the following C function into LC-2 assembly language.

```
main()
{
    int a[5], i;

    i = 4;
    while (i >= 0) {
        a[i] = i;
        i--;
    }
}
```

17.9.   The following code contains a call to the function **triple**. What is the minimum size of the activation record of **triple**?

```
main()
{
    int array[3];

    array[0] = 1;
    array[1] = 2;
    array[2] = 3;

    triple(array);
}
```

17.10. For this question, refer to the following C program:

```c
int FindLen(char *);

main()
{
    char str[10];

    printf("Enter a string : ");
    scanf("%s", str);

    printf("%s has %d characters\n", str, FindLen(str));
}

int FindLen(char * s)
{
    int len=0;

    while (*s != '\0') {
        len++;
        s++;
    }

    return len;
}
```

1. For the C program written below, what is the size of the activation record for the function **main** and **FindLen**?

2. Show the contents of the stack just before the function **FindLen** returns if the input string is **apple**.

3. What would the activation record look like if the program were run and the user typed a string of length greater than 10 characters? What would happen to the program?

17.11. Write a program to remove any duplicates from a sequence of numbers. For example, if the list consisted of the numbers 5, 4, 5, 5, and 3, the program would output 5, 4, 3.

17.12. Write a program to find the median of a set of numbers. Recall that the median is a number within the set in which half the numbers are larger and half are smaller. *Hint:* To perform this, you may need to sort the list first.

18

I/O in C

18.1 INTRODUCTION

Whether it be to the screen or to a file, output is generated by all useful programs. Most programs also require input. In order to program in a programming language effectively, you need to understand how it carries out input and output. Input and output is not directly supported by C, instead it is handled by a set of standard library functions. The behavior of these functions is precisely defined by the ANSI C standard.

In this chapter, we will discuss six functions in the C standard I/O library. The functions **putchar** and **printf** write output to the monitor and the functions **getchar** and **scanf** get input from the keyboard. The more general functions **fprintf** and **fscanf** perform file I/O. We have used most of these functions in the many examples throughout the second half of this book. In this chapter, we examine the details of how these functions work.

18.2 A BRIEF NOTE ABOUT THE C STANDARD LIBRARY

We have encountered the C standard library in passing several times already. The C standard library is a major part of the C programming language. It provides support for I/O, character string manipulations, math functions, system functions, file access functions, and other useful things that are not specific to any single program but required by many. More information on the C standard library can be found in Appendix D.8. The library's functions are typically written by designers of the compiler, operating system, and hardware platform because writing them requires intimate knowledge of the underlying hardware and system software.

To use a function defined within the C standard libraries, the proper header file (.h file) must be included. The functions within the library are grouped by the tasks they perform, and each of these groups has a header file associated with it. The standard I/O functions use the header file **stdio.h**. This header files contain several things such as the function declarations for the I/O functions and preprocessor macros relating to I/O. A library header file does *not* contain the source code for library functions.

If the header files do not contain source code, then how does the machine code for, say, **printf** get added to our programs? Each library function called within a program is linked in when the executable image is formed. The object files containing the library functions are stored somewhere on the system and are accessed by the linker, which links together our program and all the library functions required by it into an executable image. A preview for a future course: often nowadays, programs can be linked using dynamically linked libraries (DLLs) or *shared* libraries. With these types of libraries, the machine code for a library routine does not appear within the executable image but is "linked" in while the program executes.

18.3   I/O, ONE CHARACTER AT A TIME

Let's start by examining general characteristics of I/O using some of the simplest I/O capabilities that C provides. The functions **getchar** and **putchar** perform input and output *one character at a time*. They provide no conversion functionality; input is read in as ASCII and output is written out as ASCII, in a manner similar to the **IN** and **OUT** TRAP routines of the LC-2.

Conceptually, C performs all input and output on ASCII *text streams*. In fact, many other popular languages provide a similar abstraction for I/O. The sequence of ASCII characters typed by the user at the keyboard is an example of an input stream. The sequence of ASCII characters printed by a single running program to the computer's monitor is an example of an output stream. What this means is each character typed at the keyboard is added to the stream whenever it is detected, and it waits in the input stream, in the order it was received, until the program reads it. Similarly, whenever the program prints a character to the output device, it gets added to the output stream, and it waits until the monitor is ready to display it.

In C the standard input stream from the keyboard is referred to as **stdin**, and the standard output stream is referred to as **stdout**. By default, the functions **getchar** and **putchar** operate on these two streams.

18.3.1 putchar

The function **putchar** is the high-level language equivalent of the LC-2 **OUT** TRAP routine. The function **putchar** displays on the **stdout** output stream the ASCII value of the parameter passed to it. It performs no type conversions—the value passed to it is assumed to be ASCII and is written to the output stream. All the calls to **putchar** in the following code segment cause the same character (**h**) to be displayed. A **putchar** function call is treated like any other function call. Here the function being called resides within the standard library. Its function declaration is in the **stdio.h** header file. Its code will be linked into the executable during the compiler's link phase.

```
char c = 'h';

   :
putchar(c);
putchar('h');
putchar(104);
```

18.3.2 getchar

The function **getchar** is the high-level language equivalent of the LC-2 **IN** TRAP function. It returns the ASCII value of the next input character appearing in the **stdin** input stream. By default, the **stdin** input stream is simply the stream of characters typed at the keyboard. In the following code segment, **getchar** returns the ASCII value of the next character typed at the keyboard. This return value is assigned to the variable **c**.

```
char c;

c = getchar();
```

18.3.3 Buffered I/O

Run the C code in Figure 18.1 and you will notice something peculiar.

The program prompts the user for the first input character and waits for that input to be typed in. Type in a character (say *z*, for example) and nothing happens. The

```
#include <stdio.h>

main()
{
  char inChar1;
  char inChar2;

  printf("Input character 1:\n");
  inChar1 = getchar();

  printf("Input character 2:\n");
  inChar2 = getchar();

  printf("Character 1 is %c\n", inChar1);
  printf("Character 2 is %c\n", inChar2);
}
```

Figure 18.1   An example of buffered input

second prompt does not appear, as if the call to **getchar** has missed the keystroke. In fact, the program seems to make no progress at all until the new-line character (the Enter key) is typed in. Such behavior seems unexpected considering that **getchar** is supposed to read only a single character from the keyboard input stream.

This unexpected behavior is due to buffering of the keyboard input stream. On most computer systems, I/O streams are buffered. Every key typed on the keyboard is captured by the computer's low-level software and kept in a *buffer* until it is read via an I/O function call, say **getchar**. Conceptually, each I/O stream has its own buffer. A *buffer* is a temporary storage area containing the input stream, kept somewhere in the system's memory.

As for the input buffer, keystrokes are added only after an input line is terminated by the Enter key. On most computer systems, whenever a user types the Enter key, the sequence of characters typed since the last time the Enter key was pressed is added to the input stream. So from the previous code example, it is not until the Enter key is pressed that the program actually sees the characters the user typed in. (Notice that the Enter key also appears in the input stream as the new-line character.) There is a good reason for this behavior: Pressing the Enter key allows the user to *confirm* the input. Say you mistyped some input and wanted to correct it before the program detects it. You can edit your input using the backspace and delete keys, and then confirm your input by pressing Enter.

The output stream is similarly buffered. Observe by running the program in Figure 18.2.

On most computer systems, you will notice that the delay loop (which may have to be adjusted for your system by modifying the value of DELAY to cause a delay of a several seconds) causes a pause before any output appears on the monitor even though the first **putchar** appears before the delay loop. The output stream is not *flushed* to the output device until a new-line character appears in the stream (or the

```
#include <stdio.h>
#define DELAY 100000000

main()
{
  int sum = 0;
  int i;

  putchar('a');

  /* Generate a small delay */
  for (i = 0; i < DELAY; i++) {
    sum = sum + i;
  }

  putchar('b');
  putchar('\n');
}
```

Figure 18.2   An example of buffered output

program controlling the output stream completes). The **putchar('\n')** causes output to be flushed.

Despite the slightly complex implementation of buffered I/O streams, the underlying mechanism used to actually read the keyboard and write to the monitor is very similar to the simpler **IN** and **OUT** TRAP routines described in Chapter 8.

18.4 SLIGHTLY MORE SOPHISTICATED I/O

The functions **putchar** and **getchar** suffice for simple I/O jobs, but we require more powerful constructs for typical I/O jobs. The functions **printf** and **scanf** perform more sophisticated *formatted* I/O.

18.4.1 printf

The function **printf** writes formatted text to the output stream. Using **printf**, we can print out ASCII text embedded with values generated by the running program. The **printf** function takes care of all the necessary type conversions. We have seen many examples of this function throughout the second half of the book. This example prints out the sum of three input values:

```
int x,y,z;

printf("Enter three integer values : ");
scanf("%d %d %d", &x, &y, &z);
printf("The three values are: %d %d %d\n", x, y, z);
printf("The sum of the parameters is %d\n", x + y + z);
```

Generally speaking, **printf** writes its first parameter to the output stream. The first parameter is the *format string*. It is a character string (i.e., of type **char ***) containing text to be output. Embedded within the format string are zero or more *conversion specifications*.

The conversion specifications indicate how to print out any of the parameters that follow the format string in the function call. Conversion specifications all begin with a **%** character. As their name implies, they indicate how the values of the parameters that follow the format string should be treated when converted to ASCII. In many of the examples we have encountered so far (including the one above), integers have been printed out as decimal numbers using the **%d** specification. We could also use the **%x** specification to print integers as hexadecimal numbers, or **%b** to print them as binary numbers (represented as ASCII text, of course). Other conversions for other types of values can also be accomplished: **%c** causes a value to be interpreted as straight ASCII (how is this type conversion accomplished?), the **%s** specification is used for strings and causes characters stored consecutively in memory to be output. The end-of-string character **\0** signals the end of the string. The specification **%f** displays a floating point number. What if we wanted to print out the **%** character itself? We use the sequence **%%**. See Appendix E for a full listing of conversion specifiers.

As mentioned in Chapter 11, special characters such as a new line can also be embedded in the format string. The \n prints a new line and a \t character prints a tab; both are examples of these special characters. All special characters begin with a \ and they can appear anywhere within a format string. In order to print out a backslash character, we use a \\. See Table D.1 in the appendix for a list of special characters.

Here are some examples of various format specifications:

```
int  a = 102;
int  b = 65;
char c = 'z';
char banner[10] = "Hola!";
double pi = 3.14159;

printf("The variable 'a' decimal : %d\n", a);
printf("The variable 'a' hex : %x\n", a);
printf("The variable 'a' binary : %b\n", a);
printf("'a' plus 'b' as character : %c\n", a + b);
printf("A char %c.\t A string %s\n A float %f\n", c, banner, pi);
```

The function **printf** begins by examining the format string a single character at a time. If the current character is not a % or \, then the character is directly written to the output stream. (Remember, the stream may be buffered so the output may not appear on the monitor until a new line is written.) If the character is a \, then the next character indicates the particular special character to print out. For instance, the escape sequence \n indicates a new-line character. If the current character is a %, indicating a conversion specification, then the next character indicates how the next pending parameter should be interpreted. For instance, if the conversion specification is a %d and the next pending parameter is the bit pattern 000000001101000, then the number 104 is written to the output stream. If the conversion character is a %c, then the character h is written. A different value is printed if %f is the conversion specification. The conversion specifier indicates to **printf** how the next parameter should be interpreted. It is important to realize that, within the **printf** routine, there is no relationship between a conversion specification and the type of a parameter. The programmer is free to choose how things are to be interpreted as they are displayed to the screen. *Question:* What happens with the following function call?

```
printf("The value of nothing is %d\n");
```

There is no argument corresponding to the %d specification. The **printf** routine assumes the correct number of values were written onto the stack when it is called and blindly reads a value off the stack for the %d spec, assuming it was intentionally placed there. Here, a garbage value is displayed to the screen. It, however, is displayed in decimal.

18.4.2 `scanf`

The function **scanf** is used to read formatted ASCII data from the input stream. A call to **scanf** is similar to a call to **printf**. Both calls require a format string as the first argument followed by a variable number of other arguments. Both functions are controlled by characters within the format string. The function **scanf** differs in that all arguments following the format string *must* be pointers. We dicussed the reasons for this in Chapter 17

The format string for **scanf** contains ASCII text and conversion specifications, just like the format string for **printf**. The conversion characters are similar to those used for **printf**. A table of these specifications can be found in Appendix E. Essentially, the format string represents the format of the input stream. For example, the format string **"%d"** indicates to **scanf** that the next sequence of nonwhite space characters (white space is defined as spaces, tabs, new lines, carriage returns, vertical tabs, and form feeds) is a sequence of digits in ASCII representing an integer in decimal notation. After this decimal number is read from the input stream, it is converted into an integer and stored into the corresponding argument. Since **scanf** modifies the values of the variables passed to it, arguments are passed *by reference* using the **&** operator. In addition to conversion specifications, the format string also can contain plain text, which **scanf** attempts to match with the input stream.

We use the following code to demonstrate.

```
char name[100];
int bMonth, bDay, bYear;
double gpa;

printf("Enter : lastname birthdate grade_point_average\n");
scanf("%s %d/%d/%d %lf", name, &bMonth, &bDay, &bYear, &gpa);

printf("\n");
printf("Name : %s\n", name);
printf("Birthday : %d/%d/%d\n", bMonth, bDay, bYear);
printf("GPA : %f\n", gpa);
```

In the **scanf** statement above, the first specification is a **%s** that scans in a string from the input stream. In this context, all characters starting from the first nonwhite space character and ending with the next white space character (conceptually, the next *word* in the input stream) is stored in memory starting at the address of **name** and an **\0** character is automatically added to signify the end of the string. Since the argument **name** is an array, it is automatically passed by reference, that is, the address of the first element of the array is passed to **scanf**.

The next specification is for a decimal number, **%d**. Now, **scanf** expects to find a sequence of digits (at least one digit) as the next set of nonwhite space characters in the standard input stream. Characters from standard input are analyzed, white-space characters are discarded, and the decimal number (i.e., a sequence of digits terminated by a nondigit) is read in. The number is converted from a sequence of ASCII characters into a binary integer and stored in the memory location indicated by the argument **&bMonth**.

The next input field is the ASCII character, /. Now, **scanf** expects to find this character, possibly surrounded by white space, in the input stream. Since this input field is not a conversion specification, it is not assigned to any variable. Once it is read in from the input stream, it is simply discarded, and **scanf** moves onto the next field of the format string. Similarly, the next three input fields **%d/%d** are read in two decimal numbers separated by a /. These values are converted into integers and stored into **bDay** and **bYear**.

The last field in the format string specifies that the input stream contains a *long* floating-point number, which is the specification used to read in a value of type **double**. For this specifier, **scanf** expects to see a sequence of decimal numbers, and possibly a decimal point, possibly an **E** or **e** signifying exponential notation (see Appendix D.2.4), in the input stream. This field is terminated once a nondigit (excluding the first **E**, or the decimal point or a plus or minus sign for the fraction or exponent) or white space is detected. The **scanf** routine takes this sequence of ASCII characters and converts them into a properly expressed, double-precision floating-point number and stores it into **gpa**.

Once it is done processing the format string, **scanf** returns to the caller. It also returns an integer value. The number of format specifications that were successfully scanned in the input stream is passed back to the caller. In this case, if everything went correctly, **scanf** would return the value 5. In the code example above, we chose to ignore the return value.

So, for example, the following line of input yields the following output:

```
Enter : lastname birthdate grade_point_average
Mudd 02/16/69 3.02

Name : Mudd
Birthday : 2/16/69
GPA : 3.02
```

Since **scanf** ignores white space for this format string, the following input stream yields the same results. Remember, new-line characters are considered white space.

```
Enter : lastname birthdate grade_point_average
Mudd      02
/
16 / 69      3.02

Name : Mudd
Birthday : 2/16/69
GPA : 3.02
```

What if the format of the input stream does not match the format string? For instance, what happens with the following stream?

```
Enter : lastname birthdate grade_point_average
Mudd 02 16 69 3.02
```

Here, the input stream does not contain the / characters encoded in the format string. In this case, **scanf** returns the value 2, since the variables **name** and **birth_month** are correctly assigned before the mismatch is detected. The remaining variables go unmodified. Since the input stream is buffered, unused input is not discarded and subsequent reads of the input stream begin where this call left off.

If the next two reads of the input stream are

```
a = getchar();
b = getchar();
```

what does **a** and **b** contain? The answer ' ' (the space character) and **1** should not be puzzling.

What happens if arguments are not passed to **scanf** as pointers? For example, what happens with the following call?

```
int n = 0;

scanf("%d", n);
```

Run this code and you will notice an error due to **scanf** modifying a restricted memory location.

18.4.3   Variable Argument Lists

By now, you might have noticed something different about the functions **printf** and **scanf**. Both can have a *variable* number of arguments passed to them. The number of arguments passed to **printf** and **scanf** depends on the number of items being printed or scanned. They, therefore, require a special function call mechanism.

There is a one-to-one correspondence between each conversion specification in the format string and each argument that appears after the format string in these function calls. The following **printf** statement is from a previous example:

```
printf("A char %c.\t A string %s\n A float %f\n", c, banner, pi);
```

The format string contains three format specifications; therefore, three arguments follow it in the function call. The **%c** spec in the string is associated with the first argument that follows (the variable **c**). The **%s** is associated with **banner**, and **%f** with **pi**. There are three values to be printed; therefore, this call contains four arguments altogether. If we want to print five values, the function call contains six arguments.

The compiler treats a call to **printf** or **scanf** as any other call except the number of arguments for the call is the first item placed in the activation record. Then, each argument is placed on the stack before the actual function call is performed. The format string (as are all constant strings that appear in C code) is actually a character array and, like all arrays, is passed as the address of the first element. The format string itself is stored in memory by the compiler in a special region of reserved for constants (constants within a program are also called *literal values*). The address of the format string is passed as the first argument and all other arguments follow it. Most compilers will *not* check the format string to make sure there are the same number of specifiers and arguments to print.

Since the functions **printf** and **scanf** use variable-length argument lists, they require special treatment in order for the activation record and run-time stack to work properly. A modified version of the calling mechanism described in Chapter 14 is used for functions with variable argument lists.

18.5   I/O FROM FILES

What if we wanted to process a large set of data from within a program, say the daily stock price for IBM for the last 20 years. To ask the user to type this via keyboard every time the program is run would render it very "user-unfriendly." To handle this, we require the ability to read and write ASCII data *files* from within our C programs. As we will see, I/O in C is conceptually based on file I/O.

The functions **printf** and **scanf** are really special cases of more general-purpose C I/O functions. These two functions operate specifically on the special *file pointers* **stdin** and **stdout**. For our purposes, we say that a file pointer maps a particular stream (input or output or *input and output*) to a particular file or device. In C, **stdin** and **stdout** are mapped by default to the keyboard and the monitor.

The general-purpose version of **printf** is called **fprintf** and the general-purpose version of **scanf** is called **fscanf**. The functions **fprintf** and **fscanf** work like their counterparts, with the main difference being that they allow us to specify the stream on which they act. For example, we can inform **fprintf** to write its output to a specific file. Let's see how this can be accomplished.

Before we can perform file I/O, we need to declare a file pointer for each physical file we want to manipulate. Typically, physical files are files stored on the file system of the particular computer system. In C, we can declare a file pointer called **infile** as such:

```
FILE *infile;
```

Here we are declaring a pointer to something of type **FILE**. The type **FILE** is defined within the header file **stdio.h**. Its details are not important for our discussion here.

Once the file pointer is declared, we need to map it to a physical file. The C library call **fopen** performs this mapping. Each **fopen** call requires two arguments: the name of the file to open and description of what type of operations we want to perform on the file. To follow is an example.

```
FILE *infile;

infile = fopen("ibm_stock_prices", "r");
```

The first argument to **fopen** is the string **ibm_stock_prices**. The second argument is the operation we want to perform on this file. Several useful *modes* are

"r" for reading, **"w"** for writing (a file opened with this mode will lose its previous contents), **"a"** for appending (here, previous contents are not lost; new data is added to the end of the file), **"r+"** for reading and writing. Note that both arguments must be character strings; therefore, they are surrounded by double quotes in this example. In this case, we are opening the file called **"ibm_stock_prices"** for reading.

If the **fopen** call is successful, the function returns a file pointer to the physical file. If the open for some reason fails, then the function returns a special value called the *null value*. It is defined to the preprocessor macro **NULL**. It is *always* good practice to check if the **fopen** call was successful.

```
FILE *infile;

infile = fopen("ibm_stock_prices", "r");

if (infile == NULL)
    printf("fopen unsuccessful!\n");
```

Now with the file pointer properly mapped to a physical file, we can use **fscanf** and **fprintf** to read and write it just as we used **printf** and **scanf** to read the standard devices. The functions **fscanf** and **fprintf** both require a file pointer as their first argument to indicate on which stream the operations are to be performed. The example to follow demonstrates.

```
#define LIMIT 10000

FILE *infile;
FILE *outfile;
double prices[LIMIT];
char answer[10];
int i = 0;

infile  = fopen("ibm_stock_prices", "r");
outfile = fopen("buy_hold_or_sell", "w");

if (fp != NULL && output_file != NULL) {
  /*  Read the input data */
  while ((fscanf(infile, "%lf", prices[i]) != EOF) && i < LIMIT)
    i++;

  printf("%d prices read from the data file", i);

  /* Process the data... */
  :
  :

  /* Write the output */
  fprintf(output_file, "%s", answer);
}
else {
   printf("fopen unsuccessful!\n");
}
```

Here, we are reading from an ASCII text file called **ibm_stock_prices** and writing to a file called **buy_hold_or_sell**. The input file contains a floating-point data item separated by white space. Even though the file can contain more, at most 10,000 items are read in using **fscanf**. The **fscanf** function returns a special value when no more data can be read from the input file, either indicating the end of file has been reached or the file was improperly formatted. We can check the return value of **fscanf** against this special character, which is defined to the preprocessor macro **EOF**. The condition on the **while** loop causes it to terminate if **EOF** is encountered or if the limit of input values is exceeded. After reading the input file, the program processes the input data, the output file is written with the value of the string **answer**.

The functions **printf** is equivalent to calling **fprintf** using **stdout** as the file pointer. Likewise, **scanf** is equivalent to calling **fscanf** using **stdin**.

PROBLEMS

18.1. Write an I/O function call to handle the following tasks. All can be handled by a single call.

1. Print out an integer followed by a string followed by a floating-point number.

2. Print out a phone number in (XXX)-XXX-XXXX format. Internally, the phone number is stored as three integers.

3. Print out a student ID number in XXX-XX-XXXX format. Internally, the ID number is stored as three character strings.

4. Read a student ID number in XXX-XX-XXXX format. The number is to be stored internally as three integers.

5. Read in a line of input containing **Last name, First name, Middle initial age sex**. The name fields are separated by commas. The middle initial and sex should be stored as characters. Age is an integer.

18.2. What does the value returned by **scanf** represent?

18.3. Why is buffering of the keyboard input stream useful?

18.4. What is displayed by the following function call:
`printf("The value of x is %d\n");`?

18.5. Why does the following code print out a strange value (such as 1073741824)?

```
float x = 192.27163;
printf("The value of x is %d\n", x);
```

18.6. What is the value of **input** for the following function call:

```
scanf("%d", &input);
```

if the input stream contains

> **This is not the input you are looking for.**

18.7. Consider the following program:

```
#include <stdio.h>

main()
{
  int x = 0;
  int y = 0;
  char label[10];

  scanf("%d %d", &x, &y);
  scanf("%s", label);

  printf("%d %d %s\n", x, y, label);
}
```

1. What gets printed out if the input stream is **46 29 BlueMoon**?

2. What gets printed out if the input stream is **46 BlueMoon**?

3. What gets printed out if the input stream is **111 999 888**?

18.8. Write a program to read in a C source file and write it back to a file called **"condensed_program"** with all *white space* removed.

18.9. Write a program to read in a text file and provide a count of

1. The number of strings in the file, where a string begins with a nonwhite-space character and ends with a white-space character.

2. The number of words in the file, where a word begins with an alphabetic character (e.g., a–z or A–Z) and ends with a nonalphabetic character.

3. The number of unique words in the file. Words are as defined in the previous part. The set of unique words has no duplicates.

4. The frequency of words in order of most frequent to least frequent. In other words, analyze the text file, count the number of times each word occurs, and display these counts from most frequent word to least frequent.

chapter

19

Data Structures

19.1 INTRODUCTION

The data manipulated by the programs we write almost always has some natural higher level organization to it. It is often beneficial to use this natural structure when designing the programs that use the data. If the data is organized properly within the program, the flow of the program is more intuitive and the program is easier to write, debug, and maintain. For example, if we were writing a program to manage a company's employee database, *bundling* a particular employee's data—such as name, address, job title, social security number—as one unit would be a natural way to organize the data.

Data structures are the organization of data in memory. Picking the right structure for the data a program works on is an important step in the development of the program. At a low level, we want to group related data together tightly (i.e., grouping employee data into one unit). At a higher level, we want to put the grouped data in a convenient arrangement so that the operations performed by program can be done more efficiently.

In this chapter, we will introduce the C support for structures. *Structures* are a way to group related data items together. First, we examine how to create structures in C. Then we take a brief look at dynamic allocation in C. Dynamic allocation is not directly related to the concept of data structures, but is a necessary concept for understanding the third item of this chapter, the linked list. The linked list is a fundamental abstract data structure that appears in some form in many programs and is a common high-level organization of data items. We will look at functions for adding, deleting, and searching for data items within linked lists.

19.2   STRUCTURES

19.2.1   The Basics of Structures in C

Most high-level programming languages have a way to group together related pieces of data. In C, the mechanism for accomplishing this grouping is called a **struct**, which is short for structure. Structures allow related data items to be grouped together and treated as a single data item. Structures are often called aggregate data types because the programmer defines them as a collection of simple data items such as **int**, **char**, and **double**. They are similar to arrays in that we can group data items together. They are different from arrays in that we can group data with *different* types together. Structure variables are declared in the same way variables of simple data type are declared. Before any structure variables are declared, though, the organization and naming of the data items within the structure must be defined.

Let's say we wanted to write a weather statistics program that contains information about the weather for the past 100 days. Say, for each day, we want to store the high and low temperatures, amount of precipitation, and average wind speed and direction. Each day has a certain set of data associated with it, which we can represent using the following variables:

```
int highTemp;
int lowTemp;
double precip;
double windSpeed;
int windDirection;
```

Declaring Structures   A convenient way to organize this data and associate it with a single day is to organize it as a structure, as shown:

```
struct w_type {
   int highTemp;
   int lowTemp;
   double precip;
   double windSpeed;
   int windDirection;
};
```

In the preceding declaration, we have declared a new type containing five *member* elements. We have not yet declared any storage; we have simply indicated to the compiler what we want this new type to look like. We have given the structure the *tag* **w_type**, which is necessary for referring to the structure in other parts of the code. To declare a variable of this new type, we can do the following:

```
struct w_type day;
```

We can access the individual members of this structure variable using the following syntax:

```
struct w_type day;

day.highTemp = 32;
day.lowTemp = 22;
```

The variable declaration **day** gets allocated on the stack (if it is a local variable) and occupies a contiguous region of memory big enough to hold each member element.

The allocation of the structure is straightforward. A structure is allocated the same way a variable of a basic data type is allocated: locals (by default) are allocated on the run-time stack, and globals are allocated in the global data section. Figure 19.1 shows a portion of the activation record for a function that contains the following declarations:

```
int x;
struct w_type day;
int y;
```

Generically, the syntax for a structure declaration is as follows:

```
struct tag {...members...} identifiers;
```

The **tag** provides a handle for referring to the structure again, as in the case of later declaring variables of the structure's format. It is optional, and if we do not use it, then we need to restate the members of the structure if we intend to use the structure again. The list of members defines the organization of a structure and is syntactically a list of declarations. Finally, we can optionally include identifiers in a structure's declaration to actually declare variables of that structure's type. For instance, the following declares a variable called **day**, of type **struct w_type**.

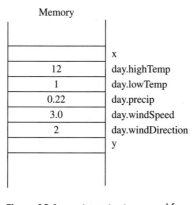

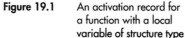

Figure 19.1   An activation record for a function with a local variable of structure type

```
struct w_type {
    int highTemp;
    int lowTemp;
    double precip;
    double windSpeed;
    int windDirection;
} day;
```

typedef   C provides a facility for letting programmers name their own types. We have just seen that structures allow programmers to define their own types by grouping types together. The **typedef** declaration allow programmers to name them. It has the general form

typedef type name;

Here, this statement causes the identifier **name** to be synonymous with the type **type**, which can be any basic type or aggregate type (e.g., a structure). So for instance,

typedef int Color;

allows us to define variables of type **Color**. These variables are actually the same as integers. For example:

Color pixels[500];

The **typedef** declaration is particularly useful when dealing with structures. For example, we can create a name for the structure we defined to hold daily weather data:

```
struct w_type {
    int highTemp;
    int lowTemp;
    double precip;
    double windSpeed;
    int windDirection;
};
```

typedef struct w_type WeatherData;

Now we can declare variables of this type by using the type name **WeatherData**. For example,

WeatherData day;

is now equivalent to the declaration **struct w_type day;** which we have seen previously.

The **typedef** declaration provides no additional functionality—we can still program effectively without it. However, most programmers invariably choose to use **typedefs**, often in conjunction with structures. Giving names to types is invaluable to writing readable code. Well-chosen type names (even if we are creating a new name for an existing basic type such as **int**) connote properties of the variables they declare (e.g., what do you think **Colors pixels[500];** declares?) beyond what can be expressed by the given names of the C basic types.

Using Structures   Now that we have seen the technique for declaring and allocating variables of structure type (and have given them new type names), we now focus on accessing the member fields and performing operations on them. For example, in the following code, the members of a structure variable of type **WeatherData** are accessed.

```
int x;
WeatherData day;
int y;

day.highTemp = 12;
day.lowTemp = 1;
day.precip = 0.22
day.windSpeed =  3.0;
day.windDirection = 2;
```

Here, the variable **day** is of type **WeatherData**, meaning it has the five member fields we defined previously. The member field labeled **highTemp** is accessed using the variable's name followed by a period, followed by the member field label. The compiler, knowing the layout of the structure, generates code that accesses the structure's member field using another offset. Figure 19.1 shows the layout of the portion of the activation record for this function. The compiler keeps track, in its symbol table, of the location of each variable and if the variable is an aggregate data type, it also tracks the position of each field within the variable. Notice that the address of the structure is the address of the first member of that structure.

Below is the code generated by the LC-2 C compiler for the first two assignments in the previous code segment.

```
AND   R1, R1, #0    ; zero out R1
ADD   R1, R1, #12   ; R1 = 12

ADD   R0, R6, #4    ; R0 contains address of day
ADD   R0, R0, #0    ; R0 contains address of day.highTemp
STR   R1, R0, #0    ; day.highTemp = 12;

AND   R1, R1, #0    ; zero out R1
ADD   R1, R1, #1    ; R1 = 1

ADD   R0, R6, #4    ; R0 contains address of day
ADD   R0, R0, #1    ; R0 contains address of day.lowTemp
STR   R1, R0, #0    ; day.lowTemp = 1;
```

19.2.2   Arrays and Pointers with Structures

For the purpose of our weather program, we want to track the weather for the last 100 days. For this, the following declaration makes sense.

```
WeatherData days[100];
```

This declaration is similar to the declaration `int d[100]`, except instead of declaring 100 integer values, we have declared a contiguous region of memory containing 100 structures, each of which is composed of the five members indicated in the structure's declaration. The reference `days[12]`, for example, would refer to the thirteenth element in the region of 100 in memory. Each element contains enough storage for the five member elements of this structure.

Each element of this array is of type **WeatherData** and can be accessed using standard array notation. Accessing the weather statistics for day 0 can be done using the identifier `days[0]`. Accessing a member field is done by accessing an element of the array and then specifying a field: `days[0].highTemp`. The following code segment provides an example. It averages the high temperatures for all 100 days:

```
int i;
int sum = 0;
int average_highTemp;

for (i = 0; i < 100; i++)
    sum = sum + days[i].highTemp;

average_highTemp = sum / 100;
```

We can also create pointers to structures. The following declaration creates a pointer variable that contains the address of a variable of type **WeatherData**.

```
WeatherData *dayPtr;
```

We can assign this variable as we would any pointer variable.

```
dayPtr = &day[34];
```

Now we introduce a new piece of syntax: dereferencing a pointer variable which points to a structure. If we want to access any of the member fields pointed to by this pointer variable, we could do the following:

```
(*dayPtr).highTemp
```

Here, we are dereferencing the variable **dayPtr**. It points to something of type **WeatherData**, and we can access one of its member fields by using the member operator (`.`). As we shall see, this is a very common operation, and since this expression is not very easy to grasp a special operator has been defined for it. The previous expression is equivalent to

```
dayPtr->highTemp
```

The program listed in Figure 19.2 shows a complete example using structures and arrays and pointers. This program uses the weather data structure defined earlier. The program takes input from the keyboard for 10 days worth of weather data (the number of days is defined via the macro **NUM_DAYS**), calculates and displays the average high temperature, and also displays the weather data for the day with the highest temperature. The two functions **inputDay** and **outputDay** perform the task of I/O for a day's worth of weather data. Notice that pointers to items of type **WeatherData** are used as arguments to these functions.

```
#include <stdio.h>

#define NUM_DAYS 10

/* Structure definition */
struct w_type {
  int highTemp;
  int lowTemp;
  double precip;
  double windSpeed;
  int windDirection;
};

typedef struct w_type WeatherData;

/* Function declarations */
int InputDay(WeatherData *day);
void OutputDay(WeatherData *day);

int InputDay(WeatherData *day)
{
  printf("High temp in deg F  : ");
  scanf("%d", &day->highTemp);

  printf("Low temp in deg F   : ");
  scanf("%d", &day->lowTemp);

  printf("Precipitation in inches : ");
  scanf("%lf", &day->precip);

  printf("Ave wind speed in mph : ");
  scanf("%lf", &day->windSpeed);

  printf("Wind direction (1=N,2=E,3=S,4=W) : ");
  scanf("%d", &day->windDirection);

  /* Check for erroneous input */
  if (day->windDirection < 1 || day->windDirection > 4)
    return -1;
  else
    return 0;
}
```

Figure 19.2   An example weather data program (Continued on page 414)

19.3   A FORAY INTO DYNAMIC ALLOCATION

Variables in C programs are allocated in one of three spots in memory: the run-time stack, the global data section, and the *heap*. Variables declared local to functions are allocated during execution on the run-time stack by default. Global variables are allocated in the global data section and are accessible by all parts of a program. Dy-

```
void OutputDay(WeatherData *day)
{
  printf("High temp       : %d deg F\n", day->highTemp);
  printf("Low temp        : %d deg F\n", day->lowTemp);
  printf("Precipitation   : %lf inches\n", day->precip);
  printf("Ave wind speed  : %lf mph\n", day->windSpeed);
  printf("Wind direction  : %d (1=N,2=E,3=S,4=W)\n", day->windDirection);
}

main()
{
  WeatherData days[NUM_DAYS];      /* main weather data database  */
  WeatherData *maxDay;             /* day with the max temperature */
  int maxTemp = 0;                 /* max temperature in all days  */
  int sumTemp = 0;                 /* the sum used to calc ave temp */
  int ii;                          /* iteration variable          */

  printf("Input data for the previous %d days\n", NUM_DAYS);
  ii = 0;
  while (ii < NUM_DAYS) {
    printf("Input information for day %d\n", ii);
    if (InputDay(&days[ii]) == 0) {
      printf("Input accepted\n\n");
      ii++;
    }
    else
      printf("Bad input!  Try again...\n");
  }

  for (ii = 0; ii < NUM_DAYS; ii++) {
    sumTemp = sumTemp + days[ii].highTemp;

    if (days[ii].highTemp >= maxTemp) {
      maxTemp = days[ii].highTemp;
      maxDay = &days[ii];
    }
  }

  printf("\nThe average temperature was : %d\n", sumTemp / NUM_DAYS);
  printf("The max temperature occurred on this day:\n");
  OutputDay(maxDay);
}
```

Figure 19.2   An example weather data program, (*Continued*)

namically allocated data items—items that are created during run-time—are allocated on the heap.

In the previous example, we declared an array that contained 10 days of weather data. But what if we wanted to create a flexible program that could handle as many days of weather data as the user was willing to enter? Or, say we were analyzing a large, but unknown, amount of weather data from a file? One possible solution would be to declare the array assuming a large upper limit to the number of days' worth of data the program might encounter. This could result in a lot of potentially wasted memory space. Another solution is to determine at run-time the number of days the program will need to manage and to declare the space for the data dynamically. If the user indicates that there is data for 100 days, then a region of memory is declared with room for 100 **WeatherData** structures.

Dynamic allocation in C is handled by the C standard library functions. Let's take a look at an example that uses the function **malloc**:

```
int numberOfDays;
WeatherData *days;

printf("How many days of weather data are in the input?");
scanf("%d", &numberOfDays);

/* A call to a dynamic allocation routine */
days = malloc(10 * numberOfDays);
```

Here we use a library call to the routine **malloc**, which is short for *memory allocate*. The function allocates a contiguous region of memory of the size in bytes indicated by the single parameter. If the call is successful, it returns a pointer to the allocated region.

Here we allocate a chunk of memory consisting of **10 * numberOfDays** bytes, where **numberOfDays** is the number indicated by the user as size of the input set, and 10 is the size of each item of type **WeatherData**. Why the 10? Recall that the structure is composed of five members—three integers and two doubles—which in the LC-2, all occupy 2 bytes each. As a necessary convenience to programmers, the C language supports a compile-time operator called **sizeof**. This operator returns the size, in bytes, of the memory object passed to it as an argument. For example, **sizeof(WeatherData)** will return the number of bytes occupied by a variable of type **struct WeatherData**, or 10. The programmer does not need to calculate the sizes of various data objects; the compiler can be instructed to perform the calculation.

The function **malloc** and other similar functions in the standard library that manages memory allocation, manages the heap region of memory. Each call updates information associated with the heap. If for some reason, the allocation cannot be accomplished, for example if all the memory of the heap has already been allocated and is in use, then **malloc** returns a **NULL** value. The symbol **NULL** is a preprocessor macro symbol, defined to a particular value depending on the particular computer system. It is always good programming practice to check that the return value from **malloc** indicates the memory allocation was successful.

The function **malloc** returns a pointer to a generic data item (or, **void *** as it is better known). We need to *type cast* the pointer returned by **malloc** to the type of the variable to which we are assigning it. In the previous example, we assigned the pointer to **days**, which is of type **WeatherData ***, so therefore we need to cast the pointer to type **WeatherData**. To do otherwise makes the code less portable across different computer systems; most compilers generate a warning message because we are assigning a pointer value of one type to a pointer variable of another. Type casting causes the compiler to treat a value of one type as if it were of another type. To type cast a value from one type to a **newType**, we use the following syntax. The variable **var** should be of **newType**.

var = (newType) expression;

Given type casting and the **sizeof** operation and the error checking of the return value from **malloc**, the correct way to write the code from the previous example is given below:

```
int numberOfDays;
Weather *days;

printf("How many days of weather data are in the input?");
scanf("%d", &numberOfDays);

/* A more correctly written call malloc */
days = (WeatherData *) malloc(sizeof(WeatherData) * numberOfDays);
if (days == NULL) {
    printf("Error in allocating the days array\n");
    :
    :
}
days[0].highTemp = ...
```

Since the region that is allocated by **malloc** is contiguous in memory, we can switch between pointer notation and array notation. Now we can use the expression **days[29]** to access the weather data for the thirtieth day (provided that **numberOfDays** was larger than 30, of course). This is an example of the flexibility that has helped make C a very popular programming language.

The function **malloc** is only one of several memory allocation functions in the standard library. The function **calloc** allocates memory and initializes it. The function **realloc** attempts to grow or shrink previously allocated regions of memory. The deallocation counterpart to these functions is called **free**, which takes as its parameter a pointer to an allocated region and *deallocates* it. After a region has been **free**'d, it is once again eligible for allocation. It is good programming practice to deallocate memory objects after we are done with them; otherwise the space on the heap available for allocation may quickly start to vanish.

19.4   THE LINKED LIST

19.4.1   What Is a Linked List?

Having the business listings in a phone book organized alphabetically by category makes looking up phone numbers quick and simple. If the listing were haphazardly placed, then finding a phone number would take too long, probably making the phone book useless. The data within the phone book is organized in a manner suited for the task we commonly use it for—looking up phone numbers. Similarly, a programmer can make a program run more quickly by choosing the right arrangement of data within memory. Choosing the correct data structure is an important part of the planning phase of writing a program. The wrong data structure could make your program overly complicated or unnecessarily slow.

In this section, we present a fundamental data structure called the linked list. To understand linked lists, we need to tie together many of the concepts we have covered in the second half of this book.

A *linked list* is a collection of nodes, where each node is one "unit" of data, such as a day's worth of weather data from the previous section. We connect these nodes together using pointers. In addition to its data, each node contains a pointer element that points to the next node in the list. Given a starting node, we can go from node to node by following the pointer in each node. As you might have guessed, we create these nodes using C structures. A critical element for the structure that defines the nodes within a linked list is that it contains a member element that points nodes like itself.

The linked list has a beginning and an end. Its beginning, or head node, is accessed using a pointer called the *head pointer*. The final node in the list, or tail, points to the **NULL** value. Figure 19.3 shows two representations of a linked list data structure: an abstract depiction where nodes are represented as blocks and pointers are represented by arrows, and a more physical representation that shows what the data structure might look like in memory.

Conceptually, a linked list and an array are similar data structures. They both hold a sequence of data items, names of students enrolled at a university, for example. However, they have some strong fundamental differences. An array can be accessed in random order. We can access element number 4, followed by element 911, followed by 45, for example. A simple linked list must be traversed starting at its head. If we wanted to access node 29, then we must start at node 0 (the head node) and then go to node 1, then to node 2, and so forth. Stated another way, a linked list can only be accessed sequentially.

However, the linked list has some strong advantages. The linked list is dynamic in nature; additional nodes can be added to it or removed from it. Arrays are static in size (but one can mimic dynamically-sized arrays using **malloc**). If more students enrolled at the university, with a linked list we can dynamically add nodes to make room for more data. A second advantage is that it is much simpler to insert and delete nodes from the middle of a linked list than from the middle of an array.

19.4.2   An Example Using Linked Lists

Say we want to write a program to manage the inventory at a used car lot. At the lot, cars keep coming and going, and the database needs to be updated continually—a new entry is created whenever a car is added to the lot and an entry deleted whenever a car is sold. Furthermore, the entries are stored in order by vehicle identification

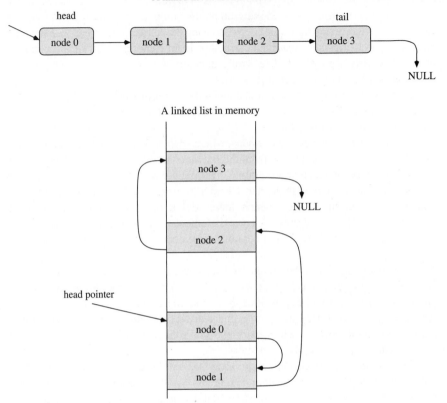

Figure 19.3   Two representations for a linked list

number so that queries from the used car salespeople can be handled quickly. The information we need to keep per car is as follows:

```
int   vehicleID;
char make[20];
char model[20];
int   year;
int mileage;
double cost;
```

In reality, a vehicle ID is a sequence of characters and numbers and cannot be stored as a single **int**. We have simplified reality for the sake of this example.

The frequent operations we want to perform—adding, deleting, and searching for entries—can be performed simply and quickly using a linked list data structure. Each node in the linked list contains all the information associated with a car in the lot, as shown above. We can now define the node structure, which is then given the name **CarNode** using **typedef**:

```
typedef struct c_node CarNode;

struct c_node {
  int   vehicleID;
  char make[20];
  char model[20];
  int   year;
  int mileage;
  double cost;

  CarNode *next;      /* Points to a car_node */
};
```

Notice that this structure contains a pointer element that points to something of type **CarNode**, meaning it points to something of the same type as the structure itself. We will use this member item to point to the next node in the linked list. If the **next** field is equal to **NULL**, then the node is the last in the list.

Now that we have defined the elementary data type and the organization of data in memory, we want to focus on the flow of the program, which we can do by writing the function **main**. The code is listed in Figure 19.4.

We have created a menu-driven interface for the used car database. The main data structure is accessed using the variable **carBase**, which is of type **CarNode**. We will use it as a dummy head node, meaning that we will not be storing any information about any particular car within the fields of **carBase**, but rather we will use **carBase** simply as a place holder for the rest of the linked list. Using this dummy head node makes the algorithms for inserting and deleting slightly simpler because we do not have to deal with the special case of an empty list. Initially, **carBase.next** is set equal to **NULL** indicating no data items are stored in the data base. Notice that we pass the address of **carBase** whenever we call the functions to insert a new car to the list (**AddEntry**), to delete a car (**DeleteEntry**), and to search the list for a particular car (**Search**).

You should note that this higher level representation of the program makes very little reference to the underlying data structure. From **main**, we can not tell that a linked list will be used to hold the data items. The data structure is abstracted away at this level in the program. The essence of the program is apparent without being cluttered by the details of the implementation.

As we shall see, the functions **AddEntry**, **DeleteEntry**, and **Search** all rely upon a basic operation to be performed on the linked list: scanning the list to find a particular node. For example, when adding the entry for a new car, we need to know where in the list the entry should be added. Since the list is kept in sorted order of increasing vehicle ID numbers, any new car node must be added before the first existing node with a larger vehicle ID. To accomplish this, we have created a support function called **ScanList** that traverses the list (which is passed as the first argument) searching for a particular vehicle ID (passed as the second argument). **ScanList** always returns a pointer to the node **just before** the node for which we are scanning. If the node we are scanning for is not in the list, then **ScanList** returns a pointer to the node **just before** the place in the list where the node would

```
main()
{
  int op;              /* Hold the current operation to be perform.    */
  CarNode carBase; /* carBase is an empty node that points to list. */

  carBase.next = NULL;              /* Initialize the main list pointer */

  printf("=========================\n");
  printf("=== Used car database ===\n");
  printf("=========================\n\n");

  do {
    printf("Enter an operation:\n");
    printf("1 - Car added to the lot. Add a new entry for it.\n");
    printf("2 - Car sold.  Remove its entry.\n");
    printf("3 - Query.  Look up a car's information.\n");
    printf("4 - Quit.\n");
    scanf("%d", &op);

    switch(op) {
       case 1:
         AddEntry(&carBase);
         break;

       case 2:
         DeleteEntry(&carBase);
         break;

       case 3:
         Search(&carBase);
         break;

       case 4:
         printf("Good bye.\n\n");
         break;

       default:
         printf("Invalid option.   Try again.\n\n");
         break;
    }
  }
  while (op != 4);
}
```

Figure 19.4   The function **main** for our used car database program

have resided. Why does **ScanList** return a pointer to the previous node? As we shall see, passing back the previous node makes inserting new nodes easier. The code for **ScanList** is listed in Figure 19.5.

The function **AddEntry** gets information from the user about a newly acquired car and inserts a node containing this information into the proper spot in the linked list. The code is listed in Figure 19.6. The first part of the function allocates a

```
CarNode *ScanList(CarNode *headPointer, int searchID)
{
  CarNode *previous;
  CarNode *current;

  /* Point to start of list */
  previous = headPointer;
  current = headPointer->next;

  /* Traverse list -- keep scanning until we find a node with a      */
  /* vehicleID greater than or equal to the one we are looking for */
  while ((current != NULL) && (current->vehicleID < searchID)) {
    previous = current;
    current  = current->next;
  }

  /* The variable previous points to one node prior to the one      */
  /* being searched for. Either current->vehicleID equals searchID */
  /* or a node with searchID does not exist.                       */
  return previous;
}
```

Figure 19.5   A function to scan through the linked list for a particular vehicle ID

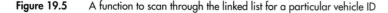

CarNode sized chunk of memory on the heap using **malloc**. If the allocation fails, an error message is displayed and the program exits using the **exit** library call, which terminates a running program. The second part of the function reads in input from the standard keyboard and assigns it the proper fields within the new node. The third part performs the insertion by calling **ScanList** to find the place in the list to insert the new node. If the node already exists in the list then an error message is displayed and the new node is deallocated by a call to the **free** library call.

Let's take a closer look at how a node is inserted into the linked list. Figure 19.7 shows a pictorial representation of this process. Once the proper spot to insert is found (using **ScanList**), then the **prevNode**'s **next** pointer is updated to point to the new node and the new node's **next** pointer is updated to point to **nextNode**. Also shown in the figure is the degenerate case of adding a node to an empty list. Here, **prevNode** points to the empty head node. The head node's **next** pointer is updated to point to the new node.

The routine to delete a node from the linked list is very similar to **AddEntry**. Functionally, we want to first query the user about which vehicle ID to delete and then use **ScanList** to locate a node with that ID. Once the node is found, the list is manipulated to remove the node. The code is listed in Figure 19.8. Notice that once a node is deleted, its memory is added back to the heap using the **free** function call. Figure 19.9 shows a pictorial representation of the deletion of a node.

The **Search** operation is very similar to the **AddEntry** and **DelEntry** functions, except that the node is not removed from the list. The code is listed in Figure 19.10. The support function **ScanList** is used to locate the requested node.

```
void AddEntry(CarNode *headPointer)
{
  CarNode *newNode;        /* Points to the new car information */
  CarNode *nextNode;       /* Points to car to follow new one   */
  CarNode *prevNode;       /* Points to car before this one     */

  /* dynamically allocate memory for this new entry.  Memory    */
  /* for this node will come from the heap                      */
  newNode = (CarNode *) malloc(sizeof(CarNode));

  if (newNode == NULL) {
     printf("Error: could not allocate a new node\n");
     exit(1);
  }

  /* Get input data from the keyboard */
  printf("Enter the following information about the car.\n");
  printf("Separate each field by whitespace:\n");
  printf("vehicle_id make mode year mileage cost\n");

  scanf("%d %s %s %d %d %lf",
        &newNode->vehicleID, &newNode->make, &newNode->model,
        &newNode->year, &newNode->mileage, &newNode->cost);

  prevNode = ScanList(headPointer, newNode->vehicleID);

  nextNode = prevNode->next;

  if (nextNode == NULL || nextNode->vehicleID != newNode->vehicleID) {
     /* Found the place to insert. Insert between prev and next */
     prevNode->next = newNode;
     newNode->next = nextNode;
     printf("Entry added.\n\n");
  }
  else {
     printf("That car already exists in the Car Database!\n");
     printf("Entry not added.\n\n");
     free(newNode);
  }
}
```

Figure 19.6   A function to add an entry to the database

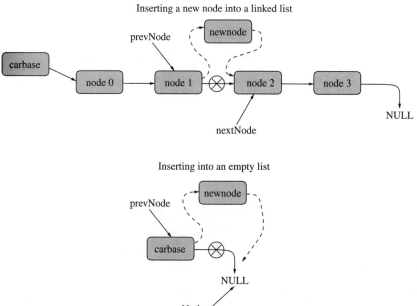

Inserting a new node into a linked list

Inserting into an empty list

Figure 19.7   Inserting a node into a linked list. The dashed lines indicate newly formed links.

```
void DeleteEntry(CarNode *headPointer)
{
  int vehicleID;
  CarNode *delNode;        /* Points to node to delete to follow */
  CarNode *prevNode;       /* Points to car before one to delete */

  printf("Enter the vehicle ID number of the car to delete:\n");
  scanf("%d", &vehicleID);

  prevNode = ScanList(headPointer, vehicleID);
  delNode  = prevNode->next;

  /* Either there is the car does not exist in the list or     */
  /* delNode points to the car to be deleted.                  */
  if (delNode != NULL && delNode->vehicleID == vehicleID) {
    prevNode->next = delNode->next;
    printf("Vehicle with id %d deleted.\n\n", vehicleID);
    free(delNode);
  }
  else {
    printf("The vehicle id %d was not found in the database.\n\n",
           vehicleID);
  }
}
```

Figure 19.8   A function to delete an entry from the database

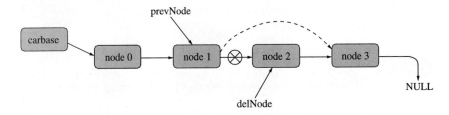

Figure 19.9   Deleting a node from a linked list. The dashed line indicates a newly formed link

```
void Search(CarNode *headPointer)
{
  int vehicleID;
  CarNode *searchNode;     /* Points to node to delete to follow */
  CarNode *prevNode;       /* Points to car before one to delete */

  printf("Enter the vehicle ID number of the car to search for:\n");
  scanf("%d", &vehicleID);

  prevNode = ScanList(headPointer, vehicleID);
  searchNode  = prevNode->next;

  /* Either there is the car does not exist in the list or     */
  /* searchNode points to the car we are looking for.          */
  if (searchNode != NULL && searchNode->vehicleID == vehicleID) {
    printf("vehicle ID : %d\n", searchNode->vehicleID);
    printf("make       : %s\n", searchNode->make);
    printf("model      : %s\n", searchNode->model);
    printf("year       : %d\n", searchNode->year);
    printf("mileage    : %d\n", searchNode->mileage);

    /* The following printf has a field width specification on  */
    /* %f specification.  The 10.2 indicates that the floating  */
    /* point number should be printed in a 10 character field   */
    /* with two units after the decimal displayed.              */
    printf("cost        : $%10.2f\n\n", searchNode->cost);
  }
  else {
    printf("The vehicle id %d was not found in the database.\n\n",
           vehicleID);
  }
}
```

Figure 19.10   A function to query the database

19.5   CONCLUSION

The primary objective of this chapter was to introduce the linked list data structure. But along the way, we covered several topics that are necessary and important ingredients: C structures and dynamic memory allocation. C structures allow us to create new data types by grouping together data of different types. C structures are a convenient way to create the nodes of a linked list. Dynamic memory allocation is a means for allocating variables and structures from within a running program. C provides several library functions to dynamically allocate memory, for example **malloc**.

Why is the linked list such an important data structure? For one thing, it is a dynamic structure that can be expanded or shrunk during execution. This dynamic quality makes it appealing to use in certain situations where the static nature of arrays would be wasteful. The concept of connecting data elements together using pointers is fundamental. It is applied very frequently in computer programming. Understanding the linked lists will help you understand more elaborate structures such as hash tables and trees.

PROBLEMS

19.1. Is there a bug in the following program? Explain.

```
struct node {
  int count;
  struct node *next;
};

main()
{
  int data = 0;
  struct node *getdata;

  getdata->count = data + 1;
  printf("%d", getdata->count);
}
```

19.2. The following are a few lines of a C program:

```
struct node {
    int count;
    struct node *next;
};

main()
{
    int data = 0;
    struct node *getdata;

              :
              :

    getdata = getdata->next;

              :
              :
}
```

Write, in LC-2 assembly language, the instructions that are generated by the compiler for the line `getdata = getdata->next;`.

19.3. The program shown below is compiled on a machine where each basic data type (pointer, character, integer, floating point) occupies one location of memory.

```
struct element {
    char  name[25];
    int   atomic_number;
    float atomic_mass;
};

is_it_noble(struct element t[], int i)
{
    if ((t[i].atomic_number==2)  ||
        (t[i].atomic_number==10) ||
        (t[i].atomic_number==18) ||
        (t[i].atomic_number==36) ||
        (t[i].atomic_number==54) ||
        (t[i].atomic_number==86))
      return 1;
    else
      return 0;
}

main()
{
    int x, y;
    struct element periodic_table[110];

              :
              :
    x = is_it_noble(periodic_table, y);
              :
              :
}
```

1. How many locations will the activation record of the function `is_it_noble` contain?

2. Assuming that **periodic_table**, **x**, and **y** are the only local variables, how many locations in the activation record for **main** will be devoted to local variables?

19.4. The following C program is compiled into the LC-2 machine language and executed. The run-time stack begins at x4000. The user types the input **abac** followed by a return.

```c
#include <stdio.h>
#define MAX 4

struct char_rec {
  char ch;
  struct char_rec *back;
};

main()
{
  struct char_rec *ptr, pat[MAX+2];
  int i = 1, j = 1;

  printf("Pattern: ");
  pat[1].back = pat;
  ptr = pat;

  while ((pat[i].ch = getchar()) != '\n') {

    while ((ptr != pat) && (ptr->ch != pat[i].ch))
      ptr = ptr->back;
    ptr[++i].back = ++ptr;

    if (i > MAX) break;
  }

  while (j <= i)
    printf("%d ", pat[j++].back - pat);

  /* Note the pointer arithmetic here: subtraction
     of pointers to structures gives the number of
     structures between addresses, not the number
     of memory locations */
}
```

1. Show the contents of the activation record for **main** when the program terminates.

2. What is the output of this program for the input **abac**?

A

The LC-2 ISA

A.1 OVERVIEW

The Instruction Set Architecture (ISA) of the LC-2 is defined as follows:

Memory address space 16 bits, corresponding to 2^{16} locations, each consisting of one word (16 bits). Addresses are numbered from 0 (i.e, x0000) to 65,535 (i.e., xFFFF). Addresses are used to identify memory locations and memory-mapped I/O device registers. For convenience, these locations are partitioned into 2^7 pages of 2^9 words each.

General purpose registers Eight 16-bit registers, numbered from 000 to 111.

Program counter A 16-bit register.

Bit numbering Bits of all quantities are numbered, from right to left, starting with bit 0.

Instructions Instructions are 16 bits wide. Bits [15:12] specify the opcode (operation to be performed), bits [11:0] provide further information that is needed to execute the instruction. Section A.3 provides further information on each of the 16 instructions.

Condition codes The load instructions (LD, LDI, LDR, LEA) and the operate instructions (ADD, AND, and NOT) set the three condition codes, depending on whether the result is negative (N = 1, Z = 0, P = 0), zero (N = 0, Z = 1, P = 0), or positive (N = 0, Z = 0, P = 1).

Memory mapped I/O Input and output are handled by standard load/store instructions using memory addresses to designate each I/O device register.

Table A.1 lists each of the relevant device registers, along with the memory address it has been assigned in the LC-2.

Table A.1   Device register assignments

Location	I/O Register Name	I/O Register Function
xF3FC	CRT status register	Also known as CRTSR. The ready bit (bit [15]) indicates if the video device is ready to receive another character to print on the screen.
xF3FF	CRT data register	Also known as CRTDR. A character written in the low byte of this register will be displayed on the screen.
xF400	Keyboard status register	Also known as KBSR. The ready bit (bit [15]) indicates if the keyboard has received a new character.
xF401	Keyboard data register	Also known as KBDR. Bits [7:0] contain the last character typed on the keyboard.
xF402	Machine control register	Also known as MCR. Bit [15] is the clock enable bit. When cleared, instruction processing stops.

A.2   NOTATION

The notation in Table A.2 will be helpful in understanding the descriptions of the LC-2 instructions (Section A.3).

A.3   THE INSTRUCTION SET

The 16 LC-2 instructions are summarized in Figure A.1 (page 432). On the following pages, the instructions are described in greater detail. For each instruction, we show the assembly language representation, the actual format of the 16-bit instruction, the operation of the instruction, an English-language description of the operation, and one or more examples of the instruction.

Table A.2   Notational Conventions

Notation	Meaning
xNumber	The number in hexadecimal notation.
#Number	The number in decimal notation.
A[l:r]	The *field* delimited by bit[l] on the left and bit[r] on the right, from the datum A. For example, if PC contains 0011001100111111, then PC[15:9] is 0011001. PC[2:2] is 1. If l and r are the same bit number, the notation is usually abbreviated PC[2].
A @ B	Concatenation of A and B. For example, if A is 0011 001 and B is 1 1100 1100, A @ B = 0011 0011 1100 1100.
BaseR	Base Register; one of R0..R7, used in conjunction with a six-bit offset to compute Base+offset addresses.
page	The set of 2^9 consecutive memory locations whose addresses share the same high seven address bits.
DR	Destination Register; one of R0..R7, which specifies where the result of an instruction should be written.
imm5	A five-bit immediate value; bits [4:0] of an instruction, when used as a literal (immediate) value. Taken as a 5-bit, 2's complement integer, it is sign-extended to 16 bits before it is used. Range: $-16..15$.
index6	Six-bit immediate value; bits [5:0] of an instruction, when used in a Base+offset instruction. Taken as a six-bit unsigned integer, it is zero-extended to 16 bits before it is used. Range: 0..63.
LABEL	An assembler construct that identifies a location symbolically (i.e., by means of a name, rather than its 16-bit address).
L	Link bit; differentiates JSR from JMP and JSRR from JMPR instructions. If L = 1 (JSR, JSRR), the value of the PC will be saved in R7. If L = 0, the PC is *not* saved in R7.
mem[address]	Denotes the contents of memory at the given address.
PC	Program Counter; 16-bit, processor-internal register which contains the memory address of the *next* instruction to be fetched. For example, during execution of the instruction at address A, the PC contains address A+1.
pgoffset9	Nine bits that differentiate the 2^9 locations on a page. PC[15:9] is concatenated with pgoffset9 to form a 16-bit memory address. Range 0..511.
setcc(X)	Indicates that condition codes N, Z, and P are set based on the value of X. If X is negative, N = 1, Z = 0, P = 0. If X is zero, N = 0, Z = 1, P = 0. If X is positive, N = 0, Z = 0, P = 1.
SEXT(A)	Sign-extend A. The most significant bit of A is replicated as many times as necessary to extend A to 16 bits. For example, if A = 110000, then SEXT(A) = 1111 1111 1111 0000.
SR, SR1, SR2	Source Register; one of R0..R7 which specifies from where an instruction operand is obtained.
trapvect8	Eight-bit trap number used in the TRAP instruction. Range 0–255.
ZEXT(A)	Zero-extend A. Zeroes are appended to the left-most bit of A to extend it to 16 bits. For example, if A = 110000, then ZEXT(A) = 0000 0000 0011 0000.

	15 14 13 12	11 10 9	8	7 6 5	4	3	2 1 0

ADD⁺ — `0001` | DR | SR1 | 0 | 00 | SR2

ADD⁺ — `0001` | DR | SR1 | 1 | imm5

AND⁺ — `0101` | DR | SR1 | 0 | 00 | SR2

AND⁺ — `0101` | DR | SR1 | 1 | imm5

BR — `0000` | n | z | p | pgoffset9

JSR — `0100` | L | 00 | pgoffset9

JSRR — `1100` | L | 00 | BaseR | index6

LD⁺ — `0010` | DR | pgoffset9

LDI⁺ — `1010` | DR | pgoffset9

LDR⁺ — `0110` | DR | BaseR | index6

LEA⁺ — `1110` | DR | pgoffset9

NOT⁺ — `1001` | DR | SR | 111111

RET — `1101` | 000000000000

RTI* — `1000` | 000000000000

ST — `0011` | SR | pgoffset9

STI — `1011` | SR | pgoffset9

STR — `0111` | SR | BaseR | index6

TRAP — `1111` | 0000 | trapvect8

Figure A.1   Formats of the 16 LC-2 instructions. NOTE: + indicates instructions that modify condition codes; * indicates that meaning and use of RTI is beyond the scope of this book.

ADD   **Addition**

Assembler Formats

ADD DR, SR1, SR2
ADD DR, SR1, imm5

Encodings

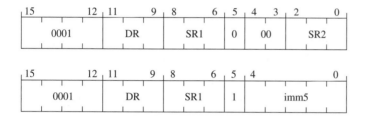

Operation

```
if (bit[5] == 0)
  DR = SR1 + SR2;
else
  DR = SR1 + SEXT(imm5);
setcc(DR);
```

Description

If bit [5] is 0, the second-source operand is obtained from SR2. If bit [5] is 1, the second-source operand is obtained by sign-extending the imm5 field to 16 bits. In both cases, the second source operand is added to the contents of SR1, and the result stored in DR. The condition codes are set, based on whether the result is negative, zero, or positive.

Examples

ADD   R2, R3, R4   ;   R2 ← R3 + R4
ADD   R2, R3, #7   ;   R2 ← R3 + 7

AND   Bitwise logical AND

Assembler Formats

AND DR, SR1, SR2
AND DR, SR1, imm5

Encodings

15			12	11		9	8		6	5	4	3	2		0
0101				DR			SR1			0	00		SR2		

15			12	11		9	8		6	5	4				0
0101				DR			SR1			1		imm5			

Operation

```
if (bit[5] == 0)
  DR = SR1 AND SR2;
else
  DR = SR1 AND SEXT(imm5);
setcc(DR);
```

Description

If bit [5] is 0, the second-source operand is obtained from SR2. If bit [5] is 1, the second-source operand is obtained by sign-extending the imm5 field to 16 bits. In either case, the second-source operand and the contents of SR1 are bitwise ANDed, and the result stored in DR. The condition codes are set, based on whether the binary value produced, taken as a 2's complement integer, is negative, zero, or positive.

Examples

AND	R2, R3, R4	;	R2 ← R3 AND R4
AND	R2, R3, #7	;	R2 ← R3 AND 7

BR Conditional Branch

Assembler Formats

```
BR     LABEL
BRn    LABEL
BRz    LABEL
BRp    LABEL
BRnz   LABEL
BRnp   LABEL
BRzp   LABEL
BRnzp  LABEL
```

Encoding

Operation

if ((n AND N) OR (z AND Z) OR (p AND P))
  PC = PC[15:9] @ pgoffset9;

Description

Test the condition codes specified by the state of bits [11:9]. If bit [11] is set, test N; if bit [11] is clear, do not test N. If bit [10] is set, test Z, etc. If any of the condition codes tested is set, branch to the location specified by pgoffset9 on the same page as the branch instruction,

Example

BRzp   LOOP   ;   Branch to LOOP if the last result was zero or positive.

JSR
JMP

Jump to Subroutine

Jump

Assembler Formats

JSR LABEL   (L = 1)
JMP LABEL   (L = 0)

Encoding

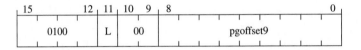

15	12	11	10	9	8								0
0100		L	00					pgoffset9					

Operation

if (L == 1)
  R7 = PC;
PC = PC[15:9] @ pgoffset9;

Description

Unconditionally jump to the location specified by pgoffset9 on the same page as the JSR/JMP instruction. If the link bit L is set, the PC is saved in R7, enabling a subsequent return to the instruction physically following the JSR instruction.

Examples

JSR   FOO   ;   Jump to FOO, put return PC into R7.
JMP   FOO   ;   Jump to FOO.

JSRR   Jump to Subroutine, Base+Offset
JMPR   Jump, Base+Offset

Assembler Formats

JSRR BaseR, index6   (L = 1)
JMPR BaseR, index6   (L = 0)

Encoding

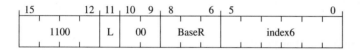

Operation

if (L == 1)
     R7 = PC;
PC = BaseR + ZEXT(index6);

Description

Unconditionally jump to the location specified by adding ZEXT(index6) to the contents of the base register. If the link bit L is set, the PC is saved in R7, enabling a subsequent return to the instruction physically following the JSRR instruction.

Examples

JSRR   R2, #10   ;   Jump to R2 + #10, put return PC into R7.
JMPR   R2, #10   ;   Jump to R2 + #10.

LD   **Load Direct**

Assembler Format

LD DR, LABEL

Encoding

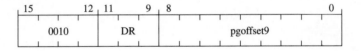

Operation

DR = mem[PC[15:9] @ pgoffset9];
setcc(DR);

Description

Load the register specified by DR from the location specified by pgoffset9 on the
same page as the LD instruction. The condition codes are set, based on whether the
value loaded is negative, zero, or positive.

Example

LD   R4, COUNT   ;   R4 ← mem[COUNT].

LDI   Load Indirect

Assembler Format

LDI DR, LABEL

Encoding

Operation

DR = mem[mem[PC[15:9] @ pgoffset9]];
setcc(DR);

Description

Load the register specified by DR as follows: Construct an address by concatenating
the top seven bits of the program counter with the pgoffset9 field of the LDI instruction.
The contents of memory at that address is the address of the data to be loaded into
DR. The condition codes are set, based on whether the value loaded is negative, zero,
or positive.

Example

LDI   R4, POINTER   ;   R4 ← mem[mem[POINTER]].

LDR   Load Base + Index

Assembler Format

LDR DR, BaseR, index6

Encoding

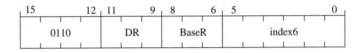

Operation

DR = mem[BaseR + ZEXT(index6)];
setcc(DR);

Description

Load the register specified by DR from the location specified by a base register and
index, as follows: The index is zero-extended to 16 bits and added to the contents of
BaseR to form a memory address. The contents of memory at this address are loaded
into DR. The condition codes are set, based on whether the value loaded is negative,
zero, or positive.

Example

LDR   R4, R2, #10   ;   R4 ← contents of mem[R2 + #10].

LEA   **Load Effective Address**

Assembler Format

LEA DR, LABEL

Encoding

Operation

DR = PC[15:9] @ pgoffset9;
setcc(DR);

Description

Load the register specified by DR with the address formed by concatenating the top seven bits of the program counter with the pgoffset9 field of the instruction. The condition codes are set, based on whether the value loaded is negative, zero, or positive.

Example

LEA   R4, FOO   ;   R4 ← address of FOO.

NOT Bitwise Complement

Assembler Format

NOT DR, SR

Encoding

15	12	11	9	8	6	5	0
1001		DR		SR		111111	

Operation

DR = NOT(SR);
setcc(DR);

Description

Perform the bitwise complement operation on the contents of SR and place the result in DR. The condition codes are set.

Example

NOT   R4, R2   ;   R4 ← NOT(R2).

RET   **Return from Subroutine**

Assembler Format

RET

Encoding

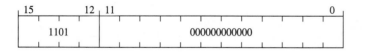

Operation

PC = R7;

Description

Load the PC with the value in R7. This causes a return from a previous JSR or JSRR instruction.

Example

RET   ;   PC ← R7.

RTI   Return from Interrupt

Assembler Format

RTI

Encoding

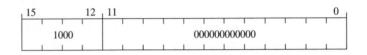

Operation

NZP = mem[R6];
R6 = R6 - 1;
PC = mem[R6];
R6 = R6 - 1;

Description

Pop the top two elements off the stack; load them into NZP, PC.

Example

RTI   ;   NZP, PC ← top two values popped off stack.

Notes

On an external interrupt, the initiating sequence pushes the current PC onto the stack before loading the PC with the starting address of the service routine. The last instruction in the service routine is RTI, which returns control to the interrupted program by popping the stack and loading the value popped into the PC. (This instruction is included in this appendix for completeness. Its purpose and use are beyond the scope of what is normally covered in an introductory textbook.)

ST   Store Direct

Assembler Format

ST SR, LABEL

Encoding

Operation

mem[PC[15:9] @ pgoffset9] = SR;

Description

Store the contents of the register specified by SR into the memory location specified by pgoffset9 on the same page as the ST instruction.

Example

ST   R4, COUNT   ;   mem[COUNT] ← R4.

STI

Store Indirect

Assembler Format

STI SR, LABEL

Encoding

Operation

mem[mem[PC[15:9] @ pgoffset9]] = SR;

Description

Store the contents of the register specified by SR into the memory location whose address is obtained as follows: Construct an address by concatenating the top seven bits of the program counter with the pgoffset9 field of the STI instruction. The contents of memory at that address is the address of the location to which the data in SR is to be stored.

Example

STI   R4, POINTER   ;   mem[mem[POINTER]] ← R4.

STR   Store Base+Offset

Assembler Format

STR SR, BaseR, index6

Encoding

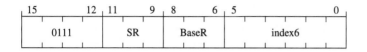

Operation

mem[BaseR + ZEXT(index6)] = SR;

Description

Store the contents of the register specified by SR into the memory location whose address is specified as follows: The six-bit offset is zero-extended to 16 bits and added to the contents of BaseR to form a memory address. This is the address of the location into which the contents of SR is to be stored.

Example

STR   R4, R2, #10   ;   mem[R2 + #10] ← R4.

TRAP   Operating System Call

Assembler Format

TRAP trapvector8

Encoding

15	12	11	8	7	0
1111		0000		trapvect8	

Operation

R7 = PC;
PC = mem[ZEXT(trapvect8)];

Description

Load the PC with the contents of the memory location obtained by zero-extending trapvector8 to 16 bits. This is the starting address of the system call specified by trapvector8. Load R7 with the PC, which enables a return to the instruction physically following the TRAP instruction in the original program after the service routine has completed.

Example

TRAP   x23   ;   Direct the operating system to execute the
               ;   **IN** system call.

Notes

Memory locations x0020 through x00FF, 192 in all, are available to contain starting addresses for system calls specified by their corresponding trapvectors. This region of memory is called the trap vector table. See Table A.3. Memory locations x0000 through x001F are not part of the trap vector table; therefore, x00 through x1F may not be used as trapvectors.

Table A.3   TRAP vector table

TRAP Number	Assembler Name	Description
x20	GETC	Read a single character from the keyboard. The character is not echoed onto the console. Its ASCII code is copied into R0. The high eight bits of R0 are cleared.
x21	OUT	Write a character in R0[7:0] to the console.
x22	PUTS	Write a string pointed to by R0 to the console.
x23	IN	Print a prompt on the screen and read a single character from the keyboard. The character is echoed onto the console, and its ASCII code is copied into R0. The high eight bits of R0 are cleared.
x25	HALT	Halt execution and print a message on the console.

B

From LC-2 to IA-32

As you know, the ISA of the LC-2 explicitly specifies the interface between what the LC-2 machine language programmer or LC-2 compilers produce and what a microarchitecture of the LC-2 can accept and process. Among those things specified are the address space and addressability of memory, the number and size of the registers, the format of the instructions, the opcodes, the data types which are the encodings used to represent information, and the addressing modes that are available for determining the location of an operand.

The ISA of the microprocessor in your PC also specifies an interface between the compilers and the microarchitecture. However, in the case of the PC, the ISA is not the LC-2. Rather it is the IA-32. IA stands for Intel architecture. Intel introduced the first member of this ISA in 1979. It was called the 8086, and the "normal" size of the addresses and data elements it processed was 16 bits. The number 32 in IA-32 identifies a typical size of addresses and data today: 32 bits.

Until recently, IA-32 was referred to as x86, to reflect the early microprocessors that were built to execute instructions from that ISA, starting with the 8086, and continuing with the 80286 (in 1982), 386 (in 1985), and 486 (in 1989). Intel continues to produce microprocessors for this ISA to the present time, for example the Pentium (in 1992), Pentium-Pro (in 1995), Pentium-II (in 1997), and Pentium-III (in 1999).

The ISA of the IA-32 is much more complicated than that of the LC-2. There are more opcodes, more data types, more addressing modes, a more complicated memory structure, and a more complicated encoding of instructions into 0s and 1s. However, fundamentally, they have the same basic ingredients.

You have spent a good deal of time understanding computing within the context of the LC-2. Some may feel that it would be good to learn about a *real* ISA. One way to do that would be to have some company such as Intel mass-produce LC-2s, some other company like Dell use them in their PCs, and a third company such as Microsoft compile Windows NT into the ISA of the LC-2. An easier way to introduce you to a *real* ISA is by way of this Appendix.

We present here elements of the IA-32, a very complicated ISA. We do so in spite of its complexity, because it is the most pervasive of all ISAs available in the marketplace.

We make no attempt to provide a complete specification of the IA-32 ISA. That would require a whole book by itself, and to appreciate it, a deeper understanding of operating systems, compilers, and computer systems than we think is reasonable at this point in your education. If one wants a complete treatment, we recommend *Intel Architecture Software Developer's Manual, volumes 1, 2, and 3*, published by Intel Corporation, 1997. In this appendix, we restrict ourselves to some of the characteristics that are relevant to application programs. Our intent is to give you a sense of the richness of the IA-32 ISA. We introduce these characteristics within the context of the LC-2 ISA, an ISA with which you are familiar.

B.1 LC-2 FEATURES AND CORRESPONDING IA-32 FEATURES

B.1.1 Instruction Set

An instruction set is made up of instructions, each of which has an opcode and zero or more operands. The number of operands depends on how many are needed by the corresponding opcode. Each operand is a data element and is encoded according to its data type. The location of an operand is determined by evaluating its addressing mode.

The LC-2 instruction set contains one data type, 16 opcodes, and three addressing modes: direct (LD, ST), indirect (LDI, STI), and register-plus-offset (LDR, STR). The IA-32 instruction set has more than a dozen data types, over a hundred opcodes, and more than two dozen addressing modes (depending on how you count).

Data Types   Recall that a data type is a representation of information such that the ISA provides opcodes that operate on information that is encoded in that representation.

The LC-2 supports only one data type, 32-bit 2's-complement integers. This is not enough for efficient processing in the real world today. Scientific applications need numbers that are represented by the floating-point data type. Multimedia applications require information that is represented in a different data type. Commercial applications written years ago, but still active today, require an additional data type, referred to as *packed decimal*. Some applications require a greater range of values and a greater precision of each value than other applications.

As a result of all the above requirements, the IA-32 is designed with instructions that operate on (for example) 8-bit integers, 16-bit integers and 32-bit integers, 32-bit floating point numbers and 64-bit floating point numbers, 64-bit multimedia values and 128-bit multimedia values. Figure B.1 shows some of the data types present in the IA-32 ISA.

Integer:

Unsigned Integer:

BCD Integer:

Packed BCD:

Floating Point:

Bit String:

MMX Data Type:

Figure B.1 A sample of IA-32 data types

Opcodes   The LC-2 comprises 16 opcodes; the IA-32 instruction set comprises more than 200 opcodes. Recall that the three basic instruction types are operates, data movement, and control. Operates process information, data movement opcodes move information from one place to another (including input and output), and control opcodes change the flow of the instruction stream.

In addition, we should add a fourth category to handle functions that must be performed in the real world because a user program runs in the context of an operating system that is controlling a computer system, rather than in isolation. These instructions deal with computer security, system management, hardware performance monitoring, and various other issues that are beyond what the typical application program pays attention to. We will ignore those instructions in this appendix, but please note that they do exist, and you will see them as your studies progress.

Here we will concentrate on the three basic instruction types: operates, data movement, and control.

Operates   The LC-2 has three operate instructions: ADD, AND, and NOT. The ADD opcode is the only LC-2 opcode that performs arithmetic. If one wants to subtract, one obtains the negative of an operand and then adds. If one wants to multiply, one can write a program with a loop to ADD a number some specified number of times. However, this is too time-consuming for a real microprocessor. So, the IA-32 has separate SUB and MUL, as well as DIV, INC (increment), DEC (decrement), and ADC (add with carry), to name a few.

A useful feature of an ISA is to extend the size of the integers on which it can operate. To do this one writes a program to operate on such *long* integers. The ADC opcode, which adds two operands plus the carry from the previous add, is a very useful opcode for extending the size of integers.

In addition, the IA-32 has, for each data type, its own set of opcodes to operate on that data type. For example, multimedia instructions (collectively called the MMX instructions) often require *saturating arithmetic*, which is very different from the arithmetic we are used to. PADDS is an opcode that adds two operands with saturating arithmetic.

Saturating arithmetic can be explained, as follows: Suppose we represent the degree of grayness of an element in a figure with a digit from 0 to 9, where 0 is white and 9 is black. Suppose we want to add some darkness to an existing value of grayness of that figure. An element could start out with a grayness value of 7, and we might wish to add a 5 worth of darkness to it. In normal arithmetic, $7 + 5$ is 2 (with a carry), which is lighter than either 7 or 5. Something is wrong! With saturating arithmetic, when we reach 9, we stay there, we do not generate a carry. So, for example, $7 + 5 = 9$ and $9 + n = 9$. Saturating arithmetic is a different kind of arithmetic, and the IA-32 has opcodes (MMX instructions) that perform this type of arithmetic.

Scientific applications require opcodes that operate on values represented in the floating-point data type. FADD, FMUL, FSIN, FSQRT are examples of floating point opcodes in the IA-32 ISA.

The AND and NOT opcodes are the only LC-2 opcodes that perform logical functions. One can construct any logical expression using these two opcodes. However, as is the case with arithmetic, this also is too time-consuming. The IA-32 has in addition separate OR, XOR, AND-NOT, as well as separate logical operators for different data types.

Furthermore, the IA-32 has a number of other operate instructions that set and clear registers, convert a value from one data type to another, shift or rotate the bits of a data element, and so on.

Table B.1 lists some of the operate opcodes present in the IA-32 instruction set.

Data Movement   The LC-2 has seven data movement opcodes: LD, LDI, ST, STI, LDR, STR, and LEA. Except for LEA, which loads an address into a register, they copy information between memory (and memory-mapped device registers) and the eight general-purpose registers, R0 to R7.

The IA-32 has, in addition to these, many other data movement opcodes. XCHG can swap the contents of two locations. PUSHA pushes all eight general-purpose registers onto the stack. IN and OUT move data between input and output ports and the processor. CMOVcc copies a value from one location to another only if a previously computed condition is true.

Table B.2 lists some of the data movement opcodes present in the IA-32 instruction set.

Control   The LC-2 has six control opcodes: BR, JSR, JSRR, RET, RTI, and TRAP. IA-32 has all these and more. Table B.3 lists some of the control opcodes present in the IA-32 instruction set.

Two Address vs Three Address   The LC-2 is a three-address ISA. This description reflects the number of operands explicitly specified by the ADD instruction. An add operation requires two source operands (the numbers to be added) and one destination

Table B.1   Operate instructions, IA-32 ISA

Instruction	Explanation
ADC x, y	x, y, and the carry retained from the last relevant operation (in CF) are added and the result stored in x.
MUL x	The value in EAX is multiplied by x, and the result is stored in the 64-bit register formed by EDX, EAX.
SAR x	x is arithmetic right shifted n bits, and the result stored in x. The value of n can be 1, an immediate operand, or the count in the CL register.
XOR x, y	A bitwise exclusive-OR is performed on x, y and the result is stored in x.
DAA	After adding two packed decimal numbers, AL contains two BCD values, which may be incorrect due to propagation of the carry bit after 15, rather than after 9. DAA corrects the two BCD digits in AL.
FSIN	The top of the stack (call it x) is popped. The $\sin(x)$ is computed and pushed onto the stack.
FADD	The top two elements on the stack are popped, added, and their result pushed onto the stack.
PANDN x, y	A bitwise AND-NOT operation is performed on MMX values x, y and the result is stored in x.
PADDS x, y	Saturating addition is performed on packed mmx values x, y and the result is stored in x.

Table B.2   Data movement instructions, IA-32 ISA

Instruction	Explanation
MOV x, y	The value stored in y is copied into x.
XCHG x, y	The values stored in x and y are swapped.
PUSHA	All the registers are pushed onto the top of the stack.
MOVS	The element in the DS segment pointed to by ESI is copied into the location in the ES segment pointed to by EDI. After the copy has been performed, ESI and EDI are both incremented.
REP MOVS	Perform the MOVS above. Then decrement ECX. Repeat this instruction until ECX = 0. (This allows a string to be copied in a single instruction, after initializing ECX.)
LODS	The element in the DS segment pointed to by ESI is loaded into EAX, and ESI is incremented or decremented, according to the value of the DF flag.
INS	Data from the I/O port specified by the DX register is loaded into the EAX register (or AX or AL, if the size of the data is 16 bits or 8 bits, respectively).
CMOVZ x, y	If ZF = 1, the value stored in y is copied into x. If ZF = 0, the instruction acts like a no-op.
LEA x, y	The address y is stored in x. This is very much like the LC-2 instruction of the same name.

Table B.3   Control instructions, IA-32 ISA

Instruction	Explanation
JMP x	IP is loaded with the address x. This is very much like the LC-2 instruction of the same name.
CALL x	The IP is pushed on the stack, and a new IP is loaded with x.
RET	The stack is popped, and the value popped is loaded into IP.
LOOP x	ECX is decremented. If ECX is not 0 and ZF = 1, the IP is loaded with x.
INT n	The value n is an index into a table of descriptors that specify operating system service routines. The end result of this instruction is that IP is loaded with the starting result of the corresponding service routine. This is very much like the TRAP instruction in the LC-2.

operand, to store the result. In the LC-2, all three must be specified explicitly, hence the name three-address ISA.

Even if the same location is to be used both for one of the sources and for the destination, the three addresses are all specified. For example, the LC-2 ADD R1,R1,R2 identifies R1 as both a source and the destination.

The IA-32 is a two-address ISA. Since the add operation needs three operands, the location of one of the sources must also be used to store the result. For example, the corresponding ADD instruction in the IA-32 ISA would be ADD EAX, EBX. (EAX and EBX are names of two of the eight general-purpose registers.) EAX and EBX are the sources, and EAX is the destination.

Since the result of the operate is stored in the location that originally contained one of the sources, that source operand is no longer available after that instruction is executed. If that source operand is needed later, it must be saved before the operate instruction is executed.

Memory Operands   A major difference between the LC-2 instruction set and the IA-32 instruction set is the restriction on where operate instructions can get their operands. An LC-2 operate instruction must obtain its source operands from registers and write the result to a destination register. An IA-32 instruction, on the other hand, can obtain one of its sources from memory and/or write its result to memory. In other words, the IA-32 can read a value from memory, operate on that value, and store the result in memory all in a single instruction. The LC-2 cannot.

The LC-2 program requires a separate load instruction to read the value from memory before operating on it, and a separate store instruction to write the result in memory after the operate instruction. An ISA, like the LC-2, that has this restriction, is called a **load-store** ISA. The IA-32 is not a load-store ISA.

B.1.2   Memory

The LC-2 memory consists of 2^{16} locations, each containing 16 bits of information. We say the LC-2 has a 16-bit address space, since one can uniquely address its 2^{16} locations with 16 bits of address. We say the LC-2 has an addressability of 16 bits, since each memory location contains 16 bits of information.

The IA-32 memory has a 32-bit address space and an addressability of eight bits. Since one byte contains eight bits, we say the IA-32 memory is byte addressable. Since each location contains only eight bits, four contiguous locations in memory are needed to store a 32-bit data element, say locations X, X+1, X+2, and X+3. We designate X as the address of the 32-bit data element. In actuality, X only contains bits [7:0], X+1 contains bits [15:8], X+2 contains bits [23:16], and X+3 contains bits [31:24] of the 32-bit value.

One can determine an LC-2 memory location by simply obtaining its address from the instruction, using one of the three addressing modes available in the instruction set. An IA-32 instruction has available to it more than two dozen addressing modes that it can use to specify the memory address of an operand. We examine the addressing modes in Section B.2 in the context of the IA-32 instruction format.

In addition to the larger number of addressing modes, the IA-32 contains a mechanism called *segmentation* that provides a measure of protection against unwanted accesses to particular memory addresses. The address produced by an instruction's addressing mode, rather than being an address in its own right, is used as an address within a segment of memory. Access to that memory location must take into account the segment register that controls access to that segment. The details of how the protection mechanism works will have to wait for later in your studies.

However, Figure B.2 does show how an address is calculated for the register+offset addressing mode, both for the LC-2, and for the IA-32, with segmentation. In both cases, the opcode is to move data from memory to a general purpose register. The LC-2 uses the LDR instruction. The IA-32 uses the MOV instruction. In the case of the IA-32, the address calculated is in the DS segment, which is accessed via the DS register. That access is done through a 16-bit **selector** which indexes into a segment descriptor table, yielding the **segment descriptor** for that segment. The segment descriptor contains a **segment base register** and a **segment limit register**,

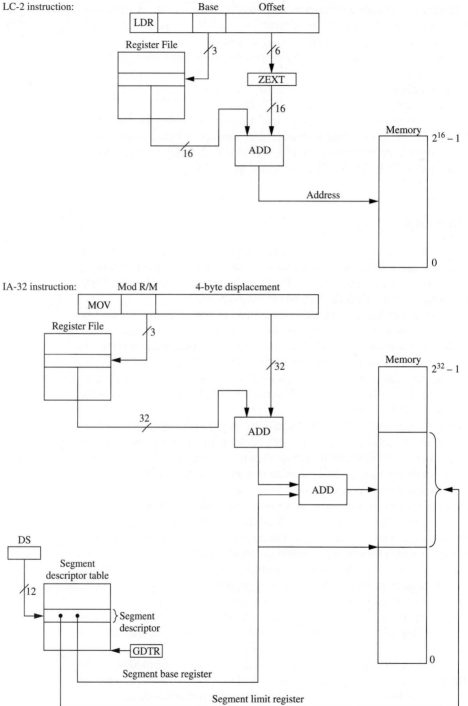

Figure B.2   Register+offset addressing mode in LC-2 and IA-32 ISAs

and the protection information. The memory address obtained from the addressing mode of the instruction is added to the segment base register to provide the actual memory address, as shown in Figure B.2.

B.1.3   Internal State

The internal state of the LC-2 consists of eight 16-bit general purpose registers, R0 to R7, a 16-bit PC, and three 1-bit condition code registers, N, Z, and P. The user-visible internal state of the IA-32 consists of application-visible registers, an Instruction pointer, a FLAGS register, and the segment registers.

Application-visible Registers   Figure B.3 shows some of the application-visible registers in the IA-32 ISA.

Corresponding to R0 through R7, the IA-32 also has eight general-purpose registers, EAX, EBX, ECX, EDX, ESP, EBP, ECI, and EDI. Each contains 32 bits, reflecting the normal size of its operands. However, since the IA-32 provides opcodes that process 16-bit operands and eight-bit operands, it should also provide 16-bit and eight-bit registers. The ISA identifies the low 16 bits of each 32-bit register as a 16-bit register and the low 8 bits and the high 8 bits of four of the registers as eight-bit

General Purpose Registers:

31		0		
	AX	EAX	AL = EAX [7:0]
	DX	EDX	DL = EDX [7:0]
	CX	ECX	CL = ECX [7:0]
	BX	EBX	BL = EBX [7:0]
	BP	EBP	AH = EAX [15:8]
	CI	ECI	DH = EDX [15:8]
	DI	EDI	CH = ECX [15:8]
	SP	ESP	BH = EBX [15:8]

Floating Point Registers:

63		0	
			FP0
			FP1
			FP2
			FP3
			FP4
			FP5
			FP6
			FP7

Multimedia Registers:

63		0	
			MM0
			MM1
			MM2
			MM3
			MM4
			MM5
			MM6
			MM7

Figure B.3   Some IA-32 application-visible registers

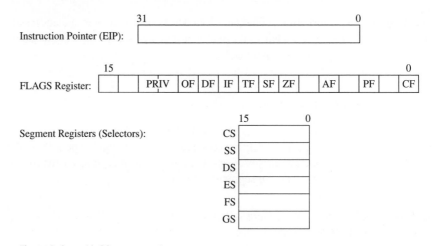

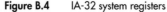

Figure B.4   IA-32 system registers

registers for use of instructions that require those smaller operands. So, for example, AX, BX, to DI are 16-bit registers, and AL, BL, CL, DL, AH, BH, CH, and DH are eight-bit registers.

The IA-32 also provides 64-bit registers for storing values needed for floating point and MMX computations. They are, respectively, FP0 through FP7 and MM0 through MM7.

System Registers   The LC-2 has two system-level registers—the PC and the condition codes N, Z, and P. The user-visible IA-32 has these and more.

Figure B.4 shows some of the user-visible system registers in the IA-32 ISA.

Instruction Pointer   The IA-32 has the equivalent of the LC-2's 16-bit program counter. The IA-32 calls it an *instruction pointer* (IP). Since the address space of IA-32 is 32 bits, IP is a 32-bit register.

FLAGS Register   Corresponding to the LC-2's N, Z, and P condition codes, the IA-32 has a one-bit SF (sign flag) register and a one-bit ZF (zero flag) register. SF and ZF provide exactly the same functions as the N and Z condition codes of the LC-2. The IA-32 does not have the equivalent of the LC-2's P condition code. In fact, the P condition code is redundant since if one knows the values of N and Z, one knows the value of P. We included it in the LC-2 ISA anyway, for the convenience of assembly language programmers and compiler writers.

The IA-32 collects other one-bit values in addition to N and Z. These one-bit values (called *flags*) are contained in a 16-bit register, called FLAGS. Several of these flags are discussed below.

The CF flag stores the **carry** produced by the last relevant operation that generated a carry. As we said earlier, together with the ADC instruction, CF facilitates the generation of procedures, which allows the software to deal with larger integers than the ISA supports.

The OF flag stores an **overflow** condition if the last relevant operate generated a value too large to store in the available number of bits. Recall the discussion of overflow in Section 2.5.3.

The DF flag indicates the **direction** that string operations are to process strings. If $DF = 0$, the string is processed from the high-address byte down (i.e., the pointer keeping track of the element in the string to be processed next is decremented). If $DF = 1$, the string is processed from the low-address byte up (i.e., the string pointer is incremented).

Two flags not usually considered as part of the application state are the IF (**interrupt**) flag and the TF (**trap**) flag. Both correspond to functions with which you are familiar.

IF is very similar to the IE (interrupt enable) bit in the KBSR and CRTSR, discussed in Section 8.5. If $IF = 1$, the processor can recognize external interrupts (like keyboard input, for example). If $IF = 0$, these external interrupts have no effect on the process that is executing. We say the interrupts are *disabled*.

TF is very similar to *single-step mode* in the LC-2 simulator, only in this case, it is part of the ISA. If $TF = 1$, the processor halts after every instruction, so the state of the system can be examined. If $TF = 0$, the processor ignores the trap, and processes the next instruction.

Segment Registers   When operating in its preferred operating mode (called **protected mode**), the address calculated by the instruction is really an offset from the starting address of a segment, which is specified by some *segment base register*. These segment base registers are part of their corresponding *data segment descriptors*, which are contained in the *segment descriptor table*. At each instant of time, six of these segments are active. They are called, respectively, the *code segment* (CS), *stack segment* (SS), and four data segments (DS, ES, FS, and GS). The six active segments are accessed via their corresponding segment registers shown in Figure B.4, which contain pointers to their respective segment descriptors.

B.2   THE FORMAT AND SPECIFICATION OF IA-32 INSTRUCTIONS

The LC-2 instruction is a 16-bit instruction. Bits[15:12] always contain the opcode; the remaining 12 bits of each instruction are used to support the needs of that opcode.

The length of an IA-32 instruction is not fixed. It consists of a variable number of bytes, depending on the needs of that instruction. A lot of information can be packed into one IA-32 instruction. Figure B.5 shows the format of an IA-32 instruction. The instruction consists of anywhere from 1 to 16 bytes, as shown in the figure.

The two key parts of an IA-32 instruction are the opcode and, where necessary, the ModR/M byte. The opcode specifies the operation the instruction is to perform. The ModR/M byte specifies how to obtain the operands it needs. The ModR/M byte specifies one of several addressing modes, some of which require the use of registers and a one-, two-, or four-byte displacement. The register information is encoded in a SIB byte. Both the SIB byte and the displacement (if one is necessary) follow the ModR/M byte in the instruction.

Some opcodes specify an immediate operand and also specify the number of bytes of the instruction that is used to store that immediate information. The immediate value (when one is specified) is the last element of the instruction.

Finally, the instruction assumes certain default information with respect to the semantics of an instruction, such as address size, operand size, segment to be used, and so forth. The instruction can change this default information by means of one or more prefixes, which are located at the beginning of the instruction.

Each part of an IA-32 instruction is discussed in more detail below.

B.2.1   Prefix

Prefixes provide additional information that is used to process the instruction. There are four classes of prefix information, and each instruction can have from zero to four prefixes, depending on its needs. Fundamentally, a prefix overrides the usual interpretation of the instruction.

The four classes of prefixes are lock and repeat, segment override, operand override, and address override. Table B.4 describes the four types of prefixes.

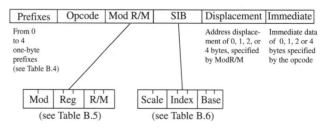

Figure B.5   Format of the IA-32 instruction

Table B.4   Prefixes, IA-32 ISA

Repeat/Lock	
xF0 (LOCK)	This prefix guarantees that the instruction will have exclusive use of all shared memory until the instruction completes execution.
xF2,xF3 (REP/REPE/REPNE)	This prefix allows the instruction (a string instruction) to be repeated some specified number of times. The iteration count is specified by ECX. The instruction is also terminated on the occurrence of a specified value of ZF.
Segment override	
x2E(CS), x36(SS), x3E(DS), x26(ES), x64(FS), x65(GS)	This prefix causes the memory access to use the specified segment, instead of the default segment expected for that instruction.
Operand size override	
x66	This prefix changes the size of data expected for this instruction. That is, instructions expecting 32-bit data elements use 16-bit data elements. And instructions expecting 16-bit data elements use 32-bit data elements.
Address size override	
x67	This prefix changes the size of operand addresses expected for this instruction. That is, instructions expecting a 32-bit address use 16-bit addresses. And instructions expecting 16-bit addresses use 32-bit addresses.

B.2.2   Opcode

The opcode byte (or bytes, some opcodes are represented by two bytes) specifies a large amount of information about the needs of that instruction. The opcode byte (or bytes) specifies, among other things, the operation to be performed, whether the operands are to be obtained from memory or from registers, the size of the operands, whether or not one of the source operands is an immediate value in the instruction, and if so, the size of that immediate operand.

Some opcodes are formed by combining the opcode byte with bits [5:3] of the ModR/M byte, if those bits are not needed to provide addressing mode information. The ModR/M byte is described in Section B.2.3.

B.2.3   ModR/M Byte

The ModR/M byte, shown in Figure B.5, provides addressing mode information for two operands, when necessary, or for one operand, if that is all that is needed. If two operands are needed, one may be in memory, the other in a register, or both may be in registers. If one operand is needed, it can be either in a register or in memory. The ModR/M byte supports all cases.

The ModR/M byte is essentially partitioned into two parts. The first part consists of bits [7:6] and bits [2:0]. The second part consists of bits [5:3].

If bits [7:6] = 00, 01, or 10, the first part specifies the addressing mode of a memory operand, and the combined five bits ([7:6],[2:0]) identify which addressing mode. If bits [7:6] = 11, there is no memory operand, and bits [2:0] specify a register operand.

Bits [5:3] specify the register number of the other operand, if the opcode requires two operands. If the opcode only requires one operand, bits [5:3] are available as a subopcode to differentiate among eight opcodes that have the same opcode byte, as described in Section B.2.2.

Table B.5 lists some of the interpretations of the ModR/M byte.

B.2.4 SIB Byte

If the opcode specifies that an operand is to be obtained from memory, the ModR/M byte specifies the addressing mode, that is, the information that is needed to calculate the address of that operand. Some addressing modes require more information than can be specified by the ModR/M byte alone. Those operand specifiers (see example 3 in Table B.5) specify the inclusion of an SIB byte in the instruction. The SIB byte (for scaled-index-base), shown in Figure B.5, provides scaling information, and identifies which register is to be used as an index register and/or which register is to be used as a base register. Taken together, the SIB byte computes scale · index + base, where base and/or index can be zero, and scale can be one. Table B.6 lists some of the interpretations of the SIB byte.

B.2.5 Displacement

If the ModR/M byte specifies that the address calculation requires a displacement, the displacement (one, two, or four bytes) is contained in the instruction. The opcode and/or ModR/M byte specifies the size of the displacement.

Figure B.6 shows the addressing mode calculation for the source operand if the instruction is as shown. The prefix x26 overrides the segment register and specifies using the ES segment. The ModR/M and SIB bytes specify a four-byte displacement

Table B.5   ModR/M byte, examples

Mod	Reg	R/M	Eff. Addr.	Reg	Explanation
00	011	000	[EAX]	EBX	EAX contains the address of the memory operand, EBX contains the register operand.
01	010	000	disp8[EAX]	EDX	Memory operand's address is obtained by adding the displacement byte of the instruction to the contents of EAX. EDX contains the register operand.
10	000	100	disp32[-][-]	EAX	Memory operand's address is obtained by adding the four-byte (32 bits) displacement of the instruction to an address that will need a SIB byte to compute. (See Section B.2.4 for the discussion of the SIB byte.) EAX contains the register operand.
11	001	110	ESI	ECX	If the opcode requires two operands, both are in registers (ESI and ECX). If the opcode requires one operand, it is in ESI. In that case, 001 (bits [5:3]) are part of the opcode.

Table B.6   SIB byte, examples

Scale	Index	Base	Computation	Explanation
00	011	000	EBX+EAX	The contents of EBX are added to the contents of EAX. The result is added to whatever is specified by the ModR/M byte.
01	000	001	$2 \cdot EAX + ECX$	The contents of EAX are multiplied by two, and the result is added to the contents of ECX. This is then added to whatever is specified by the ModR/M byte.
01	100	001	ECX	The contents of ECX are added to whatever is specified by the ModR/M byte.
10	110	010	$4 \cdot ESI + EDX$	The contents of ESI are multiplied by four, and the result is added to the contents of EDX. This is then added to whatever is specified by the ModR/M byte.

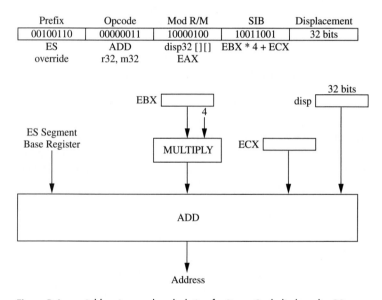

Figure B.6   Addressing mode calculation for Base+ScaledIndes+disp32

is to be added to the base register ECX + the index register EBX after its contents are multiplied by four.

B.2.6   Immediate

Recall that the LC-2 allowed small immediate values to be present in the instruction, by setting inst[5:5] to 1. The IA-32 also permits immediate values in the instruction. As stated previously, if the opcode specifies that a source operand is an immediate value in the instruction, it also specifies the number of bytes of the instruction used to represent the operand. That is, an immediate can be represented in the instruction with one, two, or four bytes. Since the opcode also specifies the size of the operand,

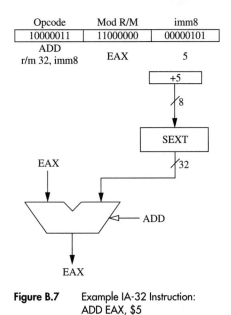

Figure B.7   Example IA-32 Instruction:
ADD EAX, $5

immediate values that can be stored in fewer bytes than the operand size are first sign-extended to their full size before being operated on. Figure B.7 shows the use of the immediate operand with the ADD instruction. The example is ADD EAX, $5. We are very familiar with the corresponding LC-2 instruction: ADD R0,R0,#5.

B.3   AN EXAMPLE

We conclude this appendix with an example. The problem is one we have dealt with extensively in Chapter 14. Given an input character string consisting of text, numbers, and punctuation, write a C program to convert all the lowercase letters to uppercase. Figure B.8 shows a C program that solves this problem. Figure B.9 shows the annotated LC-2 assembly language code that a C compiler would generate. Figure B.10 shows the corresponding annotated IA-32 assembly-language code. For readability, we show assembly-language representations of the LC-2 and IA-32 programs, rather than the machine code.

```c
#include <stdio.h>

void UpcaseString(char inputString[]);

main ()
{
    char string[8];

    scanf("%s", string);
    UpcaseString(string);
}

void UpcaseString(char inputString[])
{
  int i = 0;

  while(inputString[i]) {
    if (('a' <= inputString[i]) && (inputString[i] <= 'z'))
      inputString[i] = inputString[i] - ('a' - 'A');
    i++;
  }
}
```

Figure B.8   C source code for the upper/lowercase program

```
; uppercase:  converts lower- to uppercase
            .ORIG   x3000
            LEA     R6, STACK
MAIN        ADD     R1, R6, #3
READCHAR    IN                      ; read in input string: scanf
            OUT
            STR     R0, R1, #0
            ADD     R1, R1, #1
            ADD     R2, R0, x-A
            BRnp    READCHAR
            ADD     R1, R1, #-1
            STR     R2, R1, #0      ; put in NULL char to mark the "end"
            ADD     R1, R6, #3      ; get the starting address of the string
            STR     R1, R6, #14     ; pass the parameter
            STR     R6, R6, #13
            ADD     R6, R6, #11
            JSR     UPPERCASE
            HALT
UPPERCASE   STR     R7, R6, #1
            AND     R1, R1, #0
            STR     R1, R6, #4
            LDR     R2, R6, #3
CONVERT     ADD     R3, R1, R2      ; add index to starting addr of string
            LDR     R4, R3, #0
            BRz     DONE            ; Done if NULL char reached
            LD      R5, a
            ADD     R5, R5, R4      ; 'a' <= input string
            BRn     NEXT
            LD      R5, z
            ADD     R5, R4, R5      ; input string <= 'z'
            BRp     NEXT
            LD      R5, asubA       ; convert to uppercase
            ADD     R4, R4, R5
            STR     R4, R3, #0
NEXT        ADD     R1, R1, #1      ; increment the array index, i
            STR     R1, R6, #4
            BR      CONVERT
DONE        LDR     R7, R6, #1
            LDR     R6, R6, #2
            RET
a           .FILL   #-97
z           .FILL   #-122
asubA       .FILL   #-32
STACK       .BLKW   100     $0
            .END
```

Figure B.9   LC-2 assembly-language code for the upper/lowercase program

```
.386P
.model FLAT

_DATA    SEGMENT                ; The NULL-terminated scanf format
$SG397   DB       '%s', 00H     ; string is stored in global data space.
_DATA    ENDS

_TEXT    SEGMENT

_string$ = -8                   ; Location of "string" in local stack
_main    PROC NEAR
         sub    esp, 8          ; Allocate stack space to store "string"
         lea    eax, DWORD PTR _string$[esp+8]
         push   eax             ; Push arguments to scanf
         push   OFFSET FLAT:$SG397
         call   _scanf

         lea    ecx, DWORD PTR _string$[esp+16]
         push   ecx             ; Push argument to UpcaseString
         call   _UpcaseString

         add    esp, 20         ; Release local stack space
         ret    0
_main    ENDP

_inputString$ = 8              ; "inputString" location in local stack
_UpcaseString PROC NEAR
         mov    ecx, DWORD PTR _inputString$[esp-4]
         cmp    BYTE PTR [ecx], 0
         je     SHORT $L404      ; If inputString[0]==0, skip the loop
$L403:   mov    al, BYTE PTR [ecx]  ; Load inputString[i] into AL
         cmp    al, 97          ; 97 == 'a'
         jl     SHORT $L405
         cmp    al, 122         ; 122 == 'z'
         jg     SHORT $L405
         sub    al, 32          ; 32 == 'a' - 'A'
         mov    BYTE PTR [ecx], al
$L405:   inc    ecx             ; i++
         mov    al, BYTE PTR [ecx]
         test   al, al
         jne    SHORT $L403      ; Loop if inputString[i] != 0
$L404:   ret    0
_UpcaseString ENDP
_TEXT    ENDS
END
```

Figure B.10   IA-32 assembly-language code for the upper/lowercase program

C

The Microarchitecture of the LC-2

We have seen in Chapters 4 and 5 the several stages of the instruction cycle that must occur in order for the computer to process each instruction. If a microarchitecture is to implement an ISA, it must be able to carry out this instruction cycle for every instruction in the ISA. This appendix illustrates one example of a microarchitecture that can do that for the LC-2 ISA. Many of the details of the microarchitecture and the reasons for each design decision are well beyond the scope of an introductory course. However, for those who want to understand *how* a microarchitecture can carry out the requirements of each instruction of the LC-2 ISA, this appendix is provided.

C.1 OVERVIEW

Figure C.1 shows the two main components of an ISA: the *data path*, which contains all the components that actually process the instructions, and the *control*, which contains all the components that generate the set of control signals that are needed to control the processing at each instant of time.

We say, "at each instant of time," but we really mean: *during each clock cycle*. That is, time is divided into **clock cycles**. The cycle time of a microprocessor is the duration of a clock cycle. A common cycle time for a microprocessor today is 1.25 nanoseconds, which corresponds to 800 million clock cycles each second. We say that such a microprocessor is operating at a frequency of 800 megahertz.

At each instant of time—or, rather, during each clock cycle—the 39 control signals (as shown in Figure C.1) control both the processing in the data path and the generation of the control signals for the next clock cycle. Processing in the data path is controlled by 29 bits, and the generation of the control signals for the next clock cycle is controlled by ten bits.

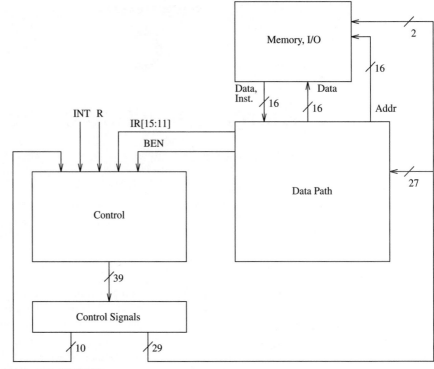

Figure C.1   Microarchitecture of the LC-2, major components

Note that the hardware that determines which control signals are needed each clock cycle does not operate in a vacuum. On the contrary, the control signals needed in the "next" clock cycle depend on all of the following:

1. What is going on in the current clock cycle.
2. The LC-2 instruction that is being executed.
3. If that LC-2 instruction is a BR, whether the conditions for the branch have been met (i.e., the state of the relevant condition codes).
4. Whether or not an external device is requesting that the processor be interrupted.
5. If a memory operation is in progress, whether it is completing during this cycle.

Figure C.1 identifies the specific information in our implementation of the LC-2 that corresponds to these five items. They are, respectively:

1. J[5:0], COND[1:0], INT.TEST, and IRD—10 bits of control signals provided by the current clock cycle.
2. inst[15:12], which identifies the opcode, and inst[11:11], which differentiates JSR(R) from JMP(R).

3. BEN to indicate whether or not a BR should be taken.

4. INT to indicate that some external device of higher priority than the executing process requests service.

5. R to indicate the end of a memory operation.

C.2   THE STATE MACHINE

The behavior of the LC-2 microarchitecture during a given clock cycle is completely determined by the 39 control signals, combined with eight bits of additional information (inst[15:11], BEN, INT, and R), as shown in Figure C.1. We have said that during each clock cycle, 29 of these control signals determine the processing of information in the data path and the other 10 control signals combine with the eight bits of additional information to determine which set of control signals will be required in the next clock cycle.

We say that these 39 control signals specify the *state* of the control structure of the LC-2 microarchitecture. We can completely describe the behavior of the LC-2 microarchitecture by means of a directed graph that consists of nodes (one corresponding to each state) and arcs (showing the flow from each state to the next). We call such a graph a *state machine*.

Figure C.2 is the state machine for our implementation of the LC-2. The state machine describes what is to happen during each clock cycle in which the computer is running. Each state is active for exactly one clock cycle before control passes to the next state. The state machine shows the step-by-step (clock cycle by clock cycle) process that each instruction goes through from the start of its FETCH phase to the end of that instruction, as described in Section 4.2.2. Each node in the state machine corresponds to the activity that the processor will carry out during a single clock cycle. The actual processing that is performed in the data path is contained inside the node. The step-by-step flow is conveyed by the arcs that take the processor from one state to the next.

For example, recall from Chapter 4 that the instruction FETCH phase starts with a memory access to read the instruction at the address specified by the PC. Note that in state 1, the MAR is loaded with PC, the PC is incremented in preparation for the FETCH of the next LC-2 instruction, and, if there is no interrupt request present (INT = 0), the flow passes to state 2. We will describe in Section C.6 the flow of control if INT = 1, that is, if an external device is requesting an interrupt.

Note that in state 2, the memory is read, and in state 3, the instruction is loaded into the instruction register (IR), completing the fetch phase. MAR is the memory address register associated with memory. If the signal denoting that memory data is available is asserted, then the contents of the location specified by MAR are loaded into MDR (the memory data register).

Note that the arrow from the last state of each instruction cycle (i.e., the state that completes the processing of that LC-2 instruction) takes us to state 1 (to begin the instruction cycle of the next LC-2 instruction).

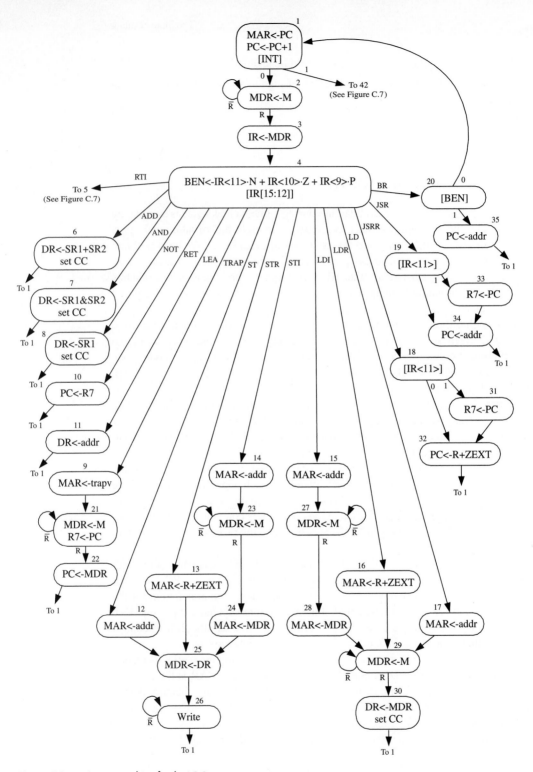

Figure C.2 A state machine for the LC-2

C.3   THE DATA PATH

The data path consists of all components that actually process the information during a cycle—the functional units (e.g., the ALU) that operate on the information, the registers that store information at the end of one cycle so it will be available for further use in subsequent cycles, and the buses and wires that carry information from one point to another in the data path. Figure C.3, a more comprehensive version of Figure 5.9, illustrates the data path of our microarchitecture of the LC-2.

Note the control signals that are associated with each component in the data path. For example, ALUK, consisting of two control signals, is associated with the ALU. These control signals determine how the component will be used each cycle. Table C.1 lists the set of control signals that control the elements of the data path, and the set of values that each control signal can have. (Actually, for readability, we list a symbolic name for each value, rather than the binary value.) For example, since ALUK consists of two bits, it can have one of four values. Which value it has during any particular clock cycle depends on whether the ALU is required to ADD, AND, NOT, or simply pass one of its inputs to the output during that clock cycle. PCMX also consists of two control signals and specifies which input to the MUX is required during a given clock cycle. LD.PC is a single-bit control signal, and is a 0 (NO) or a 1 (YES), depending on whether or not the PC is to be loaded during the given clock cycle.

During each clock cycle, corresponding to the "current state" in the state machine, the 29 bits of control direct the processing of all components in the data path that is required during that clock cycle. The processing that takes place in the data path during that clock cycle, as we have said, is specified inside the node representing the state.

C.4   THE CONTROL STRUCTURE

As described above, the state machine determines which control signals are needed to process information in the data path during each clock cycle. The state machine also determines which control signals are needed to direct the flow of control from each state to its successor state.

Figure C.4 shows a block diagram of the control structure of our implementation of the LC-2. Many implementations are possible, and the design considerations that must be studied to determine which should be used is the subject of a full course in computer architecture.

We have chosen a very straightforward microprogrammed implementation. The current state of the control structure is represented by the 29 bits that control the processing in the data path and the 10 bits that help determine which state comes next. These 39 bits are collectively known as a *microinstruction*. Each microinstruction (i.e., each state of the control structure) is stored in one 39-bit location in a special memory called the control store. Since there are 50 states in the state machine, and

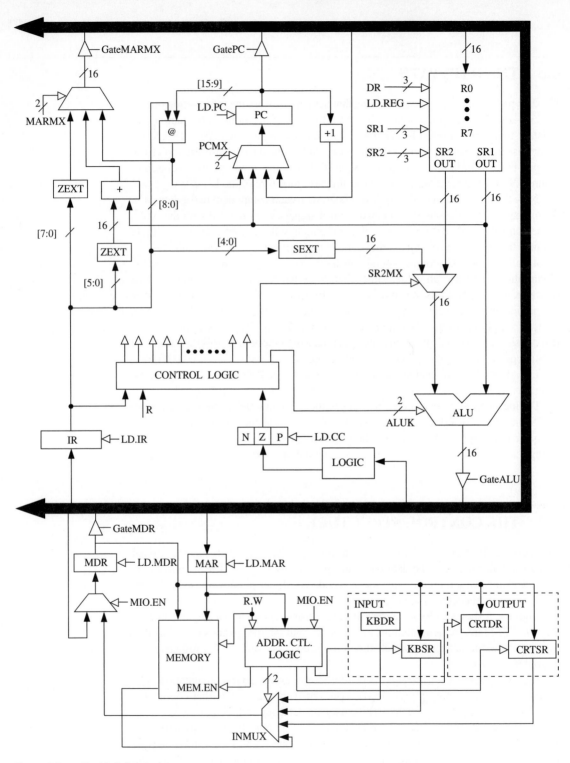

Figure C.3 The LC-2 data path

Table C.1   Data path control signals

Signal Name	Signal Values	
LD.MAR/1:	NO, LOAD	
LD.MDR/1:	NO, LOAD	
LD.IR/1:	NO, LOAD	
LD.BEN/1:	NO, LOAD	
LD.REG/1:	NO, LOAD	
LD.CC/1:	NO, LOAD	
LD.PC/1:	NO, LOAD	
GatePC/1:	NO, YES	
GateMDR/1:	NO, YES	
GateALU/1:	NO, YES	
GateMARMX/1:	NO, YES	
GateINTV/1:	NO, YES	
GatePC-1/1:	NO, YES	
GateCC/1:	NO, YES	
PCMX/2:	PC+1	;select pc+1
	BUS	;select value from bus
	REG	;select value from register file
	CONCAT	;select PC[15:9]@IR[8:0]
MIO.EN/1:	NO, YES	
R.W/1:	RD, WR	
DRMX/2:	11.9	;destination IR[11:9]
	R7	;destination R7
	R6	;destination R6
SR1MX/2:	11.9	;source IR[11:9]
	8.6	;source IR[8:6]
	R7	;source R7
	R6	;source R6
STACKMX/2:	NO	;not a stack operation
	+1	;Push
	−1	;Pop
MARMX/2:	7.0	;select IR[7:0]
	R+ZEXT	;select register +IR[5:0]
	CONCAT	;select PC[15:9]@IR[8:0]
ALUK/2:	ADD, AND, NOT, PASSA	
CCMX/1:	ALU.OUT, STACK	

since each state corresponds to one microinstruction stored in the control store, the control store for our microprogrammed implementation requires six bits to specify the address of each microinstruction.

Table C.2 lists the function of the 10 bits of control information that help determine which state comes next. Figure C.5 shows the logic of the microsequencer. The purpose of the microsequencer is to determine the address in the control store

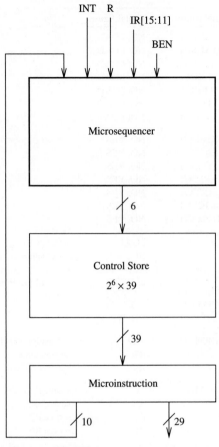

INT   R

IR[15:11]

BEN

(J, COND, IRD, INT.TEST)

Figure C.4   The control structure of a microprogrammed implementation, overall block diagram

Table C.2   Microsequencer control signals

Signal Name	Signal Values	
J/6:		
COND/2:	$COND_1$	;Unconditional
	$COND_2$	;Ready
	$COND_3$	;Branch
	$COND_4$	;Link
IRD/1:	NO, YES	
INT.TEST/1	NO, YES	

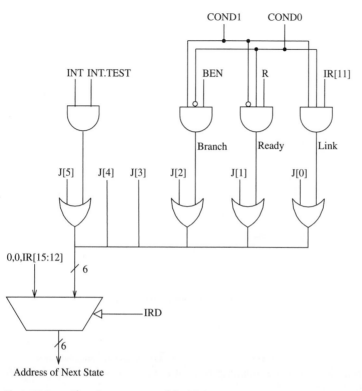

Figure C.5 The microsequencer of the LC-2

that corresponds to the next state, that is, the location where the 39 bits of control information for the next state are stored.

Note that state 4 of the state machine (Figure C.2) has 16 "next" states, depending on the LC-2 instruction being executed during the current instruction cycle. This state carries out the DECODE phase of the instruction cycle described in Chapter 4. If the IRD control signal in the microinstruction corresponding to state 4 is 1, the output MUX of the microsequencer (Figure C.5) will take its source from the six bits formed by 00 concatenated with the four opcode bits IR[15:12]. Since IR[15:12] specifies the opcode of the current LC-2 instruction being processed, the address of the control store will be one of 16 addresses, each corresponding to one of 16 "next states." That is, each of the 16 next states is the first state to be carried out after the instruction has been decoded in state 4. For example, if the instruction being processed is ADD, the address of the next state is state 6, whose microinstruction is stored at location 000001. Recall that IR[15:12] for ADD is 0001.

Several signals necessary to control the data path and the microsequencer are not among those listed in Tables C.1 and C.2. They are DR, SR1, BEN, INT, and R. Figure C.6 shows the additional logic needed to generate DR, SR1, and BEN.

The INT signal is supplied by some event external to the normal instruction processing, indicating that the normal instruction processing should be interrupted,

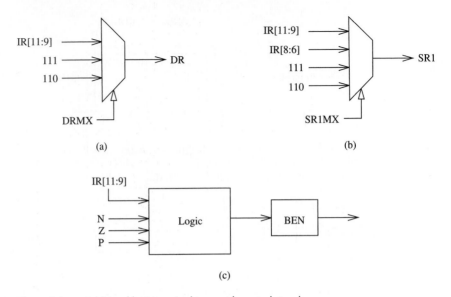

Figure C.6   Additional logic required to provide control signals

and this external event should be dealt with. The interrupt mechanism was described in Chapter 8. The corresponding flow of control, within the microarchitecture, is described in Section C.5.

The remaining signal, R, is a signal generated by the memory in order to allow the LC-2 to operate correctly with a memory that takes multiple clock cycles to read or store a value. An example should make this clear.

Consider a memory that takes five cycles to read a value. That is, once MAR contains the address to be read and the microinstruction asserts READ, it will take five cycles before MDR can contain the contents of the specified location in memory. (Note that the microinstruction asserts READ by means of two control signals: MIO.EN/YES and R.W/RD; see Figure C.3.)

States 2 and 3 of Figure C.2 show how the five cycle "read" is carried out. The microinstruction corresponding to state 2 is stored at control store address 111000. The microinstruction corresponding to state 3 is stored at control store address 111010. For the LC-2 to operate correctly, we want to execute state 2 five times before moving onto state 3. That is, until MDR contains valid data from the memory location specified by the contents of MAR, we want to reexecute state 2. After five clock cycles, the memory has completed the "read," resulting in valid data in MDR, so we can move on to state 3. Suppose the microarchitecture did not wait for the memory to complete the read operation before moving onto state 3. If that had been the case, since the information in MDR would still be garbage, the microarchitecture would have put garbage into IR in state 3.

Since the memory knows it needs five clock cycles to complete the read, it asserts a ready signal (R) at the end of the fourth clock cycle and throughout the fifth clock cycle.

The 10 microsequencer control bits for state 2 are as follows:

```
IRD/0        ; NO
INT.TEST/0   ; NO
COND/01      ; memory ready
J/111000
```

Let's examine the next state address produced by the microsequencer in Figure C.5. For each of the first four executions of state 2, since R = 0, the next state address is 111000. This causes state 2 to be executed again in the next clock cycle. In the fifth clock cycle, since R = 1, the next state address is 111010, and the LC-2 moves on to state 3.

C.5   MEMORY-MAPPED I/O

As you know from Chapter 8, the LC-2 ISA performs input and output via memory-mapped I/O, that is, with the same data movement instructions that it was to read from and write to memory. The LC-2 does this by assigning an address to each device register. Input is accomplished by a load instruction whose effective address is the address of an input device register. Output is accomplished by a store instruction whose effective address is the address of an output device register. For example, in state 29 of Figure C.2, if the address in MAR is xF401, MDR is supplied by the KBDR, and the data input will be the last keyboard character typed. On the other hand, if the address in MAR is a legitimate memory address, MDR is supplied by the memory.

The state machine of Figure C.2 does not have to be altered to accommodate memory-mapped I/O. However, something has to control when memory is being accessed and when I/O device registers are being accessed. This is the job of the address control logic shown in Figure C.3.

Table C.3 is a truth table for the address control logic, showing what control signals are generated, based on (1) the contents of MAR, (2) whether memory or I/O is being accessed (MIO.EN/NO, YES), and (3) whether a load or store is requested (R.W/Read, Write). Note that, for a memory-mapped load, data can be supplied to MDR by memory, KBDR, KBSR, or CRTSR. The address control logic provides the appropriate select signals to the IN.MUX. For a memory-mapped store, the data supplied by MDR can be written to memory, KBSR, CRTDR, or CRTSR. The address control logic supplies the appropriate enable signal to the corresponding structure.

C.6   INTERRUPT CONTROL

The final piece of the state machine to complete the LC-2 story are those states that control the initiation of an interrupt, and those states that control the return from an interrupt (the RTI instruction). Figure C.7 shows the state machine that carries out both of these processes. Figure C.8 shows the data path of Figure C.3, after adding the additional structures needed to make interrupt processing work.

Table C.3   Truth table for address control logic

MAR	MIO.EN	R.W	MEM.EN	IN.MUX	LD.KBSR	LD.CRTSR	LD.CRTDR
xF3FC	0	R	0	x	0	0	0
xF3FC	0	W	0	x	0	0	0
xF3FC	1	R	0	CRTSR	0	0	0
xF3FC	1	W	0	x	0	1	0
xF3FF	0	R	0	x	0	0	0
xF3FF	0	W	0	x	0	0	0
xF3FF	1	R	0	x	0	0	0
xF3FF	1	W	0	x	0	0	1
xF400	0	R	0	x	0	0	0
xF400	0	W	0	x	0	0	0
xF400	1	R	0	KBSR	0	0	0
xF400	1	W	0	x	1	0	0
xF401	0	R	0	x	0	0	0
xF401	0	W	0	x	0	0	0
xF401	1	R	0	KBDR	0	0	0
xF401	1	W	0	x	0	0	0
other	0	R	0	x	0	0	0
other	0	W	0	x	0	0	0
other	1	R	1	mem	0	0	0
other	1	W	1	x	0	0	0

C.6.1 Initiating an Interrupt

While a program is executing, an interrupt can be requested by some external event, such that the normal processing of instructions is preempted, and the control turns its attention to processing the interrupt. The external event requests an interrupt by asserting INT (i.e., INT = 1). Recall from Chapter 8 that the microprocessor responds to this request by initiating the interrupt. That is, it pushes the condition codes and the PC on the stack, and loads the PC with the starting address of the interrupt service routine.

The microarchitecture of the LC-2 initiates an interrupt as follows: Recall, from Figure C.2 that in state 1, while MAR is loaded with the contents of PC and PC is incremented, INT is tested.

State 1 is the only state in which the processor checks for interrupts. The reason for only testing in state 1 is straightforward: Once an LC-2 instruction starts processing, it is easier to let it finish its complete instruction cycle (FETCH, DECODE, etc.) than to interrupt it in the middle and have to keep track of how far along it was when the external device requested an interrupt (i.e., asserted INT). If INT is only tested in state 1, the current instruction cycle can be aborted early (even before the instruction has been fetched), and control directed to initiating the interrupt.

The test is enabled by the control signal INT.TEST, which is 1 in state 1, and 0 in all other states. INT.TEST and INT are two inputs to an AND gate, shown in Figure C.5. Thus, it is only in state 1 (when INT.TEST = 1), that INT = 1 will produce a 1 at the output of that AND gate. If the output of that AND gate is 1, the next state address is not 010000, corresponding to state 2, but rather is 110000, corresponding to state 42, which starts the initiation of the interrupt (see Figure C.7).

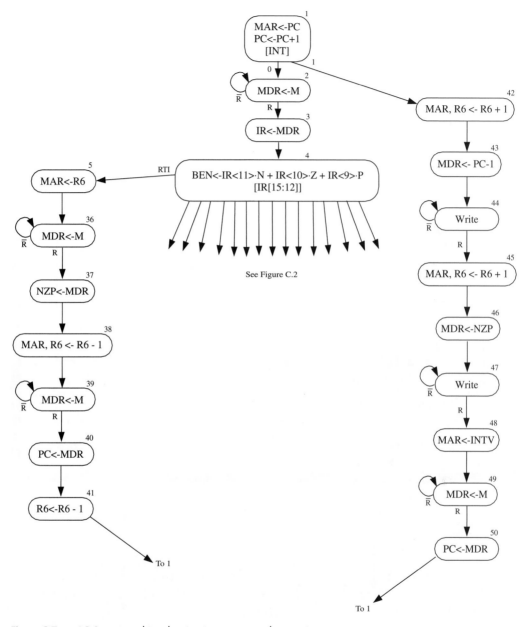

Figure C.7   LC-2 state machine showing interrupt control

In states 42, 43, and 44, the PC of the interrupted instruction is pushed on the stack. In state 42, the stack pointer is incremented (preparing for the push), and MAR is loaded with the address of the new top of the stack. In state 43, the PC is loaded into MDR. Note that state 43 says MDR is loaded with PC-1. Recall that in

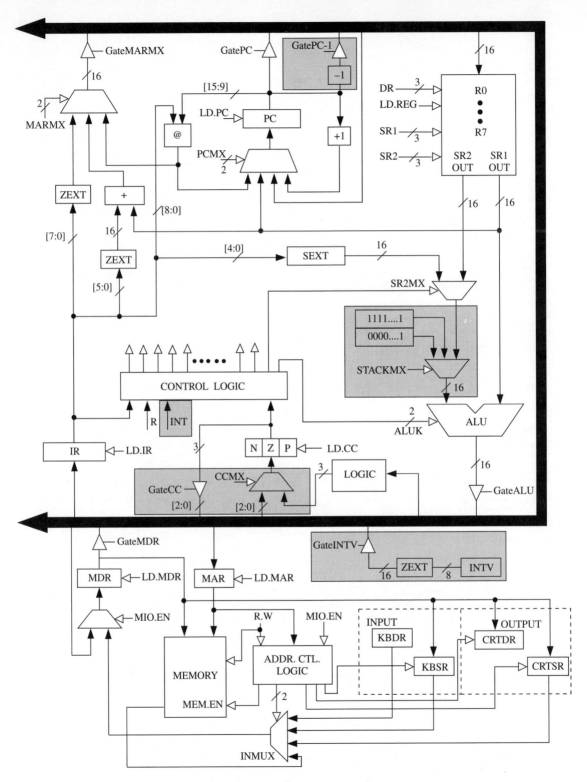

Figure C.8 LC-2 data path, including additional structures for interrupt control

state 1, at the beginning of the instruction cycle for the interrupted instruction, PC was incremented. Loading MDR with PC-1 adjusts PC to the correct address of the interrupted instruction. In state 44, the memory is enabled to WRITE (MIO.EN/YES, R.W/WR). When the write completes, signaled by R = 1, flow moves onto state 45.

In states 45, 46, and 47, the same sequence occurs, only this time, the condition codes (N, Z, and P) are pushed on the stack.

The final task to complete initiation of the interrupt is to load the PC with the starting address of the interrupt service routine. This is carried out by states 48, 49, and 50. It is accomplished in a manner similar to the loading of the PC with the starting address of a TRAP service routine. The event causing the INT request supplies an eight-bit interrupt vector, similar to the eight-bit trap vector contained in the TRAP instruction. This interrupt vector is stored in the eight-bit register INTV, shown on the data path, as in Figure C.8.

In state 48, the interrupt vector is zero-extended to 16 bits and loaded into MAR. In state 49, memory is enabled to READ. When R = 1, the read has completed and MDR contains the starting address of the interrupt service routine. In state 50, the PC is loaded with that starting address, completing the initiation of the interrupt.

C.6.2 Returning from an Interrupt, RTI

The interrupt service routine completes with the execution of the RTI instruction. The job of the RTI instruction is to restore the computer to the state it was in when the interrupt was initiated. This means restoring the values of the condition codes N, Z, P and restoring the PC. Recall that these values were pushed on the stack during the initiation of the interrupt. They must, therefore, be popped off the stack in the reverse order.

States 5, 36, and 37 restore the condition codes (NZP) to their original values. State 5 loads MAR with the address of the top of the stack. This address is contained in R6, the stack pointer. The top of the stack contains the last thing pushed (that has not been subsequently popped)—the state of the condition codes when the interrupt was initiated. In state 36, the memory is read, ending with NZP loaded into MDR. State 37 loads these condition codes into the N, Z, and P condition code registers.

States 38, 39, and 40 restore the PC to its value when the interrupt occurred. In state 38, the stack pointer is adjusted so that it points to the top of the stack after the condition codes were popped. The MAR is loaded with the address of the new top of the stack. State 39 initiates the memory READ; when the READ completes, MDR contains the address of the instruction that was to be processed next when the interrupt occurred. State 40 loads that address into the PC.

State 41 is required to adjust the stack pointer so it contains the location of the new top of the stack, after correcting for the pop of the condition codes.

C.7   CONTROL STORE

Figure C.9 completes our microprogrammed implementation of the LC-2. It shows the contents of each location of the control store, corresponding to the 39 control signals required by each state of the state machine. We have left the exact entries blank to allow you, the reader, the joy of filling in the required signals yourself. The solution is available from your instructor.

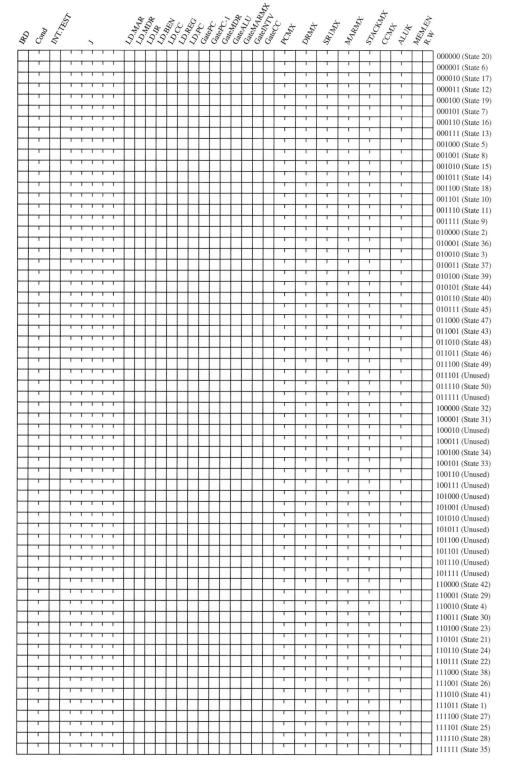

Figure C.9   Specification of the control store

D

The C Programming Language

D.1 OVERVIEW

This appendix is a C reference manual oriented toward novice C programmers. It covers a significant portion of the language, with an emphasis on the material covered in this book. Each item covered within the following eight sections contains a brief summary of a particular C feature, stated in an illustrative manner, and an example, if appropriate. The intent of this appendix is to provide a quick reference to various features of the language that may be useful during programming.

D.2 C CONVENTIONS

D.2.1 Source Files

The C programming convention is to separate programs into files of two types: source files (with the extension `.c`) and header files (with the extension `.h`). Source files, sometimes called `.c` or dot-c files, contain the C code for a group of related functions. Each `.c` file is compiled into an object file and these objects are linked together into an executable image by the linker.

D.2.2 Header Files

Header files typically never contain C statements but rather contain function, variable, and structure declarations and preprocessor macros. The programming convention is to couple a header file to the source file in which the declared items are *defined*.

For example, if the source file **stdio.c** contains the definitions for the functions **printf**, **scanf**, **getchar**, and **putchar**, then the header file **stdio.h** contains the declarations for these functions. If one of these functions is called from another .c file, then the **stdio.h** header file should be **include**d to get the proper function definitions.

D.2.3   Comments

In C, comments begin with the two character delimiter **/*** and end with ***/**. Comments within comments are not legal. Comments within strings or character literals are not recognized as comments. Comments can span multiple lines.

D.2.4   Literals

Several types of literal values can appear within a program. The type (see D.3.2) of such a value is inferred by the syntax used to express it.

Integer   Integer literal constants can be expressed either in decimal, octal, or hexadecimal notation. If the literal is prefixed by a **0** (zero), it will be interpreted as an octal number. If the literal begins with a **0x**, it will be interpreted as hexadecimal (thus it can consist of the digits **0** through **9** and the characters *a* through *f*. Uppercase *A* through *F* can be used as well). An unprefixed literal (i.e., it doesn't begin with a **0** or **0x**) indicates it is in decimal notation. All forms can be preceded by a minus sign - to indicate a negative value.

An integer literal can also be suffixed with the letter *l* or *L* to indicate that it is of type **long int**. An integer literal suffixed with the letter *u* or *U* indicated an unsigned value. Refer to D.3.3 for **long** and **unsigned** types.

The first three examples below express the same number, 87. The two last versions express it as an **unsigned int** value and as a **long int** value.

```
87
0x57
0127
-24      /* -24 in decimal */
-024     /* -20 in octal */
-0x24    /* -36 in hexadecimal */
87U
87L
```

Floating Point   Floating point literals consists of three parts: an integer part, a decimal point, and a fractional part. The fractional part and integer part are optional, but one of the two must be present. The number preceded by a minus sign indicates a negative value. Several examples are given below.

```
1.613123
.613123
1.         /* expresses the number 1.0 */
-.613123
```

Floating-point literals can also be expressed in exponential notation. The preceding form described is followed by an *e* or *E*. The *e* or *E* signals the beginning of the integer (optionally, signed) exponent, which is the power of 10 by which the part preceding the exponent is multiplied. The exponent is obviously optional (see the previous examples), and if used, then the decimal point is optional. Examples are given below:

```
6.023e23        /* 6.023 * 10^23      */
454.323e-22     /* 454.323 * 10^(-22) */
5e13            /* 5.0 * 10^13         */
```

By default, a floating-point type is a **double** or double-precision floating-point number, but this can be modified with an optional suffix. The suffix *f* or *F* indicates a **float** or single-precision floating-point number. The suffix *l* or *L* indicates a **long double** (See D.3.3).

Character   A character literal can be expressed by surrounding a particular character by single quotes, e.g., `'c'`. This converts the character into the internal character code used by the computer, which for most computers, including the LC-2, is ASCII.

Table D.1 lists special characters. Since they typically cannot be expressed with a single keystroke, the C programming language provides a means to state them via a sequence of characters. The last two forms, octal and hexadecimal, specify ways of stating an arbitrary character by using its code value, stated either octal or hex. For example, the character 'S', which has the ASCII value of 83 (decimal), can be stated as '\0123' or '\x53'.

String Literals   A string literal within a C program must be enclosed within double quote characters, **"**. String literals have the type **char** ***** and space for them is allocated in a special section of the address space reserved for literal constant values. The termination character `'\0'` is automatically added by the compiler. The following are two examples of string literals:

```
char greeting[10] = "bon jour!";
printf("This is a string literal");
```

Table D.1   Special characters in C

Character	Sequence
newline	\n
horizontal tab	\t
vertical tab	\v
backspace	\b
carriage return	\r
formfeed	\f
audible alert	\a
backslash \	\\
question mark ?	\?
single quote '	\'
double quote "	\"
octal number	\0nnn
hexadecimal number	\xnnn

D.2.5   Formatting

C is a freely formatted language. The programmer is free to add spaces, tabs, carriage returns, new lines between and within statements and declarations. This feature allows the programmer to adopt a style for coding in C, which can be helpful for making the code more readable. See 11.5.2 for more information on conventional code formatting styles.

D.2.6   Keywords

The following list is a set of reserved words which have special meaning within the C language.

```
auto        double      int         struct
break       else        long        switch
case        enum        register    typedef
char        extern      return      union
const       float       short       unsigned
continue    for         signed      void
default     goto        sizeof      volatile
do          if          static      while
```

D.3   IDENTIFIERS, TYPES, AND DECLARATIONS

D.3.1   Identifiers

A programmer can supply names for various items within a program: variables, functions, members of structures, are a few common examples. In C, identifiers can consist of letters, numbers, and the underscore character _. Uppercase letters are different from lowercase, so the identifier **sum** is different from **Sum**. There are two restrictions, however: the first character of an identifier cannot be a digit and only the first 31 characters of an identifier's name are used by the compiler to distinguish one identifier from another. Identifiers must be different from any of the C keywords (See D.2.6).

Several examples of legal identifiers follow. Each is a distinct identifier.

```
red
Blue
__green__
primary_colors
primaryColors
```

See Section 12.2 for more information.

D.3.2   Basic Data Types

In C, all identifiers and expressions (see Section D.6.1) have a type associated with them. The type indicates how the data referenced by the identifier or the value generated by the expression is to be interpreted. For instance, if the variable **kappa** is of type **int**, then the value (which is essentially just a bit pattern) referred to by **kappa** will be interpreted as a signed integer.

There are several predefined basic types within the C language: **int**, **float**, **double**, **char**. They exist automatically within all implementations of C, though their sizes and range of values depends upon the computer system being used.

Int   The binary value of something of **int** type will be interpreted as a signed whole number. Typical computers use 32 bits to represent signed integers, expressed in 2's complement form. Such integers would have the range $+2,147,483,647$ and $-2,147,483,648$.

Float   Objects declared of type **float** represent single-precision floating numbers. These numbers typically, but not always, follow the representations defined by the IEEE standard for floating-point arithmetic. See Section 2.7.1.

double   Objects declared of type **double** deal with double-precision floating numbers. Like objects of type **float**, objects of type **double** are also typically represented using the IEEE standard. The precise difference between objects of type **float** and of type **double** depends on the particular system being used; however the ANSI C standard specifies that the precision of a **double** should never be less than that of a **float**.

char   Objects of character type contain a single character, expressed in the character code used by the computer system. Typical computer systems use the ASCII character code. The size of a **char** is large enough to store a character from character set. C also imposes that the size of a **short int** must be at least the size of a **char**.

Collectively, the **int** and **char** types are referred to as integral types, whereas **float** and **double** are floating types.

See Section 12.2.1 for more information on these basic types.

Enumerated Types   C provides a way for the programmer to specify objects that take on symbolic values. For example, we may want to create a type that takes on one of four values: **Penguin**, **Riddler**, **CatWoman**, **Joker**. We can do so by using an enumerated type, as follows:

```
enum { Penguin, Riddler, CatWoman, Joker } villain;
```

The variable **villain** can take on those four symbolic values. The four symbolic values are called *enumeration constants*.

D.3.3   Type Qualifiers

The basic types can be slightly modified with the use of a type qualifier.

`signed, unsigned`   The integral types `int` and `char` can be modified with the use of the `signed` and `unsigned` qualifiers. By default, integers are signed; the default on characters depends on the particular computer system.

For example, if a particular computer uses 32-bit 2's complement signed integers, then a `signed int` can have any value in the range $+2,147,483,647$ and $-2,147,483,648$. On the same machine, an `unsigned int` can have a value in the range $+4,294,967,295$ and 0.

```
signed int c;       /* the signed modifier is redundant */
unsigned int d;

signed char j;      /* forces the char to be interpreted
                       as a signed value */

unsigned char k;    /* the char will be interpreted as an
                       unsigned number */
```

`long, short`   The qualifiers `long` and `short` allow the programmer to manipulate the physical size of an integer. Important to note is that there is no strict definition of how much larger one type of integer is than another. The C language states only that the size of a `short int` is less than or equal to the size of an `int`, which is less than or equal to the size of a `long int`. Stated more completely and precisely:

```
sizeof(char) <= sizeof(short int) <= sizeof(int) <= sizeof(long int)
```

Several new machines (particularly, machines that support 64-bit data types) make a distinction on the `long` qualifier. To check out the ranges of a particular computer, examine the standard header file `<limits.h>`. On most UNIX systems, it will be in the `/usr/include` directory. Here are several examples:

```
short int q;
long int p;
unsigned long int r;
```

The qualifier can also be used with the floating-type `double` to create a floating-point number with higher precision or larger range (if such a type is available on the particular computer) than a `double`. As stated by the ANSI C specification: the size of a `float` is less than or equal to the size of a `double`, which is less than or equal to the size of a `long double`.

```
double x;
long double y;
```

`const`   A value that does not change through the course of execution can be qualified with the `const` qualifier. For example,

```
const double pi = 3.14159;
```

The base address of an array is a `const` value. For example, if an array is declared with the declaration `int vector[100]`, then the identifier `vector` is of type `const int *`.

D.3.4   Storage Class

Variables can also have a storage class qualifier that directs the compiler where (if at all) storage for a particular item should be allocated. By default (i.e., if no storage class qualifier is specified), variables declared within functions are allocated on the stack (see Section 14.5.1); they are given *automatic* storage class by default. Variables declared globally are allocated to the global data section.

Variables declared within a function can be qualified with the `static` qualifier to indicate that they are to be allocated with other static variables, allowing their value to persist across invocations of the function in which they are declared. For example,

```
int count(int x)
{
  static int y;

  y++;
  printf("This function has been called %d times.", y);
}
```

The value of `y` will not be lost when the activation record of `count` is popped off the stack because its storage is allocated in the global data section. Every call of the function `count` updates the value of `y`.

The initial value of data items in the *static* class are guaranteed to be zero. This is not true for data items in the automatic class; they must be initialized by the programmer.

There is a special qualifier called `register` that can be applied to data items in the automatic class. This qualifier provides a hint to the compiler that the value is frequently accessed within the code, suggesting that allocation within a register may enhance performance. The compiler, however, is not bound to allocate it in a register.

Functions, as well as variables, can be qualified with the qualifier `extern`. This qualifier indicates that the function's or variable's storage is defined in another object module which will be linked together with the current module when the executable is constructed. By default, all global variables are qualified as `extern`'s.

D.3.5   Derived Types

Using the basic types as elements, different types of derived types can also be constructed within C. These derived types include pointers, arrays, and structures.

Arrays A variable declared as an array indicates that the variable exists as a contiguous sequence of values, which are individually accessible using an integer index. The elements of an array are numbered starting at 0. The size of the array, that is, the number of elements it contains, must be stated when the array is declared.

```
char string[100]; /* Declares array of 100 characters */
int  data[20];    /* Declares array of 20 integers */
```

To access a particular element within an array, an index is formed using an integer expression (see Section D.6.1) within square brackets, [ ].

```
data[0]     /* Accesses first element of array data */
data[i+3]   /* The variable i must be an integer */
string[x+y] /* x and y must be integers */
```

The compiler does not check (nor does it generate code to check) if the value of the index falls within the bounds of the array but blindly generates the machine code to make the access. The responsibility of ensuring proper access to the array is upon the programmer. See Section 17.3 for more information on arrays.

Pointers Pointers are data items that are addresses of other data items. Pointer types are declared by prefixing an identifier with an asterisk, *. The type of a pointer indicates the type of the data item being pointed to by the pointer. For example,

```
        int *v;   /* v points to an integer */
```

See Section 17.2 for more information on pointers.

C allows a restricted set of operations to be used on pointers. Pointers can be manipulated in expression, thus allowing "pointer arithmetic" to be performed. C allows assigment between pointers of the same type, or assignment, of a pointer to 0. Integer values can be added to or subtracted from a pointer value. Also, pointers of the same type can be compared (using the relational operators) or subtracted from one another, but this is meaningful only if the pointers involved point to elements of the same array. All other pointer manipulations are not explicitly allowed in C but can be done with the appropriate casting.

D.3.6 Structures

Structures are groups of data items treated as a single entity. The programmer can specify and name the data items that compose a structure using the following syntax for a structure declaration:

```
        struct tag_id {
          type1 member1;
          type2 member2;
          :
          :
          typeN memberN;
        };
```

This structure has member elements named **member1** of type **type1**, **member2** of **type2**, up to **memberN** of **typeN**. The structure is given an optional tag **tag_id**. Variables of this structure type can be declared using this tag.

```
struct tag_id x;
```

This declaration allocates storage for the structure variable **x**. This variable has all the members defined when the structure is declared. For example,

```
struct point {
  int x;
  int y;
};

/* declares an array of structure type variables */
struct point function[100];
```

See Section 19.2 for more information on structures.

D.4 DECLARATIONS

In C, variables must be declared before they can be used. Function declarations are optional. Declarations inform the compiler of characteristics (e.g., its type, storage class, etc.) of the data item so that correct machine code can be generated whenever the data item is used.

D.4.1 Variable Declarations

The format for a variable declaration is as follows:

```
[storage_class] [type_qualifier] {type} {identifier} [ = initializer];
```

The curly braces { } indicate items which are required and the square brackets [ ] indicate optional items.

The initializer for variables of automatic storage (see D.3.4) can be any expression which uses previously defined values. For variables of the static class or external variables, the initializer must be a constant expression.

Also, multiple identifiers (and initializers) can be placed on the same line, creating multiple variables of the same type, having the same storage class and type qualities.

```
static long unsigned int k = 10UL;
register char l = 'Q';
int list[100];
struct node_type n;
```
Example D.1

Declarations can be placed at the beginning of any *block* (see D.6.2), before any statements. Such declarations are visible only within the block in which they appear. Declarations can also appear at the outermost level of the program, outside of all functions. Such declarations are globally visible, that is, visible from all parts of the program. See Section 12.2 for more information on variable declarations.

D.4.2   Function Declarations

A function's declaration informs the compiler about the type of value returned by the function and the type, number, and order of arguments the function expects to receive from its caller. The format for a function declaration is as follows:

```
{type} {function_id}([type1] [, type2], ...[, typeN]);
```

The curly braces `{ }` indicate items that are required and the square brackets `[ ]` indicate items that are used if appropriate.

The *type* indicates the type of the value returned by the function and can be of any basic type (see D.2.3) or derived type (see D.3.5). If a function does not return a value, then its type must be declared as **void**.

The **function_id** can be any legal identifier that has not already been defined.

Enclosed within parentheses following the **function_id** are the types of each of the arguments expected by the function, indicated by **type1**, **type2**, **typeN**, each separated by a comma. Optionally, an identifier can be supplied for each argument, indicating what the particular argument will be called within the function's definition. For example, this is a function declaration for a function that returns the arithmetic average of an array of integers:

```
int average(int numbers[], int how_many);
```

See Section 14.3.1 for more information on function declarations.

D.4.3   Typedef

The C facility for providing a programmer-defined name for a type is called **typedef**. It has the general form

```
typedef type name;
```

Here, **type** can be any type, supported or derived. The identifier **name** can be any legal identifier. The **typedef** declaration is an important feature for enhancing code readability; a well-chosen type name conveys additional information about the object declared of that type. Following are two examples.

| | Example D.2 |

```
typedef enum {DaimlerChrysler, Ford, GM, Honda, Toyota} TheBigFive;

typedef struct {
            int xCoord;
            int yCoord;
            int color;
        } Pixel;

Pixel bitmap[1024*820];
TheBigFive carCompany;
```

D.5 OPERATORS

In this section, each of the C operators are presented, grouped by the kind of operation they perform. Within the tables is a precedence class for each operator, numbered from 1 to 18. Operators within lower numbered classes have higher precedence than operators within higher numbered classes. Within the same precedence class, operators associate left to right or right to left, as indicated by the associativity column. For example, the addition operator + and subtraction operator - are in the same class (7) and are grouped left to right. So for the expression $x - y + z$, the subtraction is performed first.

Also included for each operator is a reference to the text where a description of the operation it performs and the types of values it expects can be found.

D.5.1 Assignment Operator

Table D.2 The assignment operator

Operator Symbol	Operation	Example Usage	Precedence	Associativity	See Section
=	assignment	x = y	18	r-to-l	12.3.2

D.5.2   Arithmetic Operators

Table D.3   Arithmetic operators in C

Operator Symbol	Operation	Example Usage	Precedence	Associativity	See Section
+	positive	+x	4	r-to-l	12.3.3
-	negative	-x	4	r-to-l	12.3.3
+	addition	x + y	7	l-to-r	12.3.3
-	subtraction	x - y	7	l-to-r	12.3.3
*	multiplication	x * y	6	l-to-r	12.3.3
/	division	x / y	6	l-to-r	12.3.3
%	modulus	x % y	6	l-to-r	12.3.3

D.5.3   Bitwise Operators

Table D.4   Bitwise operators in C

Operator Symbol	Operation	Example Usage	Precedence	Associativity	See Section
&	bitwise AND	x & y	11	l-to-r	12.3.5
|	bitwise OR	x | y	13	l-to-r	12.3.5
~	bitwise NOT	~x	4	r-to-l	12.3.5
^	bitwise XOR	x ^ y	12	l-to-r	12.3.5
<<	left shift	x << y	8	l-to-r	12.3.5
>>	right shift	x >> y	8	l-to-r	12.3.5

D.5.4   Logical Operators

Table D.5   Logical operators in C

Operator Symbol	Operation	Example Usage	Precedence	Associativity	See Section
&&	logical AND	x && y	14	l-to-r	12.3.6
||	logical OR	x || y	15	l-to-r	12.3.6
!	logical NOT	!x	4	r-to-l	12.3.6

D.5.5 Relational Operators

Table D.6   Relational operators in C

Operator Symbol	Operation	Example Usage	Precedence	Associativity	See Section
==	equal	x == y	10	l-to-r	12.3.7
!=	not equal	x != y	10	l-to-r	12.3.7
>	greater than	x > y	9	l-to-r	12.3.7
>=	greater than or equal	x >= y	9	l-to-r	12.3.7
<	less than	x < y	9	l-to-r	12.3.7
<=	less than or equal	x <= y	9	l-to-r	12.3.7

D.5.6 Special Operators

Table D.7   Special operators in C

Operator Symbol	Operation	Example Usage	Precedence	Associativity	See Section
++	preincrement	++x	3	r-to-l	12.3.9
++	postincrement	x++	2	r-to-l	12.3.9
++	predecrement	--x	3	r-to-l	12.3.9
++	postdecrement	x--	2	r-to-l	12.3.9
+=	add and assign	x += y	18	l-to-r	12.3.9
-=	subtract and assign	x -= y	18	l-to-r	12.3.9
*=	multiply and assign	x *= y	18	l-to-r	12.3.9
/=	divide and assign	x /= y	18	l-to-r	12.3.9
%=	modulus and assign	x %= y	18	l-to-r	12.3.9
&=	and and assign	x &= y	18	l-to-r	12.3.9
|=	or and assign	x |= y	18	l-to-r	12.3.9
^=	xor and assign	x ^= y	18	l-to-r	12.3.9
<<=	left shift and assign	x <<= y	18	l-to-r	12.3.9
>>=	right shift and assign	x >>= y	18	l-to-r	12.3.9

D.5.7 Conditional Expression

Table D.8   Conditional expressions in C

Operator Symbol	Operation	Example Usage	Precedence	Associativity	See Section
? :	conditional expression	x ? y : z	17	l-to-r	12.3.9

D.5.8 Pointer, Array, Structure Operators

Table D.9   Pointer, array, structure operators in C

Operator Symbol	Operation	Example Usage	Precedence	Associativity	See Section
*	indirection	*x	4	r-to-l	17.2.2
&	address of	&x	4	r-to-l	17.2.2
[]	array reference	x[i]	1	l-to-r	17.3.1
.	structure member operator	x.y	1	l-to-r	19.2.1
->	structure pointer operator	p->y	1	l-to-r	19.2.1

D.5.9 Miscellaneous Operators

Table D.10   Miscellaneous operators C

Operator Symbol	Operation	Example Usage	Precedence	Associativity	See Section
sizeof	size of data item in bytes	sizeof(x)	4	r-to-l	19.3
(type_name)	cast	(int)	5	r-to-l	19.3

D.5.10 Precedence

Table D.11   Operator precedence, highest to lowest

Precedence Group	Associativity	Operators
1	l-to-r	*function call* () [ ] . ->
2	r-to-l	*postincrement* ++ *postdecrement* - -
3	r-to-l	*preincrement* ++ *predecrement* - -
4	r-to-l	*indirection* * *address* & *unary* + *unary* - ~ ! sizeof
5	r-to-l	*cast* (type)
6	l-to-r	*multiply* * / %
7	l-to-r	+ -
8	l-to-r	<< >>
10	l-to-r	< > <= >=
11	l-to-r	== !=
12	l-to-r	&
13	l-to-r	^
14	l-to-r		
15	l-to-r	&&
16	l-to-r	||
17	l-to-r	?:
18	r-to-l	= += -= *= etc.

D.6   EXPRESSIONS AND STATEMENTS

D.6.1   Expressions

An expression is any legal combination of constants, variables, operators, and function calls. An expression has an associated type, which is determined according to C typing rules. If all the elements of an expression are **int** types, then the expression is of **int** type. Below are several examples of expressions:

```
a * a + b * b
a++ - c / 3
a <= 4
q || integrate(x)
```

Example D.3

See Section 12.3 for more information on expressions.

D.6.2   Statements

In C, simple statements are expressions terminated by a semicolon, **;**. Typically, statements modify a variable or have some other side effect when the expression is evaluated.

```
c = a * a + b * b;    /* Two simple statements */
b = a++ - c / 3;
```

Related statements can be grouped together into a compound statement, or *block*, by surrounding them with curly braces **{ }**. Syntactically, the compound statement is the same as a simple statement, and they can be used interchangeably.

```
{                     /* One compound statement */
  c = a * a + b * b;
  b = a++ - c / 3;
}
```

See Section 12.3 for more information on statements.

D.7   CONTROL FLOW

D.7.1   If

An **if** statement has the format

```
if (expression)
    statement
```

If the **expression**, which can be of any basic (see D.3.2) or pointer type, evaluates to a nonzero value, then the **statement**, which can be a compound statement, is executed.

Example D.4

```
if (x < 0)
    a = b + c; /* Executes if x is less than zero */
```

See Section 13.1.1 for more examples of **if** statements.

D.7.2 If-else

An **if-else** statement has the format

```
if (expression)
    statement1
else
    statement2
```

If the **expression**, which can be of any basic (see D.3.2) or pointer type, evaluates to a nonzero value, then **statement1**, is executed. Otherwise, **statement2** is executed. Both **statement1** and **statement2** can be compound statements.

Example D.5

```
if (x < 0)
    a = b + c; /* Executes if x is less than zero */
else
    a = b - c; /* otherwise, this is executed. */
```

See Section 13.1.2 for more examples of **if-else** statements.

D.7.3 Switch

A **switch** statement has the following format:

```
switch(expression) {
case const-expr1:
    statement1A
    statement1B
    :

case const-expr2:
    statement2A
    statement2B
    :
```

```
        :
        :

case const-exprN:
    statementNA
    statementNB
        :

}
```

A **switch** statement is composed of an **expression**, which must be of integral type (See Section D.3.2), followed by compound statement (though it is not required to be compound, it almost always is). Within the compound statement exist one or more **case** labels, each with an associated constant integral expression, called **const-expr1**, **const-expr2**, **const-exprN** in the preceding example. Within a **switch**, each **case** label must be different.

When a **switch** is encountered, the controlling **expression** is evaluated. If one of the case labels matches the value of **expression**, then control jumps to the statement which follows and proceeds from there.

The special case label **default** can be used to catch the situation where none of the other case labels match. If the **default** case is not present and none of the labels match the value of the controlling expression, then no statements within the **switch** are executed.

```
char k;
```
                                                    Example D.6
```
k = getchar();
switch (k) {
case '+':
  a = b + c;
  break;        /* break causes control to leave switch */

case '-':
  a = b - c;
  break;

case '*':
  a = b * c;
  break;

case '/':
  a = b / c;
  break;
}
```

See Section 13.1.3 for more examples of **switch** statements.

D.7.4 While

A **while** statement has the following format:

while (expression)
    statement

The **while** statement is an iteration construct. If the value of **expression** evaluates to nonzero, then **statement** is executed. Control does not pass to the subsequent statement, but rather **expression** is evaluated again and the process is repeated. This continues until **expression** evaluates to 0, in which case control passes to the next statement.

Example D.7

```
x = 0;
while (x < 100) {
    printf("x = %d\n", x);
    x = x + 1;
}
```

See Section 13.2.1 for more examples of **while** statements.

D.7.5 For

A **for** statement has the following format:

for (initializer; term-expr; re-initializer)
    statement

The **for** statement is an iteration construct. The **initializer**, which is an expression, is evaluated only once, before the **loop** begins. The **term-expr** is an expression which is evaluated before each iteration of the loop. If the **term-expr** evaluates to nonzero, the loop progresses, otherwise the loop terminates and control passes to the next statement. Each iteration of the loop consists of the execution of the **statement** which makes up the loop body and the evaluation of the **reinitializer** expression.

Example D.8

```
for (x = 0; x < 100; x++) {
    printf("x = %d\n", x);
}
```

See Section 13.2.2 for more examples of **for** statements.

D.7.6 `Do-while`

A **do-while** statement has the format

```
do
    statement
while (expression);
```

The **do-while** statement is an iteration construct similar to the **while** statement. When a **do-while** is first encountered, the **statement** that makes up the loop body is executed first, then the **expression** to determine whether to execute another iteration is evaluated. If it is nonzero, then another iteration is made and **statement** is executed again. In this manner, a **do-while** always executes its loop body at least once.

```
x = 0;
do {
    printf("x = %d\n", x);
    x = x + 1;
}
while (x < 100);
```

Example D.9

See Section 13.2.3 for more examples of **do-while** statements.

D.7.7 `Break`

A **break** statement has the format

```
break;
```

The **break** statement may only be used in an iteration statement or in a **switch** statement. It passes control out of the smallest statement containing it to the statement immediately following. Typically, **break** is used to exit a loop before the terminating condition is encountered.

```
for (x = 0; x < 100; x++) {
    :
    :
    if (error)
        break;
    :
    :
}
```

Example D.10

See Section 13.2.4 for more examples of **break** statements.

D.7.8 Continue

A **continue** statement has the following format:

```
continue;
```

The **continue** statement can be used only in an iteration statement. It prematurely terminates the execution of the loop body statement of the loop, that is, it terminates the current iteration of the loop. The looping expression is evaluated to determine whether another iteration should be performed. In a **for** loop the **reinitializer** is also evaluated.

Example D.11

```
for (x = 0; x < 100; x++) {
    :
    :
    if (skip)
        continue;
    :
    :
}
```

See Section 13.2.4 for more examples of **continue** statements.

D.7.9 Return

A **return** statement has the format

```
return expression;
```

The **return** statement causes control to return to the current caller function, that is, the function which called the function which contains the **return** statement. The **expression** that follows the **return** is necessary for functions which return values. The value it evaluates to is returned to the caller function.

Example D.12

```
return x + y;
```

See Section 14.3.4 for more examples of **return** statements.

D.8   STANDARD LIBRARY FUNCTIONS

The ANSI C standard library contains over 150 functions that perform a variety of useful tasks (for example, I/O and dynamic memory allocation) on behalf of your program. Every installation of ANSI C will have these functions available, so even if you make use of these functions, your program will still be portable from one ANSI C platform to another. In this section, we will describe some useful standard library functions.

D.8.1   I/O Functions

The **<stdio.h>** header file must be included in any source file that contains calls to the standard I/O functions. Below we have provided a small sample of these functions.

getchar   This function has the following declaration:

$$\text{int getchar(void);}$$

The function **getchar** reads the next character from the standard input device, or **stdin**. The value of this character is returned (as an integer) as the return value.

The behavior of **getchar** is very similar to the LC-2 input TRAP (except no input banner is displayed on the screen).

Most computer systems will implement **getchar** using buffered I/O. This means that keystrokes (assuming standard input is coming from the keyboard) will be buffered by the operating system until the Enter key is pressed. Once Enter is pressed, the entire line of characters is added to the standard input stream.

putchar   This function has the following declaration:

$$\text{void putchar(int c);}$$

The function **putchar** takes an integer value representing an ASCII character and puts the character to the standard output stream. This is similar to the LC-2 TRAP OUT.

If the standard output stream is the monitor, the character will appear on the screen. However, since many systems buffer the output stream, the character may not appear until the system's output buffer is *flushed*, which is usually done once a newline appears in the output stream.

scanf   This function has the following declaration:

$$\text{int scanf(const char *formatString, *ptr1, ...);}$$

The function **scanf** is passed a format string (which is passed as pointer to the initial character) and a list of pointers. The format string contains format specifications that control how **scanf** will interpret fields in the input stream. For example the specification **%d** causes **scanf** to interpret the next sequence of nonwhite space characters as a decimal number. This decimal is converted from ASCII into an integer value and assigned to the variable pointed to by the next pointer in the parameter list. The number of pointers that follow the format string in the parameter list should correspond to the number of format specifications in the format string. The value returned by **scanf** corresponds to the number of variables that were successfully assigned. For a detailed description of **scanf**, refer to section 18.4.2.

printf   This function has the following declaration:

```
int printf(const char *formatString, ...);
```

The function **printf** writes the format string (passed as a pointer to the initial character) to the standard output stream. If the format string contains a format specification, then **printf** will interpret the next parameter in the parameter list as indicated by the specification, and embed the interpreted value into the output stream. For example, the format specification **%d** will cause **printf** to interpret the next parameter as a decimal value. **printf** will write the resulting digits into the output stream. In general, the number of values following the format string on the parameter list should correspond to the number of format specifications in the format string. **printf** returns the number of characters written to the output stream. However, if an error occurs, a negative value is returned. For a detailed description of **printf**, refer to section 18.4.1.

D.8.2   String Functions

The C standard library contains around 15 functions that perform operations on strings (that is, null-terminated arrays of characters). To use the string functions from within a program, include the **<string.h>** header file in each source file that contains a call to a library string function. In this section, we describe two examples of C string functions.

strcmp   This function has the following declaration:

```
int strcmp(char *stringA, char *stringB);
```

This function compares **stringA** with **stringB**. It returns a 0 if they are equal. It returns a value greater than 0 if **stringA** is lexicographically greater than **stringB** (lexicographically greater means that **stringA** occurs later in a dictionary than **stringB**). It returns a value less than 0 if **stringA** is lexicographically less than **stringB**.

strcpy   This function has the following declaration:

```
char *strcpy(char *stringA, char *stringB);
```

This function copies **stringB** to **stringA**. It copies every character in **stringB** up to and including the null character. The function returns a pointer to **stringA** if no errors occurred.

D.8.3 Math Functions

The C standard math functions perform commonly used mathematical operations. Using them requires including the **<math.h>** header file. In this section, we list a small sample of C math functions. Each of the listed functions take as parameters values of type **double**, and each returns a value of type **double**.

```
double sin(double x);   /* sine of x, expressed in radians   */
double cos(double x);   /* cosine of x, expressed in radians */
double tan(double x);   /* tan of x, expressed in radians    */
double exp(double x);   /* exponential function,  e^x        */
double log(double x);   /* natural log of x                  */
double sqrt(double x);  /* square root of x                  */
double pow(double x, double y)  /* x^y -- x to the y power   */
```

D.8.4 Utility Functions

The C library contains a set of functions that perform useful tasks such as memory allocation, data conversion, sorting, and other miscellaneous things. The common header file for these functions is **<stdlib.h>**.

malloc   As described in Section 19.3, the function **malloc** allocates a fixed-sized chunk from memory.

This function has the following declaration:

$$\text{void *malloc(size\_t size);}$$

The input parameter is the number of bytes to be allocated. The parameter is of type **size_t**, which is the same type returned by the **sizeof** operator (very often, this type is **typedef**ed as an unsigned integer). If the memory allocation goes successfully, a pointer to the allocated region of memory is returned. If the request cannot be satisfied, the value **NULL** is returned.

free   This function has the following declaration:

$$\text{void free(void *ptr);}$$

This function returns to the heap a previously allocated chunk of memory pointed to by the parameter. In other words, **free** deallocates memory pointed to by **ptr**. The value passed to **free** must be a pointer to a previously allocated region of memory, otherwise errors could occur.

rand and srand   The C standard utility functions contain a function to generate a sequence of random numbers. The function is called **rand**. It does not generate a truly random sequence, however. Instead, it generates the same sequence of varying values based on an initial *seed* value. When the seed is changed, a different sequence is generated. For example, when seeded with the value 10, the generator will always generate the same sequence of numbers. However, this sequence will be different than the sequence generated by another seed value.

The function **rand** has the following declaration:

```
int rand(void)
```

It returns a pseudo-random integer in the range 0 to **RAND_MAX**, which is at least 32,767.

To seed the pseudo-random number generator, use the function **srand**. This function has the following declaration:

```
void srand(unsigned int seed);
```

E

Useful Tables

E.1 CONVERSION SPECIFICATIONS FOR C I/O

Table E.1 `printf` conversion specifications

`printf` Conversions	Printed as
`%d`, `%i`	signed decimal
`%o`	octal
`%x`, `%X`	hexadecimal (a-f or A-F)
`%u`	unsigned decimal
`%c`	single char
`%s`	string, terminated by \0
`%f`	floating point in decimal notation
`%e`, `%E`	floating point in exponential notation
`%p`	pointer

Table E.2 `scanf` conversion specifications

`scanf` Conversions	Parameter Type
`%d`	signed decimal
`%i`	decimal, octal (leading `0`), hex (leading `0x or 0X`)
`%o`	octal
`%x`	hexadecimal
`%u`	unsigned decimal
`%c`	char
`%s`	string of nonwhite space characters, \0 added
`%f`, `%e`	floating point number

E.2 ASCII CODES

Table E.3 ASCII values represented in decimal

Character	ASCII Dec	Hex	Character	ASCII Dec	Hex	Character	ASCII Dec	Hex	Character	ASCII Dec	Hex
nul	0	00	sp	32	20	@	64	40	`	96	60
soh	1	01	!	33	21	A	65	41	a	97	61
stx	2	02	"	34	22	B	66	42	b	98	62
etx	3	03	#	35	23	C	67	43	c	99	63
eot	4	04	$	36	24	D	68	44	d	100	64
enq	5	05	%	37	25	E	69	45	e	101	65
ack	6	06	&	38	26	F	70	46	f	102	66
bel	7	07	'	39	27	G	71	47	g	103	67
bs	8	08	(	40	28	H	72	48	h	104	68
ht	9	09	)	41	29	I	73	49	i	105	69
lf	10	0A	*	42	2A	J	74	4A	j	106	6A
vt	11	0B	+	43	2B	K	75	4B	k	107	6B
ff	12	0C	,	44	2C	L	76	4C	l	108	6C
cr	13	0D	-	45	2D	M	77	4D	m	109	6D
so	14	0E	.	46	2E	N	78	4E	n	110	6E
si	15	0F	/	47	2F	O	79	4F	o	111	6F
dle	16	10	0	48	30	P	80	50	p	112	70
dc1	17	11	1	49	31	Q	81	51	q	113	71
dc2	18	12	2	50	32	R	82	52	r	114	72
dc3	19	13	3	51	33	S	83	53	s	115	73
dc4	20	14	4	52	34	T	84	54	t	116	74
nak	21	15	5	53	35	U	85	55	u	117	75
syn	22	16	6	54	36	V	86	56	v	118	76
etb	23	17	7	55	37	W	87	57	w	119	77
can	24	18	8	56	38	X	88	58	x	120	78
em	25	19	9	57	39	Y	89	59	y	121	79
sub	26	1A	:	58	3A	Z	90	5A	z	122	7A
esc	27	1B	;	59	3B	[	91	5B	{	123	7B
fs	28	1C	<	60	3C	\	92	5C	|	124	7C
gs	29	1D	=	61	3D	]	93	5D	}	125	7D
rs	30	1E	>	62	3E	^	94	5E	~	126	7E
us	31	1F	?	63	3F	_	95	5F	del	127	7F

E.3   COMMONLY USED NUMERICAL PREFIXES

Table E.4   Numerical Prefixes

Amount	Commonly Used Base-2 Approx.	Prefix	Abbreviation	Derived from
10^{24}	2^{80}	yotta	Y	Greek for eight: *okto*
10^{21}	2^{70}	zetta	Z	Greek for seven: *hepta*
10^{18}	2^{60}	exa	E	Greek for six: *hexa*
10^{15}	2^{50}	peta	P	Greek for five: *pente*
10^{12}	2^{40}	tera	T	Greek for monster: *teras*
10^{9}	2^{30}	giga	G	Greek for giant: *gigas*
10^{6}	2^{20}	mega	M	Greek for large: *megas*
10^{3}	2^{10}	kilo	k	Greek for thousand: *chilioi*
10^{-3}		milli	m	Latin for thousand: *milli*
10^{-6}		micro	μ	Greek for small: *mikros*
10^{-9}		nano	n	Greek for dwarf: *nanos*
10^{-12}		pico	p	Spanish for a little: *pico*
10^{-15}		femto	f	Danish and Norwegian for 15: *femten*
10^{-18}		atto	a	Danish and Norwegian for 18: *atten*
10^{-21}		zepto	z	Greek for seven: *hepta*
10^{-24}		yocto	y	Greek for eight: *okto*

INDEX